China's Rise
in Historical Perspective

China's Rise in Historical Perspective

Edited by
Brantly Womack

ROWMAN & LITTLEFIELD PUBLISHERS, INC.
Lanham • Boulder • New York • Toronto • Plymouth, UK

Published by Rowman & Littlefield Publishers, Inc.
A wholly owned subsidiary of The Rowman & Littlefield Publishing Group, Inc.
4501 Forbes Boulevard, Suite 200, Lanham, Maryland 20706
http://www.rowmanlittlefield.com

Estover Road, Plymouth PL6 7PY, United Kingdom

British Library Cataloguing in Publication Information Available

Library of Congress Cataloging-in-Publication Data

China's rise in historical perspective / edited by Brantly Womack.
    p. cm.
Includes bibliographical references and index.
ISBN 978-0-7425-6721-4 (cloth : alk. paper) -- ISBN 978-0-7425-6722-1
(pbk. : alk. paper) -- ISBN 978-0-7425-6723-8 (electronic)
    1. China--History--1949- 2. China--Economic policy--1949- 3. China--Politics and government--1949- 4. China--Foreign relations. I. Womack, Brantly, 1947-
    DS777.55.C44922 2010
    951--dc22   2010004021

Contents

Preface

For most of us, China has made a dramatic entrance into our concerns and into our lives over the past decade. It has moved from being a distant curiosity or a distant threat—but distant in any case—to being at the front door of American global interests. Whether as a buyer of American debt, source of imports, or collaborator on global issues, China now occupies a unique place in our national attention. China seems not as familiar as Europe, not as hostilely juxtaposed to American interests as the old Soviet Union, and growing all the time. China has arrived.

But where is China going? Will it seek to dominate Asia the way Japan did in the first half of the twentieth century? Will its economic success undermine its government the way that economic stagnation undermined the Soviet Union? Will it play by the rules of the global order, or will it attempt to lead a new revolution? How will it relate to the United States as its economy approaches parity with ours? Will it choke to death on its own pollution? Can the same communist system that failed in Europe succeed in Asia? And keep succeeding?

China is famous for its tea, but there are no tea leaves powerful enough to divine its future or that of the world. However, China was not born yesterday, and the best indicator of its future course is the dynamic created by its past. Because our interest in China is new, we tend to be unaware of the momentum created by its past. We wonder where China will step next, but we cannot see the footprints of where it has been, or the direction that its shoes are pointed. Of course China can change direction, but it is unlikely to jump out of its skin.

China's Rise in Historical Perspective provides broad-gauged reflections by leading Western scholars on China's dynamics. The historians, political scientists, and economists most knowledgeable about China's past and present were recruited for the project. The contributors are all well known for their expertise on China's historical development and also for their current engagement with Chinese scholarship and with Chinese reality. These authors have what most Americans don't have—background and engagement with China—and they are communicating the fruits of their experience. This is a task quite different from debates about being pro-China or anti-China, "panda huggers" or "dragon slayers." The task here is to explore how China feels about itself and how it deals with its people, its resources, its neighbors, and the world. China's imagination as a global actor will be informed by its own experiences, and these must be understood in order to grasp the significance of its actions.

* * *

This project began with five miniconferences sponsored by the University of Virginia's Miller Center of Public Affairs in the spring of 2009. Each miniconference featured a historian and an expert on contemporary China who addressed a major aspect of China's rise: identity, security, economy, ecology/energy, and politics. Each pair of papers was jointly presented at a public lecture and then discussed in a smaller seminar setting. The revised papers became the first ten chapters, and Qin Yaqing, vice president of China Foreign Affairs University in Beijing, contributed a final chapter on the general development of China's world perspective.

The Miller Center is best known for a broad reach of programs on contemporary issues, most prominently the Presidential Oral History Program, the Presidential Recordings Program, the Program on Governing America in a Global Era, the National Discussion and Debate Series, its Forum Program, and its National Commissions. Characteristic of the Miller Center's approach to contemporary issues is a commitment to provide a broader and deeper context by involving academics as well as experienced officials.

The miniconferences on China's Rise in Historical Perspective were a great success. The lectures attracted overflow crowds, and still more watched the webcasts on the Miller Center's website. The cross-disciplinary seminar discussions were stimulating for the speakers as well as for the other participants. History does not provide the golden key to the future, but the programs demonstrated that focusing on the long-term dynamic opened new and important avenues of understanding. It is a pleasure and an honor to present the outcome of this enterprise in book form to a broader audience.

Credit for the general idea for the project should go to Melvyn Leffler and Jeffrey Legro, and further to Bradly Reed, who helped flesh it out. Governor Gerald Baliles, director of the Miller Center, and Brian Balogh, chair of the center's Governing America in a Global Era (GAGE) program, provided strong support and encouragement, as did Sidney Milkis, the assistant director for Academic Programs. The staff of the Miller Center, and especially Anne Mulligan, made the complicated task of running the series seem effortless.

Susan McEachern of Rowman & Littlefield Publishers has been a wonderful and encouraging editor. Moreover, the contributors have been remarkably tolerant of my suggestions and punctual with their revisions. I am very grateful to Ngoc Pham and Lee Shu-Shan, who prepared the index. The students in my class that accompanied the seminars added much to the liveliness and breadth of discussion.

Last and most deeply, I would like to thank the Miller Center audiences for their enthusiasm, their critical open-mindedness, and their empathy with our subject. The most memorable moment for me was the Q&A period at the end of our session on China's economy. There were many excellent questions about China's history and about its current challenges of crossing the threshold to becoming a middle-income, middle-aged economy. None of the questions were about the front-burner American issues with the Chinese economy—will China revalue its currency, what will the Chinese do with all those Treasury bills, what about the trade deficit, and so forth. The audience was all on board with the discussion of China's own dynamic and internal challenges with its economy. We do not know what will happen in the future in the interaction between the United States and China, but with some sense of China's perspective, we will understand it better when it does happen.

Introduction

Brantly Womack

Imagine that you are standing by a railroad track as a locomotive approaches. Amid the general noise and excitement of its passing, you think that you detect a subtle shift in the sound, from a higher pitch as it approached to a lower pitch as it departed. Curious, you come back the next day and the next, and as you become used to the general confusion you are even more convinced of the shift in the sound. Excited by your discovery, you bring a few friends the next time, and most of them agree that there was a shift, though some are not quite certain. So then all of you return with an oscilloscope to measure the pitch, and sure enough, the data shows that the sound drops as the train passes.

You have been a good scientist. First, you controlled for accident and misperception by repeated observations. Then you controlled for subjective error by enlisting multiple independent observers. Finally, you collected data that measured the shift and proved that it occurred. And yet you are wrong.

From the perspective of the engineer on the train, no sound shift occurred. Moreover, if your group were spaced out along the track they would have heard the shift at different times. Lastly, if you were on a train going the opposite direction the sound shift as you passed would have been even more dramatic. What you witnessed was not a shift in the sound source, but the Doppler effect, the compression of sound waves as the distance shortens, producing a higher sound, and then the stretching of the waves as the distance lengthens, lowering the pitch.

What has this to do with China's rise? It is a simple proof that, even in the physical world, perspective counts. How much more so in the mutual perception of nations, where differences in culture, resources, and composition create complex divergences of standpoint. The crucial importance of perspective is an easy enough point to accept, but harder to digest, and almost impossible to remedy. If one is located in the United States, it can easily be granted that China is distant in every respect—geographically, historically, culturally, politically. It is a black box upon which labels can be pasted—communist, non-Western, developing country—but whose internal logic we might freely admit is beyond us.

Ironically, however, the gap between "us" and "them" can reduce our interest in understanding the other perspective. "Objectivity" concerning China, whether in journalism or in academics, is confused with distance from China's own version of its reality. China is held at the end of an analytic stick. We are not interested in what China says, only in what it does. Just the facts, please, perhaps with a projection of future best-case and worst-case scenarios. Gather around the oscilloscope, and plot a few tangents. Any differences in explanation of China's behavior must be resolvable by better empirical information. If not, then the difference lies in the subjective judgment of the individual analysts, and the consumer of analyses is free to choose.

But the problem here, just as with the train, is that unless the difference in perspective is appreciated, relative motion will be confused with absolute motion. If China moves toward us, it appears to be singing a different song than if it is moving away. And we are in motion as well. To the extent that we are moving in the same direction as China, the relative motion is reduced. In facing the global crisis of economic uncertainty, for instance, if the United States adopts a stimulus package and China does as well, then China's behavior seems "natural" and hardly in need of explanation, no matter how many tensions and doubts there might be about our own stimulus package. To the extent that our directions of movement diverge, China's change is seen as accelerated. If our economy shrinks while China's grows, then China's apparent growth is enhanced. Another example would be the founding of the People's Republic of China in 1949 during a conservative, anticommunist wave in the United States. Appropriately enough, the shift in wavelength as an object moves farther away is called a "red shift," and there was certainly a red shift in the American perception of new China. Because the entire relative motion was ascribed to China, we felt that our containment policies were only natural and defensive responses to the threatening dominoes.

As the last example suggests, the hopes and fears of the observing country heighten the Doppler effect in international politics. China has been said to be a mirror in which we mistake the reflection of ourselves for the "real" China.[1] But it is a special kind of mirror. Like Harry Potter's Mirror of Erised, it reflects our hopes and fears.[2] China's government is seen as an all-powerful totalitarianism in part because we are all too conscious (or all too subconscious?) of the weakness and vacillations of democracy. The "China threat" of challenge to American preeminence is as much a product of our anxieties concerning decline as it is an observation of China's rise. Our uncertainties about China are as much a product of uncertainties about ourselves as they are about China.

Clearly it would be a major step forward in the accurate understanding of China to attempt to understand its internal dynamic, and that is the point of this book. China's history provides the best evidence of its present dynamic and of its future direction. A consideration of China from a historical perspective is an attempt to see China's direction from the perspective of the train's engineer. Of course, the view down the tracks is no clearer for China than it is for any country trying to peer into its own foggy future. A China-centered perspective does not yield some clear, absolute truths about China's rise, but by concentrating on change in China in relationship to itself it makes possible a distinction between China's own dynamic and its relative change of position vis-à-vis other actors, including ourselves.

Just as Sun Zi's advice to "know your enemy" seems to be a truism, it might seem obvious advice to take China's perspective seriously in assessing its rise. But in fact the advice is neither easy to follow nor particularly welcome. Except for the odd China specialist (and, yes, many of them are odd), we are interested in China precisely because of its possible effect on our interests; it is China's motion relative to ourselves that counts. We are interested in the China threat *to us, our* China opportunities, *how we can meet* the China challenge. Moreover, we are all sitting on the same national bench reading the same newspapers as the China train goes by. We see the same things, and confirm each other's impressions. It is not our train, so why should we be concerned about the engineer's view? But Sun Zi is right. If the train is worth watching, it is worth knowing where it came from, and where it thinks it's going, especially in the case of a long and large train.

Even if we agree that China's own perspective is important, though, we have not solved our problems with perspective. China's perspective is privileged in the assessment of China's rise, but it is also interactive with other states and with global developments. Moreover, in any bilateral relationship, China's point of view is only one side of each story. Let us take the final essay in this volume as an illustration. Qin Yaqing presents a comprehensive overview of the political psychology of China's rise, tracing it from the tribute system through the various failed attempts to restore China's identity and finally to the successful combination of reform and openness in the current era. His survey has the authenticity of an "inside account" of China's identity and of its restoration, and as such deserves to be taken seriously by anyone interested in China's motivations and internal dynamics. However, the questions raised about the tribute system by Joseph Esherick and even more pointedly by Evelyn Rawski remain important. Historically speaking, China's traditional identity was neither as coherent nor as uncontested as contemporary China remembers. And yet both history and memory are important. And China's interactors have their histories and memories as well.

The logic of the current project follows from the above considerations. We attempt to combine an appreciation of the history of major dimensions of China's rise with analyses of its current challenges. The writers are noted Western scholars of China, and thus give a more detached and critical view of their topics than a purely inside view might yield. And Qin rounds up the discussion by returning it to the basic question of the internal dynamic of China's rise. This book attempts to provide more than a 2009 balance sheet of the current situation. Rather, it tries to follow in the steps of such works as *China in Crisis* (1968),[3] *China's Modern Economy in Historical Perspective* (1975),[4] and *Contemporary Chinese Politics in Historical Perspective* (1992).[5] Each of these anthologies tried to approach the Chinese realities of their times—the Cultural Revolution, the command economy, the aftermath of Tiananmen—with a broad appreciation of the significance of the present in terms of China's past. The current pressing task is to grasp the dynamics of China's rise.

THE BOOK IN BRIEF

The book is divided into five thematic sections, each containing two chapters, followed by Qin's comprehensive concluding chapter. The first chapter in each section presents a historically oriented analysis of its theme, and the second a more contemporary perspective. What follows is my interpretation of the themes and chapters.

The first section treats the theme of China's identity. Here two themes first raised in Joseph Esherick's historical chapter can be carried through to the reform era. The first is the inseparability of domestic and external politics— "there is no outside" (*wu wai* 无外). The second is the repressed consciousness of persistent gaps between reality and the "proper" order. As the eminent historian John King Fairbank put it, "The chief problem of China's foreign relations was how to square theory with fact, the ideological claim with the actual practice."[6]

In traditional China these themes are conjoined by China's claim to be "all under heaven" (*tianxia* 天下). The moral, hierarchical character of China's domestic governance was also the pattern of its external relationships. This is most obvious in tributary rituals, which included not only obeisance and the exchange of local products (*gong* 贡) for imperial bestowals (*ci* 賜), but also the use of the current dynastic calendar and the investiture of foreign rulers with Chinese titles of nobility. But reality was far more complex. Especially in their dealings with nomads to the north, Chinese rulers were often in the situation of coping with neighbors whom they could not control. Typically, prudent concessions would be made, but they would be presented officially as emanating from the virtuous benevolence of the emperors rather than from the force of circumstance.

With the arrival in force of the West in the mid-nineteenth century, an externally imposed treaty system replaced the China-centered tribute system. Although imperialism involved competition at the top, China was definitely not among the great powers, and it suffered the humiliations of innumerable foreign penetrations of its domestic space and interests. The mix of domestic and external politics remained, but the dynamic was reversed—from the Opium War in 1840 to the collapse of the Qing dynasty in 1911 there was less and less autonomous "inside" in China. The contradiction between official rhetoric and reality became more acute.

The third phase in the development of China's identity as described by Esherick is the rise of nationalism in the twentieth century. External failure delegitimized traditional Chinese approaches; young Chinese rallied in defense of China but not in defense of things Chinese. New ideas from the West—democracy, science, the YMCA, communism—were introduced as radical solutions to China's crisis. National humiliation was decried, but it continued at the hands of the Japanese, culminating in war in 1937. One could describe nationalist rhetoric as an antiofficialism, since it highlighted the embarrassing reality of weakness. But the gap between ideals and reality was displaced into future dreams of restored glory.

Lowell Dittmer analyzes the effect on China's identity of the establishment of the People's Republic of China (PRC) in 1949 and its subsequent politics. There were broad continuities with the past. The tone of the PRC's politics remained normative, though of course Confucianism was replaced by revolutionary values. The contradictory ambiguity remained of a transnational claim to leadership but a nonexpansionist foreign policy.

However, the turbulence of post-1949 politics gave a new twist to the idea of *wu wai*. Instead of domestic governance providing a steadying guide to foreign policy, radical changes in domestic politics led to a repeated pattern of new strategic postures displacing old ones after a period of transitional uncertainty. Dittmer describes four phases of PRC politics: socialist construction (1949–1959), the Cultural Revolution (1966–1976), reform and opening (1979–1989), and deepening of reform beginning in 1994. Each phase put its stamp on China's external posture, and, with the exception of the last, in radical juxtaposition with the previous. Success, however, presents a unique identity challenge, because China's rise changes its proportional relationship with its neighbors and with the global political economy. While a return to regional preeminence resonates with China's traditional identity, it is in contrast to the entire previous course of China's modern experience.

The theme of the second section is China's security. An underlying difference between the narratives of China's identity and of its security is that identity is primarily self-referenced while security is primarily other-referenced. From a security standpoint, there is certainly an "outside," and the problem is how to deal with it. Security focuses on threats and borders; identity on continuity.

Until the Opium War, China's most important security problems were on its northern and western frontiers. Evelyn Rawski provides a sweeping analysis of the struggles between China and its primarily nomadic neighbors during three periods of turbulence, the fourth to seventh centuries, the tenth to thirteenth centuries, and the sixteenth to seventeenth centuries. She argues that for roughly half of its existence, the Chinese empire was not in a hegemonic position in North Asia, but contended with neighbors who were its equals and sometimes its betters. Thus things were not as simple as "the hoary stereotypes of the tribute system," to use Fairbank's phrase, might suggest.[7] The "conquest dynasties" founded by the Mongols (the Yuan) and the Manchus (the Qing) further cloud the image of an all-powerful "all under heaven."

What, then, was the security situation of traditional China? Was it one among many? First among equals? In my opinion, these options, familiar from Western international relations experience, are inadequate.[8] While China was never able to control the mobile forces beyond its frontier, and sometimes was defeated by them, as an extensive and productive agricultural polity it was nevertheless in a central position in East Asia. If we separate the notion of *hegemony*, the control of others, from the notion of *centrality*, being in a unique and nontransposable relationship with others, then we could say that China was the Central Kingdom. Being central did not mean always being on top. It meant being in the middle of neighbors who could not be eliminated and were sometimes threatening. As Alexander Woodside has suggested, China felt the constant and heavy burden of its boundaries.[9] China's security challenge was that of managing a middle position.

Despite the transformed content of China's contemporary security concerns, the analysis by Michael Swaine in chapter 4 dovetails with a view of traditional China as a cautious power. Of course, China is no longer the middle power; the United States is. However, the assumption persists that security is enhanced not by subjugating other nations but rather by establishing mutually beneficial long-term relationships.

China's security outlook in the reform era has been shaped by expectations that the international environment at the global level will remain peaceful, that American unilateralism will be increasingly limited by growing multipolarity, that economic globalization is a basic trend, and that there will be growing pressure of public opinion on Chinese foreign policy. Each of these premises represents a basic change from Mao's expectations of international class struggle. The failure of revolutionary transformation not only has induced China to become socialized into a global political economy defined by the West; it also has encouraged a return to the traditional posture of reassurance to neighbors.

Swaine suggests four policy consequences for China's security. First, pragmatic emphasis on economic development, both in terms of domestic growth and in terms of international openness. Second, an overall foreign policy of "peace and development," one that emphasizes common interests and attempts to contain the influence of points of contention. Third, increased involvement in a broad range of global and regional multilateral agreements and activities. Fourth, general restraint in the use of force. China's current grand strategy differs from its traditional one in its emphasis on economic openness and in its engagement in multilateral contexts.

The United States has been and remains China's major security concern, and China's policies vis-à-vis the United States have been multipronged. On the one hand, China has pursued force modernization, with the concrete target of achieving military control of the Taiwan theater and more generally of littoral areas and islands claimed by China. On the other hand, China is concerned about stimulating a "China threat" mentality in the United States. China realizes that its current peaceful development policies presuppose the current world order. Swaine points out that the United States engages in a similar ambivalence of hedging and cooperative policies. Neither side is committed to a zero-sum game. The United States is not trying to contain China, and China is not trying to displace the United States. Nevertheless, differences of culture and interests will continue to foster security sensitivity on both sides.

China's economy is arguably the dimension of its current reality most in need of a historical perspective and an appreciation of its internal dynamic and challenges. In the third section Dwight Perkins provides a historical and comparative analysis, followed by Barry Naughton, who considers the emergence of the reform era and its current challenges.

Perkins describes what was arguably the world's most successful premodern political economy. The invention of bureaucracy facilitated the coordination and resilience of a vast agrarian economy that in turn encouraged the development of literacy, domestic trade, paper money, and banking. By contrast, China's external economic relationships were managed more with a view of avoiding trouble than of developing commerce. The tribute system stabilized political relationships, but was a rather thin reed for massive commercial development. The closing of coastal trade in the Ming and Qing dynasties was only the most extreme example of a general complacent suspicion concerning the utility of external entanglements. One might say that traditional China was centered, all too centered.

Western intrusions in the nineteenth century were both more and less than a rude awakening. Rude they were, and domestic reverberations such as the Taiping Rebellion added to the destruction and chaos. Awakening was more difficult. The inertial conservatism of the empire, embodied in the Empress Dowager, undercut early efforts to modernize, and after 1900 China as a unified political community increasingly lost control of its affairs. Some modernization occurred, but chaos does not provide a good investment environment. Possibly the most useful continuing heritage was the high value placed on education, now reoriented (with considerable help from foreign charities) toward modern subjects.

After 1949 the Chinese Communist Party (CCP) faced the novel task of creating a socialist planned economy, and they were helped by China's bureaucratic traditions as well as by the Soviet model. The rate of growth and of structural transformation in the 1950s was impressive, but Mao Zedong made the disastrous decision to shift to mass mobilization in the Great Leap Forward in 1958, and then to radical politics in the Cultural Revolution. The failure of Mao's attempts at leftist transformations was a teacher by negative example to the reform era, while the command economy provided an extensive if inefficient industrial base.

In Barry Naughton's explanation of China's amazing success in the reform era, education, rather than bureaucracy, plays a leading role. He highlights the resumption of university entrance exams in 1978 as equal in importance to the creation of special economic zones. In general, China was well positioned for rapid catch-up in 1978 because of its existing industrial base, literate and healthy population, and local institutions that could be adapted to risk-sharing and entrepreneurial activities. The CCP's prioritization of maximum growth encouraged both decentralizing policies and a redirection of official incentives away from cautious parroting of ideology and toward technical competence and practical results. Corresponding to Dittmer's discussion of the political deepening of reform, Naughton points out the continuing process of economic policy adjustment. An important example is policy toward the remaining state-owned enterprises, which have not been privatized and yet are subject to market discipline.

As the rest of the world has experienced, a major part of China's economic rise has been increased engagement with the regional and world economies. Most products are composites of capital, technology, and labor, and a characteristic of globalization has been for international production processes to emerge in which each country exploits its production advantage. China's advantage is labor, so it imports high-tech components and capital and has become the final assembly point for much of Asia's output. "Made in China" may be "Owned by Japan," featuring "Parts by Taiwan" and "Powered by Angola" before it is sold to the United States or Europe. As a result, the current economic downturn affected both China's imports and its exports, and the pain of China's export drop is shared by its many partners.

The primary challenge that China faces is in part created by its success. China has recently reached the threshold of becoming a middle-income country. However, a major resource in its swift rise was cheap labor, and China is approaching the exhaustion of its supply of rural underemployed. Beginning in 2004 in the Pearl River Delta, more jobs began to chase fewer workers, and this pattern is gradually spreading to other developed areas. Given China's scale and economic diversity, the pattern will remain uneven, but it is driven by demography as well as by economic success, and so it is likely to continue. Impressive efforts have been launched to develop western China, to raise the standards of health and education in the countryside, and to make China an economy of consumers as well as producers. But the threshold of development is not easy to cross in the best of times, and the current global crisis of economic uncertainty makes it more difficult.

The fourth section treats the composite subject of environment and energy. Mark Elvin's chapter continues his pathbreaking research on China's environmental history.[10] He paints a picture quite different from political narratives of successful traditional China followed by Western disruption and culminating in a crooked path returning to former glories. As far as the environment is concerned, according to Elvin, traditional China had worked itself into an acute impasse of unsustainability by the nineteenth century, to be rescued by Western science for a time, and now has become part of a global environmental impasse whose outcome is uncertain. Ironically, both narratives are based on the success of traditional China and its return to prominence.

China was not a pristine premodern paradise threatened by the modern forces of foreign exploitation, forced industrialization, or overpopulation. Instead, millennia of agricultural intensification and population expansion had replaced the native environment with an artificial one that was more productive, but also increasingly difficult to maintain. In his previous research Elvin detailed the effects of deforestation (China's retreating elephants were forest creatures) and of water management projects. In this chapter he explores the effect of agricultural intensification on soil, water, and population.

Traditional China showed remarkable ingenuity in maximizing the production of food per unit of land, and it built its society on its agricultural success.

Land productivity was maximized in both macro and micro senses: terracing was used to increase arable surface, and each plot of land was tended with the intensity of a garden. The output demanded was far more than the soil could sustain naturally; fertilizer (primarily night soil and mud), irrigation, and interplanting of crops made possible agrarian China. But intensification required larger and larger amounts of labor for maintenance, which in turn required more food, and it committed premodern China to an increasingly vulnerable structure of production. The effects of the environmental impasse can be seen in the population patterns of China's most productive regions.

The effect of modern science on Chinese agriculture, especially after 1949, was to vastly increase productivity and population. Chemical fertilizer and more productive crop varieties were chief contributions, further stimulated by the market incentives of the reform era. But these advances have redesigned and increased the burden on the land, and have spread China's food and resource burden to global markets. Per capita agricultural productivity in grain peaked in 1996 and has dropped dramatically in most developed provinces. Guangdong's grain productivity peaked in 1997 and in ten years declined by one-third. Its per capita grain production in 2007 was half of its 1978 figure.[11] The premodern dilemma of agrarian intensity lurks behind the current impasse: agriculture in China is necessarily labor-intensive, and as the price of labor rises the costs of production follow. To some extent contemporary China can satisfy its food needs through imports, but to what extent? And what new contingencies are created thereby for China and for the world?

Over the past few years the problem of China's energy demands has attracted more attention than food security, both inside and outside of China. As Erica Downs details in her chapter, part of the reason is the rapid and unexpected increase in China's energy imports since 2001—she rightly calls it "China's energy demand shock." Not only was China a net oil exporter until 1993, but more important, its energy demands grew only half as fast as its GDP (gross domestic product) for the first twenty years of reform. China's planners assumed that energy efficiency would continue to outpace growth, but they were wrong. From 2001 to 2007 China's energy demand increased by 90 percent, putting a great strain on the electrical grid, coal and oil production, and oil imports. Energy security became the new "fever" for China's planners.

Domestically, energy security has induced new attention to both energy conservation and supply. As Downs points out, the "power famine" of 2002–2005 was due to domestic imbalances rather than to external influences. However, the domestic crisis led to an enormous increase in oil imports. China's surge in oil imports had immediate effects on world markets, and the long-term prospect of the China factor in oil availability and pricing became a global concern. In turn, the international uncertainties of oil availability have strengthened China's determination to pursue alternative energy sources, clean energy, and energy conservation. Meanwhile China is trying to stabilize its international energy and resource expectations by means of long-term development contracts with producing states.

Rather suddenly—especially by the standards of Chinese history—energy as well as other natural resources has become a major component of China's foreign relations. They are often the centerpiece of relationships with producing countries, and indirectly they are a concern to other consuming countries. While there is no track record for China in this area, the policies pursued have fit into the traditional patterns of cautious diplomacy. But there are additional elements of strong sectoral actors, especially the major Chinese petroleum conglomerates, and comprehensive resource development projects with many countries. Clearly the "outside" is no longer far from China's concerns.

The fifth section of the book addresses China's political heritage and its relevance for contemporary China. Keith Schoppa and Joseph Fewsmith take rather different but complementary approaches to their tasks. Schoppa addresses the question of the political creativity of traditional China, an approach that necessarily highlights the internal consistency and "best practice" reality of late imperial China. Fewsmith narrates the rise of radicalism from the 1898 reaction to defeat in the Sino-Japanese War to the death of Mao Zedong, and then considers the major political challenges of the reform era. While Schoppa presents an ideal anatomy of traditional Chinese politics, Fewsmith presents a pathology of subsequent developments.

Schoppa first emphasizes the importance of the metaphor of the moral family in conceptualizing the nature of traditional government. Thus the emperor as "Son of Heaven" was the natural head of a human patrimonial order, but he also had to be filial to heaven and obey heaven's mandate of ruling benevolently. Benevolence involved active measures such as "ever-normal granaries" to provide against famine, but also a meritocratic governmental structure and a preference for light and indirect control. In accord with the family model, the roles of government stressed the importance of moral education and of education more generally. In contrast to the separation of state, church, and society in the West, in China the state oversaw ritual and encouraged education oriented toward producing a virtuous officialdom and moral subjects.

Even in its model functioning, traditional governance did not provide a final solution to problems of political order, but rather a means of negotiating the inevitable tensions of a large-scale and diverse traditional polity. Center-locality tensions were complicated in many cases by ethnic differences and almost always by the natural divergence between the interests of the center and those of the localities. Within the government, the management of the bureaucracy was a constant challenge. Most fundamentally, the informal politics of relationships (*guanxi* 关系) was ubiquitous, but in tension with the more impersonal demands of the system for efficiency. Measures such as the rule of avoidance, whereby officials were not stationed in their native places, can be viewed as attempts to prevent the instrumentality of the bureaucracy from being overwhelmed by the personal connections of its agents.

While Schoppa set himself the task of explaining the political creativity of traditional China, and implicitly the reasons for its coherence, longevity, and resilience, Fewsmith addresses the turbulence of modern and contemporary China. Although China was destabilized by external forces, its own radical response to its troubles in the twentieth century certainly contributed to the crooked path it has taken. Different doctrines guided different strands of modern Chinese politics, but until the death of Mao Zedong in 1976 the leading ones had in common a moral absolutism, what Tang Tsou called "totalism," quite different from traditional Confucian orthodoxy. Even the attempt by Jiang Jieshi (Chiang Kai-shek) to revive Confucianism in the New Life Movement of the 1930s was in spirit more akin to fascism than Confucianism.

Thus the reform era faced the challenge not only of being post-Mao, but also of being postradical. The most practical challenge created by the watershed was easily seen and enthusiastically grasped—that of economic modernization. After a false start under Hua Guofeng, Deng Xiaoping boldly led initiatives of reform and openness. As Naughton points out in his discussion of the economy, the importance of the active leadership and encouragement of new policies by the CCP should not be underrated. The deeper task was political reform. The CCP and its leading role were themselves the products of a century of radicalism, and so the task of political deradicalization was a delicate one.

An essential part of the task of postradical political reform was addressed, namely the repudiation of charisma. While Hua Guofeng tried and failed to become Mao's successor, Deng encouraged a pragmatic, collective leadership in which policy success should be judged on economic accomplishments rather than ideological correctness. Ideology defined the boundary of the permissible—one must not overtly challenge Marxism–Leninism–Mao Zedong Thought—but not its broad middle. The new ladder of success is one of knowledge. Its rungs are academic degrees and one must climb quickly because of mandatory retirement.

Fewsmith points out the rising tensions between the new standards and the old guard that came to a head with the succession struggles of the late 1980s. The sobering experience of Tiananmen and the age of the old guard led to a buffering and routinization of succession, but the more basic problem remains of the self-designation of the CCP as the governing party in a postrevolutionary age. The party has not ignored the problem of increasing its governance capacity. Many efforts have been made to oversee cadre behavior, to be more open about governance processes, and to provide for local level elections. But there is a fundamental tension between the party's presumption of a right to rule and its efforts to bind its policies and personnel to the citizenry, even at the local level. Fewsmith concludes with the pessimistic observation that the local level in general has become less important as well as less contested.

In his concluding essay, Qin Yaqing returns the book to its international concerns, but from the vantage point of the political psychology of traditional China's external posture and the struggles to return to a situation of dignity and respect in the modern era. After a number of false starts, China's embracing of the international system in the reform era has been successful because it has combined domestic reform with opening up—reform and openness, *gaige kaifang* 改革开放, are not two tasks, but one.

China's traditional identity was not defined in modern international terms, but rather in terms of its place at the center of its known world. Rather than a system of nation-states similar in structure though different in capacities, it was a hierarchical network of ritual relationships in which China was the benevolent superior. Based on the Confucian family model, the goal of politics, according to Qin, "was not only to attain law and order in society but also to establish a fiduciary community through moral persuasion and unequal love." It should be noted that regardless of the many exceptions to China's control over its international context and more cynical interpretations of its motives by neighbors, this was the Chinese view of its external role, and this conviction provided the internal resilience for restoration, correction, and reform.

Beginning with the Opium War in 1840, China's idea of its own larger identity was shattered not only by the power of the West, but by the new paradigm of a nation-state international order. The treaty system described by Esherick was not only unequal and unfair to China; it was an alien order. From 1840 to 1978, China made four efforts to reassert its identity, all of which failed. First, the Westernization Movement of the 1860s attempted to develop a modern military force, but the defeat by Japan in 1895 implied that a more radical reform was necessary.

The Reform Movement of 1898 had only a brief and unsuccessful window of opportunity in directing China's affairs, but its thinkers, including Kang Youwei and Liang Qichao, had a profound effect on reorienting China's youth toward a wider world. Sun Yat-sen's attempt to establish a modern Republic of China in 1911 seemed at first to have more promise, but the resistance of conservative forces and the dissolution of central power resulted in warlord anarchy. The May Fourth Movement of 1919 then began a more radical critique of Chinese traditions. But China's continuing weakness and the growing threat from Japan precluded a new international identity.

The problems of political weakness and internal disorder that had plagued modern China were solved in principle by the establishment of the People's Republic of China in 1949, but first the bipolar tensions of the Cold War followed by the ideological split with the Soviet Union and the Cultural Revolution brought China into deeper isolation from international society. China was still restlessly searching for an international identity.

The reform era has been a different and more successful experience in the search for a place in the world. For the first time, the rest of the world is not a threat from the outside, but an inside challenge linked inextricably with domestic reform. The most prominent dimensions of China's new international identity are the importance of economic interdependence, participation in a broad range of international regimes, and lastly a growing identity with international society as demonstrated in collaboration on common world problems.

China's new identity exists in a globalized world rather than its traditional world of neighbors, and it accepts a framework of equally sovereign states quite different from the presumptions of familial superiority embedded in the rituals of the tribute system. Nevertheless, the new global identity has deep resonance with China's traditional sense of itself, and it puts to rest the frustration and disquiet of earlier modern efforts of China to struggle against the world and against itself. The modern system poses the question of China's unity in a new form, but it is a unity with the world, not against it.

Qin's essay is a fitting conclusion to our reflections on China's rise in historical perspective. Each author has tried to situate China's concerns with identity, security, economics, environment, and politics within historical contexts, and has brought to the task a global perspective as well as an understanding of China. Ultimately, however, it is the mind of the engineer guiding China's train that will determine its future course. Qin argues convincingly that the direction China will take will be with the rest of the world rather than against it, and that is in line with the continuities of its history as well as with lessons learned from the zigzag course of the modern era.

NOTES

1. Frederick Wakeman, Jr., *History and Will* (Berkeley: University of California Press, 1973).

2. In *Harry Potter and the Philosopher's Stone*, Harry discovers the Mirror of Erised (*desire* spelled backward) and sees his parents. China is more a *camera oscura* of Erised, producing a reversed image.

3. Ping-ti Ho [He Bingdi] and Tang Tsou, eds., *China in Crisis*, 2 vols. in 3 (Chicago: University of Chicago Press, 1968).

4. Dwight Perkins, ed., *China's Modern Economy in Historical Perspective* (Stanford, CA: Stanford University Press, 1975).

5. Brantly Womack, *Contemporary Chinese Politics in Historical Perspective* (New York: Cambridge University Press, 1992).

6. John K. Fairbank, "A Preliminary Framework," in Fairbank, ed., *The Chinese World Order* (Cambridge, MA: Harvard University Press, 1968), 2–3.

7. Fairbank, *The Chinese World Order*, 1.

8. Brantly Womack, "Traditional China and the Globalization of International Relations Thinking" in *China among Unequals: Asymmetric Foreign Relations in Asia* (Singapore: World Scientific Press, 2010).

9. Alexander Woodside, "The Centre and the Borderlands in Chinese Political Theory," in Diana Lary, ed., *The Chinese State at the Borders* (Vancouver: UBC Press, 2007), 11–28.

10. Mark Elvin, *The Retreat of the Elephants: An Environmental History of China* (New Haven, CT: Yale University Press, 2004).

11. Calculated from *Guangdong Statistical Yearbook 2008*, accessed by subscription from China Data Online.

I

CHINA AND THE WORLD ORDER

Dilemmas of Identity

1

China and the World

From Tribute to Treaties to Popular Nationalism

Joseph W. Esherick

Until Western Europe's industrial revolution ushered in a new era of world trade and imperial hubris, China remained reasonably confident of its strategic centrality and cultural superiority among its Asian neighbors. China's rulers were by no means oblivious to military threats from beyond the empire's borders. The country had, after all, been repeatedly invaded and often conquered by nomadic peoples from the north. Indeed, when the West did arrive in force in the nineteenth century, China was ruled by the once "barbarian" Manchus who had conquered China in 1644 together with their Mongol allies. The Inner Asian origins of China's Manchu rulers gave a special cast to their Qing dynasty, but by the eighteenth century, the Manchus had occupied the palaces, adopted the laws, and preserved most of the structures of rule of the previous Ming dynasty, ruling China proper pretty much in accord with past dynastic practice.[1] In their relations with the outside world, the precedents of China's past shaped the official imagination and public presentation of intercourse with peoples from beyond China's borders.

THE TRIBUTE SYSTEM

In the realm of "foreign relations," the Manchus' Qing dynasty welcomed periodic tribute missions from neighboring states and expected them to conform to the norms of Chinese ritual practice. These norms were laid down in painstaking detail in the *Collected Statutes of the Qing* (*Qinding da-Qing huidian* 欽定大清會典) and the *Comprehensive Rituals of the Qing* (*Da-Qing tongli*

大清通禮), which codified the administrative and ritual practices that historians have called "the tribute system." Although the term is a "Western invention for descriptive purposes"[2] and the conception has been much disparaged by such postcolonial critics as James Hevia and Lydia Liu,[3] there was a clearly stated set of "guest rituals" governing China's relation with foreign states, with visits by tribute-bearing envoys at their heart. Chinese officials paid scrupulous attention to these protocols, and for this reason, an appreciation of the tribute system serves as a useful starting point for an understanding of the late imperial Chinese world order.

The *Collected Statutes* and *Comprehensive Rituals*, in characteristic Chinese bureaucratic form, traced the rituals to ancient precedents reaching back to the earliest recorded history. Thus a Ming dynasty version of these texts begins with the words "The kings of former times cultivated their own refinement and virtue in order to subdue persons at a distance, whereupon the barbarians (of the east and north) came to Court to have an audience. This comes down as a long tradition."[4] Ming and Qing texts then go on to relate a classically Sinocentric history of China's relations with its neighbors through all dynasties beginning with the Shang kings of the second millennium B.C., and the appropriate ceremonies that had been established for tributary missions to the Chinese court. These rituals were designed to establish a clear hierarchical relationship between the Chinese emperor as Son of Heaven and the rulers of subordinate neighboring states. In this respect, foreign relations were no different from any other Chinese social relations, where hierarchies of age, gender, social position, and official rank were understood as the natural order of things.

The Chinese conception of the world order was wrought with contradictions—or perhaps we should say that the world is such a messy and conflict-ridden place that the tribute system had a difficult time reducing it to legible order. On the one hand, the Chinese emperor was Son of Heaven presiding over all under Heaven (*tianxia* 天下). The *Book of Odes* (*Shijing* 詩經) stated clearly that "[u]nder the wide heaven, all is the king's land; within the sea-boundaries of the land, all are the king's subjects."[5] In this sense, there was no place for what we would call "foreign relations." As the Chinese texts put it, *wuwai* (無外): there was "no outer-separation."[6] Distant states that offered tribute to the Chinese emperor were his vassals and part of one continuous graded system in which proximity to the Chinese center meant enhanced degrees of bureaucratic control and distance brought greater autonomy. People from beyond China's frontiers could come and be transformed (*laihua* 來化), their ethnic difference erased as they absorbed Chinese culture.[7] On the other hand, Chinese texts from the earliest times distinguished the Chinese cultural sphere (*Hua-Xia* 華夏) from the barbarians (*yi* 夷), and it has often been noted that the characters for the various barbarian tribes on China's borders each carried an animal radical: a dog radical for the northern Di (狄), a sheep for the western Qiang (羌), an insect for the southern Man (蠻).[8] Barbarian peoples were, in a sense, subhuman, "on the edge of bestiality,"[9] and one could not expect or trust them to behave according to the proper forms of civilized (Chinese) people. Proper behavior would require firm yet patient training. Ideally, the constant repetition of established ritual would civilize these barbarians; at a minimum, the strict adherence to ritual forms of tributary relations would guarantee that untutored foreigners did not disrupt the imperial order.

The closest neighboring states of East Asia, Korea and Annam (Vietnam), presented the least problems. They had both adopted the Chinese writing system and incorporated classical Chinese learning into their cultural canon. (Japan had also adopted Chinese writing and held China's Confucian tradition in great respect. However, protected by an intervening sea, it did not accept tributary status and was left outside the formal system.) Korea and Vietnam were China's most loyal tributary states, sending regular tribute-bearing embassies to the Chinese court, adopting the Chinese calendar, and accepting seals of authority and investiture of their rulers from the Son of Heaven in Beijing. These two states lay directly on China's border; they were clearly within the Sinitic culture area; and the prominent princes, statesmen, and scholars that they sent as emissaries to China indicated a conscientious commitment to the tribute system. Their relationship with China was, in Brantly Womack's term, clearly asymmetric. As smaller states lying next to the Chinese behemoth, they purchased their autonomy at the relatively painless cost of offering ritual obeisance to the Chinese emperor. This is not to say that the Korean and Vietnamese understanding of Chinese hegemony was exactly the same as the Chinese. There was always a degree of deceit and dissimulation as they simultaneously pursued their interests vis-à-vis other states in the East Asian region.[10]

More distant states such as Siam, Champa, Khoqand, or Burma lay outside the realm of Sinitic culture but they too sent periodic tribute missions to China, though on a far less regular basis. For these states, there is even more reason to believe that their understanding of tributary practices was different from China's. Their tributary missions were allowed to trade at the borders before following a prescribed route to the capital, and trade was also permitted at controlled markets in the capital after the emissaries had been received by the emperor. Commerce was clearly the motivating force behind many tributary visits, with some Central Asian merchants posing as representatives of their rulers in order to gain access to the Chinese market. The fact that the emperor's gifts to the emissaries were expected to exceed the value of the tribute he received (as the senior partner in the exchange the emperor could hardly afford to appear stingy) gave added incentive for this practice.[11]

In the decades that have passed since the early scholarship describing the tribute system as a model for imperial China's relations with the outside world, many have noted the manifold flaws in the conception. Most important, Fairbank's Sinocentric model presented an excessively rigid and static picture of China's relations with others and ignored the significant flexibility of Chinese practice.[12] Evelyn Rawski's chapter in this volume draws on this recent scholarship to present an incisive critique of the Sinocentric model, noting the long periods of weakness in which China's hegemonic position was challenged by its neighbors. When the *Collected Statutes* presented its narrative of immutable rituals for dealing with foreign guests, all of this history was elided. Under the Qing dynasty (1644–1911), where the ruling house was Manchus from the northeast, whose leadership of their Mongol allies was based on claims to the mantle of Chinghis Khan, and whose incorporation of Tibet involved patronage of the Lamaist religion, the notion of a Sinocentric empire is particularly problematic. Far more convincing is Pamela Crossley's notion of "simultaneous emperorship" whereby Qing emperors related to different constituencies of the empire through their own cultural idioms.[13] The master of this was surely the Qianlong emperor (r. 1736–1795), who boasted of being able to greet envoys from Mongolia, Tibet, or Turkic Central Asia in their own languages.[14] The Qing court proved quite willing to adjust tributary norms in order to preserve peaceful relations with the peoples on its border. Perhaps the most notable example of this was the Treaty of Nerchinsk (1689) establishing the border with czarist Russia and the terms of trade. With the help of Jesuit intermediaries, it was negotiated on terms of equality and established a treaty settlement giving equivalent status to the two great empires of the Eurasian continent.[15]

There were, however, real limits to Qing flexibility. Qing policy exhibited a hardheaded pragmatism, which meant that adjustments of established precedent were very much contingent on historical context and the court's assessment of it. In the case of the Nerchinsk treaty, the Kangxi emperor in the 1680s was anxious to settle border disputes with the Russians along the Amur River so that he could focus attention on the increasingly disruptive activities of the Mongol leader Galdan, whom he did manage to eliminate soon after the treaty was signed.[16] Galdan's successors continued to make trouble in the eighteenth century, and when efforts to buy peace with trade concessions failed, the Qianlong emperor launched a massive expedition that by 1760 simply wiped the Zunghars off the map and vastly expanded the size of the Qing empire.[17] As a consequence, when the British came pressing for trade concessions at the end of the eighteenth century, they confronted a China that had stabilized its northern frontier and stood more confident of its place in the world than it had been for some time. The historical context had changed, and there were no longer pressing reasons for pragmatic flexibility. In addition, the Manchu rulers, themselves products of Central Asia and its conflicts, were well prepared to comprehend and address threats on the empire's northern frontier. The new seaborne barbarians on China's southern shore were a good deal more difficult to fathom, and the court's assessment of new dangers from the sea would prove fatally ill-informed.

Maintaining harmonious relations with foreign peoples was a critical concern for any Chinese dynasty. The long history of raiding and invasion by the peoples of the northern steppe required close attention to the practical matters of frontier defense. Even more important, however, was the threat to dynastic legitimacy posed by hostile forces from afar. Imperial legitimacy derived from the Mandate of Heaven, which was conferred on a virtuous ruler. Ethical rule brought order to the empire, while corruption and moral failings could trigger floods, drought, famine, or popular rebellion, all potential signs of the loss of Heaven's Mandate. It was not only domestic disasters that could herald trouble. Remember the formula cited above from the *Book of Odes*: distant people were subdued by the virtue of the ruler. By the same logic, *failure* to subdue barbarians and resultant threats to security on the frontier could portend a ruler's lack of the appropriate virtue. With no clear discursive distinction between domestic and foreign affairs, the notion of "no outerseparation" (*wuwai*) provided the philosophical basis for holding the emperor responsible for keeping foreigners properly submissive. The successful conduct of what the modern world would call "foreign affairs" was thus critical to the legitimacy of Chinese regimes. China's rulers were very conscious of this logic, which accounts for the bureaucracy's concern that foreign visitors to China's shores should demonstrate appropriate awe before the majesty of the Chinese emperor. As China entered the modern world, maintaining this ritual order would become a significant challenge.

In early modern times (seventeenth and eighteenth centuries), these considerations colored the public face of many practical adjustments in Qing policy. The Treaty of Nerchinsk with the Russians provides an instructive example. As noted above, the treaty is a much-cited example of pragmatic negotiation, on the basis of equality, with a rival empire whose rapid expansion across Siberia had brought Russian fur traders, settlers, and Cossack soldiers to the edge of the Qing frontier in Manchuria. The negotiations bore a much closer resemblance to Europe's Westphalian model of diplomatic equality between sovereign states than they did to the Chinese tributary model. But the Manchu court was careful to see that the negotiations took place at Nerchinsk on the Manchuria frontier, far from the center of power (and curious eyes) in

Beijing. In previous negotiations in the Chinese capital, the Manchu court had been much more fastidious in insisting on protocols that acknowledged its ritual superiority. The Jesuits who served as translators and mediators between Qing officials and the czar's emissaries explained to the Russians that the Manchus (then rulers of China for only a few decades) felt compelled to insist on the established tributary forms in order to impress their Chinese subjects.[18] In the Nerchinsk negotiations, while the Manchu negotiator's flexibility was evident in his secret memorials to the throne, the more public memorials and edicts ratifying the agreement spoke in terms of the emperor's indulgence of the Russians' "ignorance," his punishing them in battle when they persisted in their error, and their final "turn toward civilization" so that a border agreement could at last be reached. As a result of such rhetorical subterfuge, all of the pragmatic flexibility of Qing foreign policy was disguised from view, and the fictions of the tribute model were preserved long past the time when they were in fact operable.[19]

The dangers posed by this practice became evident roughly a century later with the Macartney Mission of 1793. In this much-studied meeting between the aging Qianlong emperor and the lordly representative of the British king, the embassy's Manchu handlers made every effort to guarantee that Macartney's movements through China and his behavior at the emperor's court conformed to proper protocol. When they felt that British conduct was recalcitrant or improper they cut back on provisions and stiffened their own attitude. When they could report that Macartney was diligently practicing for his imperial audience, they were more generous. A critical issue was always whether Macartney would perform a full kowtow of three kneelings and nine prostrations before the emperor. To this day, scholars dispute the question of whether, when he finally met the Qianlong emperor at the imperial retreat in Chengde, Macartney did or did not kowtow. It is significant, however, that the Chinese record is consistent that he did. Whatever the reality in such delicate confrontations with troublesome foreigners, the Chinese would insist for the record that the court's agents had ensured that the European envoys had conformed to Chinese protocol and offered proper obeisance to the emperor of China. When Lord Amherst returned to China in 1816, this time seeking to meet the emperor in Beijing, it was much more difficult to fudge any deviation from established protocol, and Amherst's refusal to perform the kowtow led to the failure of his mission.[20]

The tragic denouement to these interactions with the rising and aggressive British Empire was of course the Opium War. That fateful conflict has usually been studied as a violent opening of China to Western trade conducted in defense of wealthy and influential English drug-smuggling enterprises. Accurate as that account may be and shameful as the British *casus belli* surely was, a recent Chinese study of the Opium War by Mao Haijian reminds us of other important issues. Mao notes, for example, that once hostilities broke out, the imperial policy vacillated between extermination (*jiao* 剿) and appeasement (*fu* 撫). In essence these were war and peace parties, hawks and doves, but the Chinese vocabulary was exactly the same as would be used with domestic rebels. The discourse of the Qing court and its bureaucrats militated against any discussion of the British as a sovereign foreign state.[21] The Chinese conception of *wuwai* (no outer-separation) complicated all effort to devise an effective foreign policy. Mao further observes that the "appeasement" party was strongest among those who actually had to confront the British forces, and indeed members of the war party often shifted to the other side once confronted with the facts of British military superiority.[22] The Chinese officials and generals in Mao's account repeatedly report falsely to the emperor in order to cover up their failings, but more important, to make their accounts correspond to the insistent imperial commands to exterminate the enemy. For Mao Haijian, therefore, the Opium War becomes the occasion for the collapse of the Celestial Empire (*Tianchao* 天朝), the moment at which all the illusions of maintaining a hierarchical China-centered world order collapsed.

What is notable and what forms a central theme of another recent study of the Opium War by James Polachek is the minimal impact that the Opium War of 1839–1942 had on the foreign policy of the Qing state. Polachek attributes this to exaggerated reports of the success of gentry-led militia, especially in the Sanyuanli incident that would become a key local episode in the narrative of popular national resistance to Western imperialism. In the village of Sanyuanli on the outskirts of Canton (Guangzhou), a large force of local militia confronted a wayward patrol of British imperial (mostly Indian) soldiers and managed to kill a small number of them when the British flintlocks failed to fire in a driving rainstorm. It was a minor victory for the Chinese, but it received much attention at the time and achieved legendary stature in future nationalist historiography. The Qing officials' suppression of any reports of military defeat and the exaggeration of small victories over the British produced a perception in literati circles that the Opium War defeat and the humiliation of the Nanjing Treaty were the product of a traitorous sellout by such disgraced Manchu negotiators as Qiying.[23] With all accounts adjusted to conform to the perceived view of the emperor, the closed internal networks of bureaucratic communication precluded a diversity of views that might have called established truths into question.[24]

The problem is nicely illustrated in a famous letter that Lin Zexu wrote to a friend two years after the war. He told of the need for China to develop better ships and guns—in effect to embark on an early effort at military modernization—but concluded his letter by noting that he was in disgrace from his failure in the war and sternly enjoining his friend not to tell anyone of his views.[25] As a result of such self-censorship and suppression of contrary opinions, the impractical resistance to British demands continued in the second Opium War (1856–1860). As before, intransigence came not from those with actual experience in dealing with the new European threat, but from imperial censors and others who believed the Opium War myths of British vulnerability in land fighting. They adamantly resisted British demands for diplomatic residence in Beijing as a violation of all precedents for managing the barbarians. Any altering of these precedents, they feared, would damage the prestige of the dynasty in the eyes of such loyal tributaries as Korea and the Ryukyu islands (Okinawa). Such arguments strengthened the most xenophobic elements in court and brought about the Anglo-French occupation of the capital and the destruction of the Yuanmingyuan Summer Palace in 1860.[26]

THE TREATY SYSTEM

The two Opium Wars brought an end to the tribute system and replaced it with the treaty system, inaugurating what John K. Fairbank has termed the "treaty century" in modern Chinese history.[27] In all the years of negotiation leading up to this new order, the foreign powers and the British in particular had insisted that the Qing court accept the Westphalian order of diplomatic equality between sovereign states. Thus, for example, in his effort to force the Chinese to acknowledge the equivalence of the Qianlong emperor and King George, Lord Macartney had proposed that if he were required to kowtow to the emperor of China, a Chinese official of equivalent rank should kowtow to a portrait of King George.[28] Similarly, when the American envoy John Ward traveled to Beijing to exchange treaty ratifications in 1859, he proposed offering every respect and deference to the Chinese emperor that he would to his own president—a proposal rejected as placing China "on a par with the barbarians of the South and East, an arrogance of greatness which is simply ridiculous."[29] In the negotiations leading up to the Opium War, the British representatives consistently refused Chinese demands to entitle their notes to the Qing authorities, *bing* (稟), a term denoting communications from a subordinate official.[30] The intensity of the confrontations over these matters leaves no doubt of the Qing officials' fear of accepting any document that might undermine the ritual superiority of the Chinese emperor, and the British conviction that opening China to trade would require overcoming the Chinese "arrogance" that lay behind these protocols.[31] The British victory in the Opium Wars meant that the treaties of Nanjing (1842) and Tianjin (1858) would be carefully written to indicate the sovereign equality of the Chinese and British empires.

The formal diplomatic equality embodied in the treaties masked a host of provisions that disadvantaged China. Indeed, by the early twentieth century, these treaties came to be known as the "unequal treaties"—a term that has stuck in both Chinese and Western public discourse and historical writing to this day.[32] In part this result simply reflected a common characteristic of many legal regimes, where the uneven distribution of wealth and power permits the stronger party to transform formal equity into substantive injustice. There were also a number of provisions in these treaties where the utter lack of reciprocity left them unequal even in a formal sense. The low fixed tariffs required of China were not matched by any tariff concessions on the British (or other foreign signatories') side. The extraterritorial provisions for consular jurisdiction over foreigners in China were not equally applied to Chinese in Europe. The most-favored-nation provisions were also nonreciprocal. As Chinese began to study international law in the late nineteenth and early twentieth century, these gross inequities became the focus of a prolonged campaign for treaty revision—a campaign that would finally achieve some success during World War II, after Japanese attacks on Western colonialism became a propaganda embarrassment for the Allied powers.[33]

The problem, however, was far greater than specific treaty provisions. The larger system of Western and Japanese imperialism built upon a range of provisions in the unequal treaties that limited Chinese sovereignty. In fact, the treaty system, justified by an appeal to the Westphalian equality of sovereign states, created a regime in which Chinese sovereignty was threatened in ever more perilous ways.

Consider, for example, the question of Chinese tariffs. Concerned by the arbitrary way in which tariffs and fees were collected under the Canton system of trade, which preceded the Opium War, the British insisted on low fixed tariffs, usually 5 percent ad valorem, in the Treaty of Nanjing and its supplementary agreements. Since most countries in the nineteenth century relied to a significant degree on import duties to support their treasury and protect infant industries, this already left China disadvantaged in its trading regime.[34] Then, following the fall of Shanghai to the Small Swords rebels in the 1850s, the British started collecting the tariff on China's behalf, an arrangement that soon led to the establishment of the foreign-administered Chinese Imperial Maritime Customs. The Imperial Maritime Customs gradually expanded its mandate to include improving port facilities and navigation at the treaty ports, then handling China's first postal service, and finally managing tax collection of the Salt Administration. All of these measures arguably improved the efficiency and enhanced the revenue streams of the imperial government, but this was achieved at the cost of foreign control over key parts of China's fiscal apparatus.

The threat to China's sovereignty became clear in the early years of the republic, when customs and salt revenues were held in escrow in foreign banks until the great powers were satisfied that the new republic would not threaten their established interests. This was done, of course, with a heavy dose of colonial self-righteousness: "It seems to be our duty," wrote the British minister in Beijing, "to take all the measures we can to prevent China from becoming another Egypt."[35] This foreign control over the most reliable revenue source of the central government played a significant role in destabilizing politics in the early republic. Since the customs and salt revenues were paid by the customs service to the government in Beijing, warlords had every incentive to concentrate on seizing the capital and little reason to improve governance in their own provinces. The result was a decade of internal warfare in which one warlord after the other conspired to assemble a military coalition to capture Beijing and form a new government funded by the foreign-controlled customs revenues. When Sun Yat-sen's revolutionary government in South China challenged this system and demanded control of the customs collected in Canton, British antipathy to the Nationalists' anti-imperialist agenda set off the customs crisis of 1923. In the end, the Maritime Customs continued to funnel monies from Canton to the warlord government in Beijing.[36]

Extraterritoriality was another particularly sensitive provision of the treaties. Designed to protect foreigners from the vagaries of Chinese justice—particularly after a British seaman was executed for the accidental death of a Chinese from an ill-advised naval training exercise—this treaty provision called for the adjudication of cases involving foreigners by the consular authorities of the country from which the foreigner came. The provision was not without precedent in Chinese practice, and seems to have been easily accepted by the Chinese negotiators who had no desire to sit in judgment on disputes among foreigners. Since foreign merchants under the old system were confined to specific quarters of trading cities on the frontier, most disputes were likely to occur within the foreign community and it made more sense for the foreigners to settle them according to their own laws and customs.[37] Later agreements, however, permitted foreign access to the interior, a privilege initially exploited largely by Christian missionaries after China was forced to renounce the prohibitions on Christianity. These unwelcome intruders met with widespread resistance and periodic violence, incidents that then called forth "gunboat diplomacy" to protect the missionary enterprise. The most famous and fateful incident in the escalating tensions between Christians and their Chinese opponents was the Boxer Uprising of 1899–1900, which resulted in the foreign occupation of Beijing and the punitive Boxer Protocol of 1901. Since the final stage of the Boxer movement had threatened the foreign community in the capital, the great powers demanded as part of the Boxer settlement the right to place garrisons to protect foreign access to Beijing. In the twentieth century, the Japanese proved the most insistent on maintaining these garrisons and in 1932 they used their agents in Tianjin to spirit off Puyi, the last Manchu emperor, to preside over their puppet state in Manchukuo. In 1937, the Marco Polo Bridge incident that sparked the War of Resistance with Japan again involved Japanese troops stationed near Beijing to protect the railways as part of the Boxer settlement. It is clear, therefore, that the gradual expansion of treaty privileges over the course of the nineteenth and early twentieth centuries led to a situation in which foreign gunboats routinely patrolled China's rivers, foreign troops were stationed on Chinese soil, and some of the most fundamental aspects of sovereign control of Chinese territory had been grossly compromised.[38]

One of the most important and transformative products of the treaty system was the opening of trading entrepôts that came to be known as treaty ports, and the foreign-controlled concessions that grew up in these cities. The expansion of trade had always been the most important objective of the Western powers seeking access to the vast Chinese market for the manufactures of the Industrial Revolution. Frustrated by the confinement of trade to Canton, the British insisted in the Treaty of Nanjing that additional ports be opened up, the most important of which was Shanghai. Later treaties opened Tianjin in the north and Hankou (now part of Wuhan) far up the Yangzi (Yangtze) River, followed by dozens of other ports both on the coast and on China's internal waterways. The Qing state was not anxious to have Western merchants and seamen living in the midst of the Chinese population—especially when their arrival was the result of warfare that hardly endeared the alien interlopers to the local Chinese. For their part, the Europeans with their convictions of racial superiority were not anxious to live among the Chinese. So the idea of foreign concessions as a separate urban district, typically outside the old city walls, was a natural solution for both sides. Since the concessions were designed for foreigners and foreigners were beyond Chinese legal jurisdiction, the transformation of these concessions into what were in effect colonial enclaves on Chinese soil was the inevitable result. Rather quickly, however, the ban on Chinese residence proved both impractical and detrimental to the economic health of the concessions, so these colonial enclaves soon housed a substantial Chinese population.

Although Tianjin and Hankou played important roles in north and central China respectively, and the Japanese built a strategically important trading center in Dalian (Dairen) to serve their growing interests in Manchuria, Shanghai was always modern China's most important economic center, and its relative importance in China's modern economy only increased with time. In the twentieth century Shanghai also became a major center of cultural production, with most of the publishing industry, nationally circulated journals, and the new film industry concentrated in the city. By and large, the financial, manufacturing, and publishing enterprises were all based in the foreign concessions, thus illustrating the complex historical role of the foreign presence in China.

On the one hand, the concessions were colonial enclaves under foreign rule. Sikh policemen under British command kept order in the streets. Public parks had regulations that excluded dogs and unaccompanied Chinese, producing the urban legend of a sign that read "No dogs or Chinese allowed."[39] There were exclusive areas closed to Chinese at the race course, in private clubs, and in the best hotels. The treaty port English press reeked of colonial arrogance, often of an openly racist nature. In the Shanghai concessions, the privileged position of Westerners and Japanese and the second-class status of Chinese in their country's largest city was a continuously reenacted fact of everyday life.[40] On the other hand, precisely because the concessions protected economic enterprises from Chinese taxation, arbitrary exactions, and an unstable political system, they attracted capital from China and the world and hosted the most dynamic segment of the Chinese economy. In a 1937 survey of 2,435 Chinese-owned factories, nearly half of them (48.7 percent) were in Shanghai.[41] The publishing industry was attracted to the concessions by their relatively liberal press laws, which allowed editors to escape the censorship of the imperial and later the Nationalist government. And throughout early twentieth-century China, political dissidents found refuge in the concessions where in the final years of the empire they published anti-Manchu invective in radical journals, and in the 1920s they gathered for the first congress of the Chinese Communist Party.

For years, the imperial government had sought to limit the influence of foreigners on Chinese politics, culture, and society by carefully controlling tribute missions, confining merchants to trading ports on the frontier, and strictly prohibiting missionary proselytizing in the interior. By the twentieth century, the foreign presence was an integral part of the Chinese polity. To some degree, this foreign presence stimulated economic development, promoted a more cosmopolitan culture, and even created (through the refuge for radicals in the concessions) the conditions for political change. But any Chinese patriot could also see that these changes, however desirable, were accomplished at the cost of a significant loss of sovereignty.

During the course of the "treaty century" there was one final set of consequences of China's fateful confrontation with Western and Japanese imperialism that could not in any sense be considered desirable. This was the progressive loss of Chinese territory. Every defeat in war seemed to carve off another portion of the Chinese empire. The process began with the Opium War and the British seizure of Hong Kong as its colony. In the Sino-French War of 1884–1885, China lost its Vietnamese tributary to French colonialism; and a decade later, Korea fell under Japanese domination, to be incorporated into its empire in 1910. Also as a result of the Sino-Japanese War, Taiwan was ceded to Japan, the first loss of an entire Chinese province to a foreign power. Defeat in the Sino-Japanese War so convinced the European powers that China was on the verge of collapse that it set off the Scramble for Concessions in which each of the powers claimed a sphere of influence in which it would be guaranteed preferential access to railway, mining, and other projects for the exploitation of China's natural resources. Germany seized the port of Qingdao and claimed a sphere in Shandong province, and Russia claimed an ice-free port and naval base at Dalian and Port Arthur on the Liaodong Peninsula. Both of these would soon be taken over by Japan: the Liaodong concessions after the 1904–1905 Russo-Japanese War and the Shandong sphere at the outbreak of World War I. Finally, when the Qing dynasty fell in 1911, both Mongolia (with support from Russia) and Tibet (with British backing) declared their independence of China—claiming, with considerable merit, that their adherence had been to the Qing dynasty and not to a Han-nationalist Chinese Republic.[42]

THE RISE OF NATIONALISM

The accelerating assault on China's sovereignty and territorial integrity eventually sparked the nationalism that has animated China's politics ever since the early twentieth century. While a deep-seated sense of cultural superiority had informed China's early reactions to Western intrusions, by the end of the nineteenth century progressive intellectuals envisioned a social Darwinian struggle for national survival in which the fitness of China's established institutions was called into fundamental question. Where earlier generations of Chinese rulers had rejected Western demands for increased trade and diplomatic relations on grounds that they did not conform to Chinese institutional forms (*tizhi* 體制),[43] the new patriots called for a radical reform of those very institutions in order to prevent China from enduring the imperial collapse that had afflicted the Mogul empire in India, or Egypt and the Ottoman Empire in the Middle East.[44]

In the practice of Chinese politics, the most important departure of the new nationalist proponents of reform was the liberation of political discourse from the confines of bureaucratic communications and private letters to include a broader public through the new medium of the treaty port press. The process began with protests over the concessions to Japan in the wake of the Sino-Japanese War. A group of patriotic scholars who had gathered in the capital

Nationalism was the result of foreign inroads in China.

for the metropolitan examinations advocated continued resistance to Japan to avoid ceding sovereignty over Taiwan and Liaodong. To advance their cause they organized unprecedented mass memorials and published them in the Shanghai press.[45] In the years following the 1898 reforms and then the Boxer debacle of 1900–1901, the treaty port press (especially in Shanghai) and radical publications by Chinese students in Japan became a major force in Chinese politics.[46] The government could no longer confine political debate to the constrained forms and outmoded categories of official memorials and imperial edicts. Once discussion of foreign policy and national security ceased to be a state monopoly, it quickly became a weapon to attack the competence and ultimately the legitimacy of the Qing state. As the failings of the Qing were exposed to increasingly penetrating public dissection, criticism and open opposition grew to the extent that a relatively minor mutiny by radical soldiers in 1911 sparked a revolution that toppled the dynasty within a few months and established the Republic of China.

During the Republican era (1912–1949), patriotic resistance to Western and Japanese imperialism motivated every major political movement that affected the course of Chinese history. In 1919, the May Fourth Movement mobilized students to protest against the Versailles Peace Conference and its decision to grant Germany's rights in Shandong province to Japan instead of returning them to China. By this time, China had scholars and diplomats schooled in international law and they took seriously Woodrow Wilson's Fourteen Points and American promises to defend all nations' rights to self-determination. But Versailles revealed the hypocrisy of great power diplomacy and confirmed the growing conviction that China would enjoy her just rights in the international arena only when she became powerful enough to defend them on her own. What especially outraged the student demonstrators was the discovery of the Beijing government's secret assent to Japan's assuming the German concession, in return for which the warlords in power received a Japanese loan to finance their armies.[47] Here was the ultimate proof of the perils of secret diplomacy, and of the unholy alliance of warlords and imperialism that kept China weak and endangered. Thus the next stage of the revolutionary movement, the National Revolution led by the Nationalist Party (Guomindang/Kuomintang) in a united front with the Chinese Communist Party, took aim at imperialism and warlord rule and united the country in 1928.

A fundamental aim of the Nationalist regime was the abolition of the "unequal treaties" and substantial progress was made in this regard. China regained tariff autonomy and was able to raise import duties to increase revenues and protect its new industries; the number of foreign concessions in the treaty ports was reduced from thirty-three to thirteen; and a newly assertive Chinese government gained some respect in such international councils as the

League of Nations.[48] But China's rise was more than matched by an increasingly aggressive Japanese imperialism, which seized control of China's northeastern provinces in 1931 and established the puppet state of Manchukuo. From their Manchurian base, the Japanese relentlessly encroached into North China, crossing inside the Great Wall and threatening the former capital of Beijing (in 1927, the Nationalists had established their new capital in Nanjing). The National Government signed a series of agreements seeking to slow the Japanese advance, the most notable being the He-Umezu agreement signed by the minister of war, He Yingqin, in 1935. As news of this agreement, which demilitarized (and thus left undefended) the area around Beijing, reached the students, they again rose in protest against the government's pusillanimous secret diplomacy in the December Ninth Movement of 1935. Press criticism, public petitions by intellectuals, and political dissent in the National Party and military forces placed enormous pressure on the National Government. Its continued legitimacy and ability to rule was threatened by its inability to protect the nation against Japanese aggression.

Chiang Kai-shek's insistence on first crushing the Chinese Communist rebels before turning his attention to Japan was particularly unpopular. Then in December 1936, Chiang was kidnapped by one of his own generals in the Xi'an incident and forced into a new united front with the Chinese Communists. Less than a year later, on July 7, 1937, full-scale war with Japan broke out and the eight-year War of Resistance began.[49] In the early years of the war, popular support for Chiang Kai-shek and the National Government was strong, but as the war dragged on, the Nationalist Party was judged to be more concerned with its own privileges and creature comforts than with the fate of the nation. The Chinese Communists, by contrast, led an effective guerrilla resistance behind Japanese lines and by the end of the war, in the eyes of many Chinese, they had earned a reputation as the true defenders of the nation. By 1949 the Nationalist government had been driven to refuge on Taiwan, and the failure to subdue foreign threats had brought down another Chinese regime.

The emperors of late imperial China may have had an inflated and ultimately untenable view of China's place in the world order, but they did correctly perceive that their legitimacy depended, among other things, on the successful management of foreign affairs. For a substantial period, this was accomplished by keeping foreigners at a distance and ensuring that compromises that called into question the emperor's paramount position remained a confidential matter that could be covered up in official documents. An increasingly aggressive Western and Japanese imperialism dismantled the old tribute system and replaced it with the (unequal) treaty system in the years after the Opium War. But the critical change really came at the turn of the twentieth century, when the new Chinese press in the treaty ports drew back the veil of secrecy and opened up foreign affairs to widespread public scrutiny by nationalist critics. As before, regime legitimacy depended on the successful management of foreign affairs, but now the measure of success became a matter of public debate. Then as now, state news agencies and official censorship would seek to manipulate and control that debate, but mass nationalism had become an integral part of Chinese politics. It remains so today, and along with economic prosperity, nationalism has replaced Marxism-Leninism as one of the fundamental bases for the present regime's claim to political legitimacy.

NOTES

1. There is a lively debate on the nature of Manchu rule and just how "Chinese" China's last dynasty was. The debate is well represented in Evelyn Rawski's "Presidential Address: Reenvisioning the Qing: The Significance of the Qing Period in Chinese History," *Journal of Asian Studies* 55, no. 4 (November 1996): 829–50, and the response by Ho Ping-ti, "In Defense of Sinicization: A Rebuttal of Evelyn Rawski's 'Reenvisioning the Qing," *Journal of Asian Studies* 57, no 1. (February 1998): 123–55. The key monographic works are Pamela Crossley, *Orphan Warriors: Three Manchu Generations and the End of the Qing World* (Princeton, NJ: Princeton University Press, 1990) and her even more impressive *A Translucent Mirror: History and Identity in Qing Imperial Ideology* (Berkeley: University of California Press, 1999); Evelyn S. Rawski, *The Last Emperors: A Social History of Qing Imperial Institutions* (Berkeley: University of California Press, 1998); Mark C. Elliott, *The Manchu Way: The Eight Banners and Ethnic Identity in Late Imperial China* (Stanford, CA: Stanford University Press, 2001); and Edward J. M. Rhoads, *Manchus & Han: Ethnic Relations and Political Power in Late Qing and Early Republican China, 1861–1928* (Seattle: University of Washington Press, 2000).

2. Mark Mancall, "The Ch'ing Tribute System: An Interpretive Essay," in John King Fairbank, ed., *The Chinese World Order: Traditional China's Foreign Relations* (Cambridge, MA: Harvard University Press, 1968), 63.

3. James L. Hevia, *Cherishing Men from Afar: Qing Guest Ritual and the Macartney Embassy of 1793* (Durham, NC: Duke University Press, 1995), esp. xi, 9–28; Lydia H. Liu, *The Clash of Empires: The Invention of China in Modern World Making* (Cambridge, MA: Harvard University Press, 2004), 39–58. The classic study of the tribute system is J. K. Fairbank and S. Y. Teng, "On the Ch'ing Tributary System," *Harvard Journal of Asiatic Studies* 6, no. 2 (June 1941): 135–246. Fairbank is the focus of the recent critiques (Teng Ssu-yü's contribution typically being ignored). Hevia particularly objects to the functional theory that he finds behind Fairbank's analysis; Liu focuses her assault on "the theory of Chinese xenophobia" (39). In both cases the prime object seems to be to rescue China from any Orientalist disparagement so that critical analysis of the modern confrontation between China and the West can focus on the colonial sins of the European powers.

4. *Da-Ming jili* [Collected rituals of the Ming] (Palace edition, 1530) as cited in Fairbank and Teng, "On the Ch'ing Tributary System," 141. See also John E. Wills,

Jr., *Embassies and Illusions: Dutch and Portuguese Envoys to K'ang-hsi, 1666–1687* (Cambridge, MA: Harvard University Council on East Asian Studies, 1984), 5–7, on the ceremonial compilations' "extreme antiquarianism" and preoccupation with ancient precedent.

5. Cited in Kung-chuan Hsiao, *A History of Chinese Political Thought,* vol. 1: *From the Beginnings to the Sixth Century A.D.,* trans. F. W. Mote (Princeton, NJ: Princeton University Press, 1979), 23. (I have substituted "subjects" for "servants" in this translation.)

6. This translation is from Wang Gungwu, "Early Ming Relations with Southeast Asia: A Background Essay," in Fairbank, *Chinese World Order,* 56.

7. Fairbank and Teng, "On the Ch'ing Tributary System," 137–39. Cf. Kung-chuan Hsiao, *A History of Chinese Political Thought,* 1:137–42.

8. Immanuel C. Y. Hsü, *China's Entrance into the Family of Nations: The Diplomatic Phase, 1858–1880* (Cambridge, MA: Harvard University Press, 1960), 7; Lien-sheng Yang, "Historical Notes on the Chinese World Order," in Fairbank, *Chinese World Order,* 27.

9. Frank Dikötter, *The Discourse of Race in Modern China* (Stanford, CA: Stanford University Press, 1992), 4.

10. Brantly Womack, *China and Vietnam: The Politics of Asymmetry* (Cambridge: Cambridge University Press, 2005); Hae-jong Chun, "Sino-Korean Tributary Relations in the Ch'ing Period," 90–111, in Fairbank, *Chinese World Order;* Kenneth M. Swope, "Deceit, Disguise, and Dependence: China, Japan, and the Future of the Tributary System, 1592–1596," *International History Review* 24, no. 4 (December 2002): 757–82; Kenneth R. Robinson, "Centering the King of Choson: Aspects of Korean Maritime Diplomacy, 1392–1592," *Journal of Asian Studies* 59, no. 1 (February 2000): 109–25.

11. Fairbank and Teng, "On the Ching Tributary System." Cf. Wills, *Embassies and Illusions,* 23, on the "blatant commercial motivation for [tribute] embassies."

12. A nice summary and citation of the critical literature is in L. J. Newby, *The Empire and the Khanate: A Political History of Qing Relations with Khoqand, c. 1760–1860* (Leiden: Brill, 2005), 5–10.

13. Pamela Kyle Crossley, *A Translucent Mirror: History and Identity in Qing Imperial Ideology* (Berkeley: University of California Press, 1999), 11–12, ch. 5.

14. Zhang Yuxin 张羽新, "Qingdai qianqi ge minzu tongyi guannian de lishi tezheng" 清代前期各民族统一观念的历史特征 [The historical characteristics of early Qing concepts of multiethnic unity], *Qingshi yanjiu* 清史研究 2 (1996): 30–38.

15. Mark Mancall, *Russia and China: Their Diplomatic Relations to 1728* (Cambridge, MA: Harvard University Press, 1971).

16. Peter C. Perdue, *China Marches West: The Qing Conquest of Central Eurasia* (Cambridge, MA: Belknap Press of Harvard University Press, 2005), ch. 4–5.

17. Perdue, *China Marches West,* ch. 7.

18. Mancall, *Russia and China,* 109.

19. Mancall, *Russia and China,* 149–61.

20. On the Macartney mission, see in particular, Hevia, *Cherishing Men from Afar* and my own critique in "Cherishing Sources from Afar," *Modern China* 24, no. 2 (April 1998): 135–61; Earl F. Pritchard, *The Crucial Years of Early Anglo-Chinese Relations,*

1750–1800 (New York: Octagon, 1970 [originally published in 1936]) and "The Kowtow in the Macartney Embassy to China in 1793," *Far Eastern Quarterly* 2, no. 2 (February 1943): 163–203; Alain Peyrefitte, *The Immobile Empire*, trans. Jon Rothschild (New York: Knopf, 1992 [French original: 1989]); Pierre-Henri Durand (Dai Tingjie) "Jianting ze ming—Majia'erni shihua zaitan" 兼听则明—马戛尔尼使华在探 [Listening, it becomes clear: A new look at the Macartney mission], preface 89–150 in *Yingshi Majia'erni fanghua dang'an shiliao* 英使马戛尔尼访华档案史料汇编 [Collection of archival materials on the Macartney mission to China], edited by First Historical Archives (Beijing: Guoji wenhua chubanshe, 1996).

21. Mao Haijian 茅海建, *Tianchao de bengkui* 天朝的崩溃 [The collapse of the Celestial Empire] (Beijing: Sanlian, 1995), ch. 3, esp. 155.

22. Parenthetically, it is notable that Mao Haijian, himself a military historian, devotes most of his first chapter (33–46) to analyzing the failure of the Chinese military to keep up with advances in Western military technology, especially in the rifling of firearms and the working out of precise formulae for the mixing of gunpowder, essential for accurately calculating trajectories of artillery shells. That analysis contrasts strikingly with the notably positive appraisal of the Qing military in Joanna Waley-Cohen, *The Culture of War in China: Empire and the Military under the Qing Dynasty* (London: I.B. Tauris, 2006).

23. James M. Polachek, *The Inner Opium War* (Cambridge, MA: Harvard Council on East Asian Studies, 1992); cf. Mao Haijian, *Tianchao de bengkui*, 293–313.

24. This notion is inspired, in part, by Pierre-Henri Durand's essay, cited above, on the Macartney mission.

25. Lin Zexu to Wu Zixu, cited in Ssu-yü Teng and John K. Fairbank, *China's Response to the West, a Documentary Survey, 1839–1923* (New York: Atheneum, 1954), 28.

26. Hsü, *China's Entrance*, 57–58; Masataka Banno, *China and the West, 1858–1861: The Origins of the Tsungli Yamen* (Cambridge, MA: Harvard University Press, 1964), 18–27.

27. Cited in Dong Wang, *China's Unequal Treaties: Narrating National Histories* (Lanham, MD: Lexington Books, 2005), 1.

28. Pritchard, "The Kowtow," 188.

29. Banno, *China and the West*, 124.

30. Mao Haijian, *Tianchao de bengkui*, 97.

31. For an insightful study of the colonial impulses that lay behind the British attempts to overcome Chinese "arrogance," see James L. Hevia, *English Lessons: The Pedagogy of Imperialism in Nineteenth-Century China.* (Durham, NC: Duke University Press, 2003).

32. The key study here is Dong Wang, *China's Unequal Treaties*. On the popularization of the term by both Nationalist and Communist parties during the 1920s, see ch. 3.

33. Dong Wang, *China's Unequal Treaties*.

34. Dong Wang, *China's Unequal Treaties*, 14–15. In the United States in the mid-nineteenth century, 93 percent of federal revenues came from customs duties. Stanley Lebergott, *The Americans: An Economic Record* (New York: Norton, 1984), 140. (Thanks to Michael Bernstein for this reference.)

35. John Jordan to Langley, May 25, 1912, cited in Ernest P. Young, *The Presidency of Yuan Shih-k'ai: Liberalism and Dictatorship in Early Republican China* (Ann Arbor: University of Michigan Press, 1977), 47.

36. John King Fairbank, *Trade and Diplomacy on the China Coast: The Opening of the Treaty Ports, 1842–1854* (Stanford, CA: Stanford University Press, 1969), 371–461 on the establishment of the Maritime Customs; Hosea Ballou Morse, *The Trade and Administration of the Chinese Empire* (Shanghai: Kelly and Walsh, 1908); Ying-wan Cheng, *Postal Communication in China and Its Modernization, 1860–1896* (Cambridge, MA: East Asian Research Center, Harvard University, 1970); S. A. M. Adshead, *The Modernization of the Chinese Salt Administration, 1900–1920* (Cambridge, MA: Harvard University Press, 1970); Young, *The Presidency of Yuan Shih-k'ai*, 42–49; C. Martin Wilbur, *Sun Yat-sen: Frustrated Patriot* (New York: Columbia University Press, 1976), 183–90.

37. See Joseph Fletcher, "The Heyday of the Ch'ing Order in Mongolia, Sinkiang and Tibet," *The Cambridge History of China*, vol. 10: *Late Ch'ing, 1800–1911, Part 1* (Cambridge: Cambridge University Press, 1978), 378–85 and a more nuanced analysis in Newby, *Empire and Khanate*, 192–99.

38. On missionary incidents, see Paul A. Cohen, *China and Christianity: The Missionary Movement and the Growth of Chinese Antiforeignism, 1860–1870* (Cambridge, MA: Harvard University Press, 1963); on the Boxers, Joseph W. Esherick, *The Origins of the Boxer Uprising* (Berkeley: University of California Press, 1987) and Lanxin Xiang, *The Origins of the Boxer War: A Multinational Study* (London: RoutledgeCurzon, 2003); on Japan in China in the 1930s, Parks M. Coble, *Facing Japan: Chinese Politics and Japanese Imperialism, 1931–1937* (Cambridge, MA: Council on East Asian Studies Harvard University, 1991).

39. Robert A. Bickers and Jeffrey N. Wasserstrom, "Shanghai's 'Dogs and Chinese Not Admitted' Sign: Legend, History and Contemporary Symbol," *China Quarterly*, no. 142 (June 1995): 444–66.

40. Nicholas R. Clifford, *Spoilt Children of Empire: Westerners in Shanghai and the Chinese Revolution in the 1920s* (Hanover, NH: Middlebury College Press, 1991); Robert Bickers, *Britain in China: Community Culture and Colonialism, 1900–1949* (Manchester: Manchester University Press, 1999); Rhoads Murphey, *Shanghai, Key to Modern China* (Cambridge, MA: Harvard University Press, 1953) and *The Treaty Ports and China's Modernization: What Went Wrong?* (Ann Arbor: University of Michigan, Center for Chinese Studies, 1970).

41. Albert Feuerwerker, "Economic Trends, 1912–1949," in *Cambridge History of China*, vol. 12: *Republican China, Part 1* (Cambridge: Cambridge University Press, 1983), 42.

42. Immanuel C. Y. Hsü, "Late Ch'ing Foreign Relations, 1860–1905," in *Cambridge History of China*, vol. 11: *Late Ch'ing, 1800–1911, Part 2* (Cambridge: Cambridge University Press, 1980), 70–141.

43. Esherick, "Cherishing Sources," 141.

44. The literature on Chinese nationalism is now huge, but there is still no better place to start than Joseph R. Levenson, *Confucian China and Its Modern Fate*, vol. 1 (Berkeley: University of California Press, 1958). For more recent discussions, see

James Townsend, "Chinese Nationalism," 1–30, and Prasenjit Duara "De-Constructing the Chinese Nation," 31–55, in Jonathan Unger, ed., *Chinese Nationalism* (Armonk, NY: M.E. Sharpe, 1996) and Duara's *Rescuing History from the Nation: Questioning Narratives of Modern China* (Chicago: University of Chicago Press, 1995), ch. 1–2; Henrietta Harrison, *Inventing the Nation: China* (New York: Oxford University Press, 2001); Rebecca E. Karl, *Staging the World: Chinese Nationalism at the Turn of the Twentieth Century* (Durham, NC: Duke University Press, 2002); and Suisheng Zhao, *A Nation-State by Construction: Dynamics of Modern Chinese Nationalism* (Stanford, CA: Stanford University Press, 2004).

45. Luke S. K. Kwong, *A Mosaic of the Hundred Days: Personalities, Politics and Ideas of 1898* (Cambridge, MA: Harvard University Press, 1984), 73, 90–91.

46. Joan Judge, *Print and Politics: "Shibao" and the Culture of Reform in Late Qing China* (Stanford, CA: Stanford University Press, 1996); Barbara Mittler, *A Newspaper for China? Power, Identity, and Change in Shanghai's News Media, 1872–1912* (Cambridge, MA: Harvard University Asia Center, 2004); Tang Haijiang 唐海江, *Qingmo zhenglun baokan yu minzhong dongyuan: yi zhong zhengzhi wenhua de shijiao*清末政论报刊与民众动员：一种政治文化的视角 [Political newspapers and journals of the late Qing and popular mobilization: A political culture perspective] (Beijing: Qinghua daxue chubanshe, 2007).

47. The classic study of the May Fourth Movement is Chow Tse-tsung, *The May Fourth Movement: Intellectual Revolution in Modern China* (Cambridge, MA: Harvard University Press, 1960).

48. James C. Thomson, Jr., *While China Faced West: American Reformers in Nationalist China, 1928–1937* (Cambridge, MA: Harvard University Press, 1969), 5–18.

49. Coble, *Facing Japan.*

2

On China's Rise

Lowell Dittmer

While China first appeared on the global economic stage in the 1980s, the rise of China has been the dominant metanarrative since Mao announced that China had "stood up" at Tiananmen in 1949. Indeed the teleology of rising, dovetailing neatly with the inevitable stage-by-stage advance implicit in historical materialism, has laced the rhetoric of China's leadership throughout the twentieth century, whether Communist or Nationalist, radical or moderate. There is in China a pervasive (and empirically justified) consciousness of China's glorious historical legacy, the descent from which is felt to be a collective humiliation crying out for redress, for "national salvation." National salvation meant modernization, to become a "rich country, strong state." Yet while the metanarrative has been clear and consistent, it turns out that its operational semantics are as susceptible to varied interpretation as the US Constitution, and Chinese politicians have often disagreed fiercely over how to parse it and how best to put it into effect, resulting in shifts in the selection of developmental models. These shifts may be attributed not only to changing political preferences, but to the attempt to adapt to the pressures imposed by China's international environment.

This chapter considers China's rise to be the outcome of interplay among three variables: the domestic political economy (land, labor, resources, social structure, etc.), the threats and opportunities implicit in the international environment, and the political (and in China, usually ideological) synthesis between the two crafted by political leadership. This correlation of variables changes periodically over time from one modality to another in a pattern of "punctuated equilibrium." But before elaborating on the nature and dynamic

39

of these shifts, what can we say about China's rise that will apply to the entire experience? Three aspects seem relatively distinctive.

First, perhaps moved by the moralistic Confucian distinction between "kingly way" (*wang dao*) and "hegemonic way" (*ba dao*), China has placed strong emphasis on the normative dimension of rising—although legitimacy is a typical concern of elites everywhere, the normative dimension seems unusually salient in this case. Joseph Esherick's preceding chapter has stressed the importance of at least the appearance of the rule of virtue in traditional China, and it remains an imperative of diplomacy. This is evinced for example in the emphasis on "principle"—other countries may be moved by interests but China, notwithstanding its Marxist background, places greatest emphasis on principles. There is an equally strong expectation that China's diplomatic interlocutors will share and reciprocate these principles; otherwise the relationship is deemed to be "abnormal," requiring normalization. Some principles (e.g., the "five principles of peaceful coexistence") are conceived to be generally applicable, while others are tailored to fit specific bilateral relationships: for example, the "three fundamental obstacles" that impeded Sino-Soviet normalization (until the Soviet Union finally removed them), or the "basic agreements" set forth on three ceremonial occasions to govern Sino-Japanese relations, or the "three communiqués" held to govern Sino-American relations since 1982. While these normative principles are fervently and repeatedly embraced as a necessary prelude to further negotiations, practical application is often quite "realist" and flexible, though perhaps more in domestic than in foreign policy.

Closely related to this is China's penchant for comprehensive theoretical frameworks in policymaking ("theory should guide practice" [*lilun zhidao shijian*]): other countries have foreign policies, but China's foreign policy is typically conceived as part of a world order, into which it (and in principle all other nations) must fit. China's foreign policy process may thus be said to be driven by international relations theory, not necessarily in the sense of a one-to-one correspondence between program and action but in the sense that policies are informed by theory and periodically assessed in terms of their contribution to normative national objectives in an evolving international system. During the Cold War there were Three Worlds, for example, in which China became part of the Third World, and today China is part of a "harmonious world."[1] These "persuasive definitions" also have action implications—the Third World, for example, from a Maoist perspective comprised an international proletarian vanguard, destined to lead the revolution against the advanced bourgeois countries and introduce a new, just world order. And China's conception of a "harmonious world" not only enhances China's "soft" power but gives it preceptorial rights in international and bilateral relations.

Third, unlike Great Britain, France, Nazi Germany, Imperial Japan, the Soviet Union, and other great (if transitory) modern empires, China never conceived of its rise to entail the conquest and absorption of vast territorial domains designed to enhance the power and ensure the future prosperity and security of the host country. To be sure, China has conceived its national destiny to include the occupation of all contiguous territory previously claimed by antecedent dynasties, including Taiwan, Hong Kong, Tibet, the Paracel and Spratly islands, and disputed border areas. And recent rhetoric to the contrary notwithstanding, China's rise has hardly been "peaceful": partly because some claims are disputed, China's recent history has been marred by relatively frequent though limited wars (usually defined as defensive wars), as well as by long, bloody internal wars and other violent domestic altercations.[2] True, China's rise has taken place from an asymmetric position in the international order at a time when the forcible acquisition of territorial empires was no longer in fashion. And China's involvement in the project to promote Marxist-Leninist "national liberation movements" throughout the rest of the world (especially the Third World) during the Maoist era bears certain similarities to imperialist expansionism (despite its anti-imperialist rhetoric). But strictly speaking China is correct in contending that it is not encumbered by an imperialist historical legacy or propensity.[3]

These relatively invariant features of China's rise suggest a principled consistency that is part of China's currently projected national self-image but significantly understates the jarring impact of Beijing's periodic policy reconfigurations, when old principles may be abruptly discarded and new ones adopted. These reconfigurations occur periodically, usually at a point of major system crisis or leadership succession when learning from negative feedback becomes more politically acceptable. The pattern has been one of path-dependent learning, in which the "principled" path is earmarked at these crisis points and then followed over the next decade or so. Inasmuch as it is based on principle and aimed at predesignated long-term goals, Beijing is apt to adhere to these policy "lines" with relatively stubborn consistency despite setbacks. But upon reaching a critical turning point the leadership has conducted a "summary of experience" and demanded "self-criticisms" (or purges) of those held responsible for the foregoing "errors." This marks the end of the old path, but it does not specify the direction of the new one, as there are typically a number of feasible alternatives to the old path. What often ensues is a "pause" in the policy process, when the vacuum created by the critique of the old path (and by unresolved tensions among elites) is filled with pragmatic experiments that are tolerated because an authoritative new line has not yet emerged, a time when several tentative new initiatives may even be pursued simultaneously. During such periods of unclear guidelines media controls may be relaxed somewhat, allowing a "thaw" in the Chinese public realm that is beloved by intellectuals but dreaded by bureaucrats fearful of feedback overload or "chaos" (*luan*). It is resolved when elites resolve their hierarchical disputes and tire of the give-and-take of policy debate. At this point a new line is announced, at which point the emphasis shifts from innovation to faithfully executing the new line and persuading everyone else (including diplomatic counterparts) of its merits.

Since Liberation there have been four such lines, by my reckoning: the period of Socialist Construction (1949–1959); the Great Proletarian Cultural Revolution (1966–1976); the Deng Xiaoping period of Reform and Opening (1979–1989), and finally the post-Deng period of Reform "Deepening" (1994–2008). Each period is preceded by the recognition, often forced by crisis, that the previous policy parameters have exhausted their practical applicability and that fundamental change is needed, followed by a pause allowing for a summary of experience, vigorous policy debate, policy experimentation, elite personnel adjustments, and, finally, the conception and implementation of a new policy line. During each period, the leadership seeks to fashion an optimal synthesis between political economic resources and international threats and opportunities to achieve both socialist and developmental goals. But since these are transformational goals aimed at an outcome no one has yet seen, the correlation is never perfect and there are frictions, adjustments, occasionally even oblique public disputes during each period.

SOCIALIST CONSTRUCTION

After restoring civil order and introducing a new currency under centralized control of the People's Bank of China (PBC) to bring rampant inflation under control, the Chinese Communist Party (CCP) established a set of temporary political structures under the ideological aegis of Mao Zedong's (1940) concept of New Democracy, designed to function as a United Front vehicle establishing unity between the Communist Party and the noncommunist Chinese majority through a gradual process of persuasion, political education, and, if necessary, coercion. Though these United Front organs were meant to be transitional until a more fully socialist system could be introduced, it was then decided to permit them to survive indefinitely under CCP tutelage. Yet this type of goal displacement was exactly what Mao feared, allowing bourgeois opposition to become entrenched, and he pressed constantly to accelerate the supersession of New Democracy. But even during socialist transition, China "rose" along two distinct tracks: modernization (meaning industrialization, urbanization, mechanization) in the economic arena, and socialist transformation (i.e., from private property to collective or public ownership, from chaotic market competition to planned cooperation) in the political arena. This tandem arrangement assumed a congruence between ends as well as means that was held together politically only with difficulty.

The socialist transition was swift and fairly brutal, though the Chinese seem to have learned from the Soviet collectivization experience. The primary task of the state during this period, as defined in the Chinese People's Political Consultative Conference (CPPCC) Common Program, had been completed by the time of the First National People's Congress in 1954: that task was the transformation of the feudal and semifeudal property into small peasant plots and the creation of the prerequisites for industrialization.

Thus the 1954 State Constitution declared that China was now in a period of "transition to socialism," heralding major structural changes in the political system (including a new legislature) as well as more radically egalitarian redistributive policies.

The CCP leadership during this period was relatively stable, with only two major disputes (the Gao Gang-Rao Shushi purge in 1954–1955 and the purge of Peng Dehuai in 1959), taking a hybrid collegial-hierarchical form with Mao "first among equals." Every decisive turn in the CCP leadership agenda has his stamp on it, but since in most cases Mao's initiatives were consistent with common goals but charismatically stylized and did not usually wreak disaster, his colleagues concurred. The first was the decision to "lean to one side" (*yibian dao*), that is, unreserved commitment to communist revolution as organized by the communist international movement. To Mao, this was a disjunctive choice; as he put it in a speech commemorating the twenty-eighth anniversary of the CCP (June 30, 1949): "In the light of the experiences accumulated in these forty years and these 28 years, all Chinese without exception must lean either to the side of imperialism or to the side of socialism. Sitting on the fence will not do, nor is there a third road."[4] Not only was this option far more ideologically attuned to the CCP's transformational agenda; Moscow was prepared to provide China with a support package never envisaged in Washington. Though the CCP leadership had earlier expressed interest in maintaining positive relations with the United States and other Western governments, the polarization of relations between Moscow and Washington since 1947 made clear the choice had to be mutually exclusive. The choice was sealed by China's dispatch of a million "volunteers" into the Korean War to save the collapsing Democratic People's Republic of Korea (DPRK) regime in October 1950, allaying Stalin's suspicions of Chinese Titoism and foreclosing any opening to the United States. Mao made the decision to come to the defense of a small neighboring socialist country from the mightiest power on the globe against the advice of the Politburo majority, a bold choice befitting the chairman's definition of heroism:

Were rather lacking in culture;
Rather lacking in literary talent
Were the emperors Tang Tai Tsung and Sung Tai Tsu;
And Genghis Khan,
Beloved Son of Heaven for a day,
Only knew how to bend his bow at the golden eagle.
Now they are all past and gone:
To find men truly great and noble-hearted
We must look here in the present.[5]
(Chin Shih Huang and Han Wu Ti, "But alas these heroes!")

It was costly but not disastrous, ending in 1953 in a compromise that protected China's minimal security interests. True, the decision not only forfeited the recovery of Taiwan but precluded any influx of trade or investment from the capitalist world (the Seventh Fleet imposed a twenty-two-year embargo), and for the next two decades economic relations were essentially limited to the communist bloc. But given the leadership's view of international markets in terms of Lenin's theory of imperialism, being shut out of world markets did not matter; the Soviet model of socialist development in one country presented a heroic and plausible alternative. Similarly, whereas the governmental structure and socialization timetable was consensually agreed upon, Mao took it upon himself to tweak the schedule opportunistically, as in the 1955 acceleration of collectivization, or the 1958 Great Leap, in which Mao's bold assertiveness overcame collegial objections as well as (initially) objective difficulties.

The foreign policy context in which socialist construction took place was one of global bipolarity, but the trend was from tight to loose bipolarity, culminating in the "spirit of Camp David" that prevailed during Nikita Khrushchev's 1959 visit to the United States. As antagonism between the two "poles" diminished, friction between Beijing and Moscow increased, culminating in the twenty-year Sino-Soviet dispute. This was precipitated partly by bilateral issues (discomfort with the highly centralized Soviet growth model, unhappiness over Khrushchev's unilateral verdict reversal on Stalin, Soviet criticism of Mao's Leap), but triangular issues involving the United States (i.e., disagreement over détente) also emerged during Khrushchev's visit to China following his tour of the United States. As Soviet foreign policy became less militant (with a satellite in orbit, an assured nuclear second-strike capability, and confidence in the superiority of its economic system after a decade of impressive growth), Chinese foreign policy radicalized: China now scorned the "parliamentary road" advocated by the French or Italian communist parties and became increasingly selective in befriending developing regimes or endorsing national liberation wars. One can sense in Moscow a dawning perception that Beijing was proving to be more troublesome than Washington. Still, as long as

Soviet-American relations retained their edge (as they did after Francis Pow-ers's U-2 was shot down over Soviet air space in 1960, and further intensifying under Kennedy) China retained freedom of maneuver. Perhaps the field in which the Chinese exercised the greatest initiative was in recognizing and seeking to shape the emergence of a new nonaligned bloc in world politics consisting of the developing nations created upon retreat of the colonial pow-ers. It was in this context that Zhou Enlai, in concert with India's Nehru and Indonesia's Sukarno (two cofounders of this bloc), articulated the Five Prin-ciples of Peaceful Coexistence, or Panchsheel. These were subsequently incor-porated into the 1956 People's Republic of China (PRC) Constitution and have been retained in every state constitution since, helping facilitate China's rela-tions with the developing world.[6]

By the end of the First Five Year Plan (FFYP) in 1957 the CCP ambition to "rise" seemed to have met all criteria of success, whether measured by either socialization or economic modernization criteria. It was not a peaceful rise: Mao's ideology emphasized uncompromising class struggle and "national lib-eration wars," and China not only intervened in Korea but sent arms and advi- sors to North Vietnam contributing to the successful outcome there and sup-ported an unsuccessful insurgency in Malaysia, also sending very sizable military and developmental aid to various Third World movements and gov-ernments.[7] Beginning in 1957, but reaching a crescendo that culminated in the Great Proletarian Cultural Revolution and continued through to the fall of the Gang of Four, China was defined as a "socialist state of the dictatorship of the proletariat" rather than a "New Democracy" or "People's Democratic State"; this new identity was first constitutionally enshrined in the CCP Constitution of the Ninth Party Congress in 1969 and then (more appropriately) in the State Constitution of the Fourth National People's Congress in 1975. It permitted a more explicit statement of the supremacy of the CCP over the state and a more dominant role for Marxism–Leninism–Mao Zedong Thought as guiding ideol-ogy in society than was consistent with the previous formulation.

Yet in retrospect China's rise was already at this point fatally flawed. First, the rise inspired nationalist pride that was not well taken in the communist bloc, contributing even before the Leap's failure to a widening schism between China and its only patron, the Soviet Union, which despite Chinese com-plaints had contributed significantly to China's ideological and economic de-velopment. This left China strategically exposed to the threat of Soviet-American triangulation, a possibility quietly explored diplomatically by the Johnson and early Nixon administrations. Second, overconfidence led to the Great Leap Forward, an excessively ambitious and risky modernization proj-ect that failed catastrophically, precipitating one of the largest mass famines in recorded history and seriously compromising the credibility of the ruling ideology (as evinced by the spread of corruption in the early 1960s). Third, it split the leadership. The schism first emerged in Peng Dehuai's criticisms of "leftist" adventurism at the 1959 Lushan conference. Although these criticisms were indignantly repudiated and Peng and his associates purged and Leap policies revived, by 1962 the magnitude of the failure had become undeniable and Mao himself came under collegial criticism.

This in effect marked the end of the first period of rising: the Leap was quietly discontinued, the unit of production responsibility reverted from the commune down to the production team, greater entrepreneurial autonomy was permitted at local levels, and other adjustments were undertaken to facilitate economic recovery. But discontinuing one line did not necessarily specify what should replace it. The 1962–1966 period was a classic pause, during which diverse leadership initiatives were launched on both the right and the left. China's foreign policy direction was similarly mixed, including both conventional diplomatic outreach programs to Southeast Asian and African countries and vigorous support for the war in Vietnam and for other national liberation movements in the Third World. Finally, an escalating polemical feud (in which Mao was personally engaged) with the USSR split the communist bloc.

CULTURAL REVOLUTION

The Cultural Revolution (CR), now almost universally deplored (in China as elsewhere), was viewed far more favorably in its heyday, winning radical supporters around the world at the time and afterward inspiring a vast memorial and analytical literature. At once an elite power struggle and a policy coup, the policy dimension emerged not in programmatic form but initially as the obverse of the antirevisionist polemics and then in improvisatory form in a series of campaigns and "models" that made their appearance in 1966–1976. The power struggle was waged by the surprising tactic of mobilizing China's radical younger generation against their elders (and, with the help of the People's Liberation Army, or PLA, inducing the latter not to resist). Power struggle goals were for the most part achieved by 1968 (with the formal expulsion of Liu Shaoqi and Deng Xiaoping from all their posts and the former from the party itself at the Twelfth Plenum of the Eighth CCP Congress in October 1968); there would be subsequent political casualties, from Lin Biao to the Gang of Four, but their downfall was not intrinsically linked to the policy agenda. For those who took this agenda seriously (I include myself), the CR represented a major shift in priorities from economic to ideological criteria (indeed, a principled rejection of economist criteria) for rising. Mindful of the political impact of the failure of the Leap, the leadership did not

however entirely ignore economic considerations (and the economic consequences of the CR were less damaging than those of the Leap).[8] But the thrust
of policy innovation was in the ideological realm, leaving a small cadre of
surviving technocrats under Zhou Enlai on the State Council in defense of the
minimal stability to sustain economic production.

The thrust of the policy agenda was to realize the communist utopia in the
hic et nunc. Communism was defined as political-economic equality, psychosocial altruism, and cultural radicalization.[9] The psychosocial impact seems
from available evidence to have been profound but often transitory. The foreign policy impact was generally disruptive, as Chinese diplomats abroad emulated Red Guard excesses to forefend purge. Yet paradoxically by pushing Sino-
Soviet relations into dangerously polarized ground the movement inspired a
rationalization of Chinese foreign policy thinking along realist lines, leading to
the Nixon visit and hence to the end of China's ideological isolation.

The leadership was a firmly entrenched autocracy, particularly after the fall
and death of Lin Biao, after which it became impossible to introduce any stable succession arrangement. Paradoxically, although the Cultural Revolution
had eliminated all of Mao's ideological opponents, the 1969–1976 period was
one of incessant elite conflict and mass movements against imagined opponents. One reason for this is that Mao cultivated a cadre of political disciples
on both the left (the Gang of Four) and the right (Zhou Enlai and his surviving bureaucrats, later augmented by Deng Xiaoping and other rehabilitated
cadres), to keep the revolutionary dream alive and to keep the economy functioning, respectively—but given their opposing convictions, political conflict
between them was only to be expected. Particularly because both Mao and
Zhou Enlai were mortally ill during this period, giving rise to a tacit contest
to see who could outlive the other. Mao's aversion to formal succession arrangements only contrived to keep the issue (and the scheming) alive. That
Mao was the only thing holding the leadership together was demonstrated by
the swift series of coups and countercoups during his last year of life, beginning with the removal of Deng Xiaoping early in 1976 and ending after Mao's
death in September with the interim succession of Hua Guofeng and the arrest
of Mao's wife and her associates.

It was in foreign policy that Maoist ideology would have its first inescapable
encounter with political reality. All ambassadors were recalled in December
1966, but although the Red Guards seized and occupied the Ministry of Foreign Affairs for about two weeks in August 1967, Foreign Minister Chen Yi
managed to survive Red Guard criticism (with the help of Zhou Enlai), also
saving most of his diplomatic core.[10] Although relations with Burma and
Cambodia were seriously affected and there were minor incidents involving
radical demonstrators in Kenya, Ceylon (now Sri Lanka), and elsewhere, the

most sensitive problem was with the Soviet Union, one of only two nations in a position to seriously threaten China's national security. The Soviet embassy in Beijing, then the largest in the world, was picketed by Red Guards carrying inflammatory placards for nearly two years, forcing the evacuation of most diplomatic personnel. This deterioration ultimately culminated in border clashes beginning in March 1969 and continuing around six months, creating such a sense of crisis that much of Beijing's population was evacuated in the fall of 1970, anticipating a Soviet attack. The international context of this polarization was however one of loose bipolarity between the Soviet Union and the United States: Strategic Arms Limitations Talks (SALT I) began in 1969 in Helsinki, culminating in early 1971 in the outlines of an agreement on limiting antiballistic missiles, to be signed the following May. While Soviet-American détente was in full flower, Sino-Soviet relations were in such complete disrepair that Mao declared in 1965 that China was no longer part of the communist bloc. Under the circumstances, the old American idea to combine forces against China became more attractive in Moscow, and in the wake of the border clash the Kremlin made diplomatic overtures to Washington proposing either collaboration or benign neutrality during a Soviet preemptive strike on China's nuclear facilities. Fortunately for China, the Nixon administration had other plans, and the Nixon-Kissinger opening to Beijing, in conception since 1968 and diplomatically advanced by 1971, emphatically precluded any such collusion. The Nixon visit to China in February 1972 thus inaugurated a "great strategic triangle" in which China, the United States, and the USSR would henceforth weigh every bilateral relationship with a third party also in view. Reversing his earlier decision, Mao leaned not to one side but to the center of the scale. The first dawning of reform in the sense of a realistic rationalization of ideological positions, the Sino-American caesura may have contributed to the deterioration of Sino-Vietnamese relations but was otherwise provisionally isolated from Chinese foreign policy to avoid contaminating its revolutionary bona fides.

The impact of the Cultural Revolution decade on China's rise was mixed. On the one hand, it established the Chinese image in the eyes of the world as a state willing to assault the status quo and risk unpredictable chaos for the sake of revolutionary ideals. China first rose in world consciousness not because of its GDP growth rate or military prowess but on the basis of its ideas. Particularly with the publication of Lin Biao's speech "Long Live the Victory of People's War!" on the eve of the Cultural Revolution (September 3, 1965), Beijing proclaimed itself a plausible tribunal for international class war and a point of inspirational reference for the international tumult known as the Sixties (though it soon became clear it had no operational plans to follow up such a proclamation). On the other hand, by the end of the Cultural Revolution decade the experience had fairly clearly established the bankruptcy of "continuing revolution under the dictatorship of the proletariat" as a feasible way forward for the Chinese nation. This was not because it precipitated economic havoc, as in the case of the Great Leap Forward—economically the record was not bad. It was rather that the model was riddled with so many contradictions and non sequiturs as to be practically untenable. Deng Xiaoping and his colleagues were the first to recognize this and to make it the basis for an unprecedented transformation of Chinese politics, but even Hua Guofeng and the immediate beneficiaries of Mao's legacy sensed its truth, finally yielding quietly to Deng's challenge. The revolution was great; the revolution was over.

REFORM AND OPENING

The era of reform and opening is conventionally dated from the Third Plenum of the Eleventh Party Congress in December 1978, superseding the hapless Hua Guofeng's attempt to maintain the blind legitimacy of the "two whatevers," but the policy pause against continuing elite resistance actually lasted from 1976 until the Sixth Plenum (June 1981), when the Cultural Revolution, class struggle, and "politics in command" were all deemed mistaken. Although the new policy framework emerged only gradually, the pragmatic steps taken in "crossing the river feeling for stones," added up to a profound transformation of the grounding assumptions of Maoist political thinking while leaving a few of them intact. Three principal points of differences emerged: First, reversing Mao's emphasis on "productive relations" (e.g., class struggle) and the "ideological superstructure," the new position returned to the Stalinist position that "productive forces" and the "economic base" are of decisive importance. Mao's emphasis on ideological criteria for rising were thus replaced by economic criteria, with the paradoxical result that while indices of economic production exploded China regressed ideologically to the "early stage of socialism," where it might expect to remain for a hundred years or so. Ideological regression however afforded greater ambit to adopt capitalist modes of production, such as markets and private property, which proceeded to spread very rapidly. Second, in place of Mao's emphasis on striking while the iron is hot, emphasizing great leaps and smashing frames to achieve spectacular advance, Deng Xiaoping emphasized "stability above all" and cautious institution building with respect for orderly procedures as well as goals. Yet ironically the average annual economic growth rate achieved under this regime has been very fast, faster than Mao's storming approach. Third, in place of Mao's emphasis on attitudinal change ("taking the correct stand") there has been a shift to rationality and factual knowledge as proper criteria for action (*shi shi qiu shi*).

Despite these major departures, there were still some similarities. First, Deng's emphasis on pragmatism echoed Mao's own statements, made during the rural revolution when he was fighting the returned student group and other dogmatists. Second, like Mao, Deng placed great emphasis on local autonomy, building national reforms like the Household Responsibility System from successful local initiatives. Third, although Deng placed much more emphasis on formal institutionalization (the national and party legislatures now convened on schedule, officials were appointed for fixed limited tenures, iconoclastic mass mobilization was suppressed), his own ambiguous status (a vice premier who was in effect first among equals) helped ensure the survival of informal groups and elite factionalism and complicated succession arrangements.

Although domestic political reform took top priority, the reformers launched their first initiatives in foreign policy, partly because they wanted a safe and friendly international environment for reform, partly because Mao had already opened the way with his invitation to Nixon, and partly because Deng had the track record and authority for initiatives in this area. The first opportunity was to carry through Sino-US détente to formal diplomatic recognition: immediately after the Third Plenum Deng left for his tour of the United States, where normalization terms were finalized on January 1. This démarche was strategically premised on continuing Sino-US collaboration against the Soviet Union, as betokened by the simultaneous Chinese incursion into Vietnam, whose retaliatory invasion of Cambodia both Washington and Beijing opposed (and Moscow supported).

Deng took advantage of Sino-US normalization to introduce, with his "three links" and later "one country, two systems" proposals, a new policy toward Taiwan that for the first time envisaged the possibility of "peaceful reunification." The Chinese were however dismayed by Washington's continuing arms sales to Taiwan, a disappointment exacerbated by the election the following year of Ronald Reagan, who had promised during his campaign to upgrade relations with Taipei. After intensive negotiations a Third Communiqué was signed in August 1982 that purported to limit future arms sales, whereupon the CCP at its Twelfth Party Congress two months later proclaimed an "independent foreign policy of peace." From Sino-US détente, Beijing was shifting to strategic equidistance, taking advantage of polarizing Soviet-American relations (the American arms budget doubled under Reagan). While maintaining cordial relations with the United States, Beijing then moved to improve relations with the Soviet Union, declining to renew the thirty-year mutual aid treaty but opening biannual "normalization talks," which culminated in normalization in May 1989. Meanwhile, by dint of its authority to dictate ideology ex cathedra, the CCP decreed that a climactic world class war was no longer inevitable. The new foreign policy line of "peace and development" was designed to have good relations with nearly all countries (except Vietnam until 1991), and seemed well tailored to domestic policy priorities.

To say economic reform was an outstanding success is of course an understatement: the most dramatic initial effect was in agriculture, where farming families used the new initiative imparted by the Household Responsibility System and the dissolution of the commune-brigade-team network to improve output growth from less than 2 percent per annum in the 1970s to nearly 6 percent in the 1980s, resulting in a substantial improvement in their standard of living.[11] Although growth rates varied cyclically, creating a choppy political business cycle, GDP growth averaged 9.8 percent in the 1980s. The Deng formula was to begin at the bottom rather than the top, with the simplest sectors (e.g., agriculture) before moving to the more complex (e.g., banking and finance), to begin with markets before dealing with property rights reform, to deal with economics before politics, and proceed one step (or sector) at a time and to avoid "big bang" (comprehensive, syncretic) approaches. Opening to the outside world permitted trade to flourish, and foreign direct investment (FDI) was permitted, initially limited to four special economic zones (SEZs) but ultimately expanded to the entire east coast. There were some missteps, notably after urban reform was initiated at the Third Plenum of the Twelfth Congress in the fall of 1984: reluctance to undertake ownership reform allowed the "soft budget constraint" to continue, resulting in unrestrained capital investment booms followed by crashes, and the "dual track system" of price reform (allowing some prices to be determined by the market while others were fixed by the state) facilitated a form of corruption in which cadres (or their families) would buy in one market and sell in the other.

But perhaps the regime's Achilles' heel was its ambivalence about political reform and the factional tension that ambivalence encouraged. Ambivalence gave rise to social contradictions, as the reformers tended to mobilize the masses to promote further reforms during periods of relative openness while conservatives would seize upon the movement's alleged chaotic excesses to crack down. This is essentially what happened in the spring of 1989: a massive reform movement was generated in the wake of the death of Hu Yaobang, tacitly appealing for support to Zhao Ziyang and his "reform faction," but Deng Xiaoping saw only echoes of the Cultural Revolution and disdained any concessions. Zhao refused to recant, was purged, and the regime mobilized the PLA to crack down brutally on the protest movement, creating international outcry. The tragic theater of Tiananmen marked the end of naïve optimism within China regarding its world prestige as well as the end of world optimism about China's rise.

REFORM DEEPENING

Tiananmen was analogous to the Cultural Revolution in its elite consequences, consisting of a premortem succession crisis precipitated by the
incumbent leader because he had grown dissatisfied with his heir apparent.
Although Deng's position remained the same, it was structurally a reversal,
because while in the former case the heir apparent (Liu Shaoqi and Deng
Xiaoping) had organized work teams to suppress the mass movement and
the incumbent (Mao) had reversed them, in the latter case the heir apparent
(Zhao Ziyang) supported a more emancipatory policy and the incumbent
(Deng) chose to suppress the mass movement. So while the first watershed
precipitated "ten years of chaos," in the latter it resulted in ten years of political quietism. In both cases the incumbent came to rue his decision. In the
former case after purging Liu and Deng, Mao soon had a fatal confrontation
with Lin Biao, his radical heir apparent, then encouraged criticism of Zhou
Enlai, dismissed Wang Hongwen and then Deng Xiaoping, and came to re-
gret (but never rescinded) his patronage of the Gang of Four. In the latter
case Deng dismissed Zhao Ziyang as heir apparent but never promoted Li
Peng to succeed him and found the hard-line consequences of the crackdown so objectionable he seriously considered dismissing Jiang Zemin and
rehabilitating Zhao. The pause of policy uncertainty lasted from 1989 until
1992, during which many reforms were temporarily suspended, and ended
with Deng's famous "southern tour" in which he resumed de facto leadership of a revived reform movement.

Foreign affairs presented the most immediate problem in the form of
Western sanctions and the spontaneous flight of Western capital in ap-
palled response to the crackdown at Tiananmen. The immediate Chinese
reaction was to attribute Western sanctions to a Western conspiracy to destroy communism via "peaceful evolution" (*heping yanbian*), pointing for
example to the simultaneous collapse of communist regimes in Eastern
Europe and the reform excesses in the USSR. Deng Xiaoping responded
in June 1989 to what he called this "new cold war" with his famous "28-
character expression":

Lengjing guancha (watch coolly and analyze)
Wenzhu zhen jia (secure your position)
Chen zhe ying fu (deal confidently with changes)
Tao guang yang hui (hide your capabilities)
Shanyu shou zhou (keep a low profile)
Jue bu dang tou (do not assume leadership)
You suo zuo wei (make some contribution)

This admonition both assuaged and partially reinforced this resurgence of China's victim complex, implicitly affirming that China was an innocent, passive victim (i.e., never apologizing or acknowledging fault in the crackdown) while adjuring sangfroid and shrewd courage in response. As the economy bounced back in 1992 the PRC was not obliged to wait long for Western traders and investors to forget Tiananmen and return to the booming China market: whereas the original opening to China was based on strategic considerations, it now became commercially motivated. But the ambivalence about China's rise implicit in Deng's expression has continued to complicate China's approach to the issue: we are being victimized, he implies, yet there is something noble about our position and how we cope with it.

The revitalization of domestic reform was intended to continue the first decade's outstanding economic growth without its drawbacks. These drawbacks included not only the ambivalence about political reform already mentioned (henceforth, needless to say, political reform would be de-emphasized), but (1) a primitive, uncontrolled market without effective fiscal or monetary controls, resulting in a boom and bust cycle consisting of overinvestment binges followed by the imposition of tight money policy resulting in "hard landings" of unemployment and drastically reduced output. [12] And there was a tendency for this boom-bust cycle to correlate with and to reinforce the intellectual opening-and-closing (*fang shou*) cycle and its attendant mass movement cycles. (2) As marketization occurred in the context of shortage, it stimulated inflation, which in turn stimulated cadre corruption. (3) Continuing elite factionalism tended to dovetail with mass cleavages in time of crisis, forming an explosive mix (à la Tiananmen).

To eliminate the 1980s oscillation between opening and closing and the attendant cycle of mass movements followed by governmental crackdowns, the regime undertook several measures. First, elite factionalism was largely suppressed. The split between radical reform and moderate groupings was effaced by two factors: First, Zhao Ziyang and the reform grouping he led were largely purged. Second, by adopting the "socialist market economy" as an explicit model and completing economic marketization and privatization, and by opening the economy to international markets to an unprecedented degree, the radical reform agenda was essentially co-opted. Economic policy would no longer be a political football in factional disputes, but formulated more strictly according to economic criteria. And in place of the elite vacillation toward intellectual dissent of the 1980s came a more consistent repression, shifting however from the over-the-top violence of June 1989 to a more discreet regimen of selective detention and forced exile.

These countercyclical policies were reinforced by a series of measures designed to ensure social stability. There was a shift from Deng's emphasis on bottom-to-top reform initiatives to greater centralization. Vertical discipline was enforced by a major augmentation of the military budget, maintaining a series of double-digit budgetary increases throughout the 1990s (after a series of budget cuts in the 1980s), with a similar bolstering of the internal security apparatus. Along with the suppression of intellectual dissidence, academic salaries were boosted and selected policy intellectuals granted consultative relationships with the policy elite. Higher education expanded vigorously after the Fifteenth Party Congress, resulting in a threefold increase in college students from 1998 to 2002 (giving China the world's second largest college student population after the United States). The regime also launched a series of drives designed to bring the nongovernmental organizations (NGOs) that had spread like wildfire in the 1980s under the organizational control of the party. To restore political legitimacy in the wake of the collapse of the communist bloc the Jiang regime launched a new focus on the cultivation of Chinese patriotism or nationalism. Invocation of the Confucian virtues of harmony, forbearance, and respect for authority were obviously more conducive to stability than continuing revolution and class struggle.

Fundamental to the new order was a clear separation of politics from the economy: a new social contract was forged at the beginning of the 1990s, in which the regime agreed to withdraw from the economy, giving market forces full sway, in return for which the people (including erstwhile party or government officials) could plunge into commerce (*xia hai*), but were then expected to stay out of politics. People were encouraged to work hard and get rich, and by 2004 some 30 percent of China's entrepreneurs had joined the party—a process blessed by Jiang Zemin's much-heralded contribution to the ideological canon, the Three Represents, which announced that the CCP no longer represented just workers and peasants but the advanced productive forces (viz., the emerging urban middle classes), advanced culture (i.e., educated elites), and the interests of the broad masses. This meant class structure was no longer subject to political definition (as in Mao's "class struggle") but left to the case-by-case discretion of the party. Although the leadership now backed away from "party-government separation" (*dang zheng fenkai*) as a perilous loss of control, the attempt to separate party from enterprise management (*dang qi fenkai*) has continued, running the state-owned enterprises (SOEs) by market principles while transferring regulation to the government. The central leadership, though thus relieved of much economic responsibility by the market, has so much at stake in continuing productivity that its own agenda has become preoccupied with fostering favorable market conditions.

The leadership has maintained its corporate solidarity during the post-Deng period with ever-increasing stability. Jiang Zemin finally assumed the power he had formally held by Deng's grace at the Fourth Plenum of the Fourteenth Congress in 1994, and was reelected at the Fifteenth Congress in 1997. Hu Jintao's succession to Jiang at the Sixteenth Congress in 2002 proceeded still more decorously; although Hu has proceeded to build a base with his factional supporters whenever vacancies arise, he has not gone out of his way to create them. The leadership seems to have completely mastered the succession crisis, the point at which a collective dictatorship is most vulnerable. It has done so by dint of fixed, limited tenures, selection in advance of the successor (permitting socialization), and the institutionalization of a gradual shift (i.e., allowing the incumbent to cling to many of the perquisites of office after succession and intervene in case of crisis). Whereas previously succession endangered the political system, it has since become so smooth that the danger has become one of eliminating any chance for successor innovation.

What has emerged from this latest draft of reform has in many ways been a great success. The economy resumed GDP growth at a blistering pace, and although inflation revived along with growth, the 1994 financial reforms enabled the government to take more effective remedial measures, achieving a "soft landing" in 1995–1997, yet without falling victim to the Asian financial crisis that afflicted China's neighbors. Remaining barriers to the international market have fallen away and FDI has flooded in as never before, making the foreign-invested sector the leading edge in the technological upgrading of Chinese industry. Although the business cycle continues, shorn of its elite factional dimension or its intercalation with the (now defunct) mass movement cycle, it became politically innocuous. The academy has reinforced the regime's turn to nationalism with a focus on postmodernism, postcolonialism, political realism, and other analytical approaches more critical of the West. Although it is too soon to declare a victor in the ongoing struggle between Internet users and the state apparatus built to police it, the former may "win" while their discourse becomes overwhelmingly supportive and patriotic. Meanwhile the separation of politics from economics has meant that nationalism can successfully coexist with an accelerated opening to the outside world, as foreign trade, FDI, and tourism have expanded relentlessly, culminating in China's entry into the World Trade Organization (WTO) in December 2001.

CONCLUSION

Although China's rise has been going on for much of the last century, the West seems to have become aware of it only since the beginning of this one, as China's growth trajectory brings it into proximity with the orbits of the established "great powers." China's academic and intellectual community was able to extrapolate from China's aggregate "comprehensive national power" (CNP) statistics into the future as well as anyone and the aspiration to "great power" no longer seemed out of the question.[13] Thus by the late 1990s Jiang Zemin began engaging in "great power strategy" (*daguo zhanlue*) by forming "strategic partnerships" with the powers. By 2006 great power consciousness reached the public in the form of a CCTV miniseries on the "comprehensive" rise of nine established powers, a program previously vetted by the Politburo that ran three times.[14] Yet conceiving of China as a great power seemed to be at once thrilling and very problematic. Other developing countries—Germany, Japan—had become great powers only to come to grief. China's policy intellectuals felt the need to place China's rise to greatness in some positive moral context. The most famous such formulation was Party School Vice Chairman Zheng Bijian's "peaceful rise" (*heping jueqi*) formulation, first articulated at the Boao Forum in November 2003. But in September 2004 the term mysteriously disappeared from view, to be replaced by the more benign phrase "peaceful development."

This ambivalence about rising may be understood in the context of China's national self-image. China still identifies itself as a developing country—perhaps the largest and most economically successful developing country, but a developing country nonetheless—as its UN voting record attests.[15] A developing country is not yet a great power. Zhou Enlai insisted that China would never become a "hegemon" even after it became developed, as did Deng Xiaoping. True, the Chinese term for hegemony (*ba dao*) has an odious moral connotation absent in the English, but "great power" is a necessary if not a sufficient condition for hegemonic status. Finally, to become a great power is clearly incompatible with the deeply ingrained Chinese self-concept as victim, putting it in a position to function as victimizer. Thus the Chinese have some difficulty conceiving themselves to be something they dread but would dearly love to be.

If the Chinese have difficulty with the concept of rising, how do their neighbors feel? Again there is considerable ambiguity, but available public opinion polls indicate that although China's self-image in the United States is not too high, in most other countries the image of China over the past decade has been better than that of the United States. But we must make a distinction between powerful countries and second- or third-tier powers: the former might conceivably feel themselves threatened by the rise of a new power, while the latter (unless directly threatened, say by neighbors) are not in the power game and tend to be indifferent. China has used its commercial diplomacy and "soft power" quite skillfully to build friendships with its smaller trading partners, to whom China's rise has meant more trade and more opportunities, naturally inclining them to be prepared to revise negative stereotypes. For the great powers to whom China's rise might portend threat or relative loss, such as the United States, Japan, or India, the situation is more risky.

According to power transition theory, for one country to pass another in military capabilities is a very traumatic experience likely to result in war. To grow in terms of economic capabilities alone seems less sensitive—witness Japan's post–World War II ascent, having written off the use of warfare except in self-defense—or the United States' overtaking of Great Britain in the early twentieth century. What seems interesting about the China case is its ability to convince neighbors of its benign intentions—peaceful rise, responsible power, and so forth—while military spending has been increasing more rapidly than GDP growth rates. This has been achieved partly by conciliatory rhetoric, as in China's New Security Concept (NSC), which is defined in terms of mutual trust, mutual benefit, equality, and coordination. In other words, in the light of the NSC, conventional military alliances are no longer necessary. Yet China's PLA budget has increased by 15–18 percent per year since 1989. True, much of this augmented weaponry has been focused on Taiwan, to the reassurance of others. China also justifies its military expenditures in terms of the need for defense modernization to defend access to one of the globe's major trading states. China has also since the mid-1990s been increasingly willing to engage in multilateral security organizations or accords, such as signing the Association of Southeast Asian Nations (ASEAN) Treaty of Alliance and Cooperation, or the agreement with ASEAN for peaceful exploration of the Spratly Islands, jointly claimed by China and several Southeast Asian countries.

Of course those most suspicious of Chinese intentions are not disarmed by China's high-profile quest for "peaceful development." They dismiss all this ingratiating rhetoric as either deceitful or simply anachronistic, for no one (including the current PRC leadership) knows what a more powerful future China will want once it is in a position to demand it. Current indications are that it will indeed seek to play a leadership role in the region and seek to reduce the US military presence there (e.g., vide the Shanghai Cooperation Organization's 2005 request that the United States vacate its bases in Central Asia). Is this a case of the zero-sum logic of power, or a chemical aversion of unlike elements? It is true that China is not a Western democracy and shows no immediate interest in becoming one. According to democratic peace theory, democracies are much less likely to have wars with one another than they are with nondemocracies, or than nondemocracies are to have war with other nondemocracies. China has been concerned about the implications of such assumptions, as riposted in its calls for "international democracy"—meaning in effect that all states should be respected even if they are nondemocratic. On the other hand China has had noticeably cordial relations with dictatorships (in Myanmar, Zimbabwe, Sudan, Kazakhstan) while having no difficulty containing its enthusiasm for the outbreak of democracy in neighboring states (e.g., post-Suharto Indonesia, the 2005 "tulip revolution" in Kyrgyzstan).

Once China has risen, what will it want? The bottom line is, we must wait and see. China shows every intention of rising without substantial change in its existing form of government. It has vouchsafed friendly international behavior until its rise is complete. Beyond that, it will seek to avoid becoming what it calls a "hegemon," but expects "justice"—which may not be defined by bourgeois Western values.

NOTES

1. Cf. Sujian Guo and Jean-Marc Blanchard, "*Harmonious World*" *and China's New Foreign Policy* (Lanham, MD: Lexington Books, 2008).

2. On China's martial historical legacy (or "parabellum paradigm"), see Alastair Iain Johnston, *Cultural Realism: Strategic Culture and Grand Strategy in Chinese History* (Princeton, NJ: Princeton University Press, 1995); on the postliberation era, see Allen S. Whiting, *The Chinese Calculus of Deterrence: India and Indochina* (Ann Arbor: University of Michigan Press, 1975), and Andrew Scobell, *China's Use of Force: Beyond the Great Wall and the Long March* (New York: Cambridge University Press, 2003).

3. Traditional tributary relationships were the exceptions that prove the rule, if we take as an example Sino-Vietnamese relations between 1427 and 1887. Cf. Brantly Womack, *China and Vietnam: The Politics of Asymmetry* (New York: Cambridge University Press, 2006), 178–79. For a dissenting view, see Warren Cohen, "China's Rise in Historical Perspective," *Journal of Strategic Studies* 30, no. 4/5 (August 2007): 683–704.

4. Mao Zedong, "On the People's Democratic Dictatorship," in *Selected Works of Mao Tse-tung* (Peking: Foreign Languages Press, 1969), 4:411–25, at 415.

5. Mao Zedong, "Snow" (1945), in the official translation, *Mao Tsetung Poems* (Peking: Foreign Languages Press, 1976).

6. The Five Principles of Peaceful Coexistence (mutual respect for each other's territorial integrity and sovereignty; mutual nonaggression; mutual noninterference in each other's internal affairs; equality and mutual benefit; peaceful coexistence) were first articulated by Zhou Enlai in a 1953–1954 Sino-Indian forum called to resolve the issue of Tibet, and later endorsed by Sukarno in a meeting in Bandong.

7. From 1971 to 1975, China's aid budget was equal to 5.88 percent of its GDP. The highest proportion of GNP that developed nations have given for aid barely exceeds 0.5 percent (the US figure at the turn of the millennium was below 0.1 percent). During the late Maoist period, China's reached a high point of 6.92 percent (1973), the highest (in proportional terms) the world has ever known. Shi Lin, *Dangdai Zhongguo de duiwai jingji hezuo* [Contemporary China's economic cooperation] (Beijing: China Social Sciences Press, 1989), 68.

8. Indeed there was according to official statistics a respectable rate of GNP growth averaging 6.5 percent over the Cultural Revolution decade (1965–1975). Carl Riskin, *China's Political Economy: The Quest for Development since 1949* (New York: Oxford University Press, 1987), 184–86. But due to the ideological emphasis on collective

sacrifice and investment, per capita incomes (and living standards) stagnated during this period.

9. Available statistics (not very reliable) attest that economic equality was enhanced appreciably, with Gini coefficients estimated close to 0.2 and including more widely available access to rudimentary education, medical care, and other services. See also Alan Gelb, Gary Jefferson, and Interjit Singh, "Can Communist Economies Transform Incrementally?" *NBER Macroeconomic Annual*, 1993, 8:87–133; Hu Angang, Hu Linlin, and Chang Zhixiao, "China's Economic Growth and Poverty Reduction (1978–2002)," IMF Working Paper, November 2003.

10. See Melvin Gurtov, *The Foreign Ministry and Foreign Affairs in China's "Cultural Revolution,"* RAND Memorandum (Santa Monica, CA: RAND Corp), March 1969.

11. "In 1984, the income gap [between urban and rural incomes] dropped to 1:6, an historic, never-repeated low." Zhao Manhua, "The Income Gap in China," *World Bank Group Transition Newsletter*, February–March 2001.

12. See Barry Naughton, *The Chinese Economy: Transitions and Growth* (Cambridge, MA: MIT Press, 2007), 100–107.

13. See the articles compiled by Deng Yong and Sherry Gray in the special issue of *Journal of Contemporary China* 10, no. 26 (February 2001).

14. CCTV also made preparations for a sequel on China's rise, but it was aborted, no doubt due to the same apprehensions (personal communication from Brantly Womack).

15. Samuel Kim, "The People's Republic of China in the United Nations: A Preliminary Analysis," *World Politics* 26, no. 3 (April 1974): 299–330.

II

CHALLENGES OF STRATEGY AND SECURITY

3

Chinese Strategy and Security Issues in Historical Perspective

Evelyn S. Rawski

Contemporary perceptions of China's historical experience vis-à-vis its neighbors have tended to portray China as the regional hegemon in East Asia.[1] Since the 1941 publication of Fairbank and Teng's study of the tributary system, many scholars inside and outside China have accepted the model of a Sinocentric world order as a reflection of reality.[2] Although the authors focused on the evolution of a Sinocentric world order from the seventeenth to nineteenth centuries, Fairbank later placed the origins of the "Chinese world order" in the Warring States (403–221 B.C.) period. This world order was centered on Beijing (Peking), where the Son of Heaven, recipient of the Mandate to rule "all under Heaven" (the empire), received the heads of tribal groups and states. He invested vassals with hereditary titles and they in turn presented him with tribute (*gong*). Vassals were differentiated by the closeness of their ties to the imperial house. Members of the ruling lineage (*zongfan*) were first in rank; next came the heads of tribal groups within the territory directly controlled by the emperor, called *neifan* (internal vassals); and last were the *waifan* (external vassals), heads of states outside the dynasty's direct administrative control.[3]

The idea of a Sinocentric world order persists, most recently in articles by scholars in the People's Republic of China (PRC), who cite tributary missions from vassal states to argue that the current territorial boundaries of the PRC extend backward in time.[4] That actual historical circumstances frequently deviated from the tributary model was recognized in the secondary literature from an early point. *The Chinese World Order* (1968) noted that Chinese dynasties frequently could not control various Inner Asian peoples such as the Xiongnu, Uighurs, Mongols, Khitan, Tibetans, and Jurchen/Manchus. Essays in *China among Equals: The Middle Kingdom and Its Neighbors, 10th–14th Centuries* (1983)[5] challenged the assumption of Chinese hegemony for the tenth to thirteenth centuries.[6] Victoria Hui has recently argued that the decentralized multistate politics of the Warring States period resembled the situation in early modern Europe.[7] Since no one state had the military power to impose its will on its neighbors, what emerged was "an amoral interstate system characterized by constant maneuver and ruthless competition." State-to-state arrangements revealed "temporary accommodation, alliances made and abandoned, ambush and treachery, the careful cultivation of domestic resources and morale, psychological warfare, and . . . raw military power."[8] These adjectives could also be used to describe the situation in Northeast Asia during the third to seventh centuries, when a multitude of states emerged in North and South China; the tenth to thirteenth centuries, when emergent states along China's northern borders successfully challenged Chinese regimes; and the late sixteenth to early seventeenth centuries, when the Ming failed to suppress the emerging Northeast Asian state that ruled China as the Qing dynasty (1644–1911).

The security issues accompanying periods of political decentralization or weak Chinese regimes were rooted in the geography of the North China plain, where the first Chinese states emerged.[9] "Flat and featureless," without natural defensive barriers, the North China plain rendered Chinese states vulnerable to attack, especially after the introduction of the horse transformed steppe nomads into a formidable fighting force. The Mongols were not the only steppe conquest group to rule China.

Potential challengers to Chinese security also arose in Northeast Asia. Stretching eastward from the Mongolian plateau north to densely forested *taiga* and south to the fertile Liao River plain, the region consisted of three ecosystems that brought nomads, hunting/fishing peoples, and sedentary agriculturalists in contact with one another. The Khitan Liao (970–1055), Jurchen Jin (1115–1260), and, five hundred years later, the Manchu Qing conquest dynasties remind us of the dynamic political forces emanating from Northeast Asia. Chinese states from the Han dynasty until the Qing were mindful of its strategic importance.

Powerful states like Koguryŏ and Parhae extended their control from Northeast Asia into the Korean peninsula during the fourth to tenth centuries. Although Chinese military campaigns were generally linked to the threat posed by the Northeast Asian states, the peninsula remained within the periphery of Chinese interest in regional security. Japan was another actor in regional geopolitics, from a period of intense interaction in the fourth to seventh centuries, to the "Japanese piracy" of the fourteenth to sixteenth centuries, the Japanese invasion of Korea in the late sixteenth century, and the late nineteenth- and early twentieth-century Japanese invasions of Korea and China.

This chapter bypasses the contemporary perception of China as the historical regional hegemon in East Asia to argue that China's experience can equally well be presented as one in which China was forced to respond to security challenges from neighbors that it could not easily overcome by force. For over half of its recorded history, the Chinese heartland was ruled by non-Han peoples.[10] As will be shown below, even during the Han and Tang dynasties, there were occasions when Chinese rulers negotiated with their neighbors from positions of weakness. The policies they adopted belie the assumptions of the tributary model, and included the use of trade as a foreign policy tool. Chinese strategies toward Northeast Asia during the fourth to seventh centuries responded to shifts in alliances based on changing geopolitical conditions. During the tenth to twelfth centuries, the Song attempted but failed to manipulate interstate rivalries on their frontiers to their advantage. These historical precedents can be compared to the interstate maneuverings of the early modern period, centered again in Northeast Asia, which brought about the fall of the Ming dynasty. A concluding section discusses the implications of these examples for understanding the repertoire of choices adopted by Chinese states facing security issues.

POLICIES ON NORTHERN BORDERS

China's weakness vis-à-vis neighboring steppe empires in North Asia is a persistent historical theme. Even unified regimes such as the Han (206 B.C.–8 A.D.; 23 A.D.–220 A.D.) and Tang (618–907) dynasties did not always possess the power to impose their will on their neighbors.[11] Chinese courts were preoccupied with conditions on their Inner Asian frontier, where they confronted pastoral peoples whose military might equaled or surpassed their own. The Western Han state, for example, faced a Xiongnu empire that extended from the Great Wall northward past Lake Baikal, eastward to the tributaries of the Amur River, and westward past the modern-day border of Xinjiang: its territory included present-day Ningxia, Liaodong, and northern Shanxi, Shaanxi, and Hebei.[12] To the west and south of the Xiongnu, there were the Wusun, and to their south the Tibetans. The Xiongnu empire was bordered on its east by the Xianbei, the Puyǒ, and the ancestors of the Jurchen people, along the coast of Northeast Asia. As a result of the Han thrust into the northern half of the Korean peninsula, these tribes were all occupying territories bordering the Han lands.

Owen Lattimore observed that steppe power expanded when Chinese state power was weak.[13] The demise of Qin in 211 B.C. allowed the Xiongnu to expand and reoccupy the Ordos. The Han dynasty had not yet consolidated control of its own territory and was uncertain of the loyalty of frontier generals. When they came seeking peace in 198 B.C., Gaozu, the Han founder, signed a peace treaty that sent a Han princess in marriage to the Xiongnu ruler, and paid annual tribute to them. In return, the Xiongnu promised not to invade Han territory. This was the first *he qin* 和親 (peace) treaty.[14]

Treaties involved an exchange of oath-letters (*meng shi* 盟誓), which contradicted the tenets of the Sinocentric world order by constructing a bilateral relationship of equals.[15] From 198 B.C. to 135 B.C., the Han signed ten *he qin* treaties with the Xiongnu, increasing the payments when Xiongnu military power grew stronger.[16] These treaties would include "mutual recognition of equal diplomatic status even when the sedentary state was forced to pay tribute."[17] Later, treaties were signed by Chinese states that were "in great danger and under duress." In 1005, fearful of a full-scale Liao invasion, the Song and Khitan Liao exchanged oath-letters to seal the treaty of Shanyuan, by which Song agreed to pay to Liao 200,000 silk lengths and 100,000 ounces of silver a year as "contribution to military expenses" —the euphemism adopted in the face of Song refusal to allow the term "tribute" (*gong* 貢) to be applied to these annual payments.[18] Those reservations fell in a treaty concluded in 1142 with the Jurchen Jin after the Jin captured the Song capital, Kaifeng. This treaty forced Song to use the self-deprecatory terms adopted by a tributary vassal in its communications with Jin; the annual payments made by Song to Jin were called "tribute," and the Jin sent documents investing the Song emperor Gaozong as ruler of the Song state (these documents are preserved in the Jin history but not in Song records).[19]

Chinese polities often referred to "using barbarians to govern barbarians" (*yi Yi zhi Yi* 以夷制夷) and applying the "loose-rein" or *jimi* 羈縻 policy, which rationalized accommodations with border groups in terms of a long-range control strategy. *Jimi* first appeared in 52 A.D., after the Xiongnu confederation had split into two. The Southern Xiongnu became tributary vassals of Later Han in 50 A.D. and sent annual tribute to the Han court. When the Northern Xiongnu came seeking *he qin* in 52 A.D., a Later Han official, Ban Biao, recommended that the *jimi* policy be adopted: "If the barbarians came in accordance with *li* (rites and rituals), in no case should they be denied a response."[20] In actuality, however, the Han responded with coolness to the embassy and the Northern Xiongnu resumed their raids in the western regions until they were defeated by a Han army in 74 A.D.[21]

Jimi was institutionalized during the Tang dynasty, when *jimi* prefectures and departments were created in regions with non-Han subjects, to be governed by local elites who handed down their posts to descendants and did not have to report on local population or finances to the central government.[22] The *jimi fu zhou* (loose-rein prefectures and departments) seem to have been the forerunners of the *tusi* (native officials) system of the Ming and Qing periods in Southwest China.[23] *Tusi* as an institution of governance in regions dominated by non-Han populations persisted into the twentieth century in China, although many *tusi* regions were converted during the early eighteenth century to direct administration by the Qing central government.[24] Current PRC historians view *tusi* as one phase in a long-term process that incorporated non-Han minorities into a Han-centered bureaucratic system, but there are many historical counterexamples of *tusi* leaders who used their regional power base to rebel against Han rule.

TRADE AS A STRATEGIC TOOL

The desire for Chinese goods—silk textiles and tea to begin with, then Buddhist sutras, books, porcelain, and other products, including Chinese copper cash—was the powerful magnet drawing its neighbors into the Chinese orbit. Even though trade was never recognized as a central motif in Chinese visions of the world order, the way in which Chinese states allowed only tributary vassal states legitimate access to Chinese markets strongly suggests a tacit recognition that trade provided an incentive for its neighbors to seek political ties with China. Recent studies have depicted the demand for Chinese goods as the central driving force of the world economy between 1500 and 1750.[25] Fairbank and Teng noted the significant evasion of the tributary system trade monopoly by Chinese private traders during the Ming and Qing, and suggested that the expansion of private trade in the nineteenth century caused the decline of the tributary system.[26] Takeshi Hamashita's model recognizes this historical phenomenon by outlining the intra-Asian exchange network centered on China. This network, which stretched from North Asia to Southeast Asia, comprised tribute and trade. Hamashita suggested that tribute exchanges could be viewed as commercial transactions and argued that the tribute system was "in symbiosis with a network of commercial trade relations. . . .Trade relations in East and South-East Asia expanded as tribute relations expanded."[27]

Maritime trade between the Korean peninsula and Shandong goes back to the Warring States period; rice cultivation technology probably entered Japan from the Korean peninsula between 400 B.C. to 250 A.D., and Japan received emigrants during the fourth through fifth centuries A.D. from Paekche, Kaya, and even Silla.[28] After the formation of the Yamato state in the late seventh century, the Japanese engagement with the Asian continent was primarily driven by a desire for commodities, that is, by demand.

Along its Inner Asian borders Chinese states faced tribal confederations who were eager to obtain Chinese commodities, by trade or by force. Expanding steppe empires required "large amounts of external resources" obtained partly through "external tribute," payments from sedentary states. From the steppe perspective, China "was above all immensely, unbelievably wealthy and the producer of an infinite variety of goods," some of which would be consumed by tribal elites but others would be traded.[29] Beginning in the middle of the sixth century, Inner Asian steppe empires were intensely involved in long-distance and tributary trade, tapping into market networks stretching westward into the Tarim Basin. Many nomads wished to participate in market exchanges with China, selling horses in exchange for Chinese silk textiles and other goods.

Steppe empires plagued later Chinese regimes and emergent regional powers in Northeast Asia. That some of these tribal entities succeeded in conquering China only underlined the gravity of border security for the state. Even more important, the tribal confederations and China were engaged in a complex multistate geopolitics that was extremely fluid and where state options were constrained by the actions of other states. Fluctuations in power of steppe empires directly influenced the behavior of states in Northeast Asia. Analyzing interstate activity during three periods—the fourth to sixth centuries, the tenth to thirteenth centuries, and the sixteenth to seventeenth centuries—will help us to illustrate patterns of continuity amid significant historical shifts.

DECENTERING POLITICS, FOURTH TO SEVENTH CENTURIES

The pace and content of interstate diplomacy in Northeast Asia was frequently determined not by China but by neighboring states. In the fourth to sixth centuries, a series of short-lived regional regimes ruled China, several states competed for supremacy in the Korean peninsula, and Japan was in the state formation phase. The primary arena was situated not in China but in the Korean peninsula, where Koguryŏ, Paekche, and Silla sought allies in their internecine struggles. The Chinese and Yamato states were important role players but not the main actors.

The Koguryŏ kingdom arose in the first century B.C. in the Hun River drainage (in present-day Jilin province). During the reign of King Kwanggaet'o (391–413) its territory stretched westward to the Liao River, northeastward to the Sungari River, and southward to the Han and Naktong rivers. Under King Changsu (413–449), Koguryŏ maintained diplomatic ties with both the northern and southern Chinese dynasties. Its shift of the capital southward to P'yŏngyang (427) spurred Paekche and Silla to form a defensive alliance (433). Koguryŏ's expansion southward in 475 came at Paekche's expense, but in the sixth century Koguryŏ lost territory to Silla.[30]

Each Korean state sought outside allies. Koguryŏ took advantage of China's decentralization and the rivalry between northern and southern dynasties to ally with distant southern dynasties while confronting the northern dynasty on its western border. The Chinese regimes for their part awarded Chinese titles to Korean regimes to reinforce their own legitimacy as recipients of the Mandate. Paekche formed alliances with both northern and southern dynasties and with Japanese regional leaders to strengthen its hand against its major threat, Koguryŏ, and Paekche enlisted Japanese soldiers in its quarrel with Silla. Silla, which was rescued from a Paekche-Yamato attack by Koguryŏ, later found it expedient to ally with Paekche against its erstwhile savior.

The Japanese were deeply involved in the interstate rivalries of the Korean peninsula in the fourth to seventh centuries A.D., in part because of their reliance on the peninsula for precious iron implements and iron ore.[31] During this period, "wave after wave of ideas, institutions, technologies, and materials" flowed through the Korean peninsula into Japan.[32] Especially in the fifth century, Japanese chieftains came to Chinese courts seeking Chinese titles to bolster their prestige and claims over territory, not only in Japan but also in the Korean peninsula.[33] The Yamato state participated in the military struggles on the peninsula. It allied with Paekche (372) against Koguryŏ; a combined Kaya-Yamato force was defeated by Koguryŏ in 400; and Paekche, Yamato, Wa, Silla, and Kaya joint forces were defeated by Koguryŏ in 414. Yamato sent military expeditions to the peninsula six times in the sixth century. The final dispatch of military forces to assist Paekche ended in 663, when Paekche was defeated by a combined Silla-Tang army. Thereafter, the Yamato court continued to receive embassies from Parhae during the eighth and ninth centuries.[34]

The interstate rivalries in the Korean peninsula and northeast culminated in the seventh century. In the last decade of the sixth century the Sui, confronting the Turks and Koguryŏ as their rivals in Northeast Asia, attempted to subjugate Koguryŏ. Both Paekche (in 607) and Silla (608, 611) were eager to ally with Sui in a joint campaign against Koguryŏ, but the Sui military campaigns of 612, 613, and 614 resulted in Koguryŏ victories. In 626, Paekche and Silla also sent envoys to seek a military alliance with the new Tang emperors, but the Tang did not move against Koguryŏ until after the Eastern Turks were subjugated. In the interim, from 631 through 643, the Tang accepted sporadic tributary missions (four in twelve years) from Koguryŏ. In 644–648, Silla, Paekche, the Khitan, and several other allies joined Tang in attacks on Koguryŏ, but failed to obtain a decisive victory.[35]

The final round of hostilities was sparked by Koguryŏ's attack on the Khitan, who had become clients of Tang, in 654. The following year, Koguryŏ joined Paekche to capture over thirty Silla towns, causing Silla to turn to its ally, Tang, which launched new campaigns against Koguryŏ (655, 658, 659, 661). Paekche, which was allied with the Japanese Yamato state, was defeated by Silla in 663. Silla then cooperated with Tang in the final military expedition that defeated Koguryŏ. Having eliminated its major rivals and "unified" the peninsula, Silla then shifted from alliance to resistance against Chinese military expansion into the Korean peninsula. The Tang court, beset with problems in Tibet, withdrew its troops and did not seek to consolidate its hold on the Koguryŏ territories.

The 668 demise of the Koguryŏ state permitted Silla to "unify" its control over the Korean peninsula, but from the Tang perspective, this did not resolve the strategic challenge posed by regional states occupying the territory between the Korean and Chinese borders. Parhae (698–926), founded in the late seventh century by a former Koguryŏ general, faced military pressure from Tang and Silla, but survived until its destruction by the Khitan in the early tenth century. Faced with opposition from Silla and from north Chinese regimes, it attempted to ally with Japan.[36] Parhae was eventually vanquished by the Khitan Liao, in 926.

DIVIDING NORTH CHINA IN THE TENTH TO TWELFTH CENTURIES

In contrast to the fourth to seventh centuries, where the military action took place on the northeastern frontiers of the Chinese states, the arena for multistate rivalry in the tenth to twelfth centuries was the entirety of North China, from the coastline westward past the Jade Gate marking the end of the Great Wall, into the desert beyond. Leaving aside the Mongol conquest, which was part of a Eurasian "explosion of military power aimed at world conquest" that was "far grander than anything dreamed of by the Han, T'ang, or Sung, or indeed by any other Chinese regime,"[37] the other three conquest dynasties of this period shared some commonalities, even though they originated in different environments: the grasslands of North Asia for the Khitan, the steppes around present-day Qinghai for the Tangut, and the mixed ecological zones of Manchuria for the Jurchen Jin.[38] Each group was opportunistic in forming alliances. The Khitan, for example, were successively vassals of the Turks, the Sui, even (for some Khitan groups) Koguryŏ, Tang, and again the Turks, then the Uighurs, sending tribute-bearing missions to China while acknowledging Uighur overlordship.

The Tang military withdrawal from present-day Xinjiang, Turfan, Hami, and the Gansu corridor after the An Lushan rebellion (755) produced a power vacuum that was partially filled by the Khitan and the Tangut. In contrast to the fourth to sixth centuries, when, with the exception of Koguryŏ, China was surrounded by states without a permanent bureaucratic government, the Khi-tan Liao and Tangut Xia regimes each possessed literate elites who adopted a diplomatic rhetoric that drew on Chinese and nomadic traditions. The Tanguts had acquired knowledge of Chinese bureaucratic methods after the seventh century, when they had submitted to Tang and resettled in the Ordos,[39] while the Liao and Jin were "dual-administration" empires, ruling their nomadic and sedentary subjects with separate administrative structures.[40]

A stable international order in which Tang and its neighbors interacted on terms of equality was upset in 840 by the collapse of the Tibetan kingdom, followed in short order by the demise of the Uighur empire, and the destruc-tion of Tang power stemming from Huang Chao's rebellion (874–884). Tang had disintegrated into a number of independent local regimes by the early tenth century, when states in Japan, the Korean peninsula, and Northeast Asia also faced a breakdown of central authority.[41] The seeds of the loss of North China during the Song period were sown in the ninth century. It would take over a century from Huang Chao's capture of the Tang capital, Chang'an (880) to Song's conquest of the Northern Han (979) for a regime to successfully re-centralize the Chinese polity. During that period, China was divided into as many as nine or ten regional states.

The breakdown of strong centralized states throughout Asia provided op-portunities for groups like the Khitan Liao and Tangut regimes to expand their power. Moreover, the Tang *jimi* policy resulted in commanderies situated along its Inner Asian borders that were staffed with non-Han tribal peoples: through embassies and other channels of contact, tribal leaders obtained knowledge of Chinese institutions, modes of government, and the Chinese political vocabulary. These were the peoples confronting the new Song rulers after 979. Founded by border generals based on the northern frontier, the Liao and Xixia states were not outsiders to the Chinese system but rather groups that used their familiarity of Tang Chinese customs to obtain support from Han and non-Han subjects.[42]

The Song attempts to ally with non-Han states came after their repeated military defeats at the hands of the Khitan. The founder of the Song dynasty (r. 960–976) and his son Taizong (r. 976–997) had reunified the Chinese-speaking lands, but could not recapture the territory called the Sixteen Prefec-tures, going west from Datong to Yuzhou, which was ceded in 937, giving the Khitan Liao "control of all the strategic passes that defended northern China."[43] When Taizong's expedition to subjugate Liao in 979 failed, he tried to draw Koryŏ into a coordinated attack on Liao.

At first glance, such an alliance made sense: located on the southeastern fringe of the Liao empire; Koryŏ could pose the threat of a two-front war in the event of a Song-Liao conflict. But neither Song nor Koryŏ was actually willing to come to the aid of the other: Koryŏ did not send military forces to attack Liao during the Song campaign of 986, and Song did not respond to Koryŏ requests for aid during the Liao invasion of 993.[44] That invasion forced Koryŏ to become a Liao tributary vassal and removed the potential threat to Liao of a two-front (Song-Koryŏ) war. In 1990, the Tangut Xia ruler submitted to the Liao and received their investiture as king in 990,[45] freeing the Liao to focus on Song. A Song peace offer was rebuffed (994). Liao raids into Song territory in 999, 1001, 1002, 1003, and 1004 culminated in the Liao-Song treaty of Shanyuan (1005).[46]

The treaty of Shanyuan legitimized Liao occupation of part of North China.[47] The Song next sent envoys to negotiate an alliance with the Jurchen Jin against the Liao. The Jurchen leader Aguda (r. 1115–1123) had been a Liao vassal; the Liao had appointed him military governor of the Shangjing region in 1113. Shortly thereafter Aguda defeated Liao forces and declared himself master of the northeast. In 1115 he assumed the dynastic name of Jin and the title of emperor. In his relations with the Liao court after this date, he followed their example, demanding land, annual subsidies approximately equal to the payments Liao received from Song, recognition, and exchanges in which Song would address Liao as "elder brother." These demands escalated as he won more military victories.[48]

After 1117 the Jin received overtures from Song for a joint attack on Liao, which culminated in a formal treaty between the two states (1123). By that time, however, the Jin had already captured the Supreme Capital and Southern Capital of the Liao, and Song, which had hoped to recover the Sixteen Prefectures, was forced to accept Aguda's conditions. In exchange for the return of some land, Song agreed to pay Jin a "huge compensation" for the loss of tax income from these lands, and to transfer to Jin the annual payments formerly sent to Liao.[49]

Not until it had obtained the submission of Tangut Xia as a *waifan* in 1124, and ensured that the former Parhae territory was under control, did the Jin begin their campaign against Song in the autumn of 1125. Laying siege to the capital, Kaifeng, the Jin emperor Wuqimai (Taizong) demanded the cession of most of present-day Shanxi and Hebei, an indemnity that was equal to 180 years of annual payments, annual payments, and a princely hostage. In the first month of 1127, the Jin captured Kaifeng along with ex-emperor Huizong and emperor Qinzong. Further campaigns that followed the demise of the Northern Song dynasty brought the Jin to settle for all of China north of the Huai River, acknowledgment by Southern Song of its status as a Jin vassal, and tribute (*gong*) by Song to Jin.[50]

In contrast to the fourth to seventh centuries, more peoples surrounding China in the tenth to twelfth centuries had acquired written languages and political organizations based on the Tang model. Tang political collapse freed military leaders commanding border garrisons from central government control. The borderland "became the region from which new military and political forces arose to influence the rest of northern China."[51] Chinese regimes based in South China could not prevail against these military regimes, and ultimately even the south was lost to the Mongols. As a consequence of the conquests, there was a permanent northeastward shift of China's political center. Beijing, which had been a minor garrison center in the northern border region, became one of the five capitals of the Liao, remained a capital under the Jin and Mongol rulers, and, except for a brief interval in the late fourteenth and early fifteenth centuries, was the capital of the Ming and Qing dynasties. The Chinese state was "recentered" geographically.

INTERSTATE RIVALRIES IN THE EARLY MODERN PERIOD

Unlike the fourth to seventh and tenth to twelfth centuries, China was not divided into a number of regional regimes in the late sixteenth century, when it participated in a trade boom that was stimulated by the appearance of European traders. Portuguese ships reaching the Pearl River Delta in 1517 encountered a lively intra-Asian maritime trade network, conducted outside the parameters of the tributary system, which sent dyestuffs, spices, and medicinal herbs from Southeast Asia north to Japan, Japanese copper, iron, and silver to China, Korean ginseng to Japan, and Chinese cotton and silk to Asian markets. The 1550–1650 period saw silver from Japan as well as the Americas flow into China. About "half the silver production accounted for in the world between 1500 and 1800" ended up in China, where it supported, even if it did not cause, the silver monetization of the Ming economy.[52]

Oda Nobunaga's adoption of European firearms, introduced into Japan by the Portuguese, facilitated his (and later, Hideyoshi's) military drive for hegemony.[53] Japan's century-long interval of civil war, 1450–1550, coincided with a decline in Ming power on its northern frontier, where Mongols under first Dayan Khan then Altan Khan raided Chinese territory with impunity. Revolts at the Ming garrison at Datong occurred in 1524–1525, 1533, and 1545; from 1550 to 1566, there were annual Mongol raids on the capital, Beijing. These military threats coincided with fiscal crises as the state failed to expand its revenues during the commercial boom and could not even collect agrarian taxes at previously achieved levels.

The emergence of powerful Chinese maritime traders (alternatively, pirates) like Li Dan (d. 1625) and Zheng Zhilong (1604–1661), father of Zheng Chenggong (otherwise known as Koxingga), is well documented from English, Dutch, and Japanese accounts. These men were products of what Iwai Shigeki has called China's frontier society of the sixteenth and seventeenth centuries.[54] Using the concept of frontiers as dynamic regions where different cultures mingle to produce new social forces, Iwai argued that the illicit trade of the 1550–1650 period also produced their counterparts in Northeast Asia, linking the inhabitants of Sakhalin, the Kurile Islands, and Hokkaido with the Amur River basin.[55] Sable, collected in the drainage of the Sungari and Amur rivers, and ginseng were valuable regional exports, and tribal leaders who held Ming patents or trade permits monopolized and taxed the commodities moving in overland trade.

The Northeast Asian economy also received Ming military silver shipments to support border defense.[56] The Ming appointed individuals with strong local ties to regional military commands, and Ming military hereditary offices in border commanderies were filled by individuals whose loyalty to Ming wavered when asked to choose between their personal interest and the state's. Pübei, a Mongol implicated in the 1592 Ningxia uprising, Yang Yinglong, leader of a rebellion in the southwest during the 1590s, and Mao Wenlong, a Ming officer who eventually became a regional warlord on the Ming-Chosŏn-Jurchen border, are outstanding examples of such persons.[57] The same generalization could, of course, be applied to Nurhaci, who followed his father and grandfather in accepting titles from the Ming before he turned against them in 1616.

The sequence of events from 1592 to 1637, that is, from the Japanese invasion of the Korean peninsula to the second Manchu invasion of Korea, illustrates the strategic policy issues confronting the Ming state in Northeast Asia. The Ming response to the Jurchen/Manchu forces, which were emerging as a regional power, occurred within a larger context of military challenges on its southwestern, northern, and northeastern borders that stemmed from its institutionalization of border defense policies earlier in the fifteenth century.

THE JAPANESE INVASION OF KOREA

The precipitating event of a sequence that would ultimately involve Ming China, Chosŏn Korea, and the Jurchen/Manchu regime was the Japanese invasion of Korea, which was the first step toward fulfilling Hideyoshi's ambition to invade Ming China.[58] What Korean historians call the *Imjin waeran* (Invasion of the Imjin year, i.e., Hideyoshi's invasion) occurred in two phases. In May 1592, over 150,000 Japanese troops landed at Pusan and began a series of victorious engagements with the Korean army.[59] The Chosŏn king, Sŏnjo (r.

1567–1608), was forced to abandon his capital, Hansŏng (present-day Seoul), and flee to Ŭiju, right on the border with Ming. Sŏnjo then sought military aid from his overlord, the Ming Wanli emperor (Chosŏn was a Ming tributary since the late fourteenth century).

In the winter of 1591, receiving intelligence of Hideyoshi's invasion plans, the Wanli emperor had ordered a strengthening of Chinese coastal defenses and increased surveillance of the situation in the Korean peninsula. Upon hearing that the Japanese army was rapidly advancing toward the Yalu River, Wanli ordered officials in Liaodong and Shandong to begin military preparations, but the Liaodong army was engaged in suppressing a major rebellion in Ningxia from late July to late October 1592. A Ming token force of 3,000 men was annihilated by the Japanese in late August. When the first Ming troops sent to Korea were annihilated by the Japanese, the Ming negotiator Shen Weijing engaged Konishi Yukinaga, the Japanese commander occupying P'yŏngyang, in talks, staving off further military action until new forces could be committed to the Korean campaign. A more substantial army of about 44,000 men was amassed after the successful conclusion of the Ningxia campaign, and in February 1593, a combined Sino-Korean army expelled the Japanese from P'yŏngyang, an event that marked the turning point of the first phase of the invasion.

After the Japanese defeat at P'yŏngyang and the subsequent Ming failure to expel the Japanese from Hansŏng, negotiations were revived, culminating in the audience of Ming envoys with Hideyoshi (October 1595). The failed diplomacy in 1593–1595 primarily involved representatives of Ming China and Hideyoshi. The interests of the negotiators on the ground in Korea diverged significantly from those of their principals: the Japanese generals "hoped to satisfy his [Hideyoshi's] craving for power by offering him the illusion of victory," while achieving a settlement that would allow the profitable trade to resume. For his part, Shen Weijing learned that Hideyoshi's true target was Ming China but concealed that from the Wanli court. The fabrications on both sides created the diplomatic fiasco of the Hideyoshi audience, but the Ming envoys falsely reported to the Ming court that Hideyoshi had accepted Ming investiture. When Hideyoshi discovered that the envoys had come to present him with Ming regalia and documents investing him as "king of Japan," he flew into a rage and ordered another invasion. The second round of military conflict, 1597–1598, did not end until Hideyoshi's death, when Tokugawa Iyeyasu and other senior leaders ordered the withdrawal of Japanese troops from Korea.[60] The next stage in triangular interstate relations would come with the Ming response to the rise of Jurchen power in Northeast Asia. The narrative shifts to the origins of the Manchus, who would conquer the Ming and rule China as the Qing dynasty.

THE MANCHU TAKEOVER OF LIAODONG

The Manchu conquest was accomplished by a Jurchen tribal group with a long history of contact with Chinese, Korean, and Inner Asian regimes. The founder of the Qing ruling house, Nurhaci, was born into a family who were the hereditary heads of the left wing of the Jianzhou Jurchen.[61] Korean accounts furnish a great deal of information about their group, the Malgal, who were also the ancestors of the Jurchen Jin state, which ruled parts of Northeast Asia and North China (1115–1260).[62] Under Koguryŏ rule, they were "a subject people, some of whom at times were reduced to forced labor or slave status and so became an unfree class serving masters who belonged to the ruling class of Koguryŏ origins" in Parhae.[63]

Relations between Koryŏ and the Jurchen shifted in tone and intensity during the rise of the Wanyan clan under Wugunai (1021–1074), who extended Jurchen domination from the Changbaishan northward. Koryŏ's King Injong (r. 1122–1146) declared himself a vassal of Jin in 1126, even though "there were many in Koryŏ who were outraged at this," referring to the Jin demand that Koryŏ acknowledge its dominant status in the tributary relationship.[64]

Both the Ming and the Chosŏn attempted to win over the Jurchen tribes.[65] The Ming invested Jianzhou Jurchen who submitted to Ming rule with presents and titles in military guard and battalion units designed to hold off "barbarians."[66] In this manner Mŏngke Temŭr, leader of the Odori Jurchen who had previously allied himself to the Chosŏn, became the head of the left wing of the Jianzhou guard in 1410. He and the Jurchen lived in a buffer zone between the Ming and Korean authorities. While they were subjected to pressures from both sides, the recurrent Mongol threat to Ming power enabled Jurchen leaders and their followers to exercise considerable autonomy. According to his own account, the Jianzhou Jurchen leader, Nurhaci, was a descendant of Mŏngke Temŭr.

Nurhaci's early career owed much to his patron, the Ming military official Li Chengliang (1526–1618).[67] The fourth generation of his family to occupy military posts in the northeast frontier region, Li rose to become a Ming general who defended Liaodong against the Mongols and Jurchen. His authority was based not so much on the official troops under his direct command— those numbered only ten thousand—as on his private military followers, *jia ding* (several thousand in number), and on his network of real and fictive kinsmen who filled the military positions throughout the northeast. Nor did his influence stop at the regional level: he and his sons featured in virtually every major Ming campaign of the late sixteenth and early seventeenth centuries.

As a Ming appointee, Li Chengliang was able to consolidate his own regional power and use about half of the government's military allocations for Liaodong for his personal use. In addition, he tapped the profits of the trade expansion, acquiring a percentage of the transactions on horses and other commodities. With the wealth and power gleaned from his official and unofficial activities, Li created a large patronage network in Liaodong. His example was emulated by the chiefs of the Haixi Jurchen and Jianzhou Jurchen, who also obtained patents or trade permits in exchange for submitting to Ming rule.[68]

Like Li Chengliang, Nurhaci acquired profits from the growing trade to support his military activities. Feng Yuan, who served on the Liaodong-Kaiyuan Military Defense Circuit, wrote in the early seventeenth century about the competition among Jurchen in the southern tier to seize such profits by acting as middlemen and interpreters for Jurchen bearing ginseng and furs from the Sungari and Amur rivers. First the Hada chieftain built a mountain fortress at a major pass on the transport route to monopolize trade profits, but then the Yehe followed suit; now "the profits have all fallen into the hands of Nurhaci. The reason that disputes break out every year among the Jurchens is that they are fighting over patents, but in actual fact they are fighting over commercial profits."[69]

By 1618, Nurhaci was the leader of a powerful Jurchen state. Two years earlier (1616), he had declared himself the ruler (*Han*, the Manchu equivalent of *Khan*) of the Later Jin state, which claimed to be a successor to the Jin dynasty (which had ruled part of North China from 1115–1260). Nurhaci proclaimed seven grievances against the Ming, and led a ten thousand man force against the Ming garrison at Fushun (May 1618).[70] Its commander, Li Yongfang, surrendered Fushun after one attack.[71]

The fall of this strategic city aroused a military response from the Ming, who pressed the Chosŏn court to contribute military supplies and troops toward a serious military expedition against Nurhaci. Since he would face armies on his western and southern flank if Chosŏn entered the fray, Nurhaci urged Chosŏn to remain neutral in the Ming–Later Jin conflict. Caught between the Ming and the Later Jin, the Chosŏn king, Kwanghae, attempted to sit on the fence. His officials were split between a pro-Ming faction and a faction that urged caution for fear that the Jurchen would punish Chosŏn if it sided with the Ming. Kwanghae eventually sent 13,000 men to join the Ming forces in an attack on the Later Jin, but the Ming-Chosŏn forces were routed in an epic battle at Sarhū (April 1618). Nurhaci then seized control of Liaodong, the region east of the Liao River that lay directly north of Chosŏn.[72]

After Sarhū, Kwanghae successfully resisted pressure from Nurhaci for an alliance, but while remaining a tributary vassal to the Ming, he also did not respond to their demands for more troop and military aid. From a long-term perspective, Kwanghae's "adroit foreign policy" preserved Chosŏn during extremely difficult times, but his fence-sitting provoked a successful coup d'état by a pro-Ming faction in April 1723, who replaced him with Injo (r. 1623–1649). Injo's administration was marked by a "blatantly pro-Ming anti-Manchu policy." The officials of the Great Northern faction, which had dominated during Kwanghae's reign, were purged (many were executed) and the pro-Ming Westerners' faction took power.[73]

MANCHU INVASIONS OF KOREA

The immediate stimulus for the final 1636/1637 Manchu invasion was Chosŏn's refusal to formally recognize Hongtaiji, Nurhaci's successor, as Son of Heaven. On the first day of the first lunar month in 1636, Hongtaiji took two major steps toward expanding the scope of his state-building activities. He adopted a dynastic name (Qing) and took the Chinese title of "emperor" (*huangdi*). Both steps directly challenged the Ming dynasty, which was thereafter referred to in Manchu documents (rejecting the Ming as Sons of Heaven) as the "southern dynasty" (*nan chao*).[74] It was impossible for Chosŏn to recognize the Qing dynastic name and Hongtaiji's new imperial title. Two Chosŏn envoys who were present at Hongtaiji's court refused to perform the ritual of submission that followed the dynastic proclamation. Fearing punishment from their superiors, they abandoned a Qing state letter to Injo in a hostel, and fled home. The following month the Injo court also rebuffed an embassy of Mongol and Manchu banner princes that arrived in Hansŏng to invite the king to send a royal kinsman to the Qing capital, Shenyang, to congratulate Hongtaiji on his imperial title.[75]

Strategically, the invasion aimed to deny the Ming a potential military ally and thus secure the Manchu forces from an attack on their base area during their anticipated military campaigns against the Ming. Additionally, the Manchus hoped to obtain food and military supplies from Chosŏn that had been cut off by the diplomatic fracas.[76] Finally, the subjugation of Chosŏn would be a further demonstration of Manchu charisma and military power to "the world."

The 1636/1637 invasion, known in Korean history as the *Byongja horan*, was short and decisive. The Qing army crossed the Yalu River into Chosŏn territory on December 27, 1636, and Injo surrendered on February 24, 1637, so the campaign lasted about two months. The military confrontation was lopsided in favor of the Manchu army, which advanced rapidly down the peninsula; Chosŏn appealed for but failed to obtain military aid from the Ming; and Injo was finally forced to agree to the Manchu terms for peace. The Qing conditions were that Chosŏn excise the Ming reign name from its official documents, discard the Ming documents and seals of investiture, and break relations with the Ming, and that it accept the Qing calendar, and with it the tributary obligations, the quantity and types of tributary goods and local products being specified, to be delivered by embassies sent on New Year's Day, the emperor's birthday, the winter solstice, and the annual tribute-bearing mission.[77] Injo's eldest and second sons and the sons of some high ministers were taken to Shenyang as hostages. Hongtaiji also demanded that leaders of the major anti-Manchu faction should be handed over to him for punishment.[78]

The 1637 subjugation of Chosŏn freed Hongtaiji from fears of a Ming-Chosŏn alliance that would threaten him with a two-front war. The actual invasion of China proper would not occur until a Chinese rebel, Li Zicheng, occupied the Ming capital (April 25, 1644) and caused the last Ming emperor to hang himself. The Ming general Wu Sangui went over to the Qing cause; Qing troops were in Beijing on June 6, entering the final phase of a conquest that would not be completed until 1683.

CONCLUSION

As Joseph Esherick pointed out in chapter 1, the rhetoric used in court deliberations has disguised the extent to which Chinese states responded with flexibility and pragmatism to situations where they did not enjoy a military advantage over their neighbors. We have tried to demonstrate that these situations were not a rare occurrence in premodern Chinese history, and deserve serious consideration in studies of China's historical strategies of interaction with neighbors.

Whereas describing the 198 B.C. Han treaty with the Xiongnu as the court's response to the Xiongnu embassy requesting *he qin* implies that the power balance lay in China's favor, the actual agreement, necessitated by the lack of Chinese military superiority in conducting war against mounted nomads in steppe lands, was one in which the Chinese court provided payments of silver and textiles in exchange for the Xiongnu promise to cease their raids into China. Chinese records of embassies from the Japanese archipelago, the Korean peninsula, the Ryukyus, and Southeast Asia similarly portray these events as evidence of the power of the Chinese Sinocentric world order, although a more detailed examination of the embassies themselves and the historical context suggests a more complex array of motivations on both sides: ambitious regional leaders seeking Chinese titles to wield against their competitors at home, and, especially in periods of political decentralization in China, Chinese courts using the embassies as confirmation of their political legitimacy in their own domestic political struggles.

By late Tang and Song times, the states surrounding China had absorbed the Chinese political vocabulary and used it in their own foreign relations, even against Chinese states. The multistate maneuverings of the Tangut Xia, Khitan Liao, Jurchen Jin, and Song reflect a diplomatic world that employed a common language, as illustrated in the 1142 treaty that described Song as a vassal of Jin, and labeled its annual payments to Jin as tribute (*gong*). Chinese protocol was also used by other states against Chinese regimes. During the 1637 negotiations concluding the Manchu invasion of Korea, for example, Qing turned back letters from Chosŏn that did not use the same form Korean officials adopted toward the Ming emperor in addressing Hongtaiji. In the surrender ceremony, the Manchus forced the Chosŏn king, Injo, to publicly kowtow before the seated Hongtaiji to signify Chosŏn's status as a Qing vassal, and the Qing negotiators stressed that the ritual formalities must exactly follow the model stipulated by Ming.[79]

Chinese terms like *jimi* (loose-rein), which reappear throughout Chinese history, incorrectly imply that the Chinese controlled their bilateral relations with tribal groups along the frontiers, whereas the three time periods that were surveyed demonstrate that the actual reality was much more complex. All of the states made decisions on bilateral relations based on shifts in the military and economic strength of their other neighbors, and China was frequently too weak to dictate terms to its neighbors, even if its officials described their policy as *jimi*. In the same way, long-term plans to administratively absorb non-Han populations into the Chinese bureaucratic order, embodied in the Tang *jimi fu zhou* and later in the Ming and Qing *tusi* system, sometimes backfired: the An Lushan rebellion and the rise of the Khitan Liao like the sixteenth-century Ningxia and southwest rebellions and even the Jurchen challenge of Nurhaci, are examples of what can happen when "loose-rein" policies allow tribal leaders to learn Chinese political and institutional practices and emerge as leaders of incipient states.

Into the seventeenth to nineteenth centuries, when the tributary model is said to have peaked, China's neighbors challenged its claim to regional hegemony. Between 1637 and 1730, Korean officials and leaders contemplated a "northern expedition" against the Qing, erected altars to the Ming rulers, and reiterated their loyalty to the Ming by retaining the Ming calendar. In 1730, its embassy to Beijing was asked to explain why their identification plaques bore a Ming and not a Qing date.[80] Japan not only refused to participate in the Chinese tributary system but constructed an alternate Japan-centered world order: in 1715 the shogunate issued tallies and specified that only Chinese traders holding them would be permitted to dock in Nagasaki. Since domestic shortages of copper, a money metal, had driven the Kangxi court to purchase supplies in Japan, the Qing throne tacitly acquiesced in what was a direct refutation of its tributary model.[81] China's historical hegemony over Asia was by no means as complete as sometimes imagined, and

China's foreign policy stances were not as rigid as many analysts of the mid- /
nineteenth century have supposed.

The examples provided in this chapter challenge the assumption that Chinese centrality, expressed in the tributary system model, was the operative concept shaping foreign policy through the long span of Chinese history. Especially in ancient and medieval times, when Chinese regimes were centered in the North China plain, China's vulnerability to attack from its northern and northeastern neighbors would have put such a notion to constant testing. From a Sinocentric perspective, the recurring sequence of cyclical disintegration during which Chinese regimes had to deal with their neighbors as equals might be called a process of "decentering." To describe the eventual reemergence of a unified Chinese state as "recentering," however, suggests that there was a core of continuity that persisted despite the dynastic cycle. Although this notion underlies the national history written in the twentieth century, it ignores the abrupt discontinuities created by conquest. As we have shown, the ruler of the new "Chinese" state often originated in the borderlands. These rulers used the Chinese tributary model in the conduct of interstate relations but the widespread dissemination of Chinese political rhetoric does not of course mean that Chinese models were adopted without modification. From the tenth century onward, conquest dynasties skillfully blended Chinese and Inner Asian practices in order to rule a diverse array of subjects. The impact of these Inner and East Asian leaders on the formation of subsequent Chinese security strategies is itself a topic demanding further future research.

NOTES

1. In this chapter "China" refers to states occupying the region of North China (*zhongyuan*, the "central plain"), which is identified as the Chinese heartland. On the historical evolution in the meaning of terms such as *Hua* or *Xia*, the first terms found in historical documents to refer to the peoples known in contemporary times as the "Han Chinese," see Tsung-I Dow, "The Confucian Concept of a Nation and Its Historical Practice," *Asian Profile* 10, no. 4 (1982): 347–61; and Frank Dikötter, *The Discourse of Race in Modern China* (Stanford, CA: Stanford University Press, 1992), ch. 1. Also see Shao-yun Yang, "Becoming *Zhongguo*, Becoming Han: Tracing and Reconceptualizing Ethnicity in Ancient North China, 770 BC–AD 581" (MA thesis, National University of Singapore, 2007).

2. J. K. Fairbank and S. Y. Teng, "On the Ch'ing Tributary System," *Harvard Journal of Asiatic Studies* 6, no. 2 (1941): 135–246.

3. John K. Fairbank, "A Preliminary Framework," in J. K. Fairbank, ed., *The Chinese World Order: Traditional China's Foreign Relations* (Cambridge, MA: Harvard University Press, 1968), 5–11.

4. For a Korean critique of this recent literature see Kwŏn Chung-dal, "Chungguk ŭi hwakdae wa Hanjok gwan" [The expansion of China and views of the Han people], *Han'guk sahaksa hakbo* 10 (2004): 147–62; also Peter I. Yun, "Rethinking the Tribute System: Korean States and Northeast Asian Interstate Relations, 600–1600" (PhD dissertation, History Department, University of California, Los Angeles, 1998). An appraisal of the Chinese perspective is provided in Alexander Woodside, "The Centre and the Borderlands in Chinese Political Theory," in Diana Lary, ed., *The Chinese State at the Borders* (Vancouver: UBC Press, 2007), 11–28.

5. Morris Rossabi, ed., *China among Equals: The Middle Kingdom and Its Neighbors, 10th–14th Centuries* (Berkeley: University of California Press, 1983); see his "Introduction," 1–13.

6. The innovations made by the Xixia, Liao, Jin, and Yuan regimes were later analyzed: see Herbert Franke and Denis Twitchett, eds., *The Cambridge History of China*, vol. 6: *Alien Regimes and Border States, 907–1368*, (Cambridge: Cambridge University Press, 1994).

7. Victoria Tin-bor Hui, *War and State Formation in Ancient China and Early Modern Europe* (Cambridge: Cambridge University Press, 2005).

8. Michael H. Hunt, "Chinese Foreign Relations in Historical Perspective," in Harry Harding, ed., *China's Foreign Relations in the 1980s* (New Haven, CT: Yale University Press, 1980), 7–8; Hunt points out that this "realist" model also applies to the late nineteenth and early twentieth centuries.

9. Richard von Glahn, "All under Heaven," in Edward L. Shaughnessy, ed., *China: Empire and Civilization* (Oxford: Oxford University Press, 2000), 12; see also 25–26 in Brian Hook, ed., *The Cambridge Encyclopedia of China* (Cambridge: Cambridge University Press, 1991).

10. Mark Edward Lewis, *China between Empires: The Northern and Southern Dynasties* (Cambridge, MA: Belknap Press, 2009), 4, writes: "The fact that the Yellow River valley, the traditional heartland of the Chinese empire, was ruled by foreign emperors for essentially nine of the eighteen centuries after the fall of the Han dynasty in 220 (and three more centuries if the Tang ruling house is considered 'alien') dramatically demonstrates the degree to which the government of China became detached from its people and society."

11. Zhenping Wang, *Ambassadors from the Islands of Immortals: China-Japan Relations in the Han-Tang Period* (Honolulu: University of Hawai'i Press, 2005); see Mark Edward Lewis, *The Early Chinese Empires: Qin and Han* (Cambridge, MA: Belknap Press, 2007), ch. 6 on Han relations with nomadic empires.

12. Nicola Di Cosmo, *Ancient China and Its Enemies: The Rise of Nomadic Power in East Asian History* (Cambridge: Cambridge University Press, 2002), 189.

13. Owen Lattimore, *Inner Asian Frontiers of China* (Hong Kong: Oxford University Press, 1988), of a work first published in 1940. Lewis, *Early Chinese Empires*, 133, observes that the *he qin* system entailed recognition by the Han of the Xiongnu ruler's title of *chanyu* in exchange for the Xiongnu ruler's recognition of the Han *huangdi*; further, Emperor Wen's statement (162 B.C.) implied that the *chanyu* and *huangdi* shared "Heaven and Earth" (that is, they were on relations of parity).

14. Ying-shih Yü, "The Hsiung-nu," in Denis Sinor, ed., *The Cambridge History of Early Inner Asia* (Cambridge: Cambridge University Press, 1990), 118–25; Di Cosmo, *Ancient China and Its Enemies*, 190–96.

15. Gungwu Wang, "The Rhetoric of a Lesser Empire: Early Sung Relations with Its Neighbors," in Fairbank, *The Chinese World Order*, 58.

16. Yü, "Hsiung-nu," 122–25. Border markets were also opened during the second century B.C.

17. Nicola Di Cosmo, "State Formation and Periodization in Inner Asian History," *Journal of World* History 10, no. 1 (1999): 23–24. Wang, "The Rhetoric of a Lesser Empire," 58, cites the Tibetan protest when after agreeing to a treaty, Tang attempted to treat the Tibetan envoy as a tributary vassal in the late eighth century. He also contrasts the Chinese historical depiction of Tang Taizong's marriage alliance with Tibet as sealing Tibet's submission to Tang; the motivation for sending a Tang princess to marry the Tibetan king was the threat posed by the Tibetan state.

18. Denis Twitchett and Klaus-Peter Tietze, "The Liao," in Herbert Franke and Denis Twitchett, eds., *The Cambridge History of China*, vol. 6: *Alien Regimes and Border States, 907–1368* (Cambridge: Cambridge University Press, 1994), 109.

19. Herbert Franke, "The Chin Dynasty," in *The Cambridge History of China*, 6:233–34.

20. Lien-sheng Yang, "Historical Notes on the Chinese World Order," in Fairbank, *The Chinese World Order*, 32.

21. Yü, "Hsiung-nu," 131–47.

22. For a discussion of *jimi* in successive historical contexts, see Yang, "Historical Notes on the Chinese World Order," 23–25, 31–33.

23. Yang, "Historical Notes on the Chinese World Order," 23–25, 31–33; Leo Shin, *The Making of the Chinese State: Ethnicity and Expansion on the Ming Borderlands* (Cambridge: Cambridge University Press, 2006), 75; on a failed attempt to use the *jimi fu zhou* system with Tanguts, see Michael T. Dalby, "Court Politics in Late T'ang Times," in Denis Twitchett and John K. Fairbank, eds., *The Cambridge History of China*, vol. 3: *Sui and T'ang China, 589–906*, Part 1 (Cambridge: Cambridge University Press, 1979), 679.

24. On *jimi fu zhou*, see Shin, *Making of the Chinese State*, 75; on *tusi*, John E. Herman, "The Cant of Conquest: *Tusi* Offices and China's Political Incorporation of the Southwest Frontier," in Pamela Kyle Crossley, Helen E. Siu, and Donald S. Sutton, eds., *Empire at the Margins: Culture, Ethnicity, and Frontier in Early Modern China* (Berkeley: University of California Press, 2006), 135–68; on the twentieth-century *tusi*, see Jennifer T. E. Took, *A Native Chieftaincy in Southwest China: Franchising a Tai Chieftaincy under the Tusi System of Late Imperial China* (Leiden: E. J. Brill, 2005).

25. Andre Gunder Frank, *ReOrient: Global Economy in the Asian Age* (Berkeley: University of California Press, 1998), 108–17, who concludes that "the entire world economic order was—literally—Sinocentric" (117).

26. Fairbank and Teng, "The Ch'ing Tributary System," 205–6.

27. Takeshi Hamashita, "The Tribute Trade System and Modern Asia," in A. J. H. Latham and Heita Kawakatsu, eds., *Japanese Industrialization and the Asian Economy* (London: Routledge, 1994), 92.

28. Gina L. Barnes, *The Rise of Civilization in East Asia: The Archaeology of China, Korea and Japan* (London: Thames and Hudson, 1993), ch. 11, 13; William Wayne Farris, *Sacred Texts and Buried Treasures: Issues in the Historical Archaeology of Ancient Japan* (Honolulu: University of Hawai'i Press, 1998), ch. 1. See also Li Huizhu, "Handai yiqian Shandong yu Chaoxian bandao nanbu de jiaowang" [Exchanges between Shandong and the southern part of the Korean peninsula before the Han dynasty], *Beifang wenwu* 1 (2004): 16–24.

29. Twitchett and Tietze, "Liao," 54. On the importance of trade and "external tribute" for Inner Asian steppe empires, see Nicola Di Cosmo, "State Formation," 25, 30–32.

30. Ki-baik Lee, trans. Edward W. Wagner, *A New History of Korea* (Cambridge, MA: Harvard University Press, 1984), ch. 3.

31. Farris, *Sacred Texts and Buried Treasures*, 51, notes that the best source of iron was southern Korea and the demand for iron necessitated that Japan be closely linked with the states there.

32. Farris, *Sacred Texts and Buried Treasure*, 105.

33. Wang, *Ambassadors from the Islands of Immortals*.

34. Bruce L. Batten, *Gateway to Japan: Hakata in War and Peace, 500–1300* (Honolulu: University of Hawai'i Press, 2006), 18–33; Teng Hongyan, "Bohai zhi Riben liwu tanzhe" [Inquiry into the gifts presented by Bohai to Japan], *Zhongguo bianjiang shi di yanjiu* 16, no. 2 (2006): 69–76.

35. Yi-hong Pan, *Son of Heaven and Heavenly Qaghan: Sui-Tang China and Its Neighbors* (Bellingham: Western Washington Press, 1997), ch. 6.

36. Sakayori Masashi, "Tōhoku Ajia no dōkō to kodai Nihon—Botsukai no shiten kara" [Trends in Northeast Asia and Japan—from the perspective of Parhae), in Sakai Kiyotari and Hirano Kunio, eds., *Shinpan kodai no Nihon*, vol. 2: *Ajia kara mita kodai Nihon* (Tokyo: Kadokawa shoten, 1992), 295–318.

37. Herbert Franke and Denis Twitchett, "Introduction," in *The Cambridge History of China*, 6:2.

38. See the essays in *The Cambridge History of China*, vol. 6.

39. Ruth Dunnell, "The Hsi Hsia," in *The Cambridge History of China*, 6:154–214.

40. Di Cosmo, "State Formation," 32–37. Thomas Barfield, *The Perilous Frontier: Nomadic Empires and China* (Oxford: Basil Blackwell, 1989), had argued that only states emerging from the mixed ecological zones of Manchuria were successful in creating hybrid regimes that could rule both sedentary and nomadic subjects, but the essays in vol. 6 of *The Cambridge History of China* show that Inner Asian empires, including the Tangut Xia and the Mongol Yuan, learned from each other as well as from direct contact with Chinese regimes.

41. Franke and Twitchett, "Introduction," 4–7.

42. Franke and Twitchett, "Introduction," 9–14.

43. Twitchett and Tietze, "Liao," 70.

44. According to Twitchett and Tietze, "Liao," 103, a Khitan princess's daughter was married to the Koryŏ king in 996; his successor was formally invested as king by Liao in 998, and formally congratulated the Liao court on its victories over the Song in 999–1000 and 1004.

45. Twitchett and Tietze, "Liao," 104. Two years later, stimulated by news that the Xia were negotiating secretly with the Song, the Liao sent a punitive expedition into Xia territory and retained the king as a vassal. The Song refused to use the term "tribute" (*gong*) for this payment (108–10). See David C. Wright, "Party, Pedigree, and Peace: Routine Sung Diplomatic Missives to the Liao," *Journal of Sung-Yuan Studies* 26 (1996): 55–85, who analyzes the letters exchanged between Song and Liao to argue for a relationship of "diplomatic parity" after the Shanyuan treaty.

46. The Song refused to use the term "tribute" (*gong*) for this payment. Twitchett and Tietze, "Liao," 108–10.

47. Twitchett and Tietze, "Liao," 109, observe that the Song insisted that these payments not be called "tribute," but "a contribution to military expenses." The diplomatic exchanges between the two courts after this treaty were distinguished from the protocols imposed on other states.

48. Franke, "Chin," 220–22.

49. Franke, "Chin," 224–25.

50. Franke, "Chin," 226–34.

51. Franke and Twitchett, "Introduction," 10.

52. Richard Von Glahn, *Fountain of Fortune: Money and Monetary Policy in China, Fourteenth to Seventeenth Centuries* (Berkeley: University of California Press, 1996), 139–40.

53. Udagawa Takehisa, *Teppō no denrai: Heiki ga kataru kinsei no tanjō* [The transmission of firearms: What military weapons say about the birth of the early modern era] (Tokyo: Chūō koron sha, 1990); the weapons were quickly adopted by Koreans after the Hideyoshi invasion (Yonetani Hiroshi, "Jūshichi seiki zenki Nitchō kankei ni okeru buki yūshutsu" [The exportation of weapons in Japanese-Korean relations in the first half of the seventeenth century], in Fujita Satoru, ed., *Jūshichi seiki no Nihin to Higashi Ajia* [Japan and East Asia in the seventeenth century] (Tokyo: Yamakawa shuppansha, 2000), 39–67. According to Nicola Di Cosmo, "European Technology and Manchu Power: Reflections on the 'Military Revolution' in Seventeenth-Century China," in Sølvi Sogner, ed., *Making Sense of Global History: The 19th International Congress of the Historical Sciences, Oslo 2000, Commemorative Volume* (Oslog: Universitetsforlaget, 2001), 119–39, the Manchus also began to equip their army with artillery units and cannoneers.

54. Iwai Shigeki, "China's Frontier Society in the Sixteenth and Seventeenth Centuries," *Acta Asiatica* 88 (2005): 1–20.

55. Matsuura Shigeru, "Jūshichi seiki igo no Tōhoku Ajia no okeru keizai kōryu" [Economic exchange in Northeast Asia from the seventeenth century onward], in *Matsumura Jun sensi koki kinen Shindai shi ronsō* [Collected articles on Qing history, Festschrift in honor of Professor Matsumura Jun's seventieth birthday] (Tokyo: Kyūko shoin, 1994), 35–67.

56. Kishimoto Mio, "Shinchō to Yūrajia" [The Qing and Eurasia], in Rekishigaku Kenkyūkai, ed., *Kōzai sekaishi* [Lecture series on world history] (Tokyo: Tokyo University Press, 1995), 2:17–18.

57. On Pübei and Yang Yinglong, see Ray Huang, "The Lung-ch'ing and Wan-li Reigns, 1567–1720," in Frederick W. Mote and Denis Twitchett, ed., *The Cambridge*

History of China, vol. 7: *The Ming Dynasty, 1368–1644, Part 1* (Cambridge: Cambridge University Press, 1988), 566–67, 564–65; see Yang Yinglong's biography in L. Carrington Goodrich and Chaoying Fang, eds., *Dictionary of Ming Biography, 1368–1644* (New York: Columbia University Press, 1976), 1553–56; on Mao Wenlong, see Frederic Wakeman, Jr., *The Great Enterprise: The Manchu Reconstruction of Imperial Order in Seventeenth-Century China* (Berkeley: University of California Press, 1985), I:127–30.

58. The prelude to Hideyoshi's invasion is covered in Etsuko Hae-Jin Kang, *Diplomacy and Ideology in Japanese-Korean Relations from the Fifteenth to the Eighteenth Century* (New York: St. Martin's Press, 1997), ch. 3. A narrative of the invasion is provided by Samuel Hawley, *The Imjin War: Japan's Sixteenth-Century Invasion of Korea and Attempt to Conquer China* (Seoul: Royal Asiatic Society, Korea Branch, 2005).

59. Hawley, *Imjin War*, 97, states that 158,800 men were earmarked for the Korean invasion.

60. Kenneth M. Swope, "Deceit, Disguise, and Dependence: China, Japan, and the Future of the Tributary System, 1592–1596," *International History Review* 24, no. 4 (2002): 757–82; Kitajima Manji, "Jinshin waranki no Chōsen to Min" [Chosŏn and Ming during Hideyoshi's invasion], in Arano Yasunori, Ishii Masatoshi, and Murai Yōsuke, eds., *Ajia no naka no Nihon shi* [Japanese history within an Asian context], vol. 2: *Gaikō to sensō* [Foreign relations and war] (Tokyo: University of Tokyo Press, 1992), 127–60; Ronald Toby, *State and Diplomacy in Early Modern Japan: Asia in the Development of the Tokugawa Bakufu* (Princeton, NJ: Princeton University Press, 1984), 25.

61. Yan Chongnian, *Nuerhachi zhuan* [Life of Nurhaci] (Beijing: Beijing chubanshe, 1983), also his *Tianming han* [The Tianming Khan] (Changchun: Jilin wenshi chubanshe, 1930); Teng Shaozhen, *Nuerhachi pingzhuan* [Life of Nurhaci] (Shenyang: Liaoning renmin chubanshe, 1985). See also the biography in Arthur W. Hummel, ed. *Eminent Chinese of the Ch'ing Period* (Washington, DC: US Government Printing Office, 1945), 594–99.

62. Lee, *New History*, 91.

63. Lee, *New History*, 89.

64. Lee, *New History*, 229, quotation from Lee, *New History*, 128.

65. Kenneth R. Robinson, "From Raiders to Traders: Border Security and Border Control in Early Chosŏn, 1392–1450," *Korean Studies* 16 (1992): 98. In a later article, "Chōsen ō-chō—jushoku Joshinjin no kankei to 'Chōsen'" [The Chosŏn dynasty—the relationship of Jurchen holding office and 'Chosŏn'], *Rekishi hyoron* 592 (1999): 29–42, Robinson talks about the incorporation of at least part of the Jurchen population into the Korean society in the fifteenth and sixteenth centuries.

66. See Morris Rossabi, "The Ming and Inner Asia," in Denis Twitchett and Frederick W. Mote, eds., *The Cambridge History of China*, vol. 8: *The Ming Dynasty, 1368–1644, Part 2* (Cambridge: Cambridge University Press, 1998), 258–71.

67. Kenneth W. Swope, "A Few Good Men: The Li Family and China's Northern Frontier in the Late Ming," *Ming Studies* 49 (2004): 34–81; see Hummel, *Eminent Chinese of the Ch'ing Period*, I:450–52.

68. Iwai Shigeki, "China's Frontier Society," 13.

69. Quote cited in "China's Frontier Society," 11; for a description of the author of *Kaiyuan tushuo*, written ca. 1601–1619, see Lynn A. Struve, *The Ming-Qing Conflict, 1619–1683: A Historiography and Source Guide* (Ann Arbor, MI: Association for Asian Studies, 1998), 191–92.

70. These events are described in Wakeman, *The Great Enterprise*, I:49–66.

71. Wakeman, *The Great Enterprise*, I:59–62.

72. The emergence of the Manchu power in Northeast Asia is outlined in Wakeman, *The Great Enterprise*, I:49–66.

73. On the politics of the coup d'état, see Yi Yŏngch'un, *Chosŏn hugi wangwi gyesŭng yŏn'gu* [Research on royal succession in the Later Chosŏn period] (Seoul: Jib'mun tang, 1998), 124–42; on factional conflicts, see Yi Sŏngmu, *Chosŏn sidae tangjaengsa* [History of factional disputes in the Chosŏn period] (Seoul: Tongbang midio, 2000), I:155–58, 173–93.

74. *Injo sillok*, 14/6/17, #2, records Injo's "manifesto" (*kyok'mun*) to Hongtaiji: in the manifesto, the Chosŏn side refers to the Ming as "central dynasty" (*zhong chao*) while the Jurchen refer to the Ming as "southern dynasty" (*nan chao*). *Nan chao* is also found in Hongtaiji's letter of February 14, 1637 (*Injo sillok* 15/1/20, #3), and in Injo's letter to Hontaiji of February 21, 1637 (*Injo sillok* 15/1/27, #2).

75. In 1635, Hongtaiji formally changed the name of his people from "Jurchen," to "Manchu." See Pamela Kyle Crossley, *The Manchus* (Oxford: Blackwell Publishers Inc., 1997), 210–11.

76. Wakeman, *The Great Enterprise*, fn 152, 210.

77. Hae-jong Chun, "Sino-Korean Tributary Relations in the Ch'ing Period," in Fairbank, *The Chinese World Order*, 91.

78. Sun Wenliang and Li Zhiting, *Tiancong han, Chongde di* [Tiancong khan, Chongde emperor] (Changchun: Jilin wenshi chubanshe, 1993), 206.

79. *Injo sillok*, 1637/1/30 (Western date February 24, 1637) describes the surrender ceremony; also see *Taizong Wen huangdi shilu* [Veritable records of Taizong, Emperor Wen], in *Da Qing shilu* [Veritable records of the Qing dynasty), reprinted in 60 vols. under the title *Qing shilu* (Beijing: Zhonghua shuju, 1986), 432–33. The citation is from v. 2 of the reprint ed.

80. JaHyun Kim Haboush, *A Heritage of Kings: One Man's Monarchy in the Confucian World* (New York: Columbia University Press, 1988), 45–46; JaHyun Kim Haboush, "Contesting Chinese Time, Nationalizing Temporal Space: Temporal Inscription in Late Chosŏn Korea," Lynn A. Struve, ed., *Time, Temporality, and Imperial Transition* (Honolulu: University of Hawai'i Press, 2005), 115–41.

81. John W. Hall, "Notes on the Early Ch'ing Copper Trade with Japan," *Harvard Journal of Asiatic Studies* 12, no. 3–4 (1949): 452–58, describes the 1689–1723 period when Qing mints used "nothing but foreign copper" (454), and the Qing decision that the 1715 tallies were "merely a commercial procedure of no political significance" (456). See Preston M. Torbert, *The Ch'ing Imperial Household Department: A Study of Its Organization and Principal Functions, 1662–1796* (Cambridge, MA: Council on East Asian Studies, Harvard University, 1977), 94, on the Imperial Household Department's role in copper imports.

4

China's Strategy and Security in the Post–Cold War Era

Michael D. Swaine, Panda Hugger

Some observers of China's emergence as a major power in the post–Cold War period view Beijing as a highly strategic and farsighted player in the international system, fully engaged in implementing a comprehensive and detailed plan to achieve political, military, and economic dominance over Asia (and perhaps more distant regions) and thereby to displace the United States as the maritime region's premier power. Such individuals point to China's robust military modernization program—marked by steady advances in various types of power projection capabilities—and its growing diplomatic and economic presence, as providing *prima facie* evidence of an intent to achieve such dominance. Some advocates also invoke the Chinese past to support this argument, asserting that Beijing is seeking to reestablish its putative historical position as the dominant imperial power in Asia.

In contrast, other observers of China's rise argue that Beijing's approach to the outside world is largely reactive, defensive, and poorly integrated or coordinated, lacking an overall strategy beyond the enunciation of some broad principles or guidelines. To reinforce this claim, they point to the chaotic, fragmented, and often competitive structure of the Chinese political and bureaucratic systems, apparent contradictions in aspects of foreign and defense policy implementation, and the absence of any formal policy document spelling out a Chinese grand strategy.

In truth, both perspectives significantly distort a much more complex reality. There is little doubt that China's leaders have enunciated and are pursuing a clear, coherent, and largely consistent set of national objectives and priorities. Moreover, any careful examination of China's foreign and defense policies, statements, and actions confirms that China's political and military leaders are attempting to attain such goals through the application of basic diplomatic, political, economic, and military concepts and instruments. In short, they are pursuing a national strategy to attain certain national ends. They are not proceeding helter-skelter in reaction to events as they occur. On the other hand, the strategy that Beijing is pursuing does not amount to a search for hegemonic control. This chapter describes and analyzes China's current security strategy and the factors that have and likely will influence its formation and evolution over time.

CHINA'S NATIONAL OBJECTIVES
AND SECURITY ENVIRONMENT

Since at least the advent of the reform era in the late 1970s (and in some respects since the advent of the CCP regime in 1949), China's ends have included the maintenance of internal order and stability; the sustainment of high levels of growth and prosperity in order to create a "well-off society" and thus facilitate the "revival" of the nation by the middle of the century; the protection of the country against foreign and domestic threats to both territory and sovereignty; and the eventual achievement of great power status in Asia and beyond. Moreover, from the viewpoint of the senior PRC leadership, all of these objectives are bound up with the preservation of the power and legitimacy of the Chinese Communist Party (CCP). Indeed, the survival of the CCP is regarded as both the essential precondition for and an essential by-product of the attainment of all of these objectives.[1]

In the post–Cold War era, the attainment of this set of core objectives has been heavily influenced and shaped by certain specific internal and external features of China's security environment, as seen by the PRC leadership. These include, first, the expectation of peace between major powers despite smaller conflicts, second, an evolution of the distribution of international power such that American unipolarity is likely to be constrained by growing multipolarity, third, increasingly complex global economic interrelationships, and fourth, greater national self-confidence in China and consequently greater nationalist public pressure on foreign policy.

First and foremost, China expects an external threat environment marked by the low probability of a major war among the great powers. Chinese leaders use the phrase "peace and development" to characterize the current dominant feature of the international system.[2]

This assessment resulted from the end of the period of intense US-Soviet rivalry and arms racing that marked the high point of the Cold War, the subsequent collapse of the Soviet Union, and the emergence of increasing levels of political and economic cooperation and interdependence among the major powers. On the other hand, China's leaders also assert that, in place of major wars, the danger exists that local conflicts deriving from ethnic, territorial, and other disputes might erupt during the current period, especially along China's periphery. This has resulted in an external threat environment that is largely benign in terms of all-out warfare but nonetheless capable of producing serious limited conflict.

A second major feature of China's security environment consists of a perceived evolution in the distribution of power within the international system. As a result of the collapse of the Soviet empire and the emergence of rapidly industrializing nations in Asia and Europe, the Chinese leadership concluded by the 1980s that the global power structure was evolving from the bipolar strategic balance of the Cold War era, to an initial post–Cold War unipolar system dominated by the United States, to a multipolar system that could accord China greater leverage and influence. However, in recent years and at least until the advent of the current global economic crisis in 2008, the Chinese have observed that this process has slowed significantly, mainly because of America's ability to maintain its predominant position within the global system. Prolonged US dominance in the world is seen by the Chinese as preventing significant increases in China's leverage within the overall system. It also to some degree presents a serious potential threat to Beijing, given the absence—following the collapse of the Soviet Union—of an enduring strategic rationale for cooperative US-China relations, and the existence of deep-rooted ideological, political, historical, and geostrategic frictions and suspicions between the two powers.

In recent years, the Chinese leadership has increasingly viewed Washington as striving in various ways to obstruct China's emergence, to undermine the stability of the Chinese government, and to challenge the general principles— highly prized by Beijing—of national sovereignty and nonintervention in a state's internal affairs. In the military security arena, of particular concern to Beijing are US efforts to hedge against the emergence of a more powerful China by augmenting its air and naval forces in the Asia Pacific, and by US attempts to create both theater and national ballistic missile defense systems. Most recently, Beijing has become concerned that Washington could view an increasingly strong and influential China as a clear and unambiguous strategic threat requiring strenuous counterbalancing.

Despite all these concerns, the United States is also viewed by the Chinese leadership as an increasingly important—indeed essential—source of economic, financial, and technological development for Beijing. Similarly, the United States is viewed as increasingly dependent on China's expanding economy, as a source of essential goods, as a market in certain key product sectors, and as an investment destination. Moreover, despite their differences, the United States and China are also seen to share several important interests, including a strong desire for Asian stability and growth, and a common need to address a growing number of regional and global problems, such as environmental degradation, pandemics, international economic instability, and the proliferation of weapons of mass destruction (WMD). The result is a Sino-American relationship marked by both significant cooperation and periods of intense friction, along with the potential for growing strategic rivalry.[3]

Since the advent of the US global war on terrorism (GWOT), the incentives and opportunities for cooperation between Beijing and Washington, and the costs of rivalry and conflict, have arguably increased significantly. First and perhaps foremost, the GWOT has diverted US attention from the potential long-term strategic threat posed by China to American interests, thereby significantly reducing pressure on Beijing.[4] It has also greatly increased the value to the United States of maintaining good relations with Beijing, not only to minimize the chances of a distracting bilateral confrontation, but more important, to facilitate intensified efforts to combat terrorism and WMD proliferation. In such an effort, China is well positioned to offer significant assistance to the United States at relatively little cost. In fact, China's assistance has become increasingly important to the United States in several critical areas, most notably in handling the slow-motion crisis over North Korea's nuclear weapons program. Beijing's political and diplomatic support in the United Nations, the provision of important intelligence and other information on terrorist activities, and its cooperation in inspecting shipping containers bound for the United States also earn credit in Washington.[5]

Overall, in the view of many Chinese observers, the shift in US strategic priorities initiated by the events of 9/11, the resulting improvement in Sino-US relations, and China's overall increased confidence in the international arena have created a "strategic opportunity" (*zhanlue jiyu*) for strengthening the oft-strained Sino-US relationship and for advancing China's broader strategic objectives.[6]

A third, related feature of China's security environment has emerged as a result of the impact of China's rapid economic development and increased involvement with the outside world. On the negative side, the concerns posed by the prospect of local wars and the continued US dominance in maritime East Asia and elsewhere are exacerbated, in the Chinese view, by (1) an increased exposure to maritime threats as a result of the growing concentration of China's key economic and social assets along its eastern and southern coastline and a greatly increased reliance on ocean-borne import and export products; and (2) an overall increasing level of dependence upon foreign markets, investment and technology flows, and overseas energy sources for the maintenance of China's rapid rate of economic development. These two developments have together created a host of new vulnerabilities and security requirements for the PRC regime.

At the same time, Beijing's expanding economic contacts with the outside world are arguably increasing mutual incentives for cooperation while raising anxieties in some quarters over China's increasing influence. In particular, as a result of deepening bilateral trade, investment, and technology flows during the past decade or more, the Sino-American economic relationship has now become critical to the health and vitality of both nations. As a result, attempts to compel changes in the economic behavior of the other side through unilateral, broad-based sanctions or other punitive measures can no longer be undertaken without exposing oneself to very significant and potentially damaging retaliation in response.

In addition, China's deepening and expanding contact with the international system is facilitating a greater acceptance of international and even Western norms and values in many critical areas, such as global trade and investment, defense-related technology transfers, and weapons proliferation. This development is reinforced by the emergence of a new generation of political and economic leaders who possess a greater knowledge and awareness of the necessity and value of external contacts and ideas. Finally, the emergence of a growing set of Chinese domestic challenges, including generational leadership change, corruption, social unrest, economic inequalities, and environmental degradation have reinforced the need to maintain a stable and economically beneficial external environment.

A fourth set of features of China's security environment derive from both China's continued economic success and the declining ideological legitimacy of the Chinese communist regime. During the past three decades, these factors have led to the emergence and growth of a statist form of Chinese nationalism among both elites and the populace as a whole. As Lowell Dittmer describes in chapter 2, the caution of the immediate post-Tiananmen era has gradually been replaced by the self-confident optimism of "China's peaceful rise." This phenomenon reflects greater national pride and is used by the Chinese government to bolster its legitimacy. However, it can also become a source of intense elite and popular pressure on the government to defend China's national honor and interests against perceived insults and foreign threats.[7]

Moreover, the intensification of state-centric nationalism, along with the rapid growth of China's economic and military capabilities (discussed below), has generated some concern among both regional powers and the United States, thus contributing to a classic security dilemma.[8]

CHINA'S GRAND STRATEGY
AND RELATED FOREIGN AND DEFENSE POLICIES

In order to attain China's national objectives within the complex and dynamic security environment enunciated above, Beijing has adopted a set of guidelines or approaches for the application of national power and influence in the post–Cold War era that amount to a de facto grand strategy.[9]

This strategy is centered on four elements: first, a highly pragmatic, market-led economic development program—albeit with significant administrative controls in certain areas; second, an overall foreign policy of "peace and development" marked by the search for win-win outcomes, the maintenance of amicable political and security relations with virtually all nations, and the deepening of those types of interstate relationships that are most conducive to economic development; third, a steady expansion in the level of Beijing's involvement in and support for international and multilateral regimes, institutions, forums, and dialogues in a wide variety of issue areas; and fourth, a general restraint in the use of force—whether toward China's periphery or against other more distant powers. At the same time, China has worked steadily since the early 1990s to deter threats, protect growing external assets, and increase Beijing's overall international influence by modernizing and streamlining its military.[10]

In all of these areas, China is endeavoring to sustain rapid economic growth, build cooperative political relations, establish more effective means to resolve disputes and tackle common problems with other entities, and allay concerns that China's growing power requires containment or counterbalancing. On the other hand, it is also seeking to acquire greater levels of both coercive power and political/economic leverage to deter other states or international organizations from attempting to contain China, challenge its rise, or threaten its core interests, should persuasion and positive incentives fail.[11]

Such fundamental strategic guidelines have been reflected in a wide range of specific foreign and defense policies and undertakings. Many of these policies have been evident since at least the early 1990s, although some have undergone modification in the current decade in response to more recent developments in China's security environment.

At the rhetorical level, Beijing has repeatedly and emphatically enunciated an overall foreign policy of peace, cooperation, and goodwill toward all states. Under President Hu Jintao, this idea has been conveyed via the two interrelated ideas of China's peaceful development and its support for the creation of a harmonious world. The former seeks to rebut the notion that China's rise will disrupt Asian and global stability, by stressing Beijing's current and future dependence on commercial and technological globalization, its primary reliance on nonmilitary forms of contact and influence, and its historical aversion to hegemonic and expansionist behavior. The latter stresses China's unwavering support for "multilateralism" and international institutions and regimes, its increasing contribution to global humanitarian and developmental assistance programs, its respect for diverse political cultures and economic systems, its defense of the principle of national sovereignty, and the overall development of friendly relations on the basis of the 1950s notion of the Five Principles of Peaceful Coexistence.[12]

In the security realm, these ideas have been reflected in the so-called New Security Concept, unveiled in 1997, along with the notion of bilateral "strategic partnerships" with nations along China's periphery (e.g., Russia, ASEAN states, Japan, South Korea, etc.) and in other strategically important regions. In addition to their espousal of peace and harmony, both the New Security Concept and the "partnership" idea were initially intended to offer a potential alternative to the concept of bilateral security alliances (and in particular the US-centered "hub and spokes" security structure of formal alliances and forward deployed military forces in the Asia Pacific), as well as the broader notion of unilateral or non-UN-sanctioned military intervention.[13]

These concepts have obviously served a clear political and strategic purpose for Beijing by presenting, in a systematic and consistent fashion, an overall argument as to why China's rise will contribute greatly to—rather than threaten or undermine—both regional and global stability and prosperity, thus comporting with Asia's self-interests as well as with US interests in Asia. Thus Beijing advances the notion that US strategic dominance in general, and any type of US-led opposition to China's rise in particular, would be unnecessary and potentially destabilizing for the region. Multilateralism and strategic partnerships also to some extent play on the fears some states harbor of US unilateralism and intervention in domestic affairs.

On a more concrete level, these views have also provided the rhetorical foundation for China's policy of expansive involvement in and support for international and multilateral organizations, regimes, and fora, including the United Nations; a wide variety of functional regimes in areas such as economic development and WMD counterproliferation; and various regional organizations such as the Shanghai Cooperation Organization (SCO), the Association of Southeast Asian Nations (ASEAN), and the East Asian Summit (EAS). Through such extensive and deepening political, diplomatic, and economic involvement in the international system, Beijing has sought to project and maintain an image as a constructive member of the international community, to more effectively manage China's growing international challenges, and to advance collaborative solutions to common problems at a minimal cost. It has also shown a desire to use such organizations and regimes to shape regional and global views and actions in ways that advance Chinese interests, and in particular to constrain the ability of other major powers to limit Beijing's options.[14]

In addition, Beijing's involvement in the war on terror, its deepening relationships among many key European and Asian states, and the emergence of a more cooperative and interdependent Sino-US relationship have together encouraged further movement among China's elite and public toward a "great power mentality" (*daguo xintai* 大国心态) to replace the "victim mentality" (*shouhaizhe xintai* 受害者心态) of the past. Many Chinese now speak of the need to share global responsibilities among the major powers, and have proposed a variety of trade and security structures for the Asian region, including a conference to communicate, among Asian militaries, a code of conduct with ASEAN regarding territorial claims and military activities in Southeast Asia that mainly incorporates ASEAN's preferences; a joint declaration with ASEAN on nontraditional security concerns (e.g., piracy, terrorism, etc.); an initiative to form a "New Security Policy Conference" of the Asia Regional Forum (ARF)—to promote China's New Security Concept; and a series of free trade associations with various Asian nations.[15]

Another key policy derived from China's overall grand strategy focuses on the desire to resolve peacefully or defer whenever possible all major territorial disputes, avoiding the use of force if at all possible while preventing nearby states from combining to oppose Chinese territorial claims. Specifically, Beijing's strategy has resulted in a two-pronged approach in this area. First, if the territorial dispute in question is both intrinsically trivial and marginal to China's larger interests, Beijing has sought to resolve it amicably in order to pursue its larger goals. The border disputes with Russia, for example, are evidence of this approach where China's overarching interest in improving its political relationship with Moscow and securing access to Russian military technology have resulted in quick, hopefully permanent solutions to the Ussuri River dispute. Second, if the dispute in question is significant but cannot be resolved to China's advantage by peaceful means, Beijing has advocated an indefinite postponement of the basic issue. This tactic has been adopted, for example, in the case of the territorial disputes with India, Japan, and the ASEAN states. The basic logic underlying this approach has been to steadfastly avoid conceding Chinese claims with respect to the dispute, while simultaneously seeking to prevent the dispute from undermining the pacific environment that China needs to attain its current development goals.[16]

This logic has even applied to the ongoing and often intense dispute with Washington and Taipei over the status of Taiwan, in which China would prefer to resolve the issue peacefully through gradual movement toward a negotiated reunification settlement rather than employ force. To achieve this objective, Beijing pursues a multifaceted policy, including efforts to increase China's economic and cultural pull on the island while avoiding any actions that might generate alarm, to politically isolate strongly proindependence political elements, in part by deepening direct contacts with all other political forces on Taiwan, to strengthen support for China's position regarding the island among all relevant powers (and especially nearby Asian states), to limit or oversee, through direct dialogue with Taipei, the ability of Taiwan to participate in international organizations, and to avoid a confrontation with Washington over the issue while maintaining strong objections to American arms sales and official contact with the island.

With the overwhelming defeat of proindependence political forces on Taiwan in the legislative and presidential elections of early 2008, tensions over the island have abated considerably and the prospect has emerged of a more stable cross-strait situation over the longer term. However, Beijing's acquisition of military capabilities of high relevance to Taiwan continues virtually unabated, and Washington has continued to sell arms to Taipei, and to strengthen its own force deployments in the western Pacific, in an attempt to improve its overall ability to deter a future Chinese miscalculation.[17]

Another increasingly important set of strategic objectives that is highly relevant to China's foreign and defense policies involves the outward search for reliable, affordable, and efficient sources of energy. As Erica Downs describes in chapter 8, this effort is viewed by Beijing as increasingly critical to the maintenance of Chinese growth and to improvements in China's huge and growing environmental problems.[18]

To address its growing energy challenge, China has adopted a multi-pronged market- and non-market-based approach that includes the diversification of supply sources; the use of long-term energy contracts and the formation of close political and economic relationships in energy-producing areas (in Asia, Near East, Africa, and South America); equity ownership over some overseas production or refining facilities; a greater use of domestic coal and gas, and increased nuclear power; increases in energy efficiency and conservation; and additions to China's strategic oil reserves. However, it remains unclear as to whether these activities reflect the workings of a coordinated, comprehensive global energy security strategy. Although foreign-oriented activities are often associated with a so-called go-abroad energy strategy, most knowledgeable observers assert that separate (and sometimes competing) bureaucratic and commercial interests most often characterize China's search for energy security overseas. Indeed, some experts have described China's energy policymaking apparatus as "fractured" and its so-called strategy as "a collection of ad hoc initiatives."[19]

In bilateral interstate relations, China has been pursuing policies designed to reinforce and supplement the above general objectives. It has acted on several fronts (political, diplomatic, economic, military-to-military, cultural, people-to-people) to strengthen relations with all major Asian nations (e.g., South Korea, Japan, the ASEAN members, India, Russia, Indonesia, and most Central Asian states) while also establishing closer political and economic relations with key countries in Africa, Latin America, South America, and Europe.

CHINA'S APPROACH TO THE UNITED STATES

Beijing's most important relationship by far has been with the United States. At a minimum, China has required stable—if not affable—relations with Washington to continue rapid economic growth, to maintain regional stability, to achieve greater power and influence in the Asia Pacific, to minimize efforts to constrain China's emergence, and to avoid a conflict over Taiwan. Hence, it has sought to sustain cooperation with Washington and manage problems via dialogue and negotiation as far as possible.

At the same time, as indicated above, Beijing remains highly suspicious of US intentions and actions toward Chinese policies in many areas, especially China's growing power and involvement in the international order. China's leaders have thus sought to minimize the likelihood of shifts in United States' China policy toward an unambiguous position of opposition to or containment of China, strong sanctions or prohibitions on Chinese trade and investment policies, and constraints on China's global energy and trade policies. Chinese leaders have also sought to prevent the United States from providing greater support for Taiwanese independence, undertaking what they would regard as destabilizing military and diplomatic actions on the Korean peninsula, increasing greatly the US military presence in maritime Asia and South Asia, intervening politically (and perhaps militarily) in disputes between China and other Asian powers, such as India and Japan, and aggressively intervening in domestic human rights issues within China.

These and other concerns have led Beijing to undertake a variety of political and diplomatic policies or actions in the bilateral, multilateral, and international spheres to reduce US and international worries over China's growing power and reach, and to hedge against the ability or willingness of the United States (and other nations) to create and sustain policies designed to frustrate the expansion of China's capabilities, status, and influence. This hedging and deterrence strategy has also contained an increasingly prominent military component, involving a systematic, well-funded, and focused program of force modernization. During the past decade the tempo of China's force modernization program has increased significantly and the program's focus has sharpened. Driving the modernization of the Chinese military are concerns over increasing US military capabilities and growing tensions over the Taiwan issue. China has intensified efforts to acquire the military resources to deter and prevent Taiwanese attempts to attain *de jure* independence as well as US efforts to assist Taiwan militarily in the event of a conflict.

Most recently, China's force modernization effort has also begun to place a greater emphasis on acquiring more ambitious power projection capabilities beyond Taiwan, apparently for the purpose of conducting area denial and extended presence missions along the littoral of the western Pacific. In the strategic realm, Beijing has been steadily improving the survivability and potency of its small, retaliatory "counter-value" deterrent nuclear force by developing medium-, intermediate-, and intercontinental-range ballistic missiles that are more reliable, accurate, and mobile. Some of the latter are to be deployed on a new class of nuclear ballistic missile submarines. These acquisitions support China's larger efforts to deter potential aggressive actions, boost the country's image as a great power, and enhance its overall regional influence.[20]

Thus Beijing also pursues a strategy that contains both cooperative and hedging elements, as does Washington. And as in the case of the United States, these elements generate some potential tensions within Beijing's overall approach, and hence serve as the basis for domestic political differences over specific strategies and policies. In particular, the Chinese leadership is confronted with the need to strike the right balance between encouraging and facilitating cooperation with the United States and other powers on the one hand, and sending clear signals, via words and actions, that it has the capability and will to deter or prevent attempts to undermine its growth or challenge its core interests regarding issues such as Taiwan on the other hand. Too great an emphasis on the latter can obviously undermine efforts in the former area. Conversely, an excessive focus or concern with the former can arguably compromise or weaken the defense of vital Chinese interests, at least in the view of some Chinese leaders and segments of the public.

Such tensions and related domestic differences result in efforts to influence Chinese policy by both leaders and some elements of the public. At the broadest level, the balance struck between cooperation and hedging, and the specific policy approaches adopted in each of these areas, are to some extent subject to the differing outlooks and agendas of so-called hard-liners and those more moderate elements within the leadership. The former apparently believe that the United States—and perhaps other Western powers—view China's emergence as a major threat to be countered, and therefore seek not only to restrain Chinese power in many areas but to undermine and perhaps precipitate the collapse of the PRC regime altogether. Hence, hard-liners advocate policy approaches designed to weaken US influence and counter or confront US pressure in critical areas such as regional security and human rights. This

viewpoint is arguably supported, intentionally or otherwise, by some elements
of the Chinese public, who view the US government as an arrogant, overbear-
ing, and hypocritical entity that at times seeks to humiliate China and constrain China's emergence as a great power.

Moderates, on the other hand, emphasize the growing need for the United
States to cooperate with China in many areas and to avoid a confrontation
over issues such as Taiwan. They apparently argue that China's expanding
power and influence, the emergence of a growing number of serious global
problems requiring Sino-American cooperation, and the fact that the United
States is heavily distracted by crises in other regions of the world (such as the
Middle East) and the worsening global financial crisis, present Beijing with a
golden opportunity to reduce US incentives to challenge Chinese power by
promoting policies that emphasize the positive-sum aspects of bilateral relations while avoiding any overt confrontations with the United States. Advocates of this viewpoint do not argue for reductions in Chinese military power.
However, they believe that China's strategic goals can best be served by efforts
to create, among the United States and other Western nations, a set of positive
incentives to work with China, as well as a set of relationships and interactions
in global and regional institutions that increasingly limit the ability of such
powers to challenge China.

Finally, China's policy community likely contains different views over the
extent of the leadership role China should play in the foreign policy arena.
Some Chinese observers see growing opportunities for China to shape and
even lead or create various international organizations and fora. Others fear
that China is being drawn into playing a deeper, more activist role in many
foreign policy areas that potentially limit its options, expose it to increasing
levels of international scrutiny, and generally challenge its ability to keep a low
profile. The latter objective was reportedly enunciated by Deng Xiaoping in
the late 1980s or early 1990s and is summarized in the famous phrase, *tao
guang yang hui you suo zuo hui* ("hide our capacities and bide our time, but
also get some things done"). These differences do not easily translate into
contrasting or contending domestic political interests. However, they probably
influence leadership debates over specific policy issues.[21]

WHAT OF THE FUTURE?

As the above analysis suggests, although Beijing certainly has a grand strategy
for achieving clear national objectives, little solid evidence exists that its strategy comprises a deliberate, priority effort to dislodge the United States and
attain regional or global dominance. And attempts to cast Beijing as a direct,

modern-day equivalent of a hegemonic imperial China confront numerous historical problems. In fact, as Evelyn Rawski's chapter indicates, imperial China did not generally seek or demand preeminence over its known world in hard power terms, measured as the tangible subordination of others. [22]

The more relevant variables in the shaping of China's policies today and in the future are Chinese nationalism and the search for economic development, in the context of competing and powerful nation-states. In this undertaking, China is a relatively weak (in great power terms) but increasingly influential nation facing a clear need to cooperate with other nations while reducing its own vulnerability to both current and potential future threats, including (or perhaps especially) those originating from the United States.[23]

The United States, in turn, wants to enhance Beijing's ability and willingness to cooperate in facing a growing array of challenges while preserving its core interests through the maintenance of a predominant level of military, political, and economic power. In such circumstances, the most critical strategic question for the future is, as China's power and influence grow, will Beijing feel compelled to adopt policies and undertake actions designed to protect its growing interests and reduce its vulnerabilities that Washington would regard as unacceptable challenges, requiring vigorous counters that in turn prove unacceptable to China's leadership? The answer to this question is highly contingent; that is, it depends on the manner in which Beijing seeks to reduce its vulnerabilities and Washington seeks to preserve its predominance. This, in turn, depends on the extent to which worst-case, zero-sum thinking dominates the views of both leaderships, combined with their changing assessment of the practical costs and benefits that derive from continued (or enhanced) bilateral cooperation.

In this regard, fear of the unknown, distrust, and the coercive political, economic, and military capacities of the other state (as well as other major powers) are weighed against globalization, familiarity, a common interest in combating a growing number of security threats, and the overall costs of confrontation. Highly dynamic variables influence this balance: changes in relative power, the changing nature of common threats, political, social, and economic interactions, the quality of bilateral and multilateral strategic dialogues, and so on. But one point is very clear: the ability and willingness of China to adopt a more aggressive security policy that unambiguously challenges the United States depends as much on how the United States perceives its own bottom line as on any preconceived Chinese requirements for great power status or preeminence. US reaction (or overreaction) is just as likely to produce a true confrontation with China as anything Beijing does or intends to do. The US faces a major challenge in maintaining productive, nonconfrontational relations with a rising China. It cannot succeed in this effort without a clear understanding of China's interests, and the factors that influence them over time.

NOTES

1. Fei-Ling Wang defines Chinese goals as constituting a "three-P incentive structure": the political preservation of the CCP regime, China's economic prosperity, and Beijing's pursuit of power and prestige. See Fei-Ling Wang, "Preservation, Prosperity and Power: What Motivates China's Foreign Policy?" *Journal of Contemporary China* 14, no. 45 (November 2005): 669–94. Also see Michael D. Swaine and Ashley J. Tellis, *Interpreting China's Grand Strategy* (Santa Monica, CA: RAND, 2000). The goal of achieving the "great revival" of the nation by the middle of the twenty-first century through the creation of a "well-off society" was set by the Sixteenth Party Congress in November 2002. See Wang Jisi, "China's Changing Role in Asia," *The Atlantic Council Occasional Paper* (January 2004): 2–3. Also see Wang Yizhou, "Mianxiang ershiyishiji de zhongguo waijiao: Sanzhong xuqiu de xunqiu jiqi pingheng" [Chinese diplomacy in the 21st century: Achieving and balancing three needs], *Zhanlue yu Guanli* [Strategy and Management] no. 6 (1999): 18–27. Wang identifies three basic requirements or objectives for China's foreign and security policies during the twenty-first century: development, sovereignty, and responsibility (i.e., becoming a superpower). See also Thomas J. Christensen and Michael A. Glosny, "China: Sources of Stability in U.S.-China Security Relations," in Richard Ellings, Aaron Friedberg, and Michael Wills, eds., *Strategic Asia 2003–04: Fragility and Crisis* (Seattle: The National Bureau of Asian Research, 2003).

2. This important characterization was questioned by the Chinese leadership during the late 1990s, largely as a result of growing Sino-US tensions over Taiwan. But it was reaffirmed in light of the broader, enduring features of China's security environment. See David M. Finkelstein, "National Missile Defense and China's Current Security Perceptions" (Alexandria, VA: CNA Corporation, December 2001).

3. For useful analyses of Chinese views toward the reform era's international environment and the United States in particular, see Jing-dong Yuan, "The Bush Doctrine: Chinese Perspectives and Responses," *Asian Perspective* 27, no. 4 (December 2003): 124, 134–37; and Thomas Christensen, "China, the U.S.-Japan Alliance, and the Security Dilemma in East Asia," *International Security* 23, no. 4 (Spring 1999). Also see Robert Sutter, "China's Regional Strategy: An American View" (draft paper presented at the conference "China and Asia: Towards a New Regional System," George Washington University, December 5–6, 2003); He Chong, "World Peace in New Century Seen as Favoring China's Modernization," *Hong Kong Zhongguo Tongxun She* (January 19, 2000); David M. Finkelstein, "China's New Security Concept: Reading between the Lines," *Washington Journal of Modern China* 5, no. 1 (Spring 1999); Jin Canrong, "Meiguo: daodi nengzou duoyuan?" [The US: How far can it go?], *Shijie zhishi* [World Affairs], no. 11 (2003): 34–36; Han Xudong and Wei Konghu, "Tuoshi meiguo junshi zhanlue datiaozheng" [An analysis of major adjustments in US military strategies], *Liaowang* [Outlook Weekly], (May 1, 2001): 58–59; and Wu Qingli, "Meiguo yatai zhanlue maotou zhixiangshui?" [To whom is US Asia Pacific strategy aimed?], *Liaowang* [Outlook Weekly], (May 21, 2001): 60–61.

4. According to one astute Chinese scholar, China is calculating that for a "considerable period of time," any aggressiveness in US national security strategy will be

directed at international terrorism and WMD proliferation, centered largely in the Middle East, Central Asia, and South Asia. Since China will not ally with such entities and has significantly reduced its proliferation activities, "it is unlikely that the United States will regard China as its principal strategic adversary in the coming years." See Wang Jisi, "China's Changing Role."

5. The PRC made a strategic decision not to oppose the War on Terrorism and actively assisted the United States by providing intelligence and supporting post-Taliban Afghanistan. The United States branded the East Turkestan Independence Movement (ETIM) as a terrorist organization, thereby presumably weakening those in China who argued that the United States was trying to contain Beijing by supporting proindependence groups within the country. See Christensen and Glosny, "China: Sources of Stability," 58–59. See also Michael D. Swaine, "Reverse Course? The Fragile Turnaround in U.S.-China Relations," *Carnegie Policy Brief*, no. 22 (The Carnegie Endowment for International Peace, February 2003).

6. Christensen and Glosny, "China: Sources of Stability," 57. See, for example, Jia Qingguo, "The Impact of 9–11 on Sino-U.S. Relations: A Preliminary Assessment," *International Relations of the Asia Pacific* 3, no. 2 (August 2003): 159–77; Sun Jin-zhong, "Interpreting the Trend of Development of Sino-U.S. Relations," November 10, 2003, and Liu Jianfei, "'The Period of Strategic Opportunity' and Sino-U.S. Ties," January 20, 2003, *Liaowang* [Outlook Weekly]. Liu argues that America's post-9/11 emphasis on domestic security has also led Washington to de-emphasize the promotion of democracy and human rights in its security strategy, thus reducing a major source of friction in the Sino-US relationship.

7. For a discussion of the complex, double-edged nature of Chinese nationalism for China's external policies, see Zhao Suisheng, "Chinese Nationalism and Its Foreign Policy Ramifications," in Christopher Marsh and June Dreyer, eds., *U.S.-China Relations in the Twenty-First Century* (Boulder, CO: Lexington Books, 2003). As one Chinese scholar points out, excessive nationalist feelings obstruct efforts of the Chinese leadership to enhance its authority. See Wang Jisi, "China's Changing Role," 16.

8. See Christensen, "Security Dilemma in East Asia."

9. As Avery Goldstein states, China's grand strategy "does not refer to a formal and detailed plan contained in a 'smoking gun' document issued by the Chinese Communist Party's Central Committee. Instead it identifies a rough consensus on China's basic foreign policy that . . . has provided a guide for the country's international behavior." Avery Goldstein, *Rising to the Challenge: China's Grand Strategy and International Security* (Stanford, CA: Stanford University Press, 2005), 17. Also see Wang Jisi, "Some Thoughts on Building a Chinese International Strategy," *Guoji Zhengzhi Yanjiu* [International Politics Quarterly], (November 25, 2007): 1–5. Wang states that China does not have an authoritative guiding document on grand strategy. However, he argues that China's grand strategy is becoming more detailed, flexible, and sophisticated. This clearly suggests that China's leaders are following some sort of strategy.

10. Swaine and Tellis, *Interpreting China's Grand Strategy*; Michael D. Swaine, "Exploiting a Strategic Opening," in Ashley J. Tellis and Michael Wills, eds., *Strategic Asia 2004–05: Confronting Terrorism in the Pursuit of Power* (Seattle: National Bureau of Asian Research, 2004); Bates Gill, *Rising Star: China's New Security Diplomacy*

(Washington, DC: Brookings Institution Press, 2007); and Goldstein, *Rising to the Challenge,* 24, 29–30, 102–3.

11. As Kenneth Lieberthal states, China's grand strategy "is designed to both sustain high speed economic development and to blunt any concerns that other countries may have about rapidly growing PRC capabilities." Avery Goldstein conveys this point somewhat differently, stating that China's grand strategy is designed to ensure its national interests by increasing the perceived advantages of working with China while also underscoring the disadvantages of working against it. In this way, China hopes to offset fears about the so-called China threat and become a more instrumental player in the international system. See Goldstein, *Rising to the Challenge,* 118. Also see Swaine, "Exploiting a Strategic Opening"; Evan S. Medeiros, "China's International Behavior: Activism, Opportunism, and Diversification," *Joint Forces Quarterly,* no. 47 (4th Quarter 2007): 34–41; Jia Qingguo, "Learning to Live with the Hegemon: Evolution of China's Policy toward the US since the End of the Cold War," *Journal of Contemporary China* 14, no. 44 (August 2005): 395–407; Robert G. Sutter, "China's Rise: Implications for U.S. Leadership in Asia," *Policy Studies,* no. 21 (East-West Center, 2006); Robert Sutter, "China's Regional Strategy and America," in David Shambaugh, ed., *Power Shift: China and Asia's New Dynamics* (Berkeley: University of California Press, 2005): 289–305; Gill, *Rising Star,* 10.

12. The best example of such rhetoric is found in Hu Jintao, "Building towards a Harmonious World of Lasting Peace and Common Prosperity" (UN Speech, September 15, 2005), www.fmprc.gov.cn/eng/wjdt/zyjh/t213091.htm. Also see Zheng Bijian, "China's 'Peaceful Rise' to Great-Power Status," *Foreign Affairs* 84, no. 5 (September/ October 2005); and Ye Zicheng, "Carrying Forward, Developing and Pondering Deng Xiaoping's Foreign Policy Thinking in the New Situation," *Beijing Shijie Jingji Yu Zhengzhi,* no. 11 (November 14, 2004): 8–14.

13. See Swaine, "Exploiting a Strategic Opening." Also see David Finkelstein, "China's New Concept of Security" in Stephen J. Flanagan and Michael E. Marti, eds., *The People's Liberation Army and China in Transition* (Washington, DC: The Center for the Study of Chinese Military Affairs, 2003); Sutter, "China's Regional Strategy," 289–305; and David Shambaugh, *Modernizing China's Military: Progress, Problems, and Prospects* (Berkeley: University of California Press, 2002), 293.

14. Evan S. Medeiros and M. Taylor Fravel, "China's New Diplomacy," *Foreign Affairs* 82, no. 6 (November/December 2003): 25–27; David Shambaugh, "China Engages Asia: Reshaping the Regional Order," *International Security* 29, no. 3 (Winter 2004–2005): 69–70; Gill, *Rising Star,* 12–13; Sutter, "China's Rise," viii. Sutter argues that "China's Asian approach focuses on 'easy' things—the 'low-hanging fruit'—and avoids costly commitments or major risks."

15. Medeiros and Fravel, "China's New Diplomacy," 25–27; and Christensen and Glosny, "China: Sources of Stability," 57.

16. Swaine and Tellis, *Interpreting China's Grand Strategy;* Gill, *Rising Star,* ch. 2, especially p. 36; M. Taylor Fravel, "Power Shifts and Escalation: Explaining China's Use of Force in Territorial Disputes," *International Security* 32, no. 3 (2007); and M. Taylor Fravel, "Securing Borders: China's Doctrine and Force Structure for Frontier Defense," *Journal of Strategic Studies* 30, no. 4–5 (August 2007): 705–37.

17. Yun-han Chu, "The Evolution of Beijing's Policy toward Taiwan during the Reform Era," in Yong Deng and Fei-ling Wang, eds., *China Rising: Power and Motivation in Chinese Foreign Policy* (Oxford: Rowman and Littlefield Publishers, 2005); Sutter, "China's Rise"; Swaine, "China: Exploiting a Strategic Opening," 67–101; Michael D. Swaine and Oriana Skylar Mastro, "Assessing the Threat," in Michael D. Swaine, Andrew N. D. Yang, Evan S. Medeiros, and Oriana Skylar Mastro, eds., *Assessing the Threat: the Chinese Military and Taiwan's Security* (Washington, DC: Carnegie Endowment for International Peace, 2007), 219–41; Richard C. Bush and Michael E. O'Hanlon, *A War like No Other: The Truth about China's Challenge to America* (Hoboken, NJ: John Wiley & Sons, 2007); and T. J. Cheng, "China-Taiwan Economic Linkage: Between Insulation and Superconductivity," in Nancy Bernkopf Tucker, ed., *Dangerous Strait: The U.S.-Taiwan-China Crisis* (New York: Columbia University Press, 2005).

18. Oil consumption increased by almost 500,000 b/d in 2006, which was approximately 38 percent of the total growth in world oil demand. The "trade value" of the country's energy imports and exports increased by an amazing 330.5 percent between 2001 and 2006, from $23.27 billion to $100.19 billion. China's demand for energy—specifically in oil, gas, and coal—will continue to rise rapidly in the foreseeable future in order to support its fast-paced economic growth. Indeed, China is expected to increase its energy consumption by 150 percent by 2025, and most of its oil will come from outside of China's borders. For China, energy security is apparently defined as "sufficient energy to support economic growth and prevent debilitating energy shortfalls that could trigger social and political turbulence." See Daniel H. Rosen and Trevor Houser, *China Energy: A Guide for the Perplexed*, A Joint Project by the Center for Strategic Studies and the Peterson Institute for International Economics, May 2007, 1–49; Michael T. Klare, "Fueling the Dragon: China's Strategic Energy Dilemma," *Current History* 105, no. 690 (April 2006): 180–85; *Mapping the Global Future*, Report of the National Intelligence Council's 2020 Project (December 2004); Edward S. Steinfeld, Richard K. Lester, and Edward A. Cunningham, "Greener Plants, Grayer Skies? A Report from the Front Lines of China's Energy Sector" (Massachusetts Institute of Technology Industrial Performance Center, August 2008); Lee Geng, "The Saudis Take a Chinese Wife," *Energy Tribune*, November 3, 2008, www.energytribune.com/articles.cfm?aid=1007; Erica Downs, "China," *Energy Security Series* (The Brookings Institution, December 2006); and Wang Jiacheng, "Chinese Energy Security: Demand and Supply," *China Strategic Review* 11 (2005).

19. Downs, "China," 16; Downs states that "China's energy projects and agenda are often driven by corporate interests of China's energy firms rather than by the national interests of the Chinese state." See also Erica Downs, *China's Quest for Energy Security* (Santa Monica, CA: RAND, 2000); Kenneth Lieberthal and Mikkal Herberg, "China's Search for Energy Security: Implications for U.S. Policy," *NBR Analysis* 17, no. 1 (April 2006); David Shambaugh, "Beijing's Thrust into Latin America," *International Herald Tribune*, November 20, 2008; Andrew Erickson and Gabe Collins, "Beijing's Energy Security Strategy: The Significance of a Chinese State-Owned Tanker Fleet," *Obris: A Journal of World Affairs* 51, no. 4 (Fall 2007): 665–84; David Zweig and Bi Jianhai, "China's Global Hunt for Energy," *Foreign Affairs* (September/October 2005); Wenran

Jiang, "China's Global Quest for Energy Security," *Canadian Foreign Policy* 13, no. 2 (2006); Daniel Yergin, "Ensuring Energy Security," *Foreign Affairs* 85, no. 2 (March/ April 2006); and Zha Daojiang, "China's Energy Security: Domestic and International Issues," *Survival* 48, no. 1 (March 1, 2006).

20. See Michael D. Swaine, "China's Regional Military Posture," in Shambaugh, *Power Shift*; and Shambaugh, *Modernizing China's Military*; see also Robert S. Norris and Hans M. Kristensen, "Chinese Nuclear Forces, 2008," *Bulletin of the Atomic Scientists* 64, no. 3 (July/August 2008): 42–45; Bernard D. Cole, "Right-Sizing the Navy: How Much Naval Force Will Beijing Deploy?" in Roy Kamphausen and Andrew Scobell, eds., *Right Sizing the People's Liberation Army: Exploring the Contours of China's Military* (Carlisle, PA: The Strategic Studies Institute of the U.S. Army War College, 2007), 523–56; Aaron L. Friedberg, "Asia Rising," *American Interest* 6, no. 3 (Winter 2009): 53–61.

21. See Susan Shirk, *China: Fragile Superpower* (New York: Oxford University Press, 2007), 106–9. Also see Fei-Ling Wang, "Preservation, Prosperity and Power," 675.

22. Premodern China was primarily interested in securing its immediate periphery from attacks against the homeland, eliciting some level of symbolic and cultural obeisance from nearby political entities, and achieving pragmatic understandings and hence mutual accommodation based on reciprocal material benefits. Of course, if persistent and clear mortal threats could not be paid off or co-opted, they were usually militarily resisted or crushed, if possible. Moreover, this security approach was largely based on the prior attainment of geographic and administrative boundaries that essentially set the limits of Chinese territorial ambition, boundaries that were largely stable for the Tang, Song, and Ming. In short, in many ways, traditional China by and large did not function as a power-oriented regional hegemon in the sense in which that term is used in the modern era. See Swaine and Tellis, *Interpreting China's Grand Strategy*.

23. Many specific features of Beijing's current or possible future external environment would arguably prove unacceptable to a much stronger and more confident China, including (1) an expanding US military presence along China's periphery, possessing the ability to strike Chinese strategic assets using long-range, precision-guided conventional munitions; (2) an increasingly militarily capable and assertive Japan; (3) an excessively high level of reliance on US markets, technology, and capital; (4) a US commitment to democracy promotion and the strengthening of bilateral political and military alliances in Asia and beyond; and (5) an insecure, unpredictable energy supply structure. Altering this environment could require increasingly assertive efforts.

III

CHINA'S ECONOMIC TRAJECTORY

5

China's Prereform Economy in World Perspective

Dwight H. Perkins

China's thirty years of economic growth and reform beginning in 1978 did not occur in a historical vacuum. The extraordinary performance of the most recent three decades can only be understood in the context of the economic and political foundations laid both in the leftist decades immediately preceding the economic reform period and in the evolution of the Chinese economy going back as much as a millennium. This historical heritage was not all positive. In fact the two decades immediately preceding the 1978 reforms were years of pain and comparative stagnation, but pain and stagnation were nevertheless an important element in making possible the sweeping changes in the economic system that occurred after 1978. China's earlier history beginning as early as the Song dynasty (960–1279) and carrying through to the Qing dynasty (1644–1911) and the Republican period (1912–1948) did lay positive foundations for later developments, but these foundations in key respects had become calcified by the nineteenth and twentieth centuries. Much of what had been built, particularly in the political realm, had to be swept away before sustained progress was possible in the economic realm.

We will begin this chapter with a discussion of the nature of the pre-1949 Chinese economy and society. We will then move on to what occurred in the first thirty years of the People's Republic of China (PRC) from 1949 to 1978. As Barry Naughton's chapter will detail, the direction of the current reform is diametrically at odds with its past, but at the same time presupposes the context and capabilities created by its traditional heritage. Comparisons and contrasts with the rest of the world's economies will illustrate the salience of China's background.

CHINA'S PREMODERN ECONOMY

China's political leaders achieved unity over something approximating the country's current territory as early as 221 B.C. More important, the Chinese government was able to maintain control over that very large territory for much of the next two thousand years with the notable exceptions of the 206 A.D. to 581 A.D. and 1127 A.D. to 1271 A.D. periods, and for much shorter periods at later dates. Although, as Evelyn Rawski details in chapter 3, there were frequent conflicts between the agricultural heartland and the northern nomads, there was at the same time a massive and resilient political and economic central structure. China was able to maintain unity over such a large territory largely because it developed a system of government based on a bureaucracy whose members were chosen by examination rather than by aristocratic privilege or reliance on local military power. Bureaucratic rule encouraged the spread of a common written language, a unified budget and regulatory system, and a centrally controlled military. The military force was there for putting down major challenges, but military commanders were not made governors of territories (feudal lords) as occurred in Europe and Japan. Because of the nature of the European feudal system, unity over the whole of Europe was not achieved until the formation of the European Union. Japan did not become unified for the first time until the Tokugawa leadership succeeded in bringing the various feudal *han* under their rule in 1603.

The relevance of this achievement to the current period in China is that China's post-1949 political leaders did not first have to create a nation-state out of a collection of disparate political entities with different cultures and languages and no sense of national identity. They did have to fight a civil war to gain control of China, but both sides in the civil war fought to gain control of all of China, not to create a separate state in one or another region of the country.[1] The contrast is with such countries as Nigeria and the Congo and in fact much of Sub-Saharan Africa that has been torn by civil strife based on the presence of different tribes, languages, religions, and ecologies (nomad versus settled agriculture versus export crop agriculture in West Africa) within a single political entity. Within Asia, India and Pakistan became independent in 1947, and in 1971 Bangladesh split from Pakistan, and ethnic tensions remain major threats to political unity in Nepal and Sri Lanka. Indonesia, a decade after independence, had to fight a civil war for the government in Jakarta to hold on to the islands outside of Java, and its problems with Aceh have been eased only by the relief efforts following the 2004 tsunami.

In the economic sphere proper China in the millennia prior to 1949 created what by premodern standards was a sophisticated economic system. China developed a wide range of technologies in agriculture, industry, and transport.[2] In agriculture, many of the methods of cultivation in northern dryland agriculture as early as the Tang dynasty (618–907) were similar to the methods for growing similar crops in northern Europe in the eighteenth and early nineteenth centuries. Rice cultivation was transformed in the eleventh century by the introduction of early ripening varieties of rice from Champa (part of contemporary Vietnam).[3] After the European discovery of the Americas, crops from the Americas (corn, potatoes, peanuts) soon found their way to the Philippines and from there entered China spreading quickly (within a century) across much of the country. Farm equipment by the early Ming dynasty had reached a level of sophistication that could not easily be improved upon for Chinese conditions until the advent of modern farm machinery in the twentieth century. From the fourteenth century on Chinese population grew from around 65–80 million to over 400 million by 1850 and food production kept up with population as crop yields rose, although changes in agricultural technology other than the imported new crops were largely absent.[4]

In industry many of the technologies developed as early as the Song dynasty in such areas as the making of steel were as sophisticated as industrial technologies not found in Europe until the eighteenth and early nineteenth centuries.[5] As Mark Elvin argues in chapter 7, a fundamental distinction can be made between technologies that can be developed by tinkering and technologies that can only be developed after a society has developed modern science as practiced first in the West beginning in the nineteenth century. Innovations through tinkering are developed by individuals who experiment, for example, with different ways of increasing the efficiency of fuel use in the making of steel or with the speed with which one could spin cotton into yarn or weave yarn into cloth. Science-based innovations in Europe became central to continued technological advance in the latter half of the nineteenth century with the development of electric power and the modern chemical industry. Technologies that could be developed by tinkering had largely been developed in China centuries before the modern era.[6] Those that required the prior development of modern science were not present in China until they were brought in from Europe in the late nineteenth century.

The general pattern of Chinese commerce, especially in the Ming and Qing dynasties, was the opposite of that of the Mediterranean West. Typically China was suspicious of private foreign commerce and did not found trading colonies, as the West had been doing since the time of Phoenicia. To be sure, there was significant trade beyond China's overland boundaries and also maritime trade, and groups of Han Chinese moved beyond the Great Wall[7] into the northeast and by ship throughout Southeast Asia.[8] But official contact was based on the tribute system of ritual exchange of presents rather than on commerce. While private commerce undoubtedly exceeded official exchanges in volume and value, it was unrecorded and viewed with disapproval by the last two dynasties.[9] The apparent exceptions that in fact proved the rule were the famous voyages of Admiral Zheng He (seven voyages from 1405 to 1431), which were not launched to promote trade, but rather to extend and bolster the tribute system.[10] When there were troubles controlling pirates and other seagoing entrepreneurs, Beijing did not strengthen its navy but rather attempted to close down trade altogether. Similarly, Chinese who emigrated to Southeast Asia did so illegally and were treated with suspicion when they accompanied diplomatic missions from their adopted states. Hence the common picture of traditional China as a closed and anticommercial state.

But China's internal commerce was, in fact, well developed and extensive. Like many countries around the globe, China had rural and town markets that met periodically or continuously. But China also had a long distance trading system that brought grain from the interior of China to the coast or from the lower Yangzi Delta to Beijing in the north and moved silk and other industrial products from the coast back into the interior. China from early on had cities with a population as large as a million people. The supply of such cities required a sophisticated domestic commercial system utilizing an extensive array of roads and canals.

An argument can be made that this level of domestic commercial development was first achieved in the Song dynasty, was followed in the Ming dynasty by a decline in long distance commerce and in the size of cities, and then recovered in the Qing to something approximating what had been achieved earlier.[11] Regardless of fluctuation, however, there is little question that the domestic commerce of China in certain respects matched the sophistication of that found in the West prior to the advent of the railroad. If we add to the physical infrastructure the fact that ground transport across Europe might entail crossing innumerable national boundaries, China's domestic commercial prowess is doubly impressive. The best evidence for China's strength in this regard is that when the European and American traders did come to China, they did not take over major parts of the domestic trade even though they depended on that trade to obtain the silk and tea that they shipped back to Europe and America. The domestic trade remained firmly in Chinese hands although many of these domestic merchants (*compradors*) worked closely with and for the foreigners. It is not that the Europeans and Americans were uninterested in the domestic trade. It was that they could not really compete outside the treaty ports for most of this business. Europeans and Americans did control and manage the export trade to Europe and in the nineteenth century the import trade into China (much of it opium) because they understood and had better access to foreign markets.

The Chinese experience with the control of domestic commerce contrasts sharply with the situation found in much of Africa and Southeast Asia. In these latter areas the local rural markets were in the hands of local merchants, but the long distance trade, both domestic and foreign, was not in local hands for the most part. Europeans dominated foreign trade as in China, but domestic trade was typically in the hands of immigrants from elsewhere who maintained their separate identity. In West Africa these traders were often Lebanese, in East Africa they were mostly "Asians" meaning South Asians, and in colonial Southeast Asia they were mostly Chinese although in Burma they were mainly Indian.

In the financial sphere, China also developed sophisticated institutions by premodern standards. As is well known, China was the first country to use paper money on a nationwide scale. Far more important is that China developed a banking system to complement its domestic trading system. The Shanxi banks and others could transfer large sums of money over distances of hundreds or a thousand miles or more without actually having to transfer the currency itself (mainly copper coins and silver coins or ingots). Merchants and ordinary citizens could deposit money in one place for transfer to another with confidence that the funds would actually be paid out at their destination. This system required banks that could keep books and an organizational capacity that could perform and build up trust over generations.

How do we explain the relative development of China's domestic commerce and the relative backwardness of officially encouraged international commerce? China's geographic and demographic scale is certainly important. *Scale* Moreover, China's agrarian, land-bound perspective was reinforced by Confucian disparagements of merchants. One might imagine that if domestic merchants were held in high esteem they might eventually cast their gaze abroad. Also, one could argue that China's centrality in Asia affected the salience of trade. Chinese goods were more important to its neighbors than the neighbor's goods were to China, so a more cautious and defensive attitude was natural. Domestic commerce was a necessary concomitant to a prosperous China; foreign trade was not. *Lack of a felt need for imports.*

Partly related to the development of commerce and finance was the rise of literacy in China at least among a portion of the male population. One could not keep records and transfer instructions over long distances without some degree of literacy and numeracy skills. More generally, literacy in China was promoted by the Confucian value system. Confucius himself had made literacy an essential characteristic of anyone who aspired to be more than a farmer, and it later became built into the way in which China governed since the bureaucracy was selected on the basis of examinations that typically involved two or more decades of study of the Chinese classics. We do not have a reliable

Literacy a key to China's post 1978 take off.

estimate of literacy in nineteenth-century China, let alone for earlier years, but male literacy could have been as high as 50 percent.[12] That is the figure achieved by Tokugawa Japan.[13] Although commercial development may have been larger there, literacy played a much smaller role in the Tokugawa governing system than it did in China.

The specific things studied in premodern China were not very relevant to the requirements of a twentieth-century economy, but the existence of a substantial number of highly educated people and a much larger number of literate people was a foundation on which China could and did build. By the 1930s China had several hundred thousand graduates of modern universities with tens of thousands of those being in science and engineering.[14] It is difficult to conceive of a country achieving this kind of educational development starting from an education base where only a few hundred people had a university-level education and the great majority of the population was illiterate. Part of the credit for China's pre-1949 university enrollment goes to missionary-run colleges, but the case of Vietnam demonstrates that Western influence on education could be negative as well. Despite Vietnam's high cultural regard for education, under French colonialism non-French secondary enrollment in Vietnam in 1944 was only 687 students.[15] Much of Africa even in the early twentieth century had virtually no university graduates and illiteracy in the population at large was well over 90 percent. In the least developed parts of Sub-Saharan Africa such as Chad or Mali no more than a quarter of the population is literate even today. Literacy in most countries in Africa has expanded rapidly since independence was obtained (in the 1960s in most parts of the continent), but it takes generations to develop the kind of educational system that can support internationally top ranked universities such as Tsinghua or Beijing universities.

WHAT PREVENTED MODERN ECONOMIC GROWTH IN PREMODERN CHINA?

Given the sophistication of China's premodern economy and society, the logical next question is to ask why China did not begin sustained rapid economic growth long before the last decades of the twentieth century? This question is sometimes put as why did Japan start modern economic growth one-half to three-quarters of a century before China? Japan in 1868 when the Meiji Restoration started was no richer than China in terms of per capita income. Both in fact were very poor with perhaps half the per capita income of Europe when Europe entered into sustained economic growth.[16] Nor was Japan technologically more sophisticated. Its commerce and cities may have been a larger share of its GDP and population than in China but not by any dramatic amount. Furthermore, China faced the challenge of Western imperialism earlier than Japan. China had already lost a war with the Western powers by 1842 whereas Commodore Perry's Black Ships did not appear off the Japanese coast until 1854. It was the Western challenge that led Japan to topple the Tokugawa and restructure its government and economy beginning in 1868 but no such response occurred in China.

We will not try to explain in this chapter why Japan developed first, but there are two primary reasons why China was not able to enter into a sustained period of modern economic growth in the nineteenth or even the first half of the twentieth century. First, it took China over a century to jettison its traditional mode of governance and replace it with a government that would systematically promote modern economic growth, and the process involved numerous wars and civil wars that would have disrupted the best economic development plans of any government. Second, even when the Chinese government did enjoy periods of peace and stability, the dominant forces within that government vigorously resisted any fundamental change of the kind that modernization of the economy and society would have required.

The disruption caused by war and civil war in China before 1949 was massive and ongoing. China fought and lost its first war to the Western powers in 1839–1842. That war was not very disruptive of the economy and had the positive economic effect (but seen as not at all positive from a Chinese political perspective either then or now) of opening up the Chinese economy to more foreign trade. However, the Taiping Rebellion that followed and lasted for fourteen years (1850–1864) was extremely disruptive. It began in China's southern interior provinces and before it was over it had laid waste not only to parts of the interior but also to the richest area of the country at that time, the lower Yangzi River Delta. The number of people who died as a direct result of the rebellion has been estimated to have been over 20 million and the total population of China may have declined over that period by as much as 75 million. The Taiping Rebellion was eventually put down, but China toward the end of the Taiping period lost a second war to the Western powers. At the end of that three-decade period of peace China lost a war with Japan in 1895 that involved a large indemnity that the Chinese government could ill afford to pay together with the loss of Taiwan, which at that time was something of a backwater and hence not of great economic significance for the rest of China. This defeat was followed by the uprising of the Boxers in North China and the siege of the legation quarter in Beijing in 1900. The invasion and defeat of the Boxers by the Western powers plus Japan led to the Boxer Protocol of 1901, which imposed a 67 million pound indemnity on China, a very large sum for that time. The dynasty staggered on for another ten years before collapsing as a result of the Xinhai or Republican Revolution of 1911. The political maneuvering of the new republic in 1912 first produced Sun Yat-sen (Sun Zhongshan) as president but quickly moved on to make General Yuan Shikai president. Yuan Shikai's failed attempt to make himself the first emperor of a new dynasty ended with his death in 1917. There then followed more than a decade of what is generally referred to as the warlord period in modern Chinese history. Various generals controlled parts of China's northern provinces and the Nationalist Party of Sun Yat-sen together with other generals controlled various parts of the south. The nominal leader of the government recognized by the foreign powers was whoever controlled Beijing at the time. As Joseph Esherick points out in chapter 1, foreign recognition was important because customs revenues were delivered to the Beijing government. There was not all that much fighting but neither was there a government anywhere that could carry out a development program and many of the local warlord governments depended on predatory taxation for survival.

In 1927 the army created by the Nationalist Party and led by General Chiang Kai-shek (Jiang Jieshi) marched north and by a combination of military action and negotiation with some of the warlords established a kind of unity over the entire country. Chiang then turned his attention to eliminating the Communist Party, but their small rural bases proved stubborn. More important from the standpoint of any Nationalist program to promote economic growth was the Japanese seizure of China's northeastern provinces in 1931 and the formation of the puppet state of Manchukuo. This was followed in 1937 by an all-out Japanese attack on the rest of China that soon drove the Nationalist government and army out of the coastal cities into China's interior with its capital at Chongqing. The Communists controlled mountainous areas in the northwest but gradually extended their control to large parts of northern rural China surrounding the Japanese-controlled cities and transportation links. The defeat of Japan in 1945 led to all-out civil war between the Nationalists and Communists that ended in the establishment of the People's Republic of China in 1949.

This brief recitation of a century of Chinese political and military history goes a long way toward explaining why China's economy did not develop in the period between the initial challenge of the Western powers and the eventual triumph of the Communists. Long-term investors require a stable political and policy environment for their investments and China during most of this century could provide neither. Investing in a battlefield is rarely an attractive option. But neither was it possible to invest long term when government leaders and their policies changed frequently if they had any economic development policies at all. Investors other than Japanese could not count on a stable environment in Japanese-held territory even if they were willing to put aside their opposition to the Japanese invasion. The only places of stability in the country throughout most of this period were the treaty port cities with their areas set aside for foreigners and controlled by foreigners. Chinese and others did invest in these areas, but it was a poor substitute for a stable country and a development-oriented government.

Instability is thus a major part of the story of why China did not develop, but it is not the whole story. China, as already mentioned, did have a period of peace during which it might have been able to start a major development effort but it failed to do so. The period is known as the Tongzhi Restoration, so titled because that was the reign name of the emperor who was in office at the beginning of the period. The Tongzhi emperor reigned from 1860 through 1875 but the period of peace lasted much longer until the Japanese attack of 1895. And defeat by the Japanese in 1895 could have led on to a very different result from what actually happened (the Boxer Uprising) if the Guangxu emperor and his advisors (Kang Youwei and Liang Qichao) had managed to fully implement the reforms they began in 1898 soon after the young emperor came of age. There was also a considerable period between the death of the Tongzhi emperor and the coming of age of the Guangxu emperor when there were efforts at reform at the provincial level that could have been built on to become a major economic reform effort. But no such broad-based development effort occurred. Why not?

The primary reason why China was not able to take full advantage of this peaceful interregnum was that power in the Qing dynasty government rested with the Empress Dowager Ci Xi and a large number of conservative officials. The power of these individuals, however, was not a historical accident. These people to a large degree represented the values that had always governed traditional China and were still believed to be valid by large parts of the educated population and political leadership of the country in the late nineteenth century. The challenge for China, in their view, was not to fundamentally change the Chinese traditional system of governance but to restore its vitality.[17] Even these conservatives recognized that the West had better weapons and better ships and so they did not oppose the creation of the first modern industrial enterprise in China, the Jiangnan Arsenal founded in 1865. But most of the efforts of the period were devoted to making the traditional system work better by putting good men in key positions.

There were provincial governors, notably Li Hongzhang and Zhang Zhidong, who saw the Western challenge in somewhat broader terms. They did promote a few industrial enterprises in the 1870s and 1880s through a system called "official supervision merchant management" (*guandu shangban*), a hybrid that guaranteed that these enterprises would struggle to become profitable and even to survive.[18] One major problem throughout this period was that it was difficult to attract funding for industrial enterprises and for other modernization measures such as the building of railroads. The private sector was reluctant to invest and typically required guaranteed rates of return and the government itself had very limited tax revenues. China's lack of government revenue was the secondary reason why the Qing government failed to develop a successful economic modernization program. The land tax, for example, was the major tax but it amounted to no more than 2 percent of Chinese GDP at the time.[19] There was a domestic commercial tax, the *lijin*, that produced some revenue but not as much as the land tax, and then there was the customs revenue that was managed by foreign officials and produced significant revenue, much of which was tied to the repayment of foreign loans. The government in Beijing and the provincial governors had very little in the way of discretionary funds and most of these were eaten up fighting or preparing to fight various rebellions and foreign incursions. There is a striking contrast with the government of Meiji Japan that commanded revenue that amounted to over 10 percent of Japanese GDP and an even higher percentage in late Tokugawa.[20]

Japan's defeat of China in 1895 had one positive outcome from the point of view of economic development. For the first time foreign direct investment in industry and commerce was made legal in China and foreign investors did begin to enter mainly in and around the treaty ports where their investments were safer. The other "positive" impact of the loss to Japan was that it built an impetus for reform that was much broader than what had occurred up to that time. The initial reform effort, however, lasted for only "100 days" and then was snuffed out by the Empress Dowager and the court conservatives. The key reformers fled the country and the authority of the young emperor was taken away. Instead the conservatives at court made a last ditch effort to drive out foreigners and Chinese who had acquired foreign ideas (mainly from missionaries). This effort failed utterly and eventually spelled the end of the dynasty.

The defeat in 1898 of the hundred days of reform and the Boxer Uprising, however, did not bring a halt to China's growing if still feeble efforts to modernize its economy. Despite all of the disruption caused by war and civil war in the first half of the twentieth century, China did experience growth in the small modern sector of the economy. Overall GDP growth until the Japanese invasion in 1937 was only 1.8 to 2 percent per year,[21] but modern industry alone grew at 9.4 percent per year between 1912 and the end of 1936.[22] During this period a modern banking system was established and a wide variety of new laws governing the economy were passed. China's university system was also transformed into something approximating a Western-style university system, aided in no small part by Christian mission-sponsored schools. Increasing numbers of Chinese also went abroad to study. In one of the most farsighted

20th Century

gestures of American diplomacy toward China, the US portion of the Boxer indemnity was turned back to China in the form of support for study abroad in the United States. In China's northeast there was also substantial development of industry and railroads, but in the service of the Japanese empire.

Most of the industrial and infrastructure capital built during the last decade of the nineteenth century and the first four decades of the twentieth century was destroyed during China's war with Japan and its aftermath. Much Chinese-owned industry and equipment was moved inland ahead of the Japanese forces. This enabled China to continue to produce certain civilian and military essentials during the war, but most industrial capital was obsolete by the time the war ended. The capital invested in China's northeast by Japan was largely carted off to the Soviet Union as "compensation" for the Soviet entry into the war against Japan in August 1945.

physical capital

It is not clear just what the legacy of development in the first part of the twentieth century is for China's economic development after 1949 or after 1978. The topic has never been systematically studied. We do know from the experience of Germany and Japan after World War II, however, that what matters most for future development is not the physical capital—most of which was destroyed by Allied bombs in Germany and Japan—but the human capital that existed in the many workers, engineers, and managers who had survived the war. These people understood the old technology and knew how to acquire the new technology and they knew how to organize themselves to build and run new factories and infrastructure. In China after 1945 there were hundreds of thousands of people with this kind of human capital.

Human Capital

Not all of those with this kind of experience stayed in China, however. With the victory of the Communists in 1949, many with relevant skills fled to Hong Kong, Taiwan, and even farther afield. In addition, China after 1949 also adopted a very different economic system, a centrally planned command economy modeled on that of the Soviet Union. Individuals with experience in Western-style banks and other financial institutions and even many industrial managers found their skills of little relevance in the new system. On top of that the "three and five anti" movements of 1951 and 1952 during the height of the Korean War removed additional experienced personnel from positions where their skills could have been used.

In sum, although China by the 1940s was in desperate straits after the war with Japan and the ensuing civil war, intrinsically traditional China was neither a "failed state" nor a failed economy. Had British warships not appeared on its horizon, it is likely that China would have continued managing its domestic affairs as it had done for centuries even as the world balance of industrial capacity shifted more and more decisively to the West. Inevitably the disparity would have been noticed and perhaps structural reforms would have been attempted. But this imaginary course of events underlines two weaknesses of China's traditional order. It was mortally vulnerable to a modernized West, and it was not capable of internally transforming its traditional institutions and outlook. The ensuing disruption further hampered the emergence of a modern economy until order was restored in 1949.

Nevertheless, traditional China left much more than memories for its later leadership to build on. National political and economic unity, the habits of bureaucratic governance, education and a patriotic intellectual elite—all of these formed the foundation of what China could do next, and not every new state has been so fortunate.

THE POST-1949 PRE-1978
CHINESE ECONOMY AND ITS LEGACY

China in 1949 was therefore still very poor but it was not entirely "poor and blank" as Mao Zedong said in those early years of Communist Party rule. In addition to the inherited experience of the past centuries, the Communist movement that came to power brought with it skills of its own acquired in battle and in efforts to mobilize the territories it controlled to support the war effort. The Communists not only fielded a large army. They equipped that army with weapons and managed the supplies for that army in ways that were designed not to alienate the people in the territories that they controlled. Rural revolution is not easy, and Marxism provided no model for it. Mao Zedong had to generate political support and military power by transforming rural areas, village by village, into revolutionary bases. Some of the skills so acquired contributed to the development efforts that began in the early 1950s. These skills certainly contributed to the Communist Party's ability to govern a country with over 500 million people. On the other hand, as was demonstrated in the leftist era from 1957 to 1976, some of these same skills misapplied could also bring about economic and social disaster.

In the early 1950s China began to introduce a Soviet-style command economy. This way of managing an economy required information and skills very different from either a rural revolution or a market economy. The government first draws up a plan for the industrial and commercial sectors that specifies how much output of each product is required and what inputs will be needed to produce that output. These plan targets are then translated into individual production and input use targets for each individual enterprise. Even in the 1950s in China there were thousands of industrial and commercial enterprises, although most were quite small. Backing up the plan was an input distribution system that was run by a government bureaucracy and which allocated inputs according to the plan. As a further backup, the main role of the banking system (which was consolidated into one large mono-bank that performed both central bank and commercial bank roles) was to make sure that enterprises spent money in accordance with the plan. If an enterprise was in accordance with the plan, the bank would allow it to use the funds it had on deposit, or, if these funds were insufficient, the bank would lend the enterprise the difference.

This system required a planning bureaucracy staffed by thousands of individuals trained to analyze the various sectors of the economy and come up with the output and input targets. It also required an even larger administrative bureaucracy with similar skills to distribute the inputs and acquire and distribute the output of these enterprises and to manage the banking system. Such bureaucratic skills are quite different from the entrepreneurial and technical skills required in a competitive market economy. In China these planning skills had to be learned from scratch after 1949 since no such system had existed in China previously. Furthermore, these large bureaucratic organizations had to be managed in accordance with the technical requirements of planning. There was little room for senior managers to hire their unskilled friends, relatives, and political allies or to apply political as contrasted to technical criteria in the allocation of inputs or the setting of targets. Despite these strict requirements, China began to introduce this system in the early 1950s and the industrial and urban commercial economy was largely run by such as system by 1955–1956. Soviet advisors did play an important role in helping China set up this way of managing the economy, but the staffing was largely Chinese.

It would be impossible for many developing countries to introduce such a system and make it function reasonably well. A country such as Indonesia that had only a handful of university graduates at the time of independence, had an inexperienced and poorly trained bureaucracy, and a political leadership that before 1965 cared little for following technical requirements, could not have made such a system function with even a minimum of effectiveness. Much of Sub-Saharan Africa where the education base was similar to that of Indonesia and whose societies were often deeply divided along ethnic and other lines could not have made such a system function. Those few that tried to create an industrial base by moving in this direction failed without exception.

What was it that allowed China to introduce and run this system well for a time? The answer has to be the nature of China's premodern experience involving an emphasis on education, experience with running a large government bureaucracy, and a leadership that to a substantial degree could minimize politics and rent seeking in decisions that had to be made on technical grounds. China was not alone is having this capacity. India introduced many of these features into parts of its economy as did Vietnam at a somewhat later date, but in most developing economies the introduction of such a system would have led and sometimes did lead to economic disaster. Most commonly, developing countries that moved in this direction in their industrial development efforts simply failed to develop much industry and what they did develop could not compete in the international market. China's economy during the First Five Year Plan period (1953–1957), in contrast, grew at 6 percent per year and industrial output grew at 19.6 percent per year.[23]

Mao Zedong, however, was not satisfied with this performance or with the tight technical strictures that the centrally planned command economy system imposed on economic decision making in China. The system had never really been practical in the agricultural sector where most of China's labor force worked and Mao argued that the system was too restrictive for the industrial sector as well. He believed that China could do much better if it relied on the political mobilization skills that had played a central role in the Communist victory in the civil war. The result was the Great Leap Forward (1958–1960) that was designed to enable China to leap ahead of such industrial economies as Great Britain.

The method involved pressuring enterprise and local community cadres to use their imagination and the energies of their workers to expand production at an unprecedented pace. Local communities were to build their own small "backyard" iron and steel furnaces that would lead to a large jump in iron and steel output. Larger modern enterprises were encouraged to tear up their old plans and replace them with far more ambitious plans without any effort to coordinate these new plans with the rest of the economy or with the Soviet Union that would have had to supply the additional equipment required in many cases. The result, as is well known, was a collapse in industrial output and an enormous waste of China's limited resources. The backyard furnaces ended up melting down great quantities of useful iron and steel implements in order to produce large amounts of unusable low-quality crude iron and steel ingots. In the agricultural sector, a similar political mobilization effort was the primary contributor to three years of harvest failures (1959–1961) that were responsible for the deaths of around 30 million people.

In effect, the Great Leap Forward made little use of the strengths of China's premodern economy and society, the presence of substantial numbers of educated people and experience running bureaucratic organizations. Instead China's leaders turned to their revolutionary political skills that were important in winning the civil war but had little relevance to running the economy. Revolutionary leaders seldom make good managers of the economic development process. They have highly developed skills but not ones suitable to running a modern economy. The list of failed economic programs led by the founders and revolutionary leaders of newly independent countries is a long

Great Leap Forward

one and includes Sukarno in Indonesia, Nehru in India, Syngman Rhee in South Korea, Nkrumah in Ghana, Mugabe in Zimbabwe, and Le Duan in Vietnam, among others.

What worked in primitive base areas fighting for survival was an absolute failure in a large state trying to accelerate modernization. The primary problems of the Great Leap Forward were that technical criteria were abandoned in favor of political criteria in economic decision making and that there was no mechanism for coordinating these decisions even when they may have made sense at the individual enterprise level. A national economy has to have a coordinating mechanism and the only methods available are either a central plan or markets. China in 1958–1960 used neither planning or markets.

The experience of the Great Leap Forward led Mao Zedong to largely remove himself from economic decision making. The system of central planning was rehabilitated by others in the early 1960s with one important change. Much of the planning and control of the economy was now done at the provincial level and below rather than everything being centered in Beijing. In agriculture there was even experimentation with a return to household agriculture in some regions of the country.

Mao Zedong, however, soon came back into the decision-making picture in ways that had some impact, mostly negative, on the economy. Mao's goal, however, was no longer to transform the economy at a rapid pace. His stated goal was to transform Chinese society by changing its values to "all public and no private" (*da gong wu si* 大公无私). Some argue that Mao's real goals had mainly to do with keeping himself in power, but whatever his true motivation, he unleashed a movement that had a traumatic impact on Chinese society. The Great Proletarian Cultural Revolution (1966–1976) only directly disrupted the economy in a major way for two or three years in the late 1960s. Its overall impact upon Chinese politics and society was pervasive and lasted for the decade of the Cultural Revolution itself and for many years thereafter.

The main effect of the movement was that it inflicted enormous pain on large numbers of Chinese people. Anyone with ties to foreigners was persecuted. Teachers, normally an object of great respect in traditional Chinese society, were attacked by their students and driven from their jobs and sent off to the countryside to do manual labor. The students themselves were then sent off in large numbers to the countryside often for many years during the middle of the period when they otherwise would have been in school. Factory managers and chief engineers were sometimes locked in a factory room for months or a year and more. But probably most important from the standpoint of what happened after the end of the Cultural Revolution, most of the leadership of the Chinese government and of the Chinese Communist Party was persecuted, removed from their jobs, and sent off to the countryside to perform hard labor. In the course of the decade, millions of people including many who had achieved positions of power (e.g., former president Liu Shaoqi) died as a result of the treatment they received.

By 1969 Mao had lost faith in the impending transformation of China and the world. He did not repudiate the Cultural Revolution, which lasted officially until his death in 1976. However, he brought Deng Xiaoping back into the central leadership in 1973, and tried to keep a balance between returned party leaders like Deng and the Cultural Revolution leftists led by Mao's wife, Jiang Qing. Politics remained tense, and economic reform was subject to fierce criticism from the leftist Gang of Four.

Mao's death in 1976 effectively brought an end to the Cultural Revolution. The extreme leftist supporters of the movement were soon purged and the remaining party and government leadership that had been sent off to the countryside was rapidly returned to office and power. Support among most of the population and the leadership for movements such as the Cultural Revolution and the Great Leap Forward had virtually disappeared. The scene was set for a return to a more systematic and effective approach to governance in general and to governance of the economy in particular. But what kind of governance of the economy was required?

The Cultural Revolution destroyed the Maoist approach to economic and social development, but it did not itself create a constituency or a plan for a clear alternative. China could have gone back to central planning on the grounds that it had never given the command economy system a proper try except for a few years in the mid-1950s and at that time it had performed reasonably well. Indeed, Hua Guofeng in his brief period of power pursued a state-led development strategy that featured massive projects like the Baoshan steel complex in Shanghai. Deng Xiaoping, who was back in power by the end of 1978, was not committed to any particular economic system although he certainly started the reform period with a view that the challenge was to make the planned economy work better, not to abandon it altogether. Chen Yun, the other political leader with a major role in economic policy, was almost certainly of a similar mind.

The process that led to the steady abandonment of the centrally planned command economy was made possible by the horrors of the Cultural Revolution in the sense that the period created a large constituency for something different that would bring stability and prosperity to China. What ultimately led to the specific path followed involved two elements. The first was that Deng was a leader who was interested in "wealth and power" for China and was ready to support whatever changes would bring that about and the people he put in charge of the economy were willing to experiment with all kinds of radical change and these changes did work and hence were adopted and sustained. The second element was that the Soviet system of central planning by the 1980s was no longer seen as a great success as it had been so perceived in the 1950s, and not just in China. Instead, China was surrounded by neighbors who had pursued a very different strategy (Japan, South Korea, and two "greater China" economies, Hong Kong and Taiwan). This alternative strategy had lifted all of these other countries up from poverty to a level of prosperity that came as a shock to most Chinese when they were finally allowed to learn about it. Increasingly China's reforms moved in a direction that was not a copy of the Japanese or South Korean model, but with notable exceptions such as in the treatment of foreign direct investment, it was a similar approach adapted to Chinese conditions.

The most immediate and obvious contribution of prereform post-1949 China to the reform era was its role as "teacher by negative example" concerning the limits of popular mobilization as an economic strategy and of leftist dogmatism as a political direction. Maltreatment of much of the country's leadership and of most intellectuals had created a large constituency eager for change from the chaos and misery that had characterized their lives for a decade or more. On the more positive side, the 1949–1976 era did produce a large if inefficient industrial base and a major expansion in the number of educated personnel despite the closing down of the universities and the disruption of all schools during much of the Cultural Revolution.

CONCLUSION

China's rapid economic development over the three decades since the reform began in 1978 was a radical break from the past, but in a fundamental sense those reforms built on the past. China's subsequent rapid development can best be understood when that past is taken into account. The comparative sophistication of the premodern Chinese economy together with the emphasis on education in traditional society and the experience gained running organizations such as the Chinese bureaucracy are certainly part of the reason why China could introduce and run a modern industrial economy that is internationally competitive. Much the same can be said about why several other East Asian economies have done so well and why other economies with this kind of background such as Vietnam and India are beginning to experience rapid growth now that they have begun to abandon the growth stifling policies of the past.

China itself could not take full advantage of this historical heritage for a long time because of the century of political and military disruption together with foreign invasions that accompanied China's inability to transform the traditional system. When unity under a modern system was achieved in the 1950s, it was the wrong modern system for China's conditions, or at the very least it was not as effective a system as first China's neighbors and then China itself adopted after 1978. Conceivably China could have continued with that centrally planned command system after 1978, but the extreme disruptions of the Cultural Revolution together with the leadership of Deng Xiaoping created conditions that made much more fundamental change possible. That much more fundamental change in policy combined with the capacity of the Chinese people based on the heritage of both the premodern period and of the first decades of Communist rule to produce the extraordinary economic performance that the world has witnessed over the past three decades.

NOTES

1. The civil war did end, to be sure, with Taiwan as a separate political entity from the Chinese mainland, but the sustainability of this split was initially made possible by the US military presence in the Taiwan Straits in the context of the Cold War and later by the Taiwan government's success in achieving both rapid economic development and the political liberalization within its territory. This split, despite having lasted for sixty years and having been built on Taiwan's political separation from the Chinese mainland from 1895 to 1945, continues to be a source of potential instability. There are also minorities within the Chinese mainland some of whom would prefer to be independent of Chinese control but altogether they make up only 6.4 percent of the total population of the People's Republic of China.

2. The most comprehensive study of this subject is the multivolume effort by Joseph Needham, *Science and Civilization in China* [numerous volumes] (Cambridge: Cambridge University Press, 1954–).

3. Ping-ti Ho, *Studies on the Population of China, 1368–1953* (Cambridge, MA: Harvard University Press, 1959).

4. Dwight Perkins, *Agricultural Development in China, 1368–1968* (Chicago: Aldine Press, 1969).

5. Robert Hartwell, "Markets, Technology, and the Structure of Enterprise in the Development of the Eleventh Century Chinese Iron and Steel Industry," *Journal of Economic History* 26 (1966); and Mark Elvin, *The Pattern of the Chinese Past: A Social and Economic Interpretation* (Stanford, CA: Stanford University Press, 1973).

6. See, for example, the comparison of a wide variety of Chinese and European technologies in the premodern era by Kenneth Pomeranz, *The Great Divergence: China, Europe and the Making of the Modern World Economy* (Princeton, NJ: Princeton University Press, 2000). One relevant piece of evidence is that the Jesuit mission to China in the seventeenth century brought with them much of the best technology then in use in Europe. The clock and astronomical instruments and knowledge the Jesuits brought with them were superior to the technology in those areas then in use

in China, but there was little that the Jesuits had to offer in other areas of technology that the Chinese did not already have.

7. Iwai Shigeki, "China's Frontier Society in the Sixteenth and Seventeenth Centuries," *Acta Asiatica* 88 (2005): 1–20.

8. Wang Gungwu, *The Chinese Overseas* (Cambridge, MA: Harvard University Press, 2000).

9. Wang Gungwu, "Ming Foreign Relations: Southeast Asia," in Dennis Twitchet, ed., *Cambridge History of China*, vol 8: *The Ming Dynasty, 1368–1644, Part 2* (Cambridge: Cambridge University Press, 1998), 301–32.

10. Wang Gungwu, "Ming Foreign Relations."

11. Liu Guanglin, "Wrestling for Power: The Changing Relationship between the State and the Market Economy in Later Imperial China, 1000–1770" (PhD dissertation, Harvard University, 2005).

12. Evelyn Rawski, *Education and Popular Literacy in Ch'ing China*, Michigan Studies on China (Ann Arbor: University of Michigan Press, 1979).

13. Ronald Dore, *Education in Tokugawa Japan* (Berkeley: University of California Press, 1965).

14. Leo Orleans, *Professional Manpower & Education in Communist China* (Washington, DC: National Science Foundation, 1961). In the 1930s universities in China had an average enrollment of forty thousand students and that number rose to over a hundred thousand in the late 1940s just prior to the Communist Party's takeover of the government.

15. David Marr, *Vietnamese Tradition on Trial 1920–1945* (Berkeley: University of California Press, 1981), 39.

16. Angus Maddison, *Contours of the World Economy 1–2030 AD* (Oxford: Oxford University Press, 2007).

17. The major work on the Tongzhi Restoration is Mary Wright, *The Last Stand of Chinese Conservatism: The T'ung-Chih Restoration, 1862–1874* (Stanford, CA: Stanford University Press, 1957).

18. Albert Feuerwerker, *China's Early Industrialization: Sheng Hsuan-huai (1844–1916) and Mandarin Enterprise* (Cambridge, MA: Harvard University Press, 1958).

19. Wang Yeh-chien, *Land Taxation in Imperial China, 1750–1911* (Cambridge, MA: Harvard University Press, 1973).

20. Sydney Crawcour, "The Tokugawa Heritage," in William W. Lockwood, ed., *The State and Economic Enterprise in Japan* (Princeton, NJ: Princeton University Press, 1965), 31.

21. These are the preferred estimates of Thomas G. Rawski, *Economic Growth in Prewar China* (Berkeley: University of California Press, 1989), 330.

22. John K. Chang, *Industrial Development in Pre-Communist China: A Quantitative Analysis* (Chicago: Aldine Press, 1969), 60–61.

23. The official net material output (national income in Chinese) growth rate figure for the First Five Year Plan period is 8.9 percent per year, but this figure was obtained using the very high relative prices for industry that exaggerate the true growth rate if that rate is measured in market prices of a year when the market determined prices (a year such as in the 2000s for example).

6

The Dynamics of China's Reform-Era Economy

Barry Naughton

Unanticipated events repeatedly overturn our expectations: the daily news has been reinforcing this historical lesson since 2007. Yet during China's post-1978 transition to a market economy, the most unexpected thing was the sheer smoothness of the process, the absence of events that seriously derailed the process of economic development and change. In retrospect, China's rise appears to have been inexorable, and China today is much further along the developmental track than most people had anticipated. Market transition has been completed, generally successfully and with acceptable costs. As a result of this rapid progress, China in the last few years has begun to confront a new environment—and a new set of challenges—as it embarks on the further transition to a middle-income country. However, before that further transition could really get under way, the global (and Chinese) economic crisis delivered a sharp blow to the development process. While it is unlikely that China's growth will be derailed, the impact of the crisis is likely to be severe and hard to predict.

In the mid-1980s, economists began to project that China would experience growth acceleration and ultimately emerge from the transition process as a middle-income country. But how fast would this process take place, and when would China reach middle-income status? While it was clear that China had the capability to grow at 10 percent or even more per year, it seemed reckless to expect this potential to be realized without significant disruption from economic, social, or political events. Cautious optimists projected growth rates in the range of 6–8 percent per year.[1] Pessimists believed that China would do much worse, and possibly collapse. Yet in the event, growth surpassed even the optimists' expectations, averaging just over 10 percent per year through the middle of 2008. Moreover, significant growth acceleration took place after the turn of the century. As a result, China's 2008 GDP reached unanticipated levels that placed it on the threshold of middle-income status.

The transition to middle-income status is not just a matter of classification, or simply of improved living standards. To reach middle-income status, China must undergo a transition in the sources of growth. Rapid growth from a low income base was achieved through industrialization, urbanization, and the transfer of low-skilled labor from agriculture to industrial and service sector occupations. As growth is maintained in a middle-income environment, an increasing share of growth must be generated by investing in human resources and skills, creating a more efficient labor force that can earn higher incomes and still be economically competitive. Where does China stand today with respect to these long-run phases of economic transformation? We can relate China's current economic position to two arbitrary but still resonant benchmarks. China's total GDP—converted at prevailing exchange rates—hit $4.3 trillion in 2008, quite close to that of Japan, the world's second largest economy, estimated to be about $4.9 trillion in 2008.[2] China's per capita GDP is $3,250, approaching the dividing line between "lower middle income" and "upper middle income" countries, which the World Bank set at $3,595 for 2006 data.[3] Both these numbers paint a picture of China on the threshold of great power status, on the one hand, and of moderately comfortable living standards, on the other. We can no longer think of China as essentially a populous but poor country. A race has been run, and an era is over: China's transition from absolute poverty has occurred. Yet at the same time, China has not quite arrived either: not at comfortable great power status, nor at satisfactory living standards for the large majority of the population.

In this chapter, I first look backward at the policies that have led China to its current stage, outlining some of the main patterns shaping the outcome and impact. From this vantage point I consider the current state of the economy and impact on its East Asian neighbors. I then examine the notion of the "turning point," the idea that a qualitatively different period of growth begins when a country exhausts its supplies of abundant "surplus" labor. China's economic dynamism remains intact, and China's economic policies have already adapted to the challenges of this new regime. However, the current setbacks to growth may prove to be more serious than those of 1989–1990 and 1997–1999. The severity and synchronicity of the global economic crisis make it perilous to project the short-run future.

LOOKING BACKWARD

China in 1978 was extraordinarily well poised for economic development, despite the damage inflicted by the Cultural Revolution. In the preceding chapter, Dwight Perkins lays out a number of advantages that China had over other low-income countries, including widespread literacy, a critical mass of college-educated intellectuals, experience with large-scale government institutions, commercial experience, and national unity. By 1978, each of these advantages had been consolidated and built upon. Population health had increased dramatically, as shown by a life expectancy of about sixty-six. Basic literacy was widely spread. Moreover, under the socialist development strategy a network of institutions had been built that were compatible with a market economy, once they had been adapted to more effectively serve that economy. Most important were the rural Supply and Marketing Cooperatives and the Rural Credit Cooperatives. These insured that farmers were connected to networks to market their crops, and could get access to credit and modern agricultural inputs, such as fertilizer and improved seeds. Even in cities, people were organized into networks for support and control that could be mobilized for economic purpose. For example, urban youth returning from Cultural Revolution rustication were put to work in hastily organized cooperatives in 1979–1980. As a result, the initial challenge of institution creation was modest.

Equally important, the Communist Party had done an excellent job of sweeping away the forces that sometimes obstruct development in other countries. Landlords and entrenched rural interest groups had been eliminated. All rural residents had access to the land, initially through the agricultural collectives and subsequently through their own contracted land. There were no landless rural poor caught in poverty traps or seeking to overturn growth-friendly policies. Nor were there bitter political conflicts that could obstruct development through conflict over redistribution or deadlock over social policies. There were no obstacles to economic development in 1978, except, of course, for the Communist Party itself.

During the Cultural Revolution, the party had been in fact a formidable obstacle to growth. However, the Cultural Revolution itself thoroughly discredited the leftist approach to socialist development, and in that sense cleared the way for the party to remove itself as an obstacle to a growth-oriented policy package. Indeed, in some respects, the epochal shift of policy during the December 1978 Third Plenum that launched the reform era could be reduced to a single phrase, making "economic development" the central focus of party and government policy, replacing "class struggle." To be sure, if the commitment to economic construction had been halfhearted or qualified, a linguistic shift would not have made much difference. But in the event, the

Communist Party subordinated everything—all government policy and even the party's own organizational structure, reward system, and *raison d'être*—to the overriding quest for economic growth. This was the historical situation: once the Communist Party was willing to commit itself to the task of economic growth, nothing else stood in the way of growth acceleration.

From 1978 through the middle of the first decade of the 2000s, the Communist Party tinkered with every aspect of the economic system and experimented with many social policies, but always in the pursuit of economic growth. When competing objectives confronted Chinese policymakers, they invariably chose to give priority to growth over other objectives. This commitment to high-speed growth can be traced in the twists and turns of policy in many areas. The relative priority given to growth is so consistent that it is often seen as simply reflecting Chinese "pragmatism," as if there were no implicit trade-offs involved. But in fact it is not so much that Chinese policymakers are pragmatic, as that it is virtually impossible to find a "revealed value" that superseded the commitment to growth. Thus, to take one example, in energy policy, China has given de facto priority to exploitation of coal. This seems merely pragmatic, since coal is cheap and fairly ubiquitous in China. But in order to follow this policy, Chinese leaders had to be willing to discard other priorities, including the principle of national ownership of natural resources (many mines are private); worker safety (accident rates in coal mines are horrendous, especially in unregulated small and private mines); and the environment (coal is dirty).

The sustained priority to economic growth led China to gradually increase the rate at which it invests resources into new fixed capital. At the very beginning of the reform process, China cut the investment rate to give the economy "a breathing space" and allow consumption to increase. But since that time a steady accumulation of proproducer and progrowth policies has favored investment and pushed the investment rate back up. Companies are given favorable tax policies for investment; credit is cheap and bad loans are often forgiven; and governments at all levels are tireless promoters of new investment schemes. The result has been an enormous sustained mobilization of resources for investment. China's investment rate—fixed investment as a share of GDP—is higher than any other large country has ever achieved. During the decade from 1992 to 2002, China's investment rate was already around 38–39 percent, equal to the highest levels achieved in Japan, Korea, and Taiwan during their high investment and growth phases. But then, from 2003 onward, the Chinese investment rate rose further to surpass 40 percent, an absolutely unprecedented level.

The devotion of such a large volume of resources to new investment created a very powerful process of transformation that drove Chinese growth throughout the low-income stage of development. For the past thirty years, China has been undergoing exceptionally rapid structural change, as workers leave agriculture for industry or service sector jobs. During this type of structural transformation, the benefits to a high investment policy are arguably at their maximum. Each worker who leaves agriculture for a nonagricultural occupation creates a demand for new fixed capital for urban housing and infrastructure, and for tools and productive machinery. At the same time, the productivity of that investment stays high because each newly equipped worker quickly produces much more than when he or she was underemployed back on the farm. China's super-high investment and rapid structural transformation created an extremely powerful engine of economic transformation.

INSTITUTIONAL CHANGE

By itself, massive investment was not enough. It was essential that China also have a successful strategy of institutional change. The most fundamental characteristic of China's transition strategy—along with its growth orientation—has been the tentative and experimental nature of the most important institutional changes.[4] This strategy has often been called "crossing the river by groping for stepping-stones," labeling it (retrospectively) with Chen Yun's cautionary phrase. This approach must obviously imply a willingness to put together heterogeneous bits of institutions. The contrast is especially clear with the approach of reformers in Eastern Europe, who saw in the advanced capitalist welfare states of Western Europe a relatively complete and fully developed model to which they aspired. They attempted to purchase an expensive "best practice" model, and implement it as quickly as possible. Chinese reformers, by contrast, had no single goal in mind and were willing to borrow bits and pieces of institutions from many sources. Chinese reforms relied on improvisation. Reformers were willing to engage in what the anthropologist Levi-Strauss might have called "institutional *bricolage*," the do-it-yourself creation of a new structure from the bits and pieces of whatever materials are at hand. Those bits and pieces were borrowed from advanced capitalist countries, from East Asian neighbors, from international advisory organizations such as the World Bank, and from China's past, with no single source dominating.

Among the historical sources that Chinese reformers drew on was the example of a centralized bureaucracy that, at least in its ideals, was meritocratic. Perhaps as a result of this precedent, Chinese reformers were less likely than their Eastern European associates to tear down the whole hierarchical structure, and more likely to try to restructure it in a way that made sense for their economic goals. An example of one such step was the reinstatement of national college entrance exams, a momentous decision that actually preceded the full commitment to economic reform. In 1977, after Deng Xiaoping returned to the top leader group, but had not yet attained the paramount position, he assumed control over the education and technology portfolios. Higher education was in a shambles, and its rehabilitation at the top of the agenda. From August 4 to 8, 1977, Deng personally chaired a multiday meeting with thirty-three top scientists and educators, all of whom were brought in from outside the education bureaucracy. During the course of the meeting, in response to scientists' suggestions, Deng personally decided to push for immediate revival of the national college entrance examination system, which had been abolished more than a decade previously. Deng then rapidly got the approval (*pishi* 批示) of the other top leaders. The exam was subsequently opened to all comers, with only modest limitations on age and political record.[5] The revival of the examination system had enormous implications in and of itself: it gave a pathway back into society for the most talented individuals among those who had been marginalized and sent to the countryside; it provided a national merit-based standard; and it helped establish the credibility of the whole reform process. Indeed, it probably deserves to be twinned with the opening of special economic zones and trade and investment in Guangdong as being one of the dramatic opening moves that allowed the reform process to break decisively with the past and establish its own momentum. But most interesting in the current context is that this policy would clearly be inexplicable without reference to historical precedent. Deng Xiaoping can be imagined as rummaging around in a big bin for potential solutions to China's immense problems, and discovering that one potential source of solutions was China's historical experience. The solution that he found there was for a nationwide and centralized program, which he promptly adopted. In that sense, the historical experience of a centralized, but still "thin" governmental apparatus contributed to a gradualist and diverse process of economic reform.

The improvisational approach to economic reform has outperformed, by a huge margin, the alternative "big bang" approach to transition, which imposed large costs even on successful reformers (such as Poland) and led to failed transitions in many former Soviet states. Successful economic reform led to China's rise, and the conviction that a successful approach to economic reform had been forged in China—and perhaps only in China—certainly fueled Chinese self-confidence, which had been abysmally low at the beginning of reform, because of the Cultural Revolution catastrophe and the gap that had opened up between China's East Asian neighbors and China itself. The example of national college entrance exams also reminds us that China's reforms have often been centralizing. Of course, decentralization was also a very important part of reform, as economic functions and policy experimentation were vested in local governments and in the marketplace. But from the beginning, both centralizing and decentralizing initiatives coexisted, as new principles of decision making were worked out in practice. The ultimate result, of course, has been that China has emerged *both* with a market economy and with an unusually strong and centralized political and economic power.

Two strands of the overall transition process are most responsible for the strong state outcome. First, from the beginning, the search for a viable strategy of transition to a market economy was twinned with an effort to make the party/government hierarchy more effective, to, in economists' jargon, reduce the "agency loss" in the bureaucratic edifice. The type of initiative Deng Xiaoping took with college entrance exams in 1977 was extended to virtually every aspect of the hierarchical bureaucracy in subsequent years. Career paths were regularized by making education and experience requirements for promotion and by enforcing regular retirement rules for elderly cadres. Incentives were dramatically recast to reward bureaucrats for contributing to economic growth. Annual cash rewards and promotion opportunities were both tied to objective indicators of economic growth. This same process led to recasting of incentives for managers of state-owned corporations. To a remarkable and unanticipated extent, this process was successful in reinforcing the hierarchical political system that many had assumed would crumble with successful marketization. The Chinese bureaucracy is stronger today than thirty years ago, and it is more focused on tasks that it has a reasonable expectation of being able to perform successfully.

Second, the Chinese government has retained large state-owned corporations that control the "commanding heights" of the economy. The Chinese government presided over a substantial downsizing of the state sector in the mid-1990s. State industrial enterprise employment peaked at 45 million in 1992, before beginning a steady slide to 17.5 million by the end of 2007.[6] Agriculture, industry, and commerce have been dominated by private businesses since before the beginning of this century. But at the same time, large and powerful central government corporations have survived and thrived. Key natural resources, energy, telecom, and transport sectors have remained walled-off and reserved for state ownership. A watershed was the 2003 establishment of SASAC (the State Asset Supervision and Administration Commission). SASAC was part of an effort to make government oversight of state-run corporations more efficient, modern, and transparent—in that sense, a continuation of the hierarchy-improving effort described in the preceding paragraph. But the establishment of SASAC also marked the virtual end of central government enterprise privatization. Management buyouts of large firms ceased, and the central government stabilized its ownership portfolio, even while privatization continued at the local level, albeit slowly and gradually.

The Chinese government has been engaged in an active and sometimes aggressive effort to restructure these large central government firms and their competitive environment. Generally, at least two large firms compete in each market, sometimes in a pure duopoly and sometimes in a more complex market. Sinopec, PetroChina, and CNOOC divide the oil market, while China Mobile, China Unicom, and China Telecom partition the telecom space. All these firms are centrally owned. In the airline industry, there are two strong central airlines (Air China and China Southern), one weak central airline (China Eastern), and a fringe of small public and private airlines. These outcomes are not driven by unhindered market forces. Rather, they reflect the continuous structuring and restructuring initiatives of the Chinese government, itself balancing off two opposing considerations. Monopoly doesn't work: past Chinese experience shows clearly that giving any single organization monopoly control of a given sector leads to unrestrained rent seeking and subordination of efficiency gains to pursuit of the quiet life. On the other hand, with some limitations on entry and competition, the state can keep control of these strategic and sensitive sectors and also ensure that they will be quite profitable. The result is the current system of structured competition among state-owned actors.

Again, this approach has been remarkably successful. By most outside appraisals, these firms have dramatically upgraded their management effectiveness and operational efficiency. Through mid-2008, the central government corporations rode the global economic boom to unprecedented profitability. SASAC company profit exceeded 4 percent of GDP in 2007, and was heading toward 5 percent of GDP in the first half of 2008. After the crisis hit in mid-year, profits declined precipitously. Nevertheless, we can expect to see the role of these corporations continue to increase in the current troubled economic environment. Central government corporations will be prime recipients of government support as China tries to navigate the global (and domestic) financial crisis and injects resources into troubled domestic corporations. Moreover, China's highly centralized system has proven to be quick and responsive in the face of economic turbulence. Though certainly not immune to serious problems, these large, central-government-linked corporations are likely to be part of the global economic scene for the foreseeable future.

These features of China's transition directly influence the impact of China's rise. China's relative "weight" is increased, not only by its enormous population, but also by the presence within the Chinese borders of two of the largest organizations in the world: the 71 million member Communist Party and the 10.5 million member centralized government. When these organizations are able to move in concert, they greatly increase China's impact on the outside world, and give China an ability to react to situations in a prompt and decisive manner. Of course, such concerted actions only come in exceptional situations, when incentives are aligned and clear priorities are established by the center. Under normal circumstances, these huge organizations are subject to equally huge agency problems and reflect multiple inconsistent agendas.

The links between government, party, and business inevitably generate suspicion and resistance, and thus also detract from China's effective power. This complex of reactions was fully in evidence in early 2009 as China prepared to spend money to purchase global natural resource assets at distressed prices. The government had agreed to loan $25 billion to Russia in exchange for oil pipelines and a ten-year supply contract, while at the same time, a wealthy and important central-government-owned corporation, Chinalco (China National Aluminum Corporation), offered $19.6 billion to take a stake in Anglo-Australian resources giant Rio Tinto. At first welcomed because of the collapse of financing for the natural resource sector, Chinalco's bid for resources was ultimately turned away. The tentative recovery of financial markets played a role, to be sure, but at the same time, discomfort over the extent to which government and corporate interests were entangled in the Chinese bid contributed substantially to the derailing of the deal.

LOOKING OUTWARD: CHINA AND ASIA

China's opening with the outside world has, from the beginning, been the counterpart of domestic marketization. Moreover, the bold steps to allow foreign investors and traders a key role have contributed mightily to giving China a more diverse economy and society, and contributed some counterweight to the still strong position of the government and Communist Party. As China's economic policies and fortunes have fluctuated, China's relationship with the rest of Asia has changed dramatically. In the traditional Asian economy, China was at the center of a web of maritime trade, through the system of tribute trade and linked commercial exchanges. China was displaced from this centrality by the rise of a Japan-centered East Asian economy in the 1920s–1940s. Subsequently, China withdrew altogether from Pacific trade, and from the 1950s through the 1970s the East Asian economy shifted its orientation to outside, and especially American, markets. China's reemergence from the 1980s once again knit China into the fabric of the East Asian economy.

However, China's role in the East Asian economy has taken on a particular structure, which we can call triangular. China's trade with each of its most important trading partners is quite unbalanced, even today.[7] China imports about twice as much as it exports from five East Asian neighbors, including Korea and Taiwan. (In the case of Taiwan, China imports four times as much as it exports.) By contrast, China exports more than three times as much as it imports to the big three export markets of the United States, European Union, and Hong Kong. (In the case of Hong Kong, most of the imports are reexported to the United States). Only Japan straddles this divide, being at the same time the origin of significant inputs for the production chains that end in China, and a large and wealthy market of its own. (See table 6.1.) Of course, there is no presumption that any bilateral trade relationship should be balanced. It is simply that this pattern of one-way, and ultimately triangular, trade flows strongly characterizes China's insertion into the East Asian trading network. China serves as the point of final assembly for a broad array of goods that are manufactured by means of complex production chains that stretch across many jurisdictions. China's comparative advantage remains strongly in the relatively labor-intensive final assembly stages of production networks. It is true that the largest and most important production networks are increasingly those that produce sophisticated electronics hardware, rather than the garments and sporting goods in which China initially specialized. But the pattern of triangular trade has been a strong characteristic of China's foreign trade since the mid-1990s, and it remains so today.

In other words, China has emerged as the endpoint of the East Asian assembly chains, and not as the center of the East Asian economy. Compared to China, Japan's position remains more fundamental, not because of the absolute size of the Japanese economy, but because of the Japanese command of technology, especially technology in manufacturing. Japan is the source of many of the high-tech components and much of the sophisticated production machinery that make East Asian production networks possible. China is highly com-

Table 6.1   China Trade 2008, Main Trading Partners

	Export (billion USD)	Import	Surplus
East Asian Partners			
South Korea	74	112	-38
Taiwan	26	103	-77
Malaysia	21	32	-11
Philippines	9	20	-11
Thailand	16	26	-10
Japan	116	151	-35
Export Markets			
Hong Kong	191	13	178
EU	293	133	160
US	253	81	172
Total Trade	**1,429**	**1,133**	**296**

petitive as a point of final assembly, but in the final analysis, other locations, particularly in Southeast Asia, could also perform these activities at reasonable cost. The same cannot be said for Japanese technological sophistication.

What would it take for China to really reclaim a position as the center of the East Asian economy? First, China's domestic market needs to continue to grow in relative importance, and second, China needs to establish greater and deeper technological capabilities. The domestic market includes both the household consumption market and the (predominantly) business market for capital goods. These markets have evolved at very different paces. We have already discussed the fact that China invests a huge proportion of its domestic GDP. That implies that China's heavy industrial sector is quite large, since this sector furnishes most of the investment goods. For example, China in 2008 produced an astonishing 585 million tons of finished steel (for comparison, the United States at its peak, in the 1950s, never produced more than 150 million tons of finished steel). That means that China has the ability to move world markets for commodities like iron ore. In fact, we can get a better idea of China's importance by calculating the size of its investment goods sector in international comparable prices, that is, at purchasing power parities (PPP). In the investment goods sector, machinery is actually sold in China for about the same as world prices, although construction is much cheaper. Considering both these effects, the World Bank's revised International Comparison Project found that China's fixed capital formation, at world prices, was 17.9 percent of world total fixed capital formation in 2005, only a little bit behind the United States (20.7 percent) and well ahead of Japan (7.4 percent). In other words, because China invests so much, the Chinese market for investment goods is enormous.

When we look at the consumer market, a different picture emerges. First, the huge effort expended on investment and exporting inevitably implies that consumption—and particularly household consumption—is a correspondingly small part of the Chinese economy. After initially rising as a share of GDP in the 1980s, household consumption dropped to 44–45 percent of GDP in the 1990s (of course, individual consumption was still growing rapidly, just less rapidly than overall GDP). Beginning in 2002, household consumption's share of GDP slid again, to only 35 percent of GDP in 2007.[8] China in the 1990s was similar to Japan in the early 1970s, but China in the 2000s actually decreased its consumption share, whereas in Japan the early 1970s marked the last few years of the high-investment/high-growth era. But consumption goods in China are extremely cheap, both because of China's real comparative advantage in labor-intensive goods (covering most consumption goods), and because of any undervaluation of the Chinese currency. So it is especially important to adjust consumption measures to reflect differences in purchasing power. In fact the value of Chinese consumption is roughly tripled when evaluated at international prices. Even so—again according to the World Bank revised comparisons—China's total household consumption amounts to only 6.1 percent of the world total, not only far behind the United States (25.4 percent) but also behind Japan (7.0 percent). China's consumer market is large, to be sure, because of China's huge population. But with real per capita consumption at world prices only on average about 1/16th of what Americans consume (about 6 percent) the Chinese household market does not wield the kind of global influence that the Chinese steel industry, for example, does.

These numbers mean that China's influence on the world through its household market is relatively limited. There has been much discussion recently of a nation's "soft power," including the influence of culture. But cultural influence is exercised across national boundaries largely through the creation and export of attractive cultural products. In order for businesses to develop attractive export products, products that combine enjoyment and value for the money, they must first test and launch them in their domestic marketplace. Global cultural products—French perfume, Hollywood movies, or Japanese anime—were all developed first for domestic consumers. China's relatively low per capita GDP, and the allocation of GDP toward growth-fostering investment, mean that through the present, the Chinese consumption market is not yet sufficiently evolved to be a lead market in most cases. Despite the huge size of the potential Chinese market, and the obvious creativity of Chinese culture, China does not generally wield influence through culture markets. One particular example would be the case of Mandarin pop music. Even though the number of recordings of Mandarin pop music sold on the Chinese mainland is far larger than anywhere else, and that Mandarin singers come from all over the East Asian region, the production of Mandarin pop is dominated by Taiwan-based producers. Seventy-five percent of the winning records at the Global Chinese Music Awards were produced in Taiwan.[9] China's cultural creativity has not yet translated into market power.

The triangular trade pattern described above has been crucial to China's emergence as a high-tech exporter. China's dramatic opening to foreign investment and trade, though by now an old story, is still one of the most impressive parts of China's transformation. The size and speed of the transplantation of high-technology items to China is staggering. For example, in 2008, China exported $66 billion worth of laptop computers, more than 80 percent of the *world's* total production. At the same time, China still depends overwhelmingly on imported integrated circuits to run these laptops and indeed the enormous variety of electronics products that it produces, consumes, and exports. For nearly a decade, the Chinese government has invested mightily in supporting the development of China's integrated circuit (IC) industry, giving it policy priority and highly favorable tax treatment. Nevertheless, in 2008,

China consumed an estimated $135 billion worth of ICs, and at the same time imported $129 billion of ICs.[10] China's electronics industry relies on imports for over 90 percent of its integrated circuit needs.[11] The level of dependence on imports has changed little over the past ten years, despite Chinese government industrial policies.

Chinese policymakers have put strong emphasis on technological upgrading since the very beginning of the reform process. Indeed, the story of Deng Xiaoping and the revival of college entrance exams early in this paper can also serve as a tale exemplifying the motivating power of technological catch-up. Indeed, since the early 1980s, Chinese planners have rolled out a series of industrial policies and technological strategies, with relatively limited success.[12] Certainly, Chinese technological capabilities have increased dramatically in the past thirty years. With as much certainty as we can say anything about the future, we can declare that Chinese technology will continue to improve and steadily shrink the gap with world best practice. However, whether Chinese government technology promotion policy has contributed significantly to this catch-up process is still rather uncertain. The problem is the very limited correspondence between the specific targets in technology promotion programs and the actual outcomes we observe, which the IC example illustrates. Technological upgrading is still very much on the Chinese agenda.

THE TURNING POINT

China is still a majority rural society, but it is moving rapidly in the direction of a predominantly urban society. By the end of 2008, China's urban dwellers made up 46 percent of the population, and the share of the labor force in agriculture dropped below 40 percent. What difference does this transformation make? A long-standing concept from the development economics literature can illuminate the significance. According to the Lewis-Fei-Ranis "surplus labor" model, a key moment in the development process is reached when growing urban employment economy finally begins to drain the reservoir of underemployed farmers in the countryside. Before this point, the apparently inexhaustible supply of low-cost labor means that employers can hire more workers without raising wages (the supply is infinitely elastic). Even as cities grow and corporate profits soar, workers' wages stagnate and huge income gaps open up between capitalists and workers. Eventually, though, a "turning point" is reached: with labor supplies no longer inexhaustible, wages for unskilled workers begin to be pushed up by the operation of supply and demand. Worker incomes start to climb and employers have stronger incentives to hire more educated and skilled workers.[13] At the same time, with urbanization, a larger share of new entrants to the labor force will have received a high-quality urban education. The developing economy begins to make a swift transition not only to higher incomes, but also to a better skilled and more equal society.

This is a useful construct for understanding what is happening in China. To be sure, the concepts have been criticized in the development economics field. It is not clear that workers in the farm sector were truly "surplus" before they migrated to cities; and the "turning point" is more like a gradual shift in conditions rather than an abrupt change. When the supply of young workers in accessible regions is exhausted, there may still be large pools of surplus older workers, especially in remote areas.[14] But the concept still has explanatory power for China (and for other East Asian developing economies). A flood of migration from the countryside to urban factories has powered the Chinese industrial explosion of the past twenty years. Pulled by powerful economic forces, millions of rural Chinese moved to cities and factory towns each year. Throughout the 1990s the pace accelerated, until in the 2002–2007 period, around 15 million Chinese migrated *annually*. Yet through most of this period, wages for unskilled labor stayed low, because of the virtually unlimited supplies of available labor.[15]

Around 2004–2005, evidence started to appear that China might be approaching the "turning point." For the first time, factories in the Pearl River and Yangzi River deltas began to experience difficulty attracting workers. It was no longer enough to simply post a help-wanted sign. Factories found they had to institute modest improvements in working conditions and wages to attract the workers they needed. Moreover, this change in labor market conditions was plausibly connected to the exhaustion of the most accessible eligible migrants. For example, a 2006 survey by the Development Research Center of 2,750 villages in twenty provinces found that in 75 percent of villages, all of the young, able-bodied workers have already left the villages.[16] There is still surplus labor in the countryside, but in most villages the surplus labor is comprised of middle-aged and older workers. Labor recruiters began to venture to more distant and remote villages, and working conditions improved modestly.

Given China's size, and the fact that few farmers leave the land after age thirty-five, mass rural-urban migration will probably slow down before the agricultural labor force sinks below 30 percent of the labor force, with the remainder of the transformation taking place more slowly as the labor force ages. In any case, the process of transformation today is certainly not exhausted, but the bulk of it has passed astonishingly rapidly. In the Yangzi Delta, with a total population approaching 150 million, less than 20 percent of the labor force is left in agriculture; in Guangdong—with 94.9 million long-term residents in 2007, China's most populous province (!)—only 29 percent of the labor force is in agriculture. These nation-sized entities have transformed into middle-income and mostly urban economies, like Korea and Taiwan in the early 1980s. At the same time, many of China's provinces are still predominantly agricultural. In the southwest provinces of Yunnan and Guizhou, and even the central Chinese provinces of Henan and Hunan, more than half of the labor force still farms the land. China faces a new set of economic and policy challenges, while also trying to develop effective policies for those in less dynamic regions.

LOOKING FORWARD

The Chinese government has responded rapidly, and even proactively, to the new challenges and opportunities the Chinese economy faces as it crosses over to the other side of the Lewis turning point. Most obvious have been the changed policies toward human resources. Mass migration, and the recognition that it was transforming society and generating growth, led to new promigration policies. In the late 1990s, government policy changed dramatically in seeking to facilitate migration to the cities and lower the barriers posed by the urban *hukou* (residence permit) system. Local governments began to support out-migration with information and training through so-called Sunshine Projects. In the early 2000s, a series of State Council proclamations sought to reduce the discrimination that migrants face after arrival in the cities, and emphasize their rights as citizens and workers.

Moreover, massive investment in human resources began after the late 1990s. During the early stages of economic transition, China was very cautious about committing fiscal resources for education or health. School enrollment ratios fell and the collective health care system in the countryside collapsed. Perhaps most striking, education planners were very cautious in expanding the higher education system. This caution evaporated at the end of the 1990s, and new enrollments in higher education soared. In 1998, newly enrolled freshmen in colleges and junior colleges had just inched above 1 million; by 2005, the number had shot up to 5 million, then continued to increase, but more slowly, to 6 million in 2008. (By comparison, the United States enrolls around 2.5 million freshmen annually, a number that has changed little in recent years.) In the countryside, it took longer for the government to reorient the fiscal system and provide central government budgetary support, but this also began by the mid-2000s. Agricultural taxes were abolished, while the central government took financial responsibility for the increased provision of elementary education. Central government subsidies also permitted rapid expansion of the (very basic) cooperative rural health insurance system. By 2008, these subsidies had spread to 91 percent of rural counties.[17]

The emphasis on human resources was part of a broad policy reorientation. China's leaders around 2004–2005 began to ease off on the "growth above all else" policy and stress the achievement of a range of social goals. This reorientation of growth strategy—I have elsewhere referred to it as a "left tilt"—can be seen as a response to the real social problems that emerged in the course of market-oriented reform.[18] However, it probably makes more sense to see the new course as the response to a new set of demands caused by the looming transition to middle-income status. Some of this reflects new demands from the population: having experienced sharply higher incomes, especially in the big cities, China's citizens began to demand the "luxury" of greater economic security, lower inequality, and better environmental quality. Some of it reflects the new competitive challenges created by the same economic forces. With wages increasing, even for less skilled workers, the only path to sustained growth is through higher quality labor, with healthier and better educated workers. Facing these push and pull factors, China's leaders dramatically shifted their approach to development.

The leadership launched an impressively broad and multistranded effort to reorient growth. Some parts of that effort have already borne fruit: the renewed attention to rural areas, accompanied by substantial changes in the fiscal system, is probably the best example. However, many other strands of this new course were merely in the early stages of implementation by mid-2008 when the economic crisis hit. Since these changes generally had not been made prior to the crisis, the imperatives facing China's leaders have suddenly changed dramatically. Two main strands can be mentioned here. China's leaders made a commitment to more balanced growth, including not only a lower investment rate, but also a less energy-intensive production structure and a more environmentally friendly growth strategy.[19] However, as the earlier discussion implies, these measures had really not succeeded. China's investment rate continued to rise through 2008, and energy consumption grew rapidly.

A second area of concerted effort was for improved working conditions, including job safety, job security, as well as wages. A major push has been made on job safety, which has begun to bring down extraordinarily high occupational accident rates. A new national Labor Law went into effect on January 1, 2008. The Labor Law sought to improve working conditions and worker bargaining power through many of its provisions. One key provision was a requirement that workers who were laid off be given one month's severance pay for every year's seniority they had. The provision was made simple, clear, and mechanical precisely so that it would be easy to communicate to workers, and give them an opportunity to assert and mobilize in support of these newly granted rights.

What these measures have in common is the attempt to harness the vigorous growth process and channel it into ways that improve the quality of life. To some extent, these policies push against pure market forces, "tax" the production process, and redistribute income to produce more equitable social outcomes. But more important, they take advantage of the market forces being created by successful economic development—and especially by the new economic conditions created by the turning point—to shape and guide the next stage of economic development. The policy shift is an attempt to anticipate and adapt to the new opportunities and challenges created as the economy passes through the turning point. In an ideal world, these policies would have sustained growth while also pushing China forward into a new environment of heightened capabilities and better quality of life.

CONCLUSION: CRISIS, REGRESSION, AND GROWTH

Extraordinarily rapid economic growth in the past thirty years has propelled China to the threshold of major changes—to, but not over, the threshold. China stands on the brink of middle-income status, close to being an urbanized economy, on the verge of great power status, and beginning to tap resources of technological creativity. But in each of these categories, sober judgment would conclude that China has not yet crossed over into this new realm. The fact that we could even suggest this list of adjectives for China in 2009 is in itself remarkable. The road to this point has turned into a high-speed highway before our eyes.

The current crisis has come at a complicated junction on that path to development. Many of the policy initiatives of the government will face unprecedented challenges. Consider the two fields of labor law and higher education policy. The economic crisis hit within months of the implementation of the Labor Law, and employers began to downsize and lay off workers. While the government could insist that large state companies adopt a no-layoff policy in return for government support, many private businesses found themselves with no real choice. The Chinese government has had little alternative but to retreat on the Labor Law, and it is an open secret that local governments have been quietly nullifying the law's provisions, despite recurrent, if scattered, worker protest. China's college graduates face an increasingly challenging environment. In the early 2000s, the booming economy easily, even eagerly, absorbed new college graduates, even as the number of graduates more than tripled. In 2008, however, the 5.1 million new college graduates are facing an extremely challenging job market. Even more striking is the plight of rural-to-urban migrants. Temporarily, the flow of workers has gone into reverse. Urban jobs evaporated in 2008, and an estimated 20 million people stayed in their home villages after returning for the traditional Chinese New Year visit in 2009. Moreover, under current circumstances, the massive creation of industrial capacity that sustained the great boom of 2002 to 2008 has now turned into a liability. For example, China currently faces massive overcapacity in the steel industry. In the short run, declining sales and incomes make it harder to find the resources necessary to restructure the economy as it passes the turning point. Yet the crisis presses China to quickly make changes that leaders would have preferred to stretch over years, if not decades. The Chinese economy has developed enormous capabilities and tremendous resilience over the last thirty years. Those qualities will be needed in the transition through the current global crisis.

NOTES

1. Dwight Perkins, *China, Asia's Next Economic Giant?* The Henry M. Jackson Lectures in Modern Chinese Studies (Seattle: University of Washington Press, 1986).

2. In fact, Japan's total GDP was $4.3 trillion in 2007, and then declined 1.6 percent in nominal terms between 2007 and 2008. However, the Japanese yen appreciated dramatically against the dollar in 2008, boosting the dollar GDP, measured at exchange rates, by almost 14 percent. For comparison, US GDP is about $14 trillion.

3. World Bank, *World Development Report 2008* (Washington, DC: World Bank and Oxford University Press, 2007).

4. Sebastian Heilman, "Policy Experimentation in China's Economic Rise," *Studies in Comparative International Development* 43, no. 1 (March 2008): 1–26.

5. Long Pingping and Zhang Xiao, "Deng Xiaoping Juece huifu gaokao" [Deng Xiaoping establishes the policy to revive college entrance exams], in Zhang Shengen and Duanmu Qinghua, eds., *Gaige Kaifang 30 Nian Zhongda Juece Shimo 1978–2008* [The full story of Major Policies during the 30 years of Reform and Opening 1978–2008] (Chengdu: Sichuan Renmin), 1–9.

6. This count is based on the most inclusive definition of state enterprises, including state-controlled joint stock companies.

7. General Administration of Customs of the People's Republic of China, "Trade Statistics by Main Country or Region, December 2008," January 11, 2009, www.customs.gov.cn/publish/portal0/tab400/module15677/info155558.htm.

8. For comparison, in the United States, household consumption has been just above 70 percent of GDP since 2001. The United States is something of an outlier, and the recent US figure has been high even by US standards. In the 1950s through the early 1980s, US household consumption was about 62 percent of GDP. China is, of course, much more similar to Japan in the early 1970s than to the United States. Between 1970 and 1973, Japan devoted 49 percent of its GDP to household consumption, and 37 percent to fixed capital formation. Net exports were only 2 percent of GDP, and

government consumption, at 11 percent of GDP, was lower than in China. World Bank, *World Development Indicators* (Oxford: Oxford University Press, 2009).

9. Hitoradio, "Global Chinese Music Awards," hitoradio.im.tv/.

10. In addition, domestic firms produced $30 billion in ICs, and $24 billion was exported. Domestic firms export more than two-thirds of their output, as these are generally less sophisticated cheaper products that don't necessarily meet domestic needs.

11. Ministry of Industry and Information Technology, "2008年我国电子信息产品进出口回顾和2009年展望," February 20, 2009,   www.miit.gov.cn/n11293472/n11295057/n11298508/11990360.html; Ministry of Industry and Information Technology, "2008年我国集成电路行业发展回顾和2009年展望," February 23, 2009, www.miit.gov.cn/n11293472/n11295057/n11298508/11993762.html.

12. Barry Naughton, *The Chinese Economy: Transitions and Growth* (Cambridge, MA: MIT Press, 2007), ch. 15.

13. Arthur Lewis, "Economic Development with Unlimited Supplies of Labor," *The Manchester School of Economic and Social Studies* 22 (1954): 139–91; John C. H. Fei and Gustav Ranis, *Development of the Labor Surplus Economy* (New Haven, CT: Yale University Press, 1975).

14. Kam Wing Chan, "Introduction: Population, Migration and the Lewis Turning Point in China," in Cai Fang and Du Yang, eds., *The China Population and Labor Yearbook*, vol. 1: *The Approaching Lewis Turning Point and Its Policy Implications* (Leiden: Brill, 2009).

15. Cai Fang, "A Turning Point for China and Challenges for Further Development and Reform," *Zhongguo Shehui Kexue* (2007): 3, 4–12.

16. Han Jun, "Nongcun laodongli gongqiu guanxi de xinbianhua" [Recent changes in the supply and demand for rural labor], *Zhongguo Jingji Guancha* [China Economic Survey] (2007): 2, 165–75.

17. National Bureau of Statistics, "Statistical Communique of the People's Republic of China on the 2008 National Economic and Social Development," February 26, 2009, www.stats.gov.cn/enGliSH/newsandcomingevents/t20090226_402540784.htm.

18. Barry Naughton, "China's Left Tilt: Pendulum Swing or Mid-course Correction?" in Cheng Li, ed., *China's Changing Political Landscape: Prospects for Democracy* (Washington, DC: Brookings Institution Press, 2008), 142–58.

19. Nicholas Lardy, "Sustaining Economic Growth in China," in C. Fred Bergsten, Charles Freeman, Nicholas R. Lardy, and Derek J. Mitchell, eds., *China's Rise: Challenges and Opportunities*, ch. 6 (Washington, DC: Peterson Institute and CSIS, 2008); Barry Naughton, "The New Common Economic Program: China's Eleventh Five Year Plan and What It Means," *China Leadership Monitor* 16 (Fall 2005), www.hoover.org/publications/clm/issues.

IV

CHINA'S ECOLOGICAL AND RESOURCE INTERACTION

7

The Environmental Impasse in Late Imperial China

Mark Elvin

Contemporary China's environmental problems are well known to the rest of the world, but their provenance is not well understood.[1] The current ecological crisis is often attributed to the forced industrialization of the Maoist era,[2] and to the pressures of a rapidly swelling population only curbed but not fully contained by the policies of birth limitation later introduced in the 1970s,[3] followed by the inability of the reform era that followed to prevent the wastage of resources and the health-threatening pollution caused by resurgent market forces. While each of these factors is significant, these explanations imply that had China been spared these problems it would be ecologically a relatively happy place.

Not so. By the nineteenth century, late traditional China, the inheritor of millennia of refashioning nature for economic ends, had reached an environmental impasse. The original flora and fauna had all but vanished;[4] and the soil and water supply had, in a sense, become artifices of human ingenuity, creations that required increasingly costly and precarious efforts to ensure system maintenance.[5] And because of the nearly complete demographic filling in of most of farmable China by the end of the eighteenth century, there was almost no place to go, until in the later nineteenth century, Manchuria was opened, and migration overseas became easier.[6] With only the tools already at hand, and no homegrown scientific revolution of practical use, premodern China had no choice but to work ever harder for diminishing returns per person.

There was a dark side to the arrival of the imperial West: China's deep, if transient, political and cultural humiliation.[7] Nonetheless, it was the West's provision of China with access to modern science, modern technological productivity, and modern techniques of government and communication that made possible the escape from the environmental prison house that late imperial China had, with sophisticated premodern ingenuity, built for itself. But for this Western contribution, the huge current population of China and its aggregate wealth, for all the lopsidedness of its allocation, would not have been possible. But, now, it must be asked whether this modernity has not in the end only created a more complex, and perhaps more implacably pad-locked, environmental box, and one with global implications. *De nobis quoque fabula narratur.**

MODERNITY

My own approach to the definition of "modernity" is not the standard one, and needs some brief explanation. More than forty years of looking at China's historical economy, which for a large part of the Middle Ages was arguably the most advanced in the world, persuaded me, via a process of elimination, that the only element of importance in the European story of the period from about 1600 to 1800 that was missing in China was modern science, and the much vaster, pervasive, and commonly underestimated penumbra of ways of thinking and seeing that are, in the last analysis, anchored in "modern" sci-ence.[8] Late premodern China crossed the boundary line into modern science on a few occasions,[9] but an insufficient socio-intellectual density of interest in all but a few topics inhibited the development of the networks of communica-tion, cooperation, criticism, and cross-generational continuation needed to create self-sustaining progress. The use of a historical cultural-anthropological perspective to explain such phenomena as this lack of adequate density of interest in China is useful, but it is an error to think that it can be used in relativist fashion to blur the different quality of the validities of the different explanatory frameworks developed in these two areas. The simplest demon-stration of this arises from looking at the absurdity of postulating different rates of success or failure, given different understandings of the probabilities and payoffs, in gambling games that had effectively the same rules in both Chinese and European culture, of which there were quite a number.[10]

This point may seem a diversion. In fact it is central. If late imperial China had had the capacity to create even some useful homegrown modern science, then an early escape from the high-level equilibrium trap that immobilized farming and many other parts of the economy might well have been possible, at least for some considerable time, by raising the production function with

---

* Loosely, "It's a story that refers to us as well."

new scientifically generated inputs and techniques. It is striking that even in areas where no sophisticated instruments or mathematics were needed, the Chinese accomplished nothing in the later centuries of the empire. To take a simple example, there seem to have been no systematic observations of earthworms and their effects on the soil such as that pioneered in eighteenth-century England by Gilbert White, and then famously in the nineteenth century by Charles Darwin, who also demonstrated by exquisitely simple experiments that it makes good sense to attribute something like a "mind" to worms, however rudimentary. Li Shizhen, the great sixteenth-century naturalist, was only able to note from his own observations of earthworms that "these days they are everywhere where there is level, moist land and rich soil."[11]

As early as the sixth century A.D., the Chinese had some preliminary insight into the link between the emission of pollen by the male hemp plant and its maturation, but they never pursued this to obtain knowledge of the function of pollination. In Europe, in spite of scattered clues from antiquity in the works of Theophrastus, this topic remained unexplored until some observations by seventeenth-century English botanists, and then the proof of sex in plants by Rudolf Camerarius in 1694, followed by the experimental demonstrations of Jacob Koelreuter some decades later.[12] All that a Chinese botanist would have initially needed both for the study of worms and pollination was a good hand lens (though a simple microscope would have been better), and these had been made in China, though possibly only for a time, in the seventeenth century.[13] What mattered more than instrumentation or math was often simply an attitude of mind. One that was largely missing in China in this period.

A SUMMARY OF CHINA'S PREMODERN ENVIRONMENTAL HISTORY

Over a period of about three thousand years, the greater part of China's original forest cover was removed.[14] With its removal, the greater part of the habitats of wild animals was lost, and so hunting also gradually disappeared as a significant part of the economy except in some frontier zones, and the wood needed for houses, boats, and fuel slowly became scarcer, with the eighteenth century being in many areas the time of visible crisis.[15] With the loss of most of the forests and their wild foods, the environmental buffer that had provided against years of bad harvests was similarly lost. A parallel tale was the long-term draining of the vast swamps of what are now the North China plain and the central and lower Yangzi valley, and their conversion to farmland. If drainage work was neglected for long, however, the swamps tended to reassert their presence. The large rivers were flanked by levees to stop flooding and the smaller ones channeled and diverted to use their water for irrigation. The deposition of sediments on the beds of the first required the building of the levees ever higher and higher, and inevitably they broke from time to time until the river in the end established a new course for itself. The irrigation systems on the lesser rivers had very variable lifetimes depending on local factors, but hydrological instability required constant maintenance engineering. Long lengths of the eastern Chinese coast were also sealed off by seawalls and lock-gates across rivers from around the middle of the first millennium A.D. They were originally made mostly of earth and were very vulnerable to storms, but became increasingly strong in Ming and Qing times as techniques of stone construction on deep foundations were perfected. Saline coastal environments and freshwater inland ones thus became almost hermetically separated, dooming most anadromous fish.

Rice farming became more and more common in the later first millennium A.D. Over the centuries, most of lowland central and southern China became a mosaic of leveled paddy fields surrounded by low mud walls that needed rebuilding to some extent each year, as those not reinforced with concrete still do today. On the slopes the need to prevent the loss of soil led to the building of terraces on which rainfall ponded, and walls stopped the earth slipping downhill.[16]

As the population grew, human labor gradually stopped being the factor of farm production that was in shortest supply. The new scarcest factor was now good-quality farmable land. Part of the same process was a long-term trend toward labor intensification. This meant concentrating on growing more per acre, rather than per hour of work. Having growing numbers to feed was another reason for this shift of emphasis, but the taxation system also played its part. With only a few exceptions, from the twelfth and thirteenth centuries on, Chinese farm taxation was based on the area farmed, with an adjustment for the estimated quality of the land.[17] It would thus seem evident that as a result it paid economically to intensify, as a large harvest from the same fields did not increase the tax burden by even a single cash. Thus multicropping and intercropping expanded dramatically, and fallowing disappeared on lowland lands. These developments required shifts in institutional structures and farming practices, as animals could no longer be allowed to graze—and fertilize—stubble fields following a harvest; hence, with less grazing freely available, the Chinese farm economy became relatively "de-animalized" in so far as larger animals like cows and water buffalo were concerned. The quantity of water needed each year increased, and put pressure on communities for collective action to expand and control their hydraulic networks; and there was a pressing urgency to find additional sources of fertilizer.[18]

Some tasks could not in any case be done by animals in this garden-style farming. An example is the planting out of clumps of rice seedlings into partially flooded paddy fields. Evenly spaced rows made possible an optimal use of growing space in a level, irrigated field that had needed much hard work to prepare. Hoeing was required for banking up and weeding; and, after the initial application of manure at the time of planting, the further applications of two to four doses as top-dressing demanded care. Putting on too much manure at any one time, especially in northern dry-land farming, risked wasting too much of the nutrient supply by drainage.

From the sixteenth century on, beans, rape, or peas were increasingly grown before the rice harvest, and this helped to restore the loss of usable nitrogen in the soil.[19] By the seventeenth century farming land was in such short supply that numerous hillslopes were opened for cultivation. This led to large losses of topsoil, and at times to the choking of irrigation systems downstream, though some of the soil ended up in deltas in lakes and along the coasts where it could be reclaimed and sown. The two most important crops grown in these upland areas were recent arrivals from the New World, sweet potatoes and maize.[20] These arrived via European ships, and also represent a historical economic debt—of a sort—owed by China to the West.

Bai Shichen tried to solve the problems of the marginal hill lands with the following recommendations:

> From the summit of the hill downward divide [the land] into seven levels. The fifth level, and those below it, may be opened for cultivation. One begins with the lowest level. (. . . *Whenever there is a heavy rain, the mountain streams break forth in torrents, and sweep the rich topsoil away downstream.* Therefore [the land] becomes unusable after three years. Furthermore, the richness of the hills adheres to the surface; once streams have been opened up to flow through them, the richness dries up within. . . .) When one first opens up the land . . . one begins by planting a crop of turnips everywhere. These plants are good at loosening the soil, and guaranteeing a harvest. . . . Next one plants maize and darnel mixed together with sweet sorghum. . . . In every case one must [also] choose some moderately level ground and dig ten or more pits in which to grow taro, yams, melons, and greens to serve as vegetables and prepare [the soil] for grains. (If there are many people in the mountain hut, there will be no shortage of [human] manure. . . .) After every two years, one changes one level, proceeding gradually upward. . . . The fertility of the soil moves downward from above. If the upper half of the land is not opened up, its fertility . . . will [? percolate slowly and so] be retained by the lower levels. . . . Furthermore, one should estimate the point at which the mountain streams are at about the same height as the ground that has been opened up, and excavate winding [contour-line] ditches to these streams, using stones and mud to dam the waters. . . . When the fifth level has been reached, the richness from the top four levels [that is, 4, 3, 2, and 1?] will

have flowed down every day to the lower levels, and one can start the cycle again from the beginning.[21]

In other words, there was a combination of terracing, irrigation, and rotation of crops. Even so, cultivation in the hills had often to be abandoned as unsustainable.[22]

Apart from the dung provided by pigs, which, being scavengers, could be kept in small numbers by most families, there was a shortage of animal manure except high in the hills where there was adequate coarse grazing for stock. The two most important means of restoring fertility to the hard-pressed fields were mud dredged from the ditches for irrigation and drainage, and human excrement, both liquid and solid, assiduously collected and sometimes purchased. If we wished to be vulgar, but truthful, we could say that the survival of Chinese civilization depended on mud and shit.[23]

Water

Control of water has been at the center of much of China's economic and environmental history. Here, more than anywhere else, politics, society, and the economy met the environment head-on.[24] There were conflicts over its rival uses. These included irrigation, transportation, drinking water supply for cities, and the powering of machinery. Water-driven mills were sometimes ordered shut, having the lowest priority politically. Ponder the implications of this for any possible industrial revolution. There were also conflicts about who had access to how much. As almost everywhere in the world, upstream farmers were commonly at loggerheads with farmers lower down. There could also be arguments about whose fields were to serve as the overflow basin when a river flooded. A local war was even fought over the last issue as in the middle of the nineteenth century, at Mianyang, where the Han River joins the Yangzi. At other times, local water control could lead to a local protodemocracy, as occurred in Shanghai after 1775. The magistrates here would summon meetings of gentry to advise what hydraulic works should be undertaken, who should manage them, which landowners should pay, and how much per acre. In the polders, diked enclosures with fields below the water-level in some seasons, and where an entire community could be at all-or-none risk from flooding, there was *per contra* a spirit of community and cooperation. In a few places in the drier north, such as Baotou in the nineteenth century, there were, however, commercialized systems of water control; and it was even possible to buy shares in water without owning any land.[25]

Water-control works did not inevitably lead to what Karl Wittfogel called "hydraulic despotism," but there is truth in aspects of his old theory even so.

Commoners were conscripted for a limited time to perform essential routine tasks such as the repair of crumbling seawalls, or the draining of lakes, not just exceptional projects like cutting sections of the Grand Canal. The concentrations of workers, the dangerous and exhausting work, and the stress of the discipline, led to deaths from infectious diseases, as well as sickness from contaminated drinking water and food. Moving down the scale of size, the state also commonly promulgated rules governing the proper running of middle-level systems, and supervised their implementation. It would usually only intervene if there were chronic problems, and avoided direct bureaucratic management. An example was the Puyang River in Zhejiang province during the late Ming and the Qing. Rules remained unchanging in official proclamations, often carved on stone, but the real-life waterways were perpetually changing—silting up storage basins, or altering their meanders—in a way that soon made the details out of date.[26]

The hydrological instability of man-made water systems made the burden of maintenance perpetual. Far more had to be spent, over the long run, on keeping a system going than in creating it in the first place. A well-maintained water system may pay for itself, but it is inherently developmentally static after a certain point determined by environment and technology. There are limits to rainfall, hence to available run-off, and indeed to topography of a kind suitable for hydraulic schemes. Ground water, too, is only replenished at a fixed rate. Once the environmental opportunities have been used up, going further is a waste of time, energy, and money. This limit seems to have been close to being reached by about the middle of the Qing dynasty.

Why was it impossible to double-track the Ming and Qing Grand Canal from Hangzhou in the southeast to its terminus in the north just outside Beijing? Because, in a key section, where the Canal went up and down a stairway of locks over the spur of the Mount Tai massif, not enough usable water flowed off the hills. In fact, even one track could not be kept open all year round. The summer floods carried so heavy a load of sediment that directing them into the Canal would soon have silted it up, with unacceptable costs for clearance. Summer water was therefore diverted into the sea by an alternative channel. The clearer, but less abundant, winter and spring water was stored at the canal summit in a reservoir. When the convoys laden with grain for Beijing were coming north, a temporary dike was built across the mouth of the alternative channel and reservoir water directed into the Canal until there was a level at which the grain ships could float. Once the flotilla had passed, this dike was demolished, only to be rebuilt again the following year. Engineering work was also needed to restrain the feeder-river for the Canal from shifting its course entirely into the alternative channel that led to the sea.[27]

Although the Chinese invented the pound lock, with its double openable and closable gates, so that boats could be lifted or lowered merely by using sluices to pour in or drain out the water enclosed by the gates, the limited supply meant that, in order to avoid waste, permanently closed locks, bypassed by haulovers over which the boats were dragged, had to be used instead. Here, too, was an additional cost in labor. Likewise, smaller, lighter boats, carrying smaller cargoes, had to be used—smaller than would have been possible to handle with pound locks. The limits placed by the local environment on the further development of a water-based transport system would not have presented problems to a Grand Railroad.

The longevity of the great water systems varied. The basic Min River system in Sichuan province had already been built at the latest in the fourth century B.C., but, with some improvements, is still flourishing today. The Zheng-Bai complex of irrigation canals in Shaanxi province started in the middle of the third century B.C., but ran into difficulties quite rapidly. Immense efforts kept it going in a much diminished form until the eighteenth century, when the government gave up on the attempt.[28] Out of the many factors causing these different fates, it seems that the most important was the downcutting of the Jing River that fed the Zheng-Bai. This both led to difficulties with securing an adequate supply of water, and also over time changed the character of sediment load from fertile topsoil loess to more nearly sterile lower layers, reducing the benefit to crops that it watered. It may also have been significant that its main channel was a contour traverse that transferred water from one subcatchment to another, crossing gullies and subject to rockslides and other damage. The Min, in contrast, conformed somewhat more closely to the existing pattern of the supply river, simply diverting its water through distribution channels and then returning what was left. It nonetheless required a huge annual input of labor to keep these channels clear, as the deceleration of the current caused by the system caused a heavy rate of sediment deposition. Each year was, in a sense, precarious.

Earth

While it is generally recognized that premodern Chinese farmers performed a remarkable feat in sustaining the viability of their continuously cultivated soils for as long as they did, this admiration can blind us to the strong likelihood that there was, even so, a slow but insidious crisis undermining late imperial agriculture. At the end of his description of farming methods and soils in the early 1920s, the agronomist Wilhelm Wagner, who lived for over a decade in China, understood the Chinese language, and maintained his own laboratory there, observed in his *Die Chinesische Landwirtschaft* [The Chinese rural economy]:

"One may draw the conclusion from these reflections that a balance between the plant nutrients withdrawn from the fields by the harvests, and returned in the form of fertilizers, is not possible, and that, in consequence, the Chinese rural economy has been living off its capital stock for many centuries." He went on: "Under the circumstances relating to fertilizers that have been described here, any rise in productivity in the Chinese rural economy, or more precisely any increase in the harvest yields of individual crops as the foundation of a general upsurge by the entire operation [i.e., national farming] is not to be contemplated. The shortage of the means of fertilization constitutes for such a process an insurmountable obstacle." He stressed that traditional Chinese methods of fertilization could not be more than marginally improved within the existing framework. "I will only emphasize," he concluded, "that progress within the present-day system of plant-nutrient replacement is not possible."[29] The only way out that he could see was the widespread introduction of chemical fertilizers; and this was of course what happened later under the PRC. The initially impressive results were, however, not well sustained, due to application in a way that did not judiciously balance the three principal ingredients;[30] and there was also some concomitant damage to the soil structure.[31]

Wagner noted two other aspects of the Chinese treatment of the soil with which he was not comfortable. First, they were not sensitive to the advantages of balancing the acidic and alkaline elements in a soil, to make it what the English traditionally called "mellow" and the Germans as having the quality of "die Gare." Second, he observed that in North China a hard layer often developed between the topsoil and the subsoil, which greatly limited the rise of any subsurface water. He went on to note that in northern China, "it seems to me that the structure of Chinese field soil, as a consequence of a centuries-long removal of all remains of stubble, and the shortage of straw manures, has become of a wholly peculiar nature. It is characterized by an exceptionally low content of humus [i.e., roughly speaking, organic materials that decompose only relatively slowly], and, as a result of this, by a shortage of soil bacteria. Whereas the European farm economy sees field soils, in addition to being a location for their crops, also as a source of nutrients, the Chinese only consider the first of these purposes in respect of areas that have been farmed for centuries. The shallow topsoil has become, over the course of time, so impoverished in dissolved plant nutrients that only by means of painstaking manuring is it possible to obtain adequate harvests. It has ensued that in the arid climate of North China the very high soil content of harmful alkalis obstructs its proper working, this being the result of the unfavorable impact of its topsoil formation."[32]

We can supplement these remarks with the judgments of James Thorp on southern Chinese soils about a decade later. Because of the leaching out of lime, mostly as the result of the heavy southern rainfall, Chinese soils south of the line of the Huai River, and that are untransformed by human action, are mainly acid, or in other words contain a relatively high concentration of hydrogen ions in solution. This southern rainfall is, he says, "sufficiently heavy to . . . remove a large share of soluble mineral plant foods, and the soils tend to become infertile. This is the reason why there are such tremendous areas of infertile [*sic*] land in South China." They are "kept in a productive condition only by dint of constant fertilization . . . and painstaking cultivation." These include the regular addition of lime and "increments of rich soil materials brought down by the rivers" freshly eroded from the mountains in the Tibetan borderlands and local ranges. The southern soils that hold water well enough to allow rice to be grown are "worked and cultivated and fertilized until they become well adapted to rice culture, *regardless of their original characteristics*."[33] The soil that supported late imperial China was *artificial*.

Manure was thus the lifeline of Chinese farming. The types used in premodern times, the ceaseless efforts put into their gathering and preparation, plus the manner of their application, were the most distinctive features of the system of food production. As already noted, the main materials used were the mud from ponds, canals, and rivers, and human feces and urine. Ferdinand Von Richtofen wrote a famous passage on human excrement in the farmers' daily lives: "The first sight in the morning, when I left the ship, was a procession of people bringing sewage to the fields in buckets; the next was that of the pails and other receptacles both large and small by the doors of nearly every house in the villages in which the precious stuff had been left to ferment; and, finally, the little open cabins on the sides of the streets where the passer-by was silently begged to bestow alms of an especial sort on the owner of the nearby field."[34] Nightsoil was an important article of trade in the cities, with prices highest in spring and lowest in the winter months. It had to be processed by fermentation and dilution and, on the whole, used fairly quickly as the long storage of unthinned ordure leads to a loss of nitrogen. At times, though, the excrement was also mixed with earth, dried, and made into briquettes for later use. The dung of larger animals played a minor role as there were too few of them, except in mountainous areas. Even there, cattle dung was also often needed for fuel when compounded into blocks with items such as roots, leaves, bark, and pine needles. This was particularly true in the north with its general shortage of firewood. As often in a situation under environmental stress, different requirements competed for the same limited resource.

The use of mud was largely confined to rice-growing regions. It was collected with long-handled wickerwork ladles, or clam-shell-shaped dredges opened and closed like tongs, after which it was put into boats, and taken to the fields, where it was dumped in small mounds. Once it had dried, it was plowed into the soil of the field. Or it might be mixed with the residues of an intercrop such as peas to make a green manure for restoring land after a fertility-exhausting crop such as cotton.

Carefully matured compost was as distinctive a feature of northern farming as coarse compost was of southern. Compost is produced by the action of bacteria on decomposable waste organic matter, and generates a certain amount of heat as the action proceeds. The final product is very variable, but broadly resembles humus.[35] The rough-and-ready southern compost was a mass of straw and other matter held together by mud and feces, with the components still clearly identifiable. The ingredients were heaped into a pile on top of earth from the fields as a "starter," and usually also covered with earth. This pile needed to be turned and worked over repeatedly for the best results, another heavy burden on labor. In contrast to southern soils, northern agricultural soils had very nearly no humus, and so the use of carefully made compost was a way of remedying this, and providing crops with easily assimilable nutrients. A variety of materials went into it including street sweepings, ashes, the roots of cereal plants, and organic household rubbish. Even the matured pulverized dust from the unfired bricks used to make the *kang* oven-beds in northern peasant houses was employed when they were broken up in the springtime after a few years' use; as, after some years, was the matured "cob" or trodden clay that constituted the floors of peasant houses. The *kang* bed bricks were also rich in soot, which was valued for its ability to destroy pests. Green manures, such as Chinese clover and winter peas, were widely used; and high-quality manures such as oilcakes were applied to particularly valuable crops such as tobacco and opium poppies. Rotations of crops were commonplace, as has been noted, but the "rotation" of soils (by removal and replacement) was also practiced, especially where trees like mulberries were concerned.

Every crop was manured. Most was given to the seeds, sometimes individually, a hallmark of the Chinese farming style; the remainder was applied as a top-dressing on the plants once they were already growing. Attention was paid to applying the fertilizer individually to individual plants, or bunches of seedlings, rather than to the field. This additional manure was normally not applied on a single occasion, but, especially in North China, in two, three, or even four doses to limit the loss of nitrogen through seepage or percolation.

The main concern in plowing rice fields was not to turn the soil, which the traditional type of paddy-field plow did very incompletely, but to loosen the soil, which it did well enough. Since draft animals were expensive, these plows were often pulled by one or more humans with a plowman guiding it from behind. The northern dry-farming plow could be effective, if well designed, but Wagner thought that mostly it plowed too shallowly, and failed to turn the soil fully. Care was given, however, to fragmenting and leveling the surface soil with harrows, rake-forks, and rollers. Hard clods were broken up with mallets or flails. In Wagner's view, shallow plowing reduced the volume of soil drawn on for plant nutrients, limited how far the roots went down, and retained less moisture in the soil when dry weather tended to evaporate it. In wet weather, deeper plowing also made the use of nutrients supplied by manure more efficient, by limiting the quantity washed away by rain. Compared to the care bestowed later in the growing cycle, soil preparation was thus poor, at least by European standards. A Chinese proverb adjured, revealingly in this respect, "there is no need to be greatly concerned about the tilling of the field, but only about weeding, hoeing a lot, and spreading a lot of manure." But we may suspect that this reflected folk wisdom about the different returns from the different sorts of work.

The Chinese attached great importance to leveling fields, and small fields are simpler to level than large ones. The spread of small fields may originally have been connected with the cultivation of wet-field rice, where the flooding of the field in the early stage of seedling growth makes leveling and circumvallation essential, but it was widely applied even to dry-land farming. The point in dry farming was to stop topsoil being washed away by rainfall, because a level surface reduces the speed and hence the carrying power of any flow of water, which is proportional to the fourth power of its celerity. It also helps to retain water, as well as allowing plowing to be lighter. Thus terracing occurred widely on slopes even when there was no irrigation system attached. Obviously, though, small fields were also less suitable for the use of draft animals to pull plows, harrows, and rollers.

Von Richtofen left a description of some minute terrace fields on the lower Yangzi that he called "the most amazing example of the characteristic bustling industriousness of the Chinese." These terraces were built by filling the gaps between numerous vertical slabs of limestone on a steep slope and backfilling the spaces behind them with soil. He noted that "the people carried the soil, and not just the manure, there on their shoulders up steep paths." The fields were small, often only a few square meters in size. "If one looks at them from below," he concluded, "one sees nothing but a limestone cliff, but if one looks down on them from above, there appears a tangle of green fields. In the winter, wheat is grown there, and, in the summer, rice."[36] Whenever terraces were used for rice, the irrigation water at each level was prevented from draining away too fast to the level below by installing an impermeable layer about forty to fifty centimeters below the surface. Clay, or loam (that is a mixture of silt and sand with a smaller proportion of clay), was pressed down as tightly as possible; and when bricks or tiles were cheap, these were laid down instead.

It would clearly be possible in principle to increase yields from such a system with modern fertilizers, but whether the input of labor could be more than moderately reduced with modern technology seems problematic.

Population Growth

It has been known for at least the last half-century that the Chinese population was growing at a steady pace during the eighteenth century and the first half of the nineteenth.[37] Though the most likely rate is still a matter of dispute, as is the most plausible size of the base from which it should be calculated, there can be no doubt that *any* nontrivial positive rate, given that most potentially good arable land, apart from that in Manchuria, was already in use, would have led in the course of time to disaster if the production function had remained essentially static, let alone slightly worsening as I have suggested it may have been doing, due to the slow deterioration of the soil. Crisis here is simply a matter of the laws of compound interest.[38] For the record, my view is that 0.43 percent a year growth from 1700 to 1850 is a reasonable guess, but there is no justification for assigning to this number any more than a rough validity.[39]

Why wasn't the rate of population growth higher? Around 1800, Chinese women in the lower Yangzi area married at a median age of 16.8 years, with a mean of 17.3. Though the expectancy of life at birth for girls here was only 27.2 years, it rose to 41.1 more years by the age of 10, and one would therefore have expected a substantially higher growth rate in the absence of some form of birth limitation *within* marriage. In fact it has been possible to show good reasons for thinking the figures show that there *was* such limitation, though the behavioral means (such as possibly *coitus interruptus*) and the technical means (such as contraceptive drugs and abortifacients) are unclear for the moment; and also, more roughly, that there was a rate of female infanticide of at least 10.4 out of every 100 live female births.

Could the rate of birth limitation within marriage have been strengthened further to reach a point of approximate demographic balance? It seems, not impossible of course, but doubtful when one considers the probable parental psychological mechanism behind the limitation that did occur. There were, as has been indicated, two contrasting patterns of mortality: first, that around birth and the few years following birth, which was severe; and, second, that of adults, which was much milder, being—loosely speaking—at the level of early modern Western Europe. In the year from age 0 to 1, some 312 female Chinese babies died out of every 1,000 born. From age 12 to 13, only 4 out of every 1,000. Even up to the age of 37 the rate stayed below 20. The interest of the parents was in optimizing their chances of replacing the family's male farm labor force as fast as possible but not overstretching its resources by having too many to support on too little land. Once the survival of one or two sons was relatively assured, because they had made the transition from the high infant to the low adult probability of dying, one would have expected the birthrate to fall. And this is exactly what the data for the lower Yangzi show: after a rapid start to childbearing there is a slowdown in births once a marriage has lasted from five to ten years. Insufficient data for longer marriages make the period after this impossible to call with any conviction, but it may have risen again somewhat.

This is of course only demonstrable at the moment for a single region, albeit the most important one economically in Qing China. The pattern may well not have been universal.

The roots of China's present-day demographic problems clearly lie in this phase of massive late imperial population growth. But there is an even more lethal implication probably hidden in the story that has just been summarized, though at the moment it has to be presented as no more than a plausible hypothesis. With the coming of modern medicine, it was initially relatively easy, once its key contributions in this field had become fairly widespread through Chinese society, to reduce infant mortality on a large scale. If late imperial childbearing habits and assumptions had changed relatively more slowly than improvements in the practice of perinatal medicine, there would have been a period during which population growth was drastically accelerated. And this, as is well known, is precisely what happened. Such changes are rarely, if ever, monocausal, but the impact of the legacy of the inherited late imperial pattern of two-speed survival at different ages, and its twentieth-century modification, is worth considering seriously as having had a significant impact.

THE FUTURE

The foregoing observations have focused on the environment of China as it was in the centuries just before its economy, in a rough-and-ready sense, "joined" the modern world, though to degrees that varied widely according to location and sector, as they still do today. What lies ahead? In the first half of the last century under the Republic there were some remarkable if mostly somewhat localized economic achievements. An example is the capacity in Shanghai before the Pacific War to design and make certain quite sophisticated producer's goods to a standard fit for international export.[40] The environmental history of this period, Taiwan perhaps excepted,[41] is however still inadequately explored. For the Maoist era from the early 1950s to the middle 1970s there remains a still inadequately resolved economic question: how far, and in what ways, did the changes in this period actually help or damage China's performance and prospects? There is little doubt, though, that the environment was seriously further degraded, and that official hostility to population limitation for a generation[42] made for unnecessarily severe demographic pressure. There remain differences of opinion about the interactions in China, following the post-reform production explosion in and after the 1980s, between the economy and the polity on the one hand and the environment on the other.[43] The balance of probabilities seems to favor a somber perspective for the middle term.[44] Why?

As we have seen, the late imperial environmental legacy was a significantly negative one. To an important if still inadequate degree this has since been relieved, to some extent temporarily, by technologies based on modern science. The most important long-term change, however, is that China is now, for better and for worse, part of the world story.[45] This means that, for example, China is now a major global player in the scramble for resources, whether iron ore from Australia or oil from Africa. The Chinese authorities appreciate that even over the middle run the cost of energy will loom ever larger as time goes by, though China has still good reserves of coal. The resource scramble also suggests conflicts are likely with neighbors and competitors. An obvious example is rival needs of different nations over the exploitation of waterpower in Southeast Asia, notably as regards the Lancang/Mekong River.

Domestic political pressures from both ordinary people and commercial interests will hinder the proper, and ultimately unavoidable, economic pricing of most water in China, and the longer the availability of artificially cheap water the more lasting the damage to sustainable water supplies. Demand for water will also increase as incomes rise. Much more efficient use, though politically perilous, nonetheless offers the only major window of time in the immediate future. The recent easing out of effective power of Pan Yue, the highest official who has been the strongest protector of the environment, is probably a symptom of the impact of the counterreactive pressure of immediate convenience on those pushing for environmental controls.[46] Severe soil erosion continues to be a menace. We may note, without being able to tell exactly what it means, that a recent official estimate puts the annual soil loss at four and a half billion tons a year.[47] It thus seems likely that, in spite of strong efforts to avoid importing basic foodstuffs other than soybeans in large quantities, China will sooner rather than later have to import substantial, and in all likelihood increasing, amounts of grains. In any future impasse that China faces, whether of resources, water, or food, the world will either be part of China's solution, or China will become a large part of a global quandary.

Inevitably, we are now all in it together.

NOTES

1. I would like to express my thanks to the services of the electronic press-clipping service of the Sinological Institute of Heidelberg University.

How in the 1970s the PRC government finally came to terms with the reality of the environmental crisis is described in Elvin, "El medio ambiente" [The environment], in Taciana Fisac and Steve Tsang, eds., *China en transición. Sociedad, cultura, política y economía* [China in transition: Society, culture, politics and economy] (Bellaterra, Spain: Barcelona, 2000), esp. 323–51. For a current general update, see *Nature* 454, no. 7203 (July 24, 2008), special survey of "China's Challenges."

2. For example, Judith Shapiro, *Mao's War Against Nature: Politics and the Environment in Revolutionary China* (New York and Cambridge: Cambridge University Press, 2001).

3. Judith Banister, "Population, Public Health and the Environment in China," in Richard Edmonds, ed., *Managing the Chinese Environment* (Oxford: Oxford University Press, 1998) gives a balanced appraisal of this issue.

4. For the early chapters in the story, see Wen Huanren, *Zhongguo lishi shiqi zhiwu yu dongwu bianqian yanjiu* [Changes in plants and animals in China during different historical periods], ed. Wen Rongsheng, rev. ed. (Chongqing: Chongqing Publishing Group and Chongqing Publishing House, 2006). For the latest chapter, see Samuel Turvey, *Witness to Extinction. How We Failed to Save the Yangtze River Dolphin* (Oxford: Oxford University Press, 2008).

5. Elvin, *The Retreat of the Elephants: An Environmental History of China* (New Haven, CT: Yale University Press, 2004).

6. Elvin, *The Pattern of the Chinese Past* (Stanford, CA: Stanford University Press, 1973).

7. Elvin, "How Did the Cracks Open? The Origins of the Subversion of China's Late-traditional Culture by the West," *Thesis Eleven* 57 (1999).

8. The character of "modern" science may be summarized as an understanding of the observable world that is expressed by the construction and use of conceptual models that are, as far as possible, formally explicit, based on quantified data, logically internally consistent and consistent with other relevant current models, besides being to the extent possible mathematically summarized, and—crucially—continually subject to observational, experimental, and logical testing in the public domain, with the goal of continual improvement.

9. Elvin, "Some Reflections on the Use of 'Styles of Scientific Thinking' to Disaggregate and Sharpen Comparisons Between China and Europe from Song to Mid-Qing Times (960–1859 BCE)," in Ian Inkster, ed., *History of Technology* 25 (London: Thoemmes Continuum, 2004). See especially the sections on historical phonology and acoustics.

10. Elvin, "Gerende yunqi—weishenma qiandai Zhongguo keneng meiyou fazhan gailü sixiang?" [Personal luck: Why premodern China—probably—did not develop probabilistic thinking], in Liu Dun and Wang Yangzong, eds., *Zhongguo kexue yu kexue geming* [Science and scientific revolutions in China] (Shengyang: Liaoning Jiaoyu Chubanshe, 2002), 426–96: Chinese version of a manuscript deposited with the

Needham Research Institute Library, Cambridge, scheduled for publication in Günter Dux and Hans Ulrich Vogel, eds., *The Concept of Nature in China and Europe, Sixth Century B.C. to Seventeenth Century A.D.* [working title] (Leiden: Brill, forthcoming).

11. Gilbert White, *The Natural History and Antiquities of Selborne in the County of Southampton* (1788), expanded ed. (London: Sonnenschein, 1876), 234–35, 353; Charles Darwin, *The Formation of Vegetable Mould Through the Action of Worms* (1881), repr. (Teddington, Middlesex: Echo Library, 2007); and Li Shizhen, *Bencao gangmu* [Herbal subdivided into major and minor sections], 1596, as reprinted in *Bencao gangmu tongshi* [The *Bencao gangmu* with comprehensive explanations], ed. Chen Guiting et al., 2 vols. (Beijing: Xuefan chubanshe, 1992), vol. 2, 1902–03.

12. Jia Sixie, *Qimin yaoshu* [Essential techniques for the common people], following the extracts cited and translated by Shi Shenghan in *A Preliminary Survey of the Book* Ch'i Min Yao Shu, *An Agricultural Encyclopaedia of the 6th Century* (Beijing: Science Press, 1962), 64; Bastiaan Meeuse and Sean Morris, *The Sex Life of Flowers* (London: Faber and Faber, 1984), 7–8; V. Zarsky and J. Tupy, "A Missed Anniversary: 300 Years after Rudolf Jakob Camerarius . . ." *Sex Plant Reproduction* 8 (1995): 375–76; Lois Magner, *A History of the Life Sciences*, 3rd ed. (New York: Dekker, 2002), 374.

13. Joseph Needham and Lu Gwei-Djen, "The Optick Artists of Chiangsu," in Jerome Ch'en and Nicholas Tarling, eds., *Studies in the Social History of China & Southeast Asia. Essays in Memory of Victor Purcell* (Cambridge: Cambridge University Press, 1970), 197–224.

14. Elvin, *The Retreat of the Elephants*. Documented from literary sources in chapters 3 and 4. The scientific part of the story still largely remains to be established.

15. For a sampling of evidence, see *The Retreat of the Elephants*, chapters 8 (Guizhou in the southwest) and 9 (Zunhua in the northeast), and pages 356–61, and also some of the poems in chapter 12 (439–44).

16. Terraces of course retained water, but their importance for the retention of soil on steeper slopes is noted for China by David Montgomery, *Dirt: The Erosion of Civilizations* (Berkeley: University of California Press, 2007), 24, 182; Wilhelm Wagner, *Die Chinesische Landwirtschaft* (Berlin: Parey, 1926), 186, gives soil retention as the primary purpose. That the peasants' conscious objective in terracing loess land was to conserve soil was the view of James Thorp, author of the chapter "Soils" in John Buck, ed., *Land Utilization in China* (Nanjing: University of Nanjing, 1937; New York: Paragon, 1964), 140. Citations are to the Paragon edition.

17. On origins of the system in the mid-twelfth century, see Sudô Yoshiyuki, *Sôdai keizai-shi kenkyû* [Studies on the economic history of the Song dynasty] (Tokyo: Tôkyô Daigaku shuppankai, 1962), 474–79. On the initial rates of land tax under the Ming, see Wada Sei, *Minshi shokka-shi yakuchû* [Annotated text and translation of the economic monograph of the *Ming History*] (Tokyo: Tôyô Bunko, 1957), 151; and on how the real burden was much worse by the sixteenth century, see Kiyomizu Taiji, *Mingdai tochi seido-shi kenkyû* [Researches on the history of the land system under the Ming] (Tokyo: Daian, 1968), 504–5. The background of the Southern Song system was various proposals and initiatives both to make taxes more equitable between families and between different areas, and to find a way to regularize and generalize the government's bureaucratic control over the farmed area. See Liu Daoyuan, *Liang-Song tianfu*

zhidu [The land-tax systems of the two Song dynasties] (Shanghai: Xin shengming shuju, 1932; Taibei: Shihuo chubanshe, 1978), esp. 108–12. See also Liang Gengyao, *Nan Song-de nongcun jingji* [The rural economy of the Southern Song] (Taibei: Lian-jing chuban shiye gongsi, 1984), ch. 5.

18. Parts of this story for a peripheral, and thus late-adapting, area are told in Peter Perdue, *Exhausting the Earth: State and Peasant in Hunan, 1500–1850* (Cambridge, MA: Harvard University Press), esp. 110–35, 234–52.

19. On these so-called "spring flowers" see Kawakatsu Mamoru, *Min-Shin Kônan nôgyô keizai-shi kenkyû* [Studies on the economic history of farming in Jiangnan un-der the Ming and Qing], ch. 2.

20. Ping-ti Ho [He Bingdi], *Studies on the Population of China, 1368–1953* (Cam-bridge, MA: Harvard University Press, 1959).

21. Bao Shichen, *Qimin sishu* [Four arts for the governance of the common people], in *Anwu sizhong* [Four works by Bao Shichen] 1846, rev. ed. 1851; (repr., Taibei: Wen-hai, 1966), 1661, 1702, 1704. Citations are to the 1966 volume.

22. A. Osborne, "Highlands and Lowlands: Economic and Ecological Interactions in the Lower Yangzi Region under the Qing," in M. Elvin and T-J. Liu, eds., *Sediments of Time: Environment and Society in Chinese History* (New York: Cambridge University Press, 1998), 203–30.

23. Human manure was of course used on fields in parts of Europe. For a case study on its rise and fall in Paris, see Sabine Barles, *L'invention des déchets urbains. France: 1790–1970* (Paris: Champ Vallon, 2005).

24. Elvin, "Introduction," in Elvin, H. Nishioka, K. Tamura, and J. Kwek, *Japanese Studies on the History of Water Control in China. A Selected Bibliography* (Canberra and Tokyo: Institute of Advanced Studies, Australian National University, and The Centre for East Asian Cultural Studies for UNESCO, 1994), 3–35; Elvin, "Water in China Past and Present: Competition and Cooperation," *Nouveaux Mondes* 12 (2003): 103–28.

25. Elvin, review of Morita Akira's *Studies in the History of Water-Management under the Qing, Ch'ing-Shih wen-t'i* 3, no. 3 (November 1975): 82–103. On Shanghai see also Elvin, "The Gentry Democracy in Shanghai, 1905–1914" (PhD dissertation, Cambridge University, 1968; microfilm available from Cambridge University Library), 18–19, 29–32.

26. Morita Akira, "Water Control in Zhedong during the Late Ming," trans. Mark Elvin and Tamura Keiko, *East Asian History* 2 (1991).

27. Shuili shuidian kexue yanjiuyuan and Wuhan shuili dianli xueyuan, eds., *Zhongguo shuili shigao* [Draft history of water control in China] 2nd of 3 planned vols. (Beijing: Shuili dianli chubanshe, 1979), 2–12.

28. Summaries of the history of the two systems may be found in Elvin, "Water in China Past and Present: Competition and Cooperation," 108–12; for the second see also Pierre-Étienne Will, "Clear Waters versus Muddy Waters: the Zheng-Bai Irriga-tion System of Shaanxi Province in the Late-Imperial Period," in Mark Elvin and Liu Ts'ui-jung, eds., *Sediments of Time: Environment and Society in Chinese History* (Cam-bridge and New York: Cambridge University Press, 1998).

29. Wagner, *Die Chinesische Landwirtschaft*, 238–39. The account in this section relies extensively on Wagner's, 178–260, and individual page references are mostly not

given. It has also been cross-checked against the earlier Franklin King, *Farmers of Forty Centuries, or Permanent Agriculture in China, Korea and Japan* (Madison: University of Wisconsin, 1911).

30. Nitrogen, phosphorus, and potassium (K).

31. Vaclav Smil, *The Bad Earth: Environmental Degradation in China* (Armonk, NY: M. E. Sharpe:, 1984), 74–77, who stresses a lack of adequate green manures to preserve soil structure.

32. Wagner, *Die Chinesische Landwirtschaft*, 208–9.

33. Thorp, "Soils," 143–44, 156 (emphasis added).

34. Cited in Wagner, *Die Chinesische Landwirtschaft*, 187.

35. Ronald M. Atlas and Richard Bartha, *Microbial Ecology: Fundamentals and Applications* (Menlo Park, CA: Benjamin Cummings, 1998), 472.

36. Cited in Wagner, *Die Chinesische Landwirtschaft*, 215.

37. Ping-ti Ho [He Bingdi], *Studies on the Population of China*, chapters 3 and 4 generally, and page 278 specifically, justifying the description of "steady" by allowing for a substantial if still not exactly quantifiable percentage of "statistical growth" due to better coverage in the earlier part of this period.

38. Thus a rate of a mere half a percent per year over a century will increase the starting population by 65 percent.

39. This figure, like the discussion that follows, is based on M. Elvin and J. Fox, "Marriages, Births, and Deaths in the Lower Yangzi Valley during the Later Eighteenth Century," in Clara Ho, ed., *Windows on the Chinese World: Reflections by Five Historians* (Lanham, MD: Lexington Books, 2009), and Elvin and Fox, "Local Demographic Variations in the Lower Yangzi Valley during Mid-Qing Times," in Thomas Hirzel and Nanny Kim, eds., *Metals, Monies, and Markets in Early Modern Societies: East Asian and Global Perspectives*, vol. 1: *Monies, Markets, and Finance in China and East Asia* (Berlin: Lit Verlag, 2008; US distributor: Transaction Publishers, Piscataway, NJ). Our data and scripts are available free on gis.sinica.edu.tw/QingDemography.

40. Elvin, "Le transfert des techniques en Chine avant la seconde guerre mondiale," *Nouveaux Mondes* 2 (1993).

41. See, for example, the chapter on deforestation by Kuo-tung Ch'en and that on hydropower by An-chi Tung in Elvin and Liu, *Sediments of Time*.

42. Shapiro, *Mao's War Against Nature*, 42–44.

43. Contrast, for example, the disastrous scenario sketched by He Bochuan in *China on the Edge: The Crisis of Ecology and Development* (San Francisco: China Books and Periodicals, 1991) and the relatively less doom-laden prognoses of many of the contributors to Richard Edmonds, ed., *Managing the Chinese Environment* (Oxford: Oxford University Press, 1998).

44. See Elvin, "El medio ambiente."

45. See the reconceptualization of this story in Charles Hall and John Day, Jr., "Revisiting the Limits to Growth after Peak Oil," *American Scientist* 97, no. 3 (May–June 2009).

46. *The Guardian*, March 12, 2009.

47. *Xinhua News Agency* November 21, 2008.

8

China's Energy Rise

Erica S. Downs

James Kynge, the former China bureau chief of the *Financial Times*, has observed that "the rise of a great nation will result in great appetites."[1] Indeed, one of the most visible manifestations of China's reemergence as a global power is the extraordinary surge in the country's energy demand during the first decade of the twenty-first century. Rapid economic growth and an unexpected increase in the energy intensity of the Chinese economy contributed to the near doubling of China's energy demand from 2001 to 2007, accounting for 50 percent of the growth in world energy demand over this period.[2] Although China's energy demand growth slowed in 2008 because of the economic downturn, China still provided three-quarters of the increase in global energy demand.[3] China, the world's second largest energy consumer, is projected to displace the United States as number one within the next decade.[4]

China's voracious appetite has heightened anxiety in Beijing that energy, which has literally fueled China's rise to international prominence, may derail its further ascent. To be sure, successive generations of Chinese leaders have regarded China's low level of energy resources per capita as a constraint on the country's development. However, China's "runaway" energy demand growth after the turn of the century hastened the realization among the Chinese leadership that if such unrestrained consumption of energy continues, then resource shortages and environmental degradation will jeopardize China's future prosperity. Consequently, a top priority for Beijing is to ensure that China's appetite for energy does not prove to be its downfall.

The effects of China's hunger for energy are also being felt far beyond China's borders. The growth and volatility of China's energy demand have made

China a major force in global energy markets. China's impact has been greatest on the oil market, where both the explosion in Chinese demand and the international expansion of China's national oil companies (NOCs) have captivated market watchers and policymakers around the globe. Moreover, China's heavy coal use is contributing to the warming of the planet. Additionally, China's worldwide search for energy is increasing its global activism and changing the geopolitics of energy.

This chapter assesses China's "energy rise." The first section examines China's dramatic energy demand growth since the turn of the century from both a Chinese historical and a global perspective. The second section discusses the global impacts of China's energy appetite, and the third section analyzes China's domestic and international responses to its energy demand surge.

CHINA'S ENERGY DEMAND SHOCK

At the turn of the century, neither Chinese nor international energy experts anticipated the surge in Chinese energy demand that was about to occur. After all, China had just accomplished the remarkable and unprecedented feat of quadrupling its GDP while only doubling its energy use between 1980 and 2000.[5] This achievement was remarkable because energy consumption usually grows more rapidly than GDP in early stages of economic development. It was also unprecedented because no other large developing country at a similar stage of economic development has experienced a decline in energy intensity, the amount of energy required to produce one unit of GDP. In fact, energy intensity tends to increase in the early stages of economic development because the infrastructure build out that occurs during industrialization and urbanization is an energy-intensive activity.

Why did the energy intensity of the Chinese economy fall from 1980 to 2000? First, China's energy intensity had nowhere to go but down. During the first three decades of the People's Republic, Beijing pursued a development strategy of rapid industrialization, pouring resources into heavy industries such as cement and steel.[6] The increase in heavy industry's share of economic output also increased the energy intensity of the Chinese economy because heavy industry requires much more energy to produce a unit of GDP than other economic sectors. Moreover, Western export controls that denied China access to advanced technologies and a command economy that provided state-owned enterprises (SOEs) with little motivation to control energy costs also contributed to the development of some of the world's most energy-intensive heavy industry in China.[7] As a result, there was an enormous amount of inefficiency. Second, reform and opening up gave SOEs incentives and tools to improve energy intensity. The introduction of the right to retain profits and limited competition focused attention on energy cost management. Additionally, falling trade barriers enabled Chinese SOEs to obtain energy efficient technologies.[8] Third, and most important, beginning in the 1980s, Beijing implemented a large-scale effort to reduce energy intensity. The main components included the allocation of capital to energy efficiency projects, the creation of a system of quotas for both the amount of energy provided to SOEs and the energy intensity of manufacturing processes, and the establishment of nationwide energy conservation service centers.[9]

Chinese planners intended to maintain the decoupling of energy and economic growth into the new millennium. They set the broad goal of once again quadrupling GDP while only doubling energy use over the period 2001–2020.[10] This objective reflected a mix of aspiration and optimism. Repeating this achievement would ensure that China, which had long equated self-sufficiency with security of supply, would continue to be able to meet most of its growing energy needs with domestic supplies. Moreover, the overcapacity in China's electric power sector and the overproduction in its coal sector at the turn of the century, the result of slower economic growth due to the Asian financial crisis, probably buoyed the confidence of Chinese planners that China's industrialization would continue to require less energy than the experience of other large countries would suggest. Indeed, both Chinese and foreign energy experts expected that China's energy demand would grow much more slowly than its GDP through 2020.[11]

Much to everyone's surprise, China's economic and energy growth "recoupled" at the start of the new millennium. Not only did China's economy grow faster than expected, but energy consumption rose even more rapidly than GDP. Between 1980 and 2000, GDP grew by 11 percent per year, while energy demand increased by only 4 percent per year. In contrast, between 2001 and 2007, the average annual growth rates for GDP and energy demand were 10.4 percent and 10.8 percent respectively (see figure 8.1).[12]

The principal driver of this rise in energy intensity was the same as that responsible for the growth in energy intensity from 1949 to 1980, an increase in the share of GDP provided by heavy industry.[13] However, as Trevor Houser and Daniel Rosen argue, the recent shift in the structure of the Chinese economy toward heavy industry differs from the one that occurred in the 1950s and 1960s in that it is the result of economic incentives rather than political dictate. The recent boom in investment in energy-intensive heavy industries occurred because those industries simply were more profitable than light industries. Cheap land offered by local governments competing against each other to grow GDP, energy prices that exclude environmental costs, and distortions in the Chinese financial system facilitated the stampede of inves-

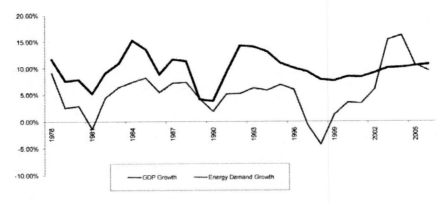

Figure 8.1.   China's GDP and Energy Demand Growth

tors into energy-intensive heavy industries. The expansion of the economy and the rise in energy intensity caused China's appetite for energy to surge. By 2007, China's energy demand reached the levels that some prominent Chinese and foreign institutions had earlier projected for 2020. In the six years between 2001 and 2007, China's demand for energy increased by 90 percent. About three-quarters of this growth came from coal, which meets more than two-thirds of China's energy requirements.[14]

China was ill-equipped to handle the demand shock. The strain placed on China's energy supply manifested itself in shortages of electricity, coal, and oil. The electric power sector was hardest hit. Shortages started to appear in 2002, with twelve of the country's thirty-one provinces reporting inadequate electricity supplies. By 2004, the number of provinces experiencing prolonged power shortages had increased to twenty-four and the national power deficit reached an estimated 30 gigawatts (GW), equivalent to the total installed capacity of Poland in that year.[15] Around the country, factories shifted production to off-peak hours, traffic lights went dark, and children did homework by candlelight.[16]

The power "famine" was partly rooted in the power "feast" of the late 1990s. In 1997, after decades of chronic electricity shortfalls, China suddenly found itself with a glut of power-generating capacity resulting from the economic slowdown associated with the Asian financial crisis. The supply overhang probably bolstered the confidence of China's planners in projections made during the late 1990s of single-digit electricity demand growth during the Tenth Five Year Plan period (2001–2005).[17] Indeed, when officials from the State Development and Planning Commission drafted the Five Year Plan in 2000, they expected electricity demand to increase by less than 7 percent per year.[18] Concerned about overcapacity, the State Council announced a three-year moratorium on the construction of new power plants in 1999. This effort to eliminate excess capacity soon came back to haunt them: electricity use increased at an annual rate of 14 percent from 2001 to 2005, more than twice as fast as China's planners had anticipated.

A "shortage" of coal, which accounts for about 70 percent of China's power generation mix, exacerbated the electricity crisis. Although China is rich in coal, transportation bottlenecks and price controls limited the delivery of coal to power plants. More than half of China's coal is moved by rail, and coal takes up more than half of freight capacity.[19] Rail, however, has long been the weak link of China's transportation. The shortage in rail cars made it difficult to transport coal from mines in the north to power plants in the south and east. Additionally, as discussed below, tightly controlled electricity prices that prevented power generators from passing on rising coal costs to consumers prompted some power plants to purchase less coal and produce less electricity.

China's power shortage also had a knock-on effect on the country's demand for oil. China's oil use soared in 2003 and 2004 as consumers who could not get the electricity they needed from the grid ran backup diesel generators and coal producers shipped more coal by road because of the lack of rail capacity. Over these two years, China's oil demand grew by 28 percent, rising from 5.3 million barrels per day (b/d) to 6.8 million b/d. Most of this growth was met with imports, which increased from 1.9 million b/d to 3.3 million b/d between 2002 and 2004.[20]

INTERNATIONAL IMPACTS

The extraordinary growth in China's energy demand from 2001 to 2007 was felt around the world as China emerged as a key source of growth and volatility in global energy markets. The surge in China's energy consumption also exacerbated the threat of global warming. In addition, China's efforts to access energy abroad are changing the geopolitics of energy.

Energy Markets

China's increasing reliance on global energy markets has made China a major factor at the margin in these markets. China accounted for almost 40 percent of the growth in world oil demand from 2001 to 2007, adding the equivalent of a medium-sized country like Argentina or Malaysia to global oil demand each year.[21] During this period, China became the world's second largest oil consumer after the United States (2003) and the world's third largest oil importer behind the United States and Japan (2004). China especially shocked the world oil market in 2004 with its 969,000 b/d demand growth, a 17 percent increase over the previous year.

China, the world's largest coal producer and consumer, was also the most important driver of world coal demand growth from 2001 to 2007. The country supplied 75 percent of the increase in global coal demand over this period.[22] Just as China stunned the world oil market with its oil demand surge in 2004, China surprised the world coal market with its faster than expected shift toward becoming a net coal importer on an annual basis. China was the world's second largest coal exporter as recently as 2003, the year its exports peaked at 93 million tons.[23] Since then, China's coal exports have dropped by more than half while its coal imports have climbed steadily upward. China was a net importer of coal for eleven out of the twenty-four months in 2007 and 2008.[24] This volatility in China's coal trade has created considerable uncertainty about how much coal other countries can buy from or sell to China.

China is likely to remain a large force on world energy markets. The International Energy Agency (IEA) projects that China will remain the largest source of growth in world oil and coal demand through 2030. China alone is expected to account for more than 40 percent of the rise in world oil demand from 2007 to 2030 and two-thirds of the increase in world coal demand from 2006 to 2030.[25]

Environment

The most widespread impact of China's appetite for energy on the global environment is its contribution to the buildup of carbon dioxide (CO_2) in the atmosphere, the likely consequences of which include sea-level rise, more intense extreme weather events, and increased droughts and floods.[26] The primary source of China's CO_2 emissions is the combustion of coal. China's faster than expected energy demand growth after 2000 caused a faster than expected rise in China's CO_2 emissions. Indeed, China accounted for more than half of the increase in the world's energy-related CO_2 emissions from 2000 to 2006. China may have surpassed the United States to become the world's largest CO_2 emitter in 2007. However, China's per capita energy-related CO_2 emissions are less than one-quarter of those of the United States. According to the IEA, China will account for nearly half of the growth in the world's energy-related CO_2 emissions during the period 2006–2030.

China's emergence as the world's top CO_2 emitter and the projected dramatic increase in its emissions has made it, along with the United States, a pivotal actor in international efforts to stop climate change. China and the United States together are responsible for 40 percent of the greenhouse gases produced each year. Consequently, any successful international effort to address climate change requires both China and the United States to transition to low-carbon economies. If either fails to do so, then any measures adopted by other countries to control greenhouse gas emissions will fall short of preventing the amount of carbon dioxide in the atmosphere from reaching disastrous levels.[27]

Geopolitics

China's "energy rise" is reshaping the geopolitical landscape. First, China's appetite for energy is transforming China into a global power.[28] China's quest for energy has increased its presence around the world, notably in Africa, Latin America, and the Middle East. Energy investments in Central Asia have also helped expand China's footprint in its own backyard.

Second, foreign energy investments have given China a stake in the politics of host countries. When China's NOCs began operating abroad, there was an expectation in China that business and politics could be kept separate, as then vice foreign minister Zhou Wenzhong stated in 2004 in his oft-quoted remark about China's approach to Sudan.[29] Since then, Beijing and China's NOCs have learned that this is easier said than done because foreign companies—and their governments—often become entangled in political developments in host countries. Indeed, Chinese oil workers have been kidnapped or killed by rebel groups in Eritrea, Nigeria, and Sudan seeking to advance political objectives. In addition, international consternation has compelled China to play a more active role in resolving the conflict in the Darfur region of Sudan. China's status as the biggest foreign investor in Sudan's oil industry and a major buyer of Sudanese crude give China influence over Sudan. Under considerable international pressure, Beijing used that influence to play a critical role in convincing Khartoum to allow a UN–African Union hybrid peacekeeping force to deploy to Darfur.[30] China may find itself becoming even more involved in Sudanese politics to keep peace between the north and south to protect substantial Chinese oil investments in the border region.[31]

Third, major energy exporters have sought to exploit China's energy demand to attain political objectives. Saudi Arabia is a success story.[32] Since the mid-1990s, Riyadh has moved to diversify its major power relationships away from the United States in response to domestic criticism of Riyadh's close ties to Washington based on anger over America's support for Israel vis-à-vis Palestine and images of Iraqi children starving because of UN sanctions. Energy ties have strengthened Saudi Arabia's relationship with China. Saudi Arabia has been China's top crude oil supplier since 2001. Additionally, Saudi Aramco and Sinopec are building a refinery in Fujian that will run Saudi crude, providing Saudi Arabia with security of demand and China with security of supply. Riyadh's closer ties to Beijing have helped Saudi Arabia counter criticism that it is a lackey of the United States and demonstrate that it is an important player in the world.

In contrast, Iran has been less successful in capitalizing on China's energy demand to advance political goals. Tehran has been courting China's NOCs to undermine the US-led international effort to curb Iran's nuclear program, hoping for much-needed capital for the development of its oil and gas resources and a protector on the UN Security Council. As international oil companies have stalled projects in Iran under pressure from home governments, the Islamic Republic has stepped up negotiations with Chinese firms, which signed three major contracts between December 2007 and June 2009. However, Tehran has not yet received the level of diplomatic support that it desires.[33] Much to Tehran's dismay, Beijing has supported all the resolutions against Iran in the UN Security Council (albeit after watering down the content). Although Iran is attractive to China's NOCs, Beijing is torn between its opposition to Iran developing nuclear weapons and its desire to access its energy resources.

Fourth, China's demand for energy is also reshaping geopolitical relations in Eurasia, strengthening ties between China and energy-rich states in Central Asia at Russia's expense. Although China and Russia have all the ingredients for the perfect energy "marriage" (Russia is a large energy producer and China is a large energy consumer and they share a long border), they have not yet built the cross-border infrastructure necessary to substantially expand their energy trade. Russia has also prevented China's NOCs from establishing a substantial presence in its energy sector. In contrast, China National Petroleum Corporation (CNPC) has achieved a dominant position in Kazakhstan and Turkmenistan. Furthermore, oil and natural gas pipelines from these countries are binding them more closely to China and eroding Russia's influence over them.[34] The natural gas pipeline currently under construction from Turkmenistan to China via Uzbekistan and Kazakhstan, in particular, is reaffirming the autonomy of these states from Russia by providing them with a non-Russian outlet for their natural gas and greater bargaining power in gas price negotiations with Russia. Moscow has had enormous influence over the economic fortunes of those states because most of their export pipelines run north, leaving them with little choice but to sell gas to Russia at low prices. However, the Turkmenistan-China pipeline has reportedly already yielded the supplying countries higher prices for the gas they sell to Russia.[35]

Fifth, China's growing reliance on foreign oil is increasing Chinese interest in the Indian Ocean. About three-quarters of China's oil imports pass through the Indian Ocean and the Strait of Malacca. Chinese anxieties about the security of these imports is reflected in the substantial attention paid by Chinese analysts to Hu Jintao's reported reference to China's "Malacca Dilemma" during the November 2003 Economic Work Conference.[36] Even if Hu never uttered these words, Beijing's concern about the vulnerability of China's oil supplies to accidents, piracy, and interdiction by various modern navies is indicated by both the public policy debates over how to enhance the safety of China's seaborne oil imports and China's pursuit of multiple transnational oil pipelines, including one from Myanmar. These words and actions have prompted some international commentators to speculate that China's demand for oil is contributing to the emergence of the "great game" in the Indian Ocean.[37]

China's energy insecurities, however, are unlikely to result in a major Chinese naval presence in the Indian Ocean anytime soon.[38] First, the People's Liberation Army Navy (PLAN) does not possess the enormous force needed to protect Chinese oil shipments in the Indian Ocean. Second, the top strategic priority of the PLAN is to secure China's coastal waters. Projecting power to the Indian Ocean is a secondary objective. Third, even if the PLAN had the capabilities and the intention to guard China's seaborne oil imports it would be difficult for it to do so because only about 10 percent of China's oil imports are carried by Chinese-flagged tankers. Fourth, India is likely to oppose a substantial Chinese naval presence in the Indian Ocean and geography dictates that the Indian navy will probably enjoy superiority over the PLAN in its ocean.

CHINA'S RESPONSE

China's energy demand surge and the international attention it garnered have heightened anxieties that energy would become an even more serious constraint on China's continued economic rise than Beijing had previously feared. The "runaway" demand growth of the early years of the twenty-first century rendered obsolete the goal of quadrupling GDP while only doubling energy use and threatened to make just quadrupling GDP difficult. Chinese officials and energy experts warned that if energy demand continued to grow faster than GDP then China's objective of creating an affluent society (*xiaokang shehui* 小康社会)—which includes raising living standards and providing people with clean air and water—by 2020 would be at risk.[39] Energy consumption on such a large scale would require so much coal that global production and transportation would be strained to supply it. The use of such vast amounts of coal also would severely damage the environment.[40]

China's energy demand growth in 2001–2007 also reaffirmed the contention of some Chinese officials and energy experts—dating back to the 1980s—that China will not be able to follow the "old road" to industrialization based on high fossil fuel consumption and "polluting first, cleaning up later" taken by the United States and other developed countries. There is simply not enough fossil fuel in the world for China's 1.3 billion people to live like Americans. This realization reignited discussion in Beijing about the need to forge a new path to industrialization that is resource conserving and environmentally friendly.[41]

The demand shock impacted the Chinese government efforts at home and abroad to prevent energy from derailing the country's economic development. Domestically, Beijing has broadened its approach to energy security to emphasize conservation and environmental protection, attempted to strengthen the country's energy institutions, and took steps toward getting energy prices right. Internationally, Beijing has increased efforts already under way to secure energy and sought to reassure other countries that China's appetite for energy is not a threat to their well-being.

New Approach to Energy Security

Ensuring access to oil was Beijing's paramount energy security concern for the first five decades of the People's Republic. During the 1950s and early 1960s, the Western trade embargo made China dependent on the Soviet Union for all of the refined products that fueled the Chinese military.[42] The reduction in Soviet oil exports to China after the Sino-Soviet split in 1960 forced China to cut back on its military activities at a time when China's leaders perceived the international environment to be highly threatening.[43] This unhappy experience with foreign oil dependence strengthened the Chinese leadership's convictions that oil self-sufficiency was necessary for national survival and China's emergence as a major power. Fortunately for China, the discovery of the Daqing oil field in 1959 made the dream of oil independence a reality. Over the next two decades China became one of the largest oil exporters in East Asia, and even embarked on a strategy of "petroleum export-led growth" in the early 1970s, which aimed to use oil exports to purchase foreign technology and equipment needed for industrialization. However, China's oil fields failed to pump enough oil to "buy" modernization and satisfy growing domestic demand. In 1993, China shifted to a net importer of oil, ending nearly three decades of self-sufficiency and focusing Chinese energy security debates on identifying and mitigating the vulnerabilities associated with dependence on foreign oil.

Despite Beijing's long-standing preoccupation with imported oil as the Achilles' heel of China's energy security, most of the country's energy crises, including that of 2002–2005, have resulted from actions taken by the Chinese government, not foreign ones, and have involved widespread shortages of electric power rather than oil. The brownouts that China suffered in the early 2000s originated, as mentioned above, with the failure of China's economic planners not only to anticipate the surge in electricity demand that occurred after the turn of the millennium but also their imposition of a moratorium on the construction of new power plants. The fact that the country's worst energy crisis in two decades was entirely of domestic origin helped to broaden the focus of China's energy security concerns beyond foreign oil dependence. Specifically, the energy shortages helped expose the limits of the "growth at any cost" model of economic development and forged a consensus among the senior Chinese leadership that curbing the country's voracious appetite for energy was necessary to meet the material and environmental needs of future generations.

The shift in the Chinese leadership's thinking about China's energy security is reflected in the Eleventh Five Year Plan for 2006–2010, which enshrines "conserving energy and reducing emissions" (*jie neng mian pai* 节能减排) as the guiding principle for China's economic development. The document lays out a blueprint for ensuring the sustainability of economic growth over the long term.[44] The pièce de résistance is a highly ambitious target for reducing the energy intensity of the economy. Specifically, the plan calls for reducing energy consumption per unit GDP by 20 percent from 2005 to 2010, which implies an annual decrease of 4 percent.

China has made substantial progress toward achieving its energy intensity reduction goal. The decrease in energy consumption per unit GDP was 1.79 percent in 2006, 4.04 percent in 2007, and 4.59 percent in 2008; China used 10.4 percent less energy per unit GDP in 2008 than in 2005.[45] Two of the most important measures that contributed to the decrease in energy consumption per unit GDP are the Ten Key Projects for Energy Conservation, which range from coal-fired boiler renovation to the creation of an energy conservation and monitoring technical services system, and the Top 1,000 Energy Consuming Enterprises Program, which set energy consumption targets for the one thousand largest firms that account for about one-third of China's total energy consumption and about one-half of industrial energy consumption.[46] Other initiatives include the strengthening of appliance standards, the adoption of vehicle fuel efficiency standards, and the closure of small, inefficient industrial and power plants.

Beijing has also set ambitious mandates for clean energy use. On January 1, 2006, two targets for 2020 went into effect: increasing the share of renewable energy in primary energy consumption to 15 percent and raising the share of renewable energy used in electricity generation to 20 percent. Most of this growth will come from large hydropower projects, with the country's hydropower capacity expected to nearly double between 2006 and 2020. The Chinese government also has set the objective of increasing China's nuclear power generating capacity to 40 gigawatts (GW) by 2020, up from 7 GW in 2006, which would slightly increase the share of electricity produced by nuclear power from 2 percent to 2–4 percent. Although China is unlikely to meet its nuclear target by 2020 because of the long construction times and supply chain bottlenecks, the country should be able to install 40 GW of nuclear power generation capacity after 2020. There are, however, currently limits to the extent to which China will be able to substitute cleaner forms of energy for coal over the longer term because of problems of scale.

Efforts to Strengthen Energy Institutions

China's energy demand surge and the strains it put on China's energy supply highlighted the mismatch between China's energy challenges and the ability of the country's energy institutions to handle them. China's energy sector is characterized by "strong firms and weak government" (*qiang qiye ruo zhengfu* 强企业弱政府), with "strong" and "weak" referring to capacity.[47] The central government's energy bureaucracy is weak because responsibility for energy is splintered among many agencies—some of which are understaffed, underfunded, and politically weak—and poor coordination among them impedes decision making and implementation. In contrast, China's state-owned energy firms are strong because they have the institutional coherence, resources, expertise, and political clout to shape the development of China's energy sector. As a result, energy governance is undermined by both a lack of state capacity and the activities of China's energy firms, whose corporate interests do not always align with national ones.[48]

China's fractured energy bureaucracy has limited Beijing's ability to manage the energy sector. There is no single institution, such as a Ministry of Energy, with the authority to coordinate the interests of the various stakeholders. For example, a fuel tax approved by the National People's Congress in 1999 was not implemented until a decade later, in large part because of conflicts of interest. One key dispute involved the Ministries of Transportation and Finance and the State Administration of Taxation, which deadlocked over which agency should take responsibility for the toll collectors who were expected to lose their jobs when the national fuel tax replaced local road fees.[49] Similarly, turf battles among government agencies have resulted in energy laws that fail to specify the agencies responsible for the content of those laws. The use of the term "relevant departments" (*youguan bumen* 有关部门) can delay or prevent implementation by allowing disputes over who is in charge to continue or by making it difficult for the agency in charge, once selected, to acquire the resources it needs because its role as the implementing agency is not defined in the law.[50]

Beijing's ability to handle the country's energy challenges is also hampered by the fact that it is managing the energy sector with a skeleton crew. China's

National Energy Administration has just 112 people. In comparison, the US Department of Energy has about 4,000 people dedicated to energy-policy-related matters.[51] Chinese energy officials are so overwhelmed by the large number of projects requiring their approval that they have insufficient time to devote to broader issues, such as policy analysis and formulation.[52] The State Commission for Public Sector Reform—the agency that determines the functions, internal structure, and staff quotas for government institutions—has probably resisted calls for more personnel out of concern that other government bodies would press for more manpower, limiting Beijing's attempts to streamline the bureaucracy.

The policy paralysis that often plagues the energy bureaucracy stands in sharp contrast to the activism of the state-owned energy firms. These companies are relatively powerful actors due to their full and vice ministerial ranking, membership of top executives in the Central Committee of the Chinese Communist Party, industry expertise, internationally listed subsidiaries, and profitability.[53] More often than not, energy firms initiate projects that are later embraced by Beijing, such as the west-east natural gas pipeline and the acquisition of foreign energy assets. The energy firms also occasionally advance corporate interests at the expense of national ones. For example, oil and power generating companies have periodically cut back supplies to Chinese consumers to pressure the government to raise the state-set prices for refined products and electricity when those prices have lagged far behind the market prices for crude oil and coal.

Despite widespread awareness of the inadequacy of China's energy institutions, attempts to strengthen them since the turn of the century have been rather timid. Powerful vested interests that favor the status quo have ensured that calls for the establishment of a ministry of energy have gone unanswered. The National Development Research Council (NDRC) and the state-owned energy companies are two of the main sources of opposition. The NDRC fears the establishment of such a ministry would deprive NDRC of a substantial portion of its portfolio and important tools of macroeconomic control.[54] The energy firms worry a ministry of energy might become another political master that would limit their direct access to China's top leaders.[55] Such opposition and other conflicts of interest have repeatedly prevented China's consensus-driven government from taking bolder steps to reform the country's energy bureaucracy.

Working toward Getting Prices Right

The extraordinary growth in China's energy demand also resulted in lots of talk and some action on the issue of further liberalizing energy prices. State-set

prices for oil products and electricity have undermined China's energy security by spurring state-owned energy companies to prioritize protecting their
bottom lines over supplying Chinese consumers. China's energy prices also
are not compatible with promoting resource conservation and environmental
protection.

The gap between the market-determined price for crude oil and the state-
set prices for refined products lies at the heart of the oil shortages that plagued
China in recent years.[56] Domestic diesel and gasoline that failed to keep pace
with the increase in international crude oil prices caused CNPC and Sinopec
to hemorrhage billions of dollars per year from their refining operations because they could not pass rising crude costs to consumers. The companies
reduced supplies to the domestic market to limit losses and pressure the government to raise oil product prices by exporting refined products or closing
refineries for maintenance resulting in widespread shortages at the pump.[57]

Beijing responded to the oil shortages with a series of stopgap measures. As
world oil prices climbed to a high of $147 per barrel in July 2008, the govern-
ment periodically raised oil product prices to narrow the gap between domestic retail and international crude prices and handed out multi-billion-dollar
subsidies to Sinopec, the country's largest refiner. In January 2009, the NDRC
implemented a new refined product pricing regime, which, according to the
IEA, moves a step closer to aligning domestic prices with international benchmarks but does not closely resemble more conventional, market-based mechanisms.[58] Beijing also instituted an increase in fuel consumption taxes, which
is targeted at curbing oil demand growth and buffering domestic retail prices
from volatility in global crude prices.[59]

Just as the misalignment between crude oil and refined product prices resulted in oil shortages, the gap between the market-determined price for coal
and state-set prices for electricity contributed to the brownouts that have
roiled China since 2002. Until that year, coal companies sold coal to power
generators at a price well below cost determined by guideline price bands set
by the NDRC. In 2002, Beijing abolished the guidance prices for "power coal"
but left state-set electricity prices unchanged. At the annual coal procurement
conference in December 2002, coal and power producers failed to reach an
agreement on price. The coal companies sought to recoup years of losses by
demanding substantially higher prices, while the power companies resisted
price increases they wouldn't be able to absorb. About 150 million tons of coal
was not contracted for, which exacerbated the electricity shortages caused by
the government's failure to anticipate the surge in electricity demand and to
approve new power plant construction.[60]

The electricity crisis prompted Beijing to implement a new pricing mechanism under which power generators may pass 70 percent of coal price increases

to consumers.[61] However, this change has not prevented the gap between power coal and electricity prices from undermining the adequacy and reliability of China's electricity supplies. The ongoing price dispute between China's coal and power firms lay behind the brownouts that seventeen provinces suffered during the blizzard of January 2008. Chinese officials were quick to blame the weather, arguing that heavy snow prevented rail deliveries of coal to power generators.[62] However, the main reason transportation bottlenecks resulted in supply cutbacks was because power generators unable to pass rising coal costs to consumers had maintained dangerously low coal stocks.[63]

In addition to contributing to shortages, China's energy prices, especially for coal, are at odds with the leadership's objective of creating a resource-conserving and environmentally friendly society. Although the price of coal is market determined, it does not reflect the environmental and social costs associated with its mining, transportation, and consumption. One recent study estimates that in 2007 alone the total external costs of coal equaled 7.1 percent of China's GDP for that year.[64]

Although China's leaders recognize China's energy prices are incompatible with sustaining rapid economic growth over the longer term, they have moved slowly to reform energy prices. First, pricing power is an important tool of macroeconomic control; Beijing has been reluctant to raise prices in recent years because of fears about inflation.[65] Second, China's leaders are concerned about the impact of higher prices on certain constituencies, especially farmers and taxi drivers, who have been quick to protest increases at the pump.[66] Third, firms in energy-intensive heavy industries, which are huge consumers of electricity, successfully lobby local and provincial officials for rates that keep their businesses profitable.[67]

Enhance Security of Energy Imports

China's energy demand surge has increased China's reliance on energy imports and accelerated efforts already under way to enhance the security of China's foreign energy supplies. Between 2001 and 2007, China's dependence on imported energy expanded from 6 percent to 11 percent.[68] In 2007 alone, China's net energy imports were almost as much as the total primary energy consumption of the United Kingdom.[69] The IEA projects that by 2030, China's oil imports will reach 12.5 million barrels per day and supply 75 percent of total oil consumption (see figure 8.2).[70]

China's reliance on imported natural gas and coal is also expected to increase. China began importing liquefied natural gas (LNG) in 2006, and the IEA projects the country's imports of natural gas will grow from 1 billion cubic meters (bcm) in 2006 to 106 bcm in 2030, increasing China's dependence on natural gas

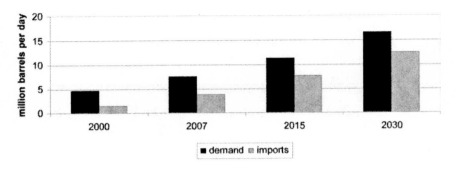

Figure 8.2.   China's Oil Demand and Imports

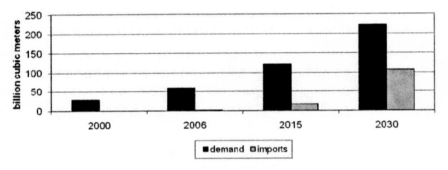

Figure 8.3.   China's Natural Gas Demand and Imports

imports from about 2 percent to almost 50 percent (see figure 8.3). China is also expected to become a net coal importer on an annual basis by 2015, although imports will only meet 3 percent of China's coal demand by 2030.[71]

Of these three fossil fuels, Beijing is most concerned about China's rising oil imports. Not only is oil the fuel for which China's import dependence is highest, but there currently is no alternative to oil in the transportation sector that is as efficient and cost-effective. While some motor vehicles can run on natural gas and electricity, there is no substitute for jet fuel for aircraft, which makes access to oil a national security issue.

The rapid growth in China's oil imports reinforced efforts to enhance supply security through the diversification of oil suppliers and transport routes. China wants to expand the number of countries from which China imports oil and to decrease dependence on the Middle East. Beijing also seeks to reduce China's reliance on the sea lines of communication (SLOCs) —through which more than 85 percent of the country's crude oil imports travel—because of their vulnerability to disruption on the high seas by various modern navies.[72]

Since China became a net oil importer in 1993, the Chinese government and oil companies have heeded the advice of Winston Churchill that "safety and certainty in oil lies in variety and variety alone."[73] China has achieved considerable success in diversifying the sources of its oil imports. In 1995 the Middle East and the Asia Pacific regions supplied almost 90 percent of China's oil imports, with Indonesia alone accounting for 31 percent. Over the past decade, the Middle East's portion of China's oil imports has hovered just below 50 percent. At the same time, growth in the share of supplies from Africa and Russia has offset a dramatic decline in the contribution of the Asia Pacific region. In 2007, the Middle East and Africa accounted for three-quarters of China's crude imports. Russia, China's fourth largest supplier of crude oil, provided 9 percent (see figures 8.4 and 8.5).

Beijing also wants to diversify China's oil import routes away from the SLOCs and especially the Strait of Malacca, one of the world's most important oil transit chokepoints.[74] Almost 80 percent of China's crude oil imports pass through this strait, and Chinese leaders are concerned about the supply disruption risks posed by piracy, tanker congestion, terrorism, and the navies of major powers.[75] Pipelines from Kazakhstan and Russia occupy a prominent place in China's diversification plans because these two countries are located outside of the Persian Gulf region and their exports ship overland to China. Russia and Kazakhstan supplied China with 412,000 b/d of oil in 2007, 13 percent of China's crude oil imports.[76] China wants to increase this

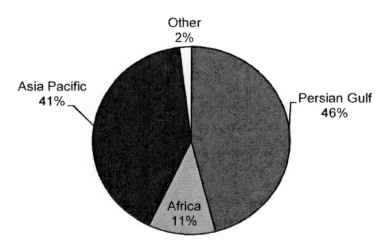

Figure 8.4.   China's Crude Oil Imports by Region, 1995

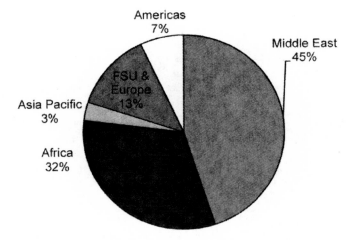

Figure 8.5.   China's Crude Oil Imports by Region, 2007

amount through two pipeline projects: a 400,000-b/d pipeline from western Kazakhstan to western China, which is being built in stages, with the eastern-most leg to the Chinese border operational, and a proposed 300,000-b/d pipeline spur to the Chinese border from the East Siberia Pacific Ocean pipeline, which is also being built in stages. China National Petroleum Corporation (CNPC) has also planned a 400,000 b/d oil pipeline from the Burmese oil port of Sittwe to Kunming and Chongqing. Although the pipeline from Burma will not reduce China's dependence on seaborne oil imports, it will provide oil tankers bound for China with an alternative to the Strait of Malacca. If all three pipelines are built and operated at design capacity, the combined throughput of 1.1 million b/d would constitute 14 percent of China's projected oil imports of 7.7 million b/d in 2015 and 9 percent of China's projected oil imports of 12.5 million b/d in 2030.[77]

The jump in China's oil demand and imports also spurred China's NOCs to acquire more exploration and production assets abroad.[78] China's oil firms have a political mandate to enhance China's energy security that includes investing in foreign oil fields.[79] There has been a fairly widespread perception within Beijing that oil pumped by China's NOCs provides a more secure supply of oil than purchases made on the international market. This idea is rooted in skepticism of the view of Western oil industry analysts that the world market will always make oil available to the highest bidder. In the late 1990s, some Chinese energy officials argued that China might one day find itself in a situation where China has money to buy oil but none is available on the international market because of war or other political turmoil.[80] In such a situation, they continued, Beijing could order China's NOCs to send their foreign oil production back to China. Despite these concerns, it is difficult to imagine a scenario in which China has money but no oil to purchase because the world is filled with buyers and sellers. Moreover, China's NOCs are unlikely to ever pump enough oil abroad to cover China's oil import requirements because more than three-quarters of the world's oil reserves are in countries that do not permit foreign equity participation.

Beijing's energy security concerns complement the strong commercial drivers that are propelling China's NOCs to expand their international portfolios. First, China's NOCs, like all other oil companies, need to continuously acquire new oil and natural gas reserves to replace what they produce, and the opportunities to do so are often more attractive abroad than at home. Second, exploration and production historically have been the most profitable sector of the oil business, and this is especially true for China's NOCs, whose refining operations have hemorrhaged billions of dollars in recent years due to rising crude costs and state-set prices for diesel and gasoline. Moreover, the compensation and future career prospects of Chinese oil executives, some of whom aspire to high-ranking positions in the Chinese Communist Party, depend in large part on the profitability of their firms. Third, if China's NOCs want to become world-class companies, and be internationally competitive, they must compete internationally. These factors have propelled China's NOCs to take advantage of the economic downturn to acquire overseas assets that might otherwise not have been available to them.

In 2007, China's NOCs pumped a combined total of 780,000 b/d of liquids abroad, an amount equal to 19 percent of China's oil imports and less than 1 percent of global oil production in that year.[81] Although China's NOCs are invested in upstream projects in more than two dozen countries, most of these assets have done little to substantially bolster their overseas output. The foreign production of China's NOCs is concentrated in two countries, Kazakhstan and Sudan, which accounted for 59 percent of the NOCs' foreign oil production in 2007.

Diplomatic Reassurance

China's extraordinary energy demand growth has prompted China's leaders to include energy in their diplomatic reassurance strategy. One of China's foreign policy priorities is to reassure other countries that China's economic growth and military modernization do not pose a threat to their economic and security interests.[82] International anxiety about China's increasing demand for energy raised concerns in Beijing that other countries, notably the United States, view China as a threat to their energy and environmental security.

Uncomfortable with being blamed for higher prices at the pump and concerned that unease in the United States and other major powers about China's
energy appetite might prompt those states to attempt to derail China's economic growth and continued emergence as a global power, China's leaders set
out to persuade the rest of the world that China is a responsible major power
with respect to global energy and environmental security.[83]

Beijing's efforts to reassure other countries about China's burgeoning appetite first took aim at disproving what Chinese officials refer to as the "China
energy threat theory," a corollary of the "China threat theory." While the
China threat theory holds that an increasingly powerful China is likely to
destabilize the international system, the China energy threat theory maintains
that China's increasing appetite for energy is likely to destabilize world energy
markets.[84] The China energy threat theory gained currency in Beijing after the
unexpected surge in Chinese oil demand in 2004 heralded China's arrival as a
major factor in the world oil market, subjecting the country to increased international scrutiny. After China's CO_2 emissions replaced China's oil demand
as the focal point of global anxieties about China's energy appetite, Chinese
officials turned their attention to refuting the China environmental threat
theory, which holds that China is not doing enough to slow global warming.
Ma Kai, the minister in charge of the NDRC from 2003 to 2008, spearheaded
both efforts.

Nobody likes to be blamed for the world's problems. This is especially true
for China when the issues are energy consumption and CO_2 emissions and
the fingers being pointed belong to the industrialized world. Chinese officials
are irritated by even mere insinuations from industrialized countries that
China and other developing countries, which contain the majority of the
world's population, should consume less energy to ensure there are enough
resources to support the high-energy-consumption lifestyles of those who
industrialized first. Moreover, it undoubtedly vexes Beijing to have China's
energy appetite criticized by countries that consume energy-intensive goods
made in China.[85] As Ma observes, "A considerable amount of the increase in
China's energy consumption is a 'substitute' for energy consumption in other
countries and regions."[86]

Similarly, Beijing is irritated by demands from the industrialized countries,
especially the United States, for China to do more to control its CO_2 emissions, especially through the adoption of hard targets for emissions for several
reasons. First, China's cumulative historical emissions of carbon dioxide,
which remains in the atmosphere for a hundred years, are only a small frac-
tion of those of the United States, which has emitted more than any other
country. Second, China's per capita emissions are very low, less than one-
quarter of the United States. Third, the industrialized countries have already

completed the high-emissions stage of industrialization while China has not. Fourth, many in China are irked by people in industrialized countries who both enjoy the energy-intensive and high-emissions products manufactured in China and criticize China for not doing more to control its emissions.[87] That 15–25 percent of China's emissions are created by Chinese exports has prompted Beijing to call for importing countries to bear responsibility for emissions generated in exporting countries.[88]

The visceral reaction of Chinese officials to the China energy threat theory and the China environmental threat theory stems from concerns that if other countries view China's energy consumption as a threat to their well-being, then those countries might seek to deny China the energy needed to fuel its continued rise to international prominence. The United States is the country China is most worried about. American unease with China's reemergence as a global power and anxiety about China's rising energy demand and the international expansion of China's NOCs has aroused suspicions in China that the United States is attempting to weaken China by making it difficult for China to access energy abroad.[89] Many in China also suspect that demands for China to adopt more aggressive measures to limit its emissions growth, when China is still in the high-emissions stage of industrialization, are a tool to slow China's economic development.[90]

China's leaders have used high-profile summits to reassure the rest of the world about China's growing energy demand. For example, during the G8 meeting in Russia in 2006, Hu Jintao discussed China's high level of energy self-sufficiency and ambitious plans to reduce the energy intensity of China's economic growth (to allay fears that China is gobbling up the word's energy resources), low per capita energy consumption (to subtly point out that the Chinese are not the world's energy gluttons), and the view that energy security is a global problem requiring a global solution (to address concerns that China views energy as the object of a zero-sum game between countries).[91] Two years later, at the global oil summit convened in Jeddah, Saudi Arabia, Hu's heir apparent, Xi Jinping, delivered a similar message.[92]

CONCLUSION

The extraordinary growth in China's appetite for energy in the early 2000s shocked China and the rest of the world. For China, the unexpected demand surge was a reminder that energy is a vulnerability that could jeopardize the country's continued economic rise. China's leaders worried that if the energy consumption binge of the early 2000s continued, then they would not achieve their long-term development of raising the living standards of the Chinese people and providing them with a healthy natural environment. For the rest of the world, China's seemingly insatiable hunger for energy was viewed as a sign of strength. International observers regarded the sudden and far-reaching impact of China's extraordinary energy demand growth on energy markets, the global environment, and geopolitics as a sign not only of China's continuing reemergence as a major power but perhaps also of that ascent occurring much more rapidly than previously expected.

The concerns voiced abroad, especially in the United States, about the impact of China's energy appetite on their ability to meet their energy and environmental requirements and foreign policy objectives heightened Chinese fears in turn that international anxiety about China's energy demand would make it more difficult for China to sustain rapid economic growth over the long term. As a result, China's efforts to ensure that energy does not undermine its continued economic rise have domestic and international dimensions. Domestically, the Chinese government is attempting to forge a path to industrialization that the world's energy resources and natural environment can support. Internationally, Beijing is trying to secure energy supplies and reassure the rest of the world that the threats associated with China's energy appetite have been greatly exaggerated in order to ensure that China has continued access to the energy it needs from abroad and is not pressured to adopt CO_2 emissions caps that would jeopardize future economic growth.

Beijing has achieved mixed results in its responses to China's energy demand surge at home and abroad. Domestically, not only have China's leaders made "conserving energy and reducing emissions" the new mantra guiding the country's economic development, but they have supported their words with aggressive measures to reduce the energy intensity of the Chinese economy and to substantially expand the role of renewable energy and nuclear power in the country's energy mix, both of which are also key components of China's climate change policy. However, these efforts have been hampered by slow movement on liberalizing energy prices and strengthening energy institutions. Internationally, China has made progress in diversifying its oil suppliers and import routes. China's NOCs have also secured a modest international upstream presence, although the oil they pump abroad is unlikely to enhance the security of China's oil supply. In terms of diplomatic reassurance, Beijing's attempts to convince other countries that China's energy appetite is not a threat have sometimes fallen on deaf ears. In some cases, this is because of genuine concerns about the impact of China's energy demand on planet earth. In other cases, it is because voicing alarm over China's energy consumption and emissions has been a useful way for some countries, notably the United States in the recent past, to divert attention from their own lackluster records of reducing energy demand and CO_2 emissions. China's efforts to ensure that its appetite for energy does not constrain its continued rise to international prominence will continue to be closely watched by other countries because China's energy challenges are also their own.

NOTES

1. James Kynge, *China Shakes the World* (Boston and New York: Mariner Books, 2006), 132.

2. *BP Statistical Review of World Energy*, June 2008, 40.

3. *BP Statistical Review of World Energy*, June 2009, 40.

4. International Energy Agency (IEA), *World Energy Outlook 2008* (Paris: OECD/ IEA, 2008), 512, 530; US Energy Information Administration, *International Energy Outlook 2008* (Washington, DC: Energy Information Administration, September 2008), 103, www.eia.doe.gov/oiaf/ieo/pdf/0484(2008).pdf.

5. This paragraph is based on Jiang Lin, Nan Zhou, Mark D. Levine, and David Fridley, "Achieving China's Target for Energy Intensity Reduction in 2010: An Exploration of Recent Trends and Possible Future Scenarios," Ernest Orlando Lawrence Berkeley National Laboratory, LBNL-61800, December 2006, 2, china.lbl.gov/files/ china.files/lbnl_61800.pdf.

6. Barry Naughton, *The Chinese Economy: Transitions and Growth* (Cambridge, MA: MIT Press, 2007); Daniel H. Rosen and Trevor Houser, "China Energy: A Guide for the Perplexed," Peterson Institute for International Economics, May 2007, 6–7.

7. Jonathan E. Sinton, Mark D. Levine, and Wang Qingyi, "Energy Efficiency in China: Accomplishments and Challenges," *Energy Policy* 26, no. 11 (1998): 814.

8. Rosen and Houser, "China Energy," 6–7.

9. Sinton, Levine, and Wang, "Energy Efficiency in China."

10. State Council Development Research Center, "National Energy Strategies and Policies," November 2003, 8.

11. Noureddine Berrah, Fei Feng, Roland Priddle, and Leiping Wang, *Sustainable Energy in China: The Closing Window of Opportunity* (Washington, DC: The World Bank, 2007) 11, 19–22; "National Energy Strategies and Policies," 8; Zhou Fengqi 周风起 and Zhou Dadi 周大地, eds., *Zhongguo zhongchangqi nengyuan zhanlue* 中国中长期能源战略 [Study on long-term energy development strategy of China] (Beijing: China Planning Press, 1999), 290; IEA, *World Energy Outlook 2002* (Paris: OECD/ IEA, 2002), 245, 462; US Energy Information Administration, *International Energy Outlook 2003* (Washington, DC: Energy Information Administration, May 2003), 181, 184, tonto.eia.doe.gov/ftproot/forecasting/0484(2003).pdf.

12. Data from the *China Statistical Yearbook* collected by CEIC Data Company Ltd. and received from the Rhodium Group.

13. Jiang Lin et al., "Achieving China's Target for Energy Intensity Reduction in 2010," 8.

14. *BP Statistical Review of World Energy*, June 2008, 35, 40–41.

15. IEA, *China's Power Sector Reforms: Where to Next?* (Paris: OECD/IEA, 2006), 58–59; US Energy Information Administration, "World Total Electricity Installed Capacity, Most Recent Annual Estimates, January 1, 1980–January 1, 2007," December 8, 2008, www.eia.doe.gov/emeu/international/electricitycapacity.html.

16. Hannah Beech, "China's Long Dark Summer," *Time*, July 5, 2004.

17. Zhou Fengqi and Zhou Dadi, *Study on Long-Term Energy Development Strategies of China*, 176. See also, "China: Facing an Electric Storm," *Petroleum Economist*, December 1, 2005.

18. Matt Pottinger, "China Paradox: Short on Power, Long on Pollution—As Brownouts Multiply, Manufacturers Scramble to Keep Factories Humming," *Wall Street Journal*, July 9, 2004.

19. Brian Ricketts, "Coal in China from a Global Perspective," in Michal Meidan, ed., *Shaping China's Energy Security: The Inside Perspective* (Paris: Asia Centre, 2007), 106.

20. *BP Statistical Review of World Energy*, June 2008, 11.

21. The data on China's oil demand growth is from *BP Statistical Review of World Energy*, June 2008, 11. The comparison to a medium-sized country is from Kenneth Lieberthal and Mikkal Herberg, "China's Search for Energy Security: Implications for US Policy," *NBR Analysis* 17, no. 1 (April 2006): 7.

22. *BP Statistical Review of World Energy*, June 2008, 35.

23. Ricketts, "Coal in China," 108.

24. *China Coal Report*, no. 57 (March 2009): 6; "Table—China 2007 Coal, Coke Import, Export," *Reuters News*, January 21, 2008; *China Coal Newsletter* 4, no. 96 (December 28, 2007): 9–12; "China Retains Net Exporter Status in Year to November by Marginal Amount: China Customs," *Platts Coal Week International*, December 17, 2007.

25. IEA, *World Energy Outlook 2008*, 93–125.

26. This paragraph is based on IEA, *World Energy Outlook 2008*, 385, 389; and Kenneth Lieberthal and David Sandalow, "Overcoming Obstacles to US-China Cooperation on Climate Change," *John L. Thornton China Center Monograph Series*, no. 1 (January 2009): 1.

27. William Chandler, "Breaking the Suicide Pact: U.S.-China Cooperation on Climate Change," Carnegie Endowment for International Peace Policy Brief, no. 57, March 2008, 1.

28. *Mapping the Global Future* (Washington, DC: National Intelligence Council, December 2004), 48, www.foia.cia.gov/2020/2020.pdf.

29. Howard W. French, "China in Africa: All Trade, with No Political Baggage," *New York Times*, August 8, 2004, 4.

30. Alfred de Montesquiou, "China's Darfur Envoy Says Beijing Has Done Its Best to Solve Crisis, Considers Sending Peacekeepers," *Associated Press*, June 21, 2007; "Senator Joseph R. Biden Jr. Holds a Hearing on the Situation in Darfur," *CQ Transcriptions*, April 11, 2007.

31. "Sudanese Tinderbox Threatens Oil Industry," *Energy Economist*, June 2008, 3–6.

32. This discussion of Saudi Arabia is based on my conversation with Fareed Mohammedi, Partner and Head of Markets and Country Strategies, PFC Energy, Washington, DC, March 11, 2009. For more on China–Saudi Arabia energy relations, see Saad Rahim, "China's Energy Strategy toward the Middle East: Saudi Arabia," in

Gabriel B. Collins, Andrew S. Erickson, Lyle J. Goldstein, and William S. Murray, eds., *China's Energy Strategy: The Impact on Beijing's Maritime Policies* (Annapolis, MD: Naval Institute Press, 2008).

33. Interview with former Chinese diplomat, Beijing, China, June 24, 2008.

34. For more information on the geopolitical changes created by China's growing energy ties to Central Asia, see Julia Nanay, Testimony before the U.S.-China Economic and Security Review Commission, Hearing on "The Impact of China's Economic and Security Interests in Continental Asia on the United States," Washington, DC, May 20, 2009.

35. John Roberts, "Turkmens Seek Chinese Cash for Developing Huge Gas Field," *Platts*, June 1, 2009; Paul Sampson, "Turkmenistan: Looking East," *Energy Compass*, December 5, 2008.

36. Shi Hongtao 石洪涛, "Nengyuan anquan zaoyu 'Maliuya kunju' ZhongRiHan nengfou xie shou" 能源安全遭遇 "马六甲困局"中日韩能否携手 [Energy security runs up against the 'Malacca Dilemma': Will China, Japan, and Korea cooperate?]," *Zhongguo qingnian bao* 中国青年报 [China Youth Daily], June 15, 2004, business .sohu.com/2004/06/15/49/article220534904.shtml.

37. Robert D. Kaplan, "Center Stage for the Twenty-first Century: Power Plays in the Indian Ocean," *Foreign Affairs* (March/April 2009): 28.

38. This paragraph is based on e-mail correspondence from Bud Cole, June 22, 2009; and James R. Holmes and Toshi Yoshihara, "China's Naval Ambitions in the Indian Ocean," in Collins, Erickson, Goldstein, and Murray, eds., *China's Energy Strategy.*

39. Study Group of the China Academy of Environmental Planning, State Environmental Protection Agency, "2020 nian Zhongguo nengyuan yu huanjing mianlin de tiaozhan yu duice" 2020年中国能源与环境面临的挑战与对策 [Challenges and countermeasures facing China's energy and environment in 2020], *Renmin Wang* 人民网 [People's Daily Online], November 5, 2005, theory.people.com.cn/GB/49154/49155/3830852.html; Zhou Fengqi 周凤起, "Zhongguo jingji fazhan zhong de nengyuan ziyuan he huanjing zhiyue" 中国经济发展中的能源资源和环境制约 [Energy resource and environmental constraints in China's economic development], August 30, 2005, www.mep.gov.cn/ztbd/lszglt/200508/t20050830_11880.htm.

40. Berrah et al., *Sustainable Energy in China*, 11–12.

41. "Chinese PM's Speech at 27 April National Teleconference on Energy Conservation," *BBC Monitoring Asia Pacific*, May 10, 2007; Ma Kai 马凯, "Zhuanbian jingji zengzhang fangshi shixian you hao you kuai fazhan—zai Zhongguo fazhan gaoceng luntan 2007 nian hui shang de yanjiang" 转变经济增长方式 实现又好又快发展—在中国发展高层论坛2007年会上的演讲 [Transform the pattern of economic growth, realize better and faster development—Speech at the China Development Forum 2007], March 18, 2007, zys.ndrc.gov.cn/wldzyjh/t20070319_121961.htm; Zheng Bijan, "China's 'Peaceful Rise' to Great-Power Status," *Foreign Affairs* (September/October 2005); Zhou Fengqi, "Energy Resource and Environmental Constraints."

42. Arthur Jay Klinghoffer, "Sino-Soviet Relations and the Politics of Oil," *Asian Survey* 16, no. 6 (June 1976): 542.

43. "Chinese Cut Back on Air Operations," *New York Times*, March 1, 1964, 29; "China: How Much Oil?" *Economist*, January 8, 1966, 197.

44. *Zhonggong zhongyang guanyu zhiding guomin jingji he shehui fazhan di shiyi ge wu nian guihua de jianyi* 中共中央关于制定国民经济和社会发展第十一个五年规划的建议 [The Communist Party Center's suggestions on setting the Eleventh Five Year Plan for national economic and social development] (Beijing: Renmin chubanshe, 2005). See also Barry Naughton, "The New Common Economic Program: China's Eleventh Five Year Plan and What It Means," *China Leadership Monitor,* no. 16 (Fall 2005).

45. This paragraph is based on Mark Levine, Lynn Price, David Fridley, Zhou Nan, Michael McNeil, Nathaniel Aden, and Hongyou Lu, "Evaluation of China's Energy-Saving and Emission-Reduction Accomplishments during the 11th Five Year Plan" (presentation at Tsinghua University, Beijing, China, June 2, 2009).

46. "Guojia fagaiwei deng bumen xia fa 'shi yi wu' shi da zhongdian jieneng gongcheng shishi yijian," 国家发改委等部门下发 '十一五' 十大重点节能工程实施意见 [Suggestions of the NDRC and other agencies on the implementation of the 10 headline energy conservation projects in the Eleventh Five-Year Plan], June 27, 2007, www.ndrc.gov.cn/xwfb/t20060727_78002.htm; Lynn Price, Xuejun Wang, and Jiang Yun, "China's Top-1,000 Energy-Consuming Enterprises Program: Reducing the Energy Intensity of the 1,000 Largest Enterprises in China," Ernest Orlando Lawrence Berkeley National Laboratory, LBNL-519E, June 2008, ies.lbl.gov/iespubs/LBNL-519E.pdf.

47. Huang Hui 黄蕙, "Guojia nengyuan lingdao xiaozu zhi shi di yi bu" 国家能源领导小组只是第一步 [The National Energy Leading Group is only the first step], *Liaowang xinwen zhoukan* 瞭望新闻周刊 [Liaowang News Weekly], no. 23 (June 6, 2005): 40–42; *China Academic Journals* (Tsinghua Tongfang Optical Disc Co. Ltd./ Eastview Publications).

48. For more information on China's energy governance, see Edward A. Cunningham, "China's Energy Governance: Perception and Reality," The Audit of Conventional Wisdom Series, MIT Center for International Studies, March 2007; Bo Kong, "Institutional Insecurity," *China Security* (Summer 2006): 65–89; Richard K. Lester and Edward S. Steinfeld, "China's Energy Policy: Is Anybody Really Calling the Shots?" Working Paper Series, Industrial Performance Center, MIT-IPC-06-002 (Cambridge, MA: MIT, January 2006); "Zhineng fensan zheng chu duo men, Woguo nengyuan guanli cunzai tizhixing quexian" 职能分散政出多门，我国能源管理存在体制性缺陷 [Dispersed functions and multiple origins of policies—structural flaws exist in our national energy management], *Jingji cankao bao* 经济参考报 [Economic Reference News], January 29, 2008, news.xinhuanet.com/fortune/2008–01/29/content_7515997.htm; Chen Xinhua 陈新华, "Nengyuan anquan yao zhongshi neibu yinsu" 能源安全要重视内部因素，强调政策体制保障 [Energy security must attach importance to internal factors], *Zhongguo nengyuan* 中国能源杂志 [Energy of China], no. 5 (2003), www.china5e .com/dissertation/policy/20050718121240.html. Xavier Xinhua Chen is a former China program manager at the International Energy Agency.

49. See, for example, Wang Qiang 王强 and Wang Mingming 王明明, "Ranyou shui de 10 nian luan xiang" 燃油税的10年乱相 [The ten years of pandemonium surrounding the fuel tax], *Shangwu Zhoukan* 商务周刊 [Business Watch Magazine], April 5, 2006, www.businesswatch.com.cn/Html/gov/zj0520/064515162897211.html.

50. E-mail correspondence from longtime analyst of China's energy sector, November 8, 2006.

51. E-mail correspondence from a former US Department of Energy official, October 10, 2008.

52. For more on the energy bureaucracy's focus on projects, see Chen Xinhua, "Energy Security."

53. For more information on the Chinese energy companies sources of power and autonomy, see Erica S. Downs, "Business Interest Groups in Chinese Politics: The Case of the Oil Companies," in Cheng Li, ed., *China's Changing Political Landscape: Prospects for Democracy* (Washington, DC: Brookings Institution Press, 2008), 121–41.

54. "Guojia nengyuanju renyuan peizhi shangwei zuihou queding, jiage guanli mianlin tupo" 国家能源局人员配置尚未最后确定，价格管理面临突破 [The National Energy Administration's personnel allocation has not been finalized: Price management facing a breakthrough], *Nangfang zhoumou* 南方周末 [Southern Weekend], March 27, 2008, finance.jrj.com.cn/news/2008–03–27/000003459178.html.

55. Liu Keyu 刘克雨, "Zujian guojia nengyuanbu tiaojian yijing jiben chengshu" 组建国家能源部条件已经基本成熟 [The conditions for establishing a national Ministry of Energy are basically ripe], *Jingji cankao bao* 政治参考报 [Economic Reference News], January 29, 2008, news.xinhuanet.com/fortune/2008–01/29/content_7516573.htm.

56. For a discussion of how domestic oil product prices were set through 2008, see IEA, *Oil Market Report*, November 10, 2006, 13.

57. IEA, *Oil Market Report*, September 9, 2005, 9; "Sinopec Gets $4.4B Handout," *International Oil Daily*, July 31, 2008.

58. For details on the new oil product pricing regime, see IEA, *Oil Market Report*, January 16, 2009, 15.

59. Ahmad Abdallah and Arthur Kroeber, *GaveKal Dragonomics China Insight*, November 26, 2008, 3.

60. "Ban yue tan tebie diaocha: nengyuan jinzhang de beihou . . ." 半月谈特别调查：能源紧张的背后 . . . [Ban Yue Tan special investigation: The background to the energy shortages . . .], *Xinhua*, March 23, 2004, news.xinhuanet.com/fortune/2004–03/23/content_1379917.htm; "You dian mei 'sanhuang' tongshi fasheng, Zhongguo mianlin nengyuan weiji?" 油点煤'三荒'同时发生，中国面临能源危机？ ['Three shortages' of oil, electricity and coal appear at the same time: Is China facing an energy crisis?], *Liaowang dongfang zhoukan* 瞭望东方周刊 [Oriental Outlook], December 18, 2003, news.xinhuanet.com/newscenter/2003–12/18/content_1237734.htm.

61. "China to Hike Electricity Price to Ease Power Shortage—NDRC," *Xinhua Financial Network News*, April 28, 2005.

62. Chen Aizhu, "China's Power Crisis Not Caused by Pricing—NDRC," *Reuters News*, January 27, 2008.

63. "Frozen Assets: China's Weather," *The Economist*, February 9, 2008.

64. Mao Yushi, Sheng Hong, and Yang Fuqiang, *The True Cost of Coal in China*, September 2008, act.greenpeace.org.cn/coal/report/TCOC-Final-EN.pdf.

65. Barry Naughton, "The Inflation Battle: Juggling Three Swords," *China Leadership Monitor*, no. 25 (Summer 2008).

66. "China Oil & Gas: Social Stability vs. Corporate Profitability," Bear Stearns Asian Equity Research, September 1, 2005.

67. Rosen and Houser, "China Energy," 25.

68. *BP Statistical Review of World Energy*, 9, 12, 25, 28, 34, 35, 40.

69. *BP Statistical Review of World Energy*, 40.

70. IEA, *World Energy Outlook 2008*, 93, 103, 106.

71. IEA, *World Energy Outlook 2008,* 110, 115, 188, 125, 129, 132.

72. The calculation of the share of China's oil imports that are seaborne is based on data from China's General Administration of Customs, cited in "Table—China Dec Crude Oil Imports and Exports," *Reuters*, January 21, 2008.

73. The Churchill quote is from Daniel Yergin, "Ensuring Energy Security," *Foreign Affairs* (March/April 2006): 69.

74. United States Energy Information Administration, "World Oil Transit Chokepoints," January 2008, www.eia.doe.gov/cabs/World_Oil_Transit_Chokepoints/Background.html.

75. Shi Hongtao 石洪涛, "Nengyuan anquan zaoyu 'Maliujia kunju' ZhongRiHan nengfou xie shou" 能源安全遭遇 '马六甲' 困局，中日韩能否携手？ [Energy security runs up against the 'Malacca Dilemma': Will China, Japan and Korea cooperate?], *Zhongguo qingnian bao* 中国青年报 [China Youth Daily], June 15, 2004, business .sohu.com/2004/06/15/49/article220534904.shtml.

76. "Table—China Dec Crude Oil Imports and Exports," *Reuters*, January 21, 2008.

77. IEA, *World Energy Outlook 2008*, 106.

78. "Nengyuan jinque yinfa youqi chujing rechao" 能源紧缺引发油企出境热潮 [The energy shortages cause an upsurge in China's oil firms going abroad], *Zhongguo shiyou bao* 中国石油报 [China Petroleum News], April 28, 2006, www.oilnews.com .cn/gb/2006-4/28/content_666191.htm.

79. See, for example, the remarks of Sinopec Corp. president Wang Tianpu in Duan Xiaoyan 段晓燕, "Women de liyi zhuyao bushi laizi longduan" 我们的利益主要不是来自垄断 [Our profits mainly are not from monopoly], *21 shiji jingji baodao* 21 世纪经济报道 [21st Century Business Herald], January 8, 2007, www.nanfangdaily.com.cn/jj/20070108/zh/200701080009.asp; and the reported remarks of Zeng Peiyan 曾培炎 in "Zhongshiyou: dang mengxiang zhaojin xianshi" 中石油：当梦想照进现实 [CNPC: Dreams may become reality], *Jinrongjie wang* 金融界网站 [Financial World Online], February 14, 2008, stock1.jrj.com.cn/news/2008-02-14/000003285143.html.

80. Zhang Yuqing 张玉清, "Shishi shiyou gongye 'zou chu qu' de fazhan zhanlüe" 实施石油工业 '走出去' 的发展战略 [Implement the 'go abroad' development strategy of the oil industry], *Hongguan jingji guanli* 宏观经济管理 [Macroeconomic Management], no. 10 (2000): 5–6; "Guojia jiwei jiaonengsi fusizhang Xu Dingming tan Woguo jingwai shiyou ziyuan de kantan kaifa" 国家计委交能司副司长徐锭明谈我国境外石油资源的勘探开发 [Xu Dingming, Deputy head of the Transportation and Energy Department of the State Planning Commission discusses China's overseas oil exploration and development], *Zhongguo jingji daobao* 中国经济导报 [China Economic Herald], October 8, 1997, *China Infobank*.

81. Data on the foreign oil production of China's NOCs provided by Wood Mackenzie, December 15, 2008; and *BP Statistical Review of World Energy*, June 2008, 8, 20.

82. Evan S. Medeiros, "China's International Behavior: Activism, Opportunism, and Diversification," *Joint Force Quarterly*, no. 47 (2007): 36.

83. The idea that concerns among the major powers about China's energy consumption may undermine China's economic growth and further rise to international prominence is reflected in Zhang Shengjun 张胜军, "Xin yi lun 'Zhongguo weixie lun' de beihou" 新一轮'中国威胁论'的背后 [Background on the new round of 'China threat theories'], *Beijng Ribao* 北京日报 [Beijing Daily], July 9, 2007, theory .people.com.cn/GB/49150/49152/5964282.html; Yu Hongyuan 于宏源, "Qingjie nengyuan he Zhongguo huanjing waijiao—Zhongguo jueqi yu guoji nengyuan tixi de lujing" 清洁能源和中国环境外交—中国崛起于国际能源体系的路径 [Clean energy and China's environmental diplomacy—the way for China to rise in the international energy system], *Lu ye* 绿叶 [Green Leaf], no. 4 (2008): 53–59; and Wang Zhongyu 王中宇, "Cong nengyuan kan 'jueqi'" 从能源看崛起 [Looking at China's 'rise' from energy], *Kexue shibao* 科学时报 [Science Times], March 19, 2008, business .sohu.com/20080319/n255799465.shtml; see also Lieberthal and Sandalow, "Overcoming Obstacles," 20.

84. For more on the China threat theory, see Denny Roy, "The 'China Threat' Issue," *Asian Survey* 36, no. 8 (August 1996): 758–71. For the Chinese government's views on the China energy and environmental threat theories, see "Ma Kai 'Qiushi' zazhi zhuanwen: bo 'Zhongguo nengyuan weixie lun,'" 马凯求是杂志撰文：驳中国能源威胁论 [Ma Kai pens an article for *Seeking Truth* magazine refuting the 'China energy threat theory'], *Renmin Wang* 人民网 [People's Daily Online], November 1, 2006, politics.people.com.cn/GB/1027/4986239.html; and "Fagaiwei: Zhongguo huanjing weixie lun meiyou shishi yiju" 发改委：中国环境威胁论没有事实依据 [NDRC: The China environmental threat theory has no basis in fact], *Xinhua*, June 4, 2007, news.xinhuanet.com/politics/2007–06/04/content_6195390.htm.

85. Guan Qingyou 管清友, "Zhongguo jueqi wei shijie zuochu juda nengyuan gongxian" 中国崛起为世界作出巨大能源贡献 [China's rise makes a major energy contribution to the world], *Dongfang zaobao* 东方早报 [Oriental Morning Post], November 17, 2007, www.gx.xinhuanet.com/dm/2007–11/17/content_11695701.htm.

86. Ma Kai, "Transform the Pattern of Economic Growth."

87. See, for example, Han Xiaoping 韩晓平, "Zhongguo cheng Mei jianpai 'dang jianpai'" 中国成美减排挡箭牌 [China has become America's excuse for not reducing emissions], *Xinhua*, June 7, 2007, news.xinhuanet.com/world/2007–06/07/content_6210685.htm.

88. "NDRC Official: Consuming Nations Should Pay for Export Emissions," *Inside US-China Trade* 9, no. 11 (March 18, 2009); Jonathan Watts, "China Says Western Nations Responsible for Its CO_2 Emissions," *The Guardian*, March 18, 2009; and "NDRC: The China Environmental Threat."

89. See, for example, Wang Zhiqiang 王志强, "Zhongguo quanqiu zhao you, Meiguo shi du shi shu?" 中国全球找油，美国是堵是疏？ [China's global search for oil—will the United States block or let through?], *Nanfengchuang* 南风窗, May 9, 2006, news.sina.com.cn/c/2006–05–09/19439812816.shtml; and "Woguo mianlin de guoji nengyuan anquan tiaozhan" 我国面临的国际能源安全挑战 [The energy security

challenges that China faces], *Nangfang yuekan* 南方月刊, July 6, 2007, www.nfyk.com/nfdj/ShowArticle.asp?ArticleID=200.

90. Lieberthal and Sandalow, "Overcoming Obstacles," 20.

91. "Hu Jintao zai ba guo jituan tong fazhan zhong guojia lingdaoren duihua huiyi shang de shumian jianghua (quanwen)" 胡锦涛在八国集团同发展中国家领导人对话会议上的书面讲话 （全文） [Hu Jintao's speech at the meeting between the G8 and leaders of developing countries (full text)], July 17, 2007, wb.boz.gov.cn/Article.asp?id=740.

92. "Xi Jinping zai Shate Jida juxing de guoji nengyuan huiyi shang de jianghua" 习近平在沙特吉达举行的国际能源会议上的讲话 [Xi Jinping's speech at the international energy meeting in Jeddah, Saudi Arabia], *Renmin Wang* 人民网 [People's Daily Online], June 23, 2008, politics.people.com.cn/GB/1024/7411044.html.

V

POLITICAL CREATIVITY
AND POLITICAL DEVELOPMENT

9

The Political Creativity
of Late Imperial China

R. Keith Schoppa

There is no older nor more justly criticized stereotype than that of "unchanging China." Yet there are certain aspects of that state that endured over time and whose continuation both defined Chinese political culture and played a role in the state's very durability. They fit under three broad rubrics: the conceptualization and nature of government, the roles of government, and governmental institutions and approaches. This chapter looks at Chinese political developments in the best-case scenario, as it were—when the state was functioning at its best. There were times, of course, when the state was functioning very badly: eighteenth-century examples are in the malfunctioning of the bureaucracy during the sorcery scare of 1768[1] or Qianlong's autocracy in his "literary inquisition."[2] But I deal here with the political creativity, even genius of the imperial state. *What went right*

THE CONCEPTUALIZATION AND NATURE
OF THE CHINESE GOVERNMENT

The conceptualization of the nature of political leadership, of the relationship between state and society, and of the basic governing focus set the course for the Chinese state as it developed. Keys were the emperor and his ministers. The *Book of History* (*Shujing*), a collection from the sixth century B.C., notes, "We do not presume to know and to say that the lords of Yin (Shang) received Heaven's Mandate for so many years. . . . But they did not reverently attend to their virtue and so prematurely threw away the Mandate. . . . Now our king has succeeded and received the Mandate."[3] Explaining that the source of political misfortunes stemmed from immoral acts, the Mandate of Heaven idea essentially "moralized the political culture."[4] Beyond simply moralizing, it cast around the emperor a religious aura. "To govern was to receive the utterance (*ming*)—the 'mandate'—of Heaven. [It was] originally related to the king's ability to communicate with (and be imbued with the morality of) the ancestral spirits."[5] Though emperors accepted the tradition of power being passed on in the family line, rule by virtue was theoretically the defining hallmark of their power. Two other related points should be noted. Having received the mandate, the emperor was the Son of Heaven; just as a son must show filial piety to a father, so the emperor must display filial piety by ruling with virtue—lest he risk losing the Mandate like the Shang. The metaphor of the family, which appeared again and again in the discourse of state and society, is significant. An emperor could lose the Mandate if he failed to do those things that marked him as emperor, if he violated, in Confucian terminology, the "rectification of names." Heaven made its will known through the people; implicit here was the sense that government was ultimately dependent on the will of the people. The people were the root of the state (*minben*).

Simple though it is, the Mandate of Heaven doctrine created a whole theory of the relationship between state and society. The be-all and end-all of the state and its leader, the Son of Heaven, and his state ministers and their staffs, making up the bureaucracy, was to rule out of benevolence for the people. A people ruled without benevolence was a society ripe for disorder. The state exhibited benevolence through various policies—prime examples are water control projects and a system of granaries to provide "subsistence security as a key element in social stability."[6] The first ever-normal granary was established in 1680, and by the 1720s granaries were widespread. Located in county seats, they lent or sold grain at reduced prices (or even gave it away) during the spring season when there were natural shortages and prices would ordinarily spike; then they bought cheaper grain in the fall to stock the granaries. In addition, charity granaries were set up in major towns; and the Yongzheng emperor expanded the granary system to include smaller community granaries (*shecang*) that were scattered across the countryside by the 1740s and 1750s.

Ever-normal granaries were managed by the staff of the magistrate, known, in the Confucian family metaphor, as the "father-mother official"—the emperor's bureaucrat who was in closest touch with the people. For the community granaries, the state was willing to enlist local gentry to establish and manage the facilities, gathering grain reserves, often by soliciting contributions from rich landowners in the area. Charity granaries differed in their function in various areas of the country; in places they functioned like the ever-normal granary, but in others they focused on doling out relief grain.[7] Evidence shows that in the eighteenth century the community and charity granary projects were especially successful. That success depended on getting local elites to "buy into" the state's "Confucian benevolent project"; the granaries were public grain reserves, not government property. This was not a case where state and society were at odds, but where notably the line between state and society appeared indistinct. This reality greatly contrasts with Western civilization where state and society developed into distinctly separate spheres, a dichotomy that, in turn, gave rise to a plurality of political and social beliefs. In the end, the granary system gives evidence of the capacity of the Chinese state to build a huge and sophisticated institution to advance material welfare across widely varying locales, with a deft touch, not with a heavy authoritarian hand. As a further indication of the morality-laced interpretations of political realities, county treasury shortfalls and partially empty granaries were denoted as moral failures of the father-mother official.[8]

Since it was perhaps *the* hallmark of the imperial political system, the centrality of the civil service examination, the institution that gave rise to the ruling meritocracy, cannot be overstressed. The emperor's bureaucracy was recruited through the examination, and local nonofficial community elites (holders of mainly lower degrees) attained a much-respected status. Imposed regional quotas at the upper level examinations meant that the educated elite was scattered throughout the country. At any time in the nineteenth century, there were around 800,000 *shengyuan* degree holders (the lowest level degree), 18,000 to 19,000 *juren*, and about 2,500 *jinshi* degree holders. Since the passage rate was so small (1 to 2 percent at each level), many more Chinese than degree holders themselves were trained in the classics; one historian has estimated that classically educated men numbered at the very minimum 5 million in the early eighteenth century (10 percent of the population).[9] Crucial also for the import of the examination was that preparations for it trained all examination takers in the discourse of Confucianism, so that, at the least, these men shared a knowledge and awareness of basic ethical values, even if not all always operating within their parameters.[10] In contrast, then, to the early modern West, where centralizing heads of state recruited officials that were especially valued for technical skills, Chinese bureaucrats were versed in broad ethical and philosophical principles. In the overall picture of Chinese political reality, the examination system "was an important element in sustaining a unified empire over such great distances under pre-modern conditions of transport and communications."[11] Finally, implicit in the system—indeed, its very engine—was the idea that social mobility was possible, that one was not mired by fate in lowly or unbearable circumstances.

The bureaucracy as meritocracy

With a few major exceptions, the government ideal was "a minimum state with maximal reach: that is, a relatively small state apparatus that succeeded in extracting substantial revenues and labor from a large population."[12] In the same vein, it has been called a model of "under-administration."[13] Minimalist government meant a relative stagnancy in the number of county magistrates over time. During the late seventeenth century, there were 1,261 counties and magistrates. While the population tripled in size in the century from 1680 to 1780, in the late nineteenth century there were only 1,303 counties and magistrates.[14] Taking the population in 1700 to be about 150 million and that of 1900 to be about 420 million (both reasonable projections), the average number to which one man served as father-mother official in 1700 was about 119,000 but was over 320,000 in 1900. By contrast, in China today, there is an official above the county level for every 2,000 people.[15]

Though counties varied widely in size and population, the figures from imperial China—estimates though they are—nevertheless suggest the minimalist reality. Clearly, imperial official presence was only the thinnest of veneers, insufficient for serving the population well. Furthermore, county governments were underfunded to a point where monies were clearly insufficient for the execution of prescribed duties. In the locality, the government was only "tenuously in control."[16] This situation is again in great contrast with the West where state making focused on state centralization built upon military power and expanded bureaucracies.

Distancing official central power from the locality even more was the law of avoidance, which specified that a magistrate could not serve in his native place: this bureaucrat of the central government was thus dependent on local subbureaucrats, clerks, and runners, many of them entrenched in their positions for years, unevaluated and often undisciplined. Indeed, the Chinese proverb had a profound truth about the relationship between the government and the people: "Heaven is high; the emperor is far away." William Rowe does not mince words: "the clerical sub-bureaucracy was compelled essentially to steal from the local population . . . not only to support itself but also to fund the entire operation of county-level government."[17] And yet despite the bad image the "government" might receive with corruption at its lowest level, the reality remained that the center was not heavy-handedly asserting itself into local communities. The government simply seemed averse to expanding the bureaucracy; the traditional ideal of a frugal government was hard to let go, as were the traditions of existing county-level administrative units. Moreover, as Philip Kuhn notes, expanding the bureaucracy "would have diluted the exclusivity of literati status."[18]

Jane Kate Leonard's study of the role of the Daoguang emperor in handling the Grand Canal crisis of the 1820s indeed speaks to the creative wisdom of the emperor's "controlling from afar."[19] The canal-riverine system so important for transporting tax grain from the lower Yangzi had fallen into severe disrepair. It was a crucial enough water control reconstruction project for the country that the Qing government had to take the lead in managing it. Yet the emperor was in Beijing, far away from the processes of canal-transport administration, the technical and practical complexities, and the often quickly changing environmental and ecological situations. In the end, "the emperor admitted the inability of the central government to design and implement practical courses of action." "The emperor's phrase 'controlling from afar' captures his particular struggle to find the correct balance between central leadership and regional initiative. . . . It encapsulates the concept of imperial direction, but regional dominance" over canal maintenance.[20]

This same kind of light, deft, and ultimately indirect touch applied as well to the state inculcation of moral values (for a fuller discussion, see below). In his study of the cult for the goddess Tianhou, James Watson noted that "members of the national elite preferred not to probe too deeply into the religious beliefs . . . of the ordinary people. Herein lies the *genius* [my emphasis] of the Chinese government's approach to cultural integration: the state imposed a structure but not the content." "The system was flexible enough to allow people at all levels of the social hierarchy to construct their own representations of state-approved deities."[21]

This Chinese model of minimal and indirect governance by its very practice in the vastness of the country created (and was continually fraught with) tensions between the poles of center and local, the forces of centralization and decentralization. The minimalist model perpetuated the age-old contention between the wisdom of a centralized imperial system (*junxian*) versus that of decentralized Chinese feudalism (*fengjian*). To keep these countervailing forces in delicate balance required creative political skills and adroitness, as well as institutions that mediated effectively and consequently facilitated workable policies. In effect, the system infused the "spirit of fengjian into the junxian structure."[22] It meant that the center had to trust local elites to act in its place at the community and county levels in the public "arena of nonstate activity that contributed to the supply of services and resources in the public good."[23] That trust had to be based on the assumption that local elites would accept the state's legitimacy and mission.

Indeed the use of community elites in this fashion suggests considerable political creativity for the Chinese state that had not been envisioned in early Chinese political philosophy. William Theodore de Bary and William Rowe have pointed out that the classic *Great Learning* (*Da xue*) completely left the local community out as a political player, going directly from the family to the state:

Central govt authority rested on the cooperation of local officials, and social acceptance of and participation in carrying out its mandates.

Role of elites

The ancients who wished clearly to exemplify illustrious virtue throughout the world would first set up good government in their states. Wishing to govern well their states, they would first regulate their families. Wishing to regulate their families, they would first cultivate their persons.

And later, "the government of the state depends on the regulation of the family."[24] Timothy Brook, however, notes the vast array of institutions in the public realm, ministered to by local elites: "schools, academies, city walls, granaries, bridges, ferry docks, hydraulic systems, orphanages, temples to state-sanctioned gods, shrines to local figures, even Buddhist monasteries." He gives an example from the Yin country (Zhejiang) gazetteer: "During the Eastern Zhejiang famine of 1751, the magistrate deputed gentry to go to the wealthy people and encourage them to make donations. Li Changyu (*jinshi* 1754) and his friend Tu Ketang (*juren* 1752) rushed about encouraging people to forward grain and were successful in amassing the required amount."[25]

The differing approaches of individual emperors compelled them to see community elites in different ways, thus underscoring the diversity of meaning and processes in the Chinese state. For the Qing's Yongzheng emperor, who was drawn to the centralizing model, local elites were state competitors. For his son, the Qianlong emperor, however, local elites were political and social associates who contributed to the management and well-being of the community and who, if literati, should certainly be given special privileges—being excused from corporal punishment and from corvee labor, having lower tax rates than the nonliterati, and frequently having a voice in the management and processes of community affairs.

Also to assist in minimal and indirect government, the central regime creatively used various social groups and networks—kinship, local markets, water control organs—to help attain its goals. Prasenjit Duara points to a "cultural nexus of power" that he argues the imperial state used to "reach into local communities" and maintain control at arm's length from those communities. Included in this nexus were "various channels, such as corporate merchant groups, temple communities, myths, and other symbolic resources embedded in popular culture."[26] It is yet another indication that approaches and policies of the late imperial Chinese government blurred the line between state and society.

ROLES OF GOVERNMENT

The Civilizing Mission

Despite the government's concern for frugality and its caution about expanding government structures, overregulating, and micromanaging, there was one arena where the state was consistently interventionist: in its civilizing agenda or its moral "ordering [of] the state."[27] In this arena, it intervened into family and individual lives. This was arguably the key role for the Qing, led, as it was, by the Manchu Other, who needed to be identified with the Chinese moral order. Jane Kate Leonard and John Watt argue that "for the Qing, the term 'state' conveys both more and less than the Western referent. While its bureaucratic functions, centering narrowly on tax collection and security, were more limited than those of modern governments, its overarching moral-cosmic functions far exceeded those of the secular state in the West," where "no one view of the moral universe could dominate."[28] British journalist Alexander Michie in 1900 drew attention to this most Chinese of state roles: "China occupies the unique position of a State resting on moral force, a conception almost as alien to the Western mind as material progress is to the Eastern."[29] Further, anthropologist Arthur P. Wolf takes the "minimalism" of the Chinese state and turns it on its head:

> Historians and political scientists often emphasize the failure of most Chinese governments to effectively extend their authority to the local level. . . . Judged in terms of its administrative arrangements, the Chinese imperial government looks impotent. Assessed in terms of its long-range impact on the people, it appears to have been one of the most potent governments ever known, for it created a religion in its own image. It is not only [China's] bureaucratic organization that is replicated in the world of the supernatural; the gods also display many of the most human characteristics of their worldly counterparts.[30]

William Rowe argues that the "civilizing" role of the Chinese state stretches back to the third century B.C. and probably earlier.[31] "Civilizing" is *jiaohua*—literally, "instructing and transforming." The mission to civilize or to become civilized defined the proper and absolutely indispensable roles of king, the literati, and the people. For the king it was the sine qua non of kingship and under the Mandate of Heaven the best measure of moral and benevolent government. Indeed, the Yongzheng emperor explicitly made the moral transformation of the Manchus the basis for their receiving Heaven's Mandate: the dynasty "had successfully assumed the vessels, rituals, and functions of the emperorship . . . ; the people were cared for; the natural processes were facilitated; and the peoples of the earth were united in their awe of and love for the ruler."[32]

For the literati, the mission was their training and their calling. For both king and the literati (those who became his ministers as well as those who emerged as nonofficial social elites), the mission was *the* crucial path for "ordering the world." The people in local communities and in families were to be receptive to instruction so that they too could be morally transformed. It should be abundantly clear that if proper ruling entailed penetrating deeply enough into people's lives to shape their morality, the structural and institutional minimalism of the state fades substantially into the background. Such a penetrative state on these issues could very easily become "meddlesome, authoritarian, and censorious." The Chinese state "promoted initiatives . . . that it saw as likely to make people take their moral and social agency seriously," like encouraging local elites to form militia units.[33] This was something that Western state builders, in a system where state was often pitted against society, would not likely have done, concerned as they were with state centralization.

Schools

There were essentially two broad strategies in the civilizing mission: education and ritual. In late imperial China there were three main types of schools, academies (*shuyuan*), community schools (*shexue*), and charity schools (*yixue*). The establishment of academies began in the Tang dynasty; these schools were established by private individuals or were joint official-private collaborations. The first Qing academy, a revival of a Ming institution, was set up in 1657, but the existence of academies was not mandated until 1733 when the Yongzheng emperor ordered that one academy "be established in the place where the governor-general or governor has his official residence" and that each would receive a thousand taels from the government.[34] In 1736, on the recommendation of the Board of Rites, academies received copies of the Confucian classics and other volumes approved by the emperor. Chen Hongmou (1696–1771), a powerful official who was a driving force in the civilizing mission, patronized academies, not only in seeking their funding but also in shaping the curriculum, appointing headmasters and teachers, and purchasing and donating books for academy libraries. Some academies were residential schools: Southern Path Academy, established in Xiaoshan county, Zhejiang province, in the late seventeenth century, for example, had attached to it a kitchen and bathhouse.[35] For well-qualified students, the academy could become the first step toward taking the civil service examination: excellent students might be awarded state stipends to move on to higher institutions (like the Imperial College in Beijing). This remains a contemporary practice: there are now three thousand administrative and Communist Party schools in China.[36] Despite the career possibilities linked to the academy, the heart of the intellectually higher-level schools remained its Confucian ethics. Many academies also transcended their purely local teaching mission, becoming important centers for philosophical, literary, and historical conversations, debate, and transmission. They were located in city and countryside.

Chen Hongmou, who also patronized lower-level schools, argued, "If we want to draw talented individuals out of every hamlet and alleyway, we must reach them when they're very small."[37] The community school (*shexue*) and charity school (*yixue*) did not differ a great deal. A government order in 1652 had specified that every area set up a community school, hire "honest and sincere" teachers, whose names would be approved by local education decision makers and who would be paid a salary. The first charity schools were begun early in the eighteenth century mostly in frontier areas where the state intended them as institutions for civilizing ethnic minorities. Local elites joined in, taking the lead in establishing charity schools in the interior as well. For the state the goal of these two kinds of schools was moral indoctrination—"to bring as many persons as possible under the influence of imperial Confucianism."[38] Textbooks used in the 650 charity schools whose establishment Chen Hongmou oversaw in Yunnan province included anthologies of political writings from the Zhou to the Song dynasties, Zhu Xi's instructions for managing households, the *Classic of Filial Piety*, and the *Sacred Edict* (see below). The state strictly controlled the textbooks and therefore the curriculum at the community and charity schools by prohibiting works filled with "trifling talks or indecent sayings"; these prohibitions were issued in 1663, 1687, 1714, 1725, 1810, 1834, and 1851, indications that this was a recurring problem or a Manchu obsession or both.[39]

The establishment and management of schools through the collaboration of officials and nonofficial elites point again to the reality that the line between state and society was indistinct, likely a crucial factor in imperial political creativity and flexibility. Lineages in both north and south played a larger role in the formation of schools than they did in the establishment and control of granaries. Significantly, the moral component of elementary education stressed the kinship relationships of corporate lineages as it celebrated the general values of the Confucian social order.

Community Lectures

At various times from the Song to the Qing, local officials and nonofficial elites tried to institute a "community compact" (*xiangyue*) that had varying components over time. The preeminent Neo-Confucian philosopher Zhu Xi had himself given rise to the efforts as he sought a "more normative, voluntarist, and societally generated alternative" to the *baojia*, the state-ordered system of social surveillance groupings.[40] With the Qing, the "compact" became twice a month "lectures" where the *Sacred Edict*, first announced by the Shunzhi emperor (1644–1661), was read by a suitable person, in the beginning of the institution a civil service degree holder, but later commoners as well. The edict set forth six maxims:

Perform filial duties to your parents.
Honor and respect your elders and superiors.
Maintain harmonious relationships with your neighbors.
Instruct and discipline your sons and grandsons.
Let each work peacefully for his own livelihood.
Do not commit wrongful deeds.[41]

Later emperors elaborated on the Shunzhi emperor's prescribed moral maxims. The Kangxi emperor in 1670 issued a list of sixteen maxims, and in 1724 the Yongzheng emperor issued a document of around ten thousand words. His glosses to that document gave the imperial rationale:

> Fearing that the stupid men and women are not fully acquainted with the profound meaning of [the emperor's] writing [in the *Sacred Edict*] and still cannot completely comprehend it, I have respectfully elaborated the royal words in common language. Thus the twice-monthly explications in the various prefectures and counties as well as the propagandizing by instructors in each village and community will be intelligible to the ear of women and children while the recalcitrant and the craven alike will be moved with enthusiasm. . . . [The ultimate goal is] to achieve for our country the blessing of peace and harmony and . . . to assist the sage Son of Heaven in the task of enlightening the people through emulating ancestors.[42]

Local gentry in many areas cooperated in this official effort at moral indoctrination by building public halls—that both housed the *Sacred Edict* and served as the lecture site. Such a hall underscored for the community the permanence and ongoing importance of the values of filial piety, respect, discipline, and harmony. As with any prescribed activity, the risk was that it would deteriorate into empty formality; as a device to inculcate the values that the state wanted to further, the community lecture was only as strong as local official support and enthusiasm. Most commentators think that the community lectures were generally not effective; for our purposes, however, it points to the relationship of state and society, in this case as parent to child or teacher to student.

Use of Models

One other educational device utilized by the state was the use of moral models. In the quotation from the glosses (above), the Yongzheng emperor notes that the task of the Son of Heaven is "enlightening the people through emulating ancestors." Confucius said, "When one sees a worthy, one should think of equaling him," and again, "When those who are in high stations perform well all their duties to their relations, the people are aroused to virtue."[43] In imperial China, teaching by words was inferior to teaching by example. William Rowe notes that the dynastic histories from the first century *Han Shu* onward included a section devoted to biographies of exemplary officials; it was, he asserts, "a highly constructed cultural institution."[44]

Early in imperial China Confucians had debated Legalists, who contended that fear of penal laws was the most effective way to induce compliance with rules. The Confucians countered that laws changed neither habits nor attitudes, but that the elevation of virtuous models did change people's thought and actions. It was the difference between the iron fist and the velvet glove. To be sure, in the large imperial and bureaucratic state, the Confucians had to compromise some on the issue of the law, but emulation of models remained the priority. Models were concrete and thus enjoyed a practical educational advantage over abstract moral values. Donald Munro has noted that Western nations have most frequently relied on material rewards or privileges to induce desired behavior. "In doing so they have neglected to tap a source of human motivation that the Chinese have understood so well and embodied in their selection of models."[45]

It is likely that almost every community had a shrine or temple remembering a local leader (or several) who displayed remarkable virtue and ability, who made outstanding contributions to society, and who could serve to motivate those in the present. There are myriad examples: here, only two. On the shore of Xiang Lake, an irrigation reservoir in Zhejiang, the twelfth-century magistrate who created the lake and benefited all the farmers in the area, Yang Shi, was remembered in a Shrine for the Virtuous and Kind. The tablets of other lake contributors over the centuries were later added to the shrine, men who were able but, more important, shone as exemplars of filial piety.[46] Prefect Peng Yi visited the shrine at its 1466 inauguration, underscoring the support of the state for such institutions. The state supported the establishment of such shrines for the living to recognize models of public spiritedness and self-sacrifice: the physical presence of the shrine in the community was important. But key also was the transmogrification of exemplars of civic virtue into beings worthy of sacrificial rituals. In Yongkang county in Zhejiang was the shrine to one Hu Zizheng, a *jinshi* degree holder from 989 and an upright and outstanding civil and military official who died in 1039. His temple, where rites were conducted in spring and autumn, was in the 1930s still drawing tens of thousands of pilgrims annually from Zhejiang, Shanghai, Jiangsu, and Fujian.[47] Pilgrimages, like models and rituals, were a part of the repertoire of the state's velvet glove for moral indoctrination. Models remain a prominent part of moral encouragement in contemporary China—the heroic soldier Lei Feng is a prime example—but to rather different values.

Rituals

Evelyn Rawski defines the transcendent importance of ritual succinctly: "Because 'the hallmark of power is the construction of reality,' rituals are important in the creation of a hegemonic order, that is, a widely accepted system of beliefs concerning the origins of power and the ethical correctness of the social order."[48] The power of ritual lies in its relationship to cosmology; according to the *Book of Rites*, "Ritual has its origins in Heaven and its movement reaches the earth. Its distribution extends to all human affairs."[49]

State rituals were most important in constructing and reasserting the dominion of the state. There were no fewer that 256 state rituals in the Qing period. Of these, 129 were "auspicious rites"—which included sacrifices to imperial ancestors, proclamation of the calendar, and imperial inspection tours. Both the Kangxi and Qianlong emperors made especially important use of the tours. The imperial diarist of the Kangxi emperor noted in 1684 that "as for rituals, none is more important than frequently embarking on tours of inspection."[50] On an eastern tour that he took in that year, he was said to punctuate the tour by "displays of ritual propriety with pointed reminders of Manchu martial prowess."[51] Michael Chang's analysis of the tours of the Kangxi and Qianlong emperors finds that the sovereigns used a "variety of hegemonic discourses" on these tours—such as "following the ancestors, avoiding luxurious ease [decadence and idleness], [and] observing the people"—all to legitimate their "ethno-dynastic rule."[52]

Among the state rituals, seventy-four "joyous rites" included ceremonies of ascending the throne, receiving foreign missions, and holding imperial audiences. Eighteen "military rites" included the emperor's review of the troops; amid twenty "guest rites" was the reception of tribute under the tributary system; and fifteen "rites of misfortune" were funeral ceremonies for people of varying social and political status.[53] Through these state rituals, displays of pomp and power, the emperor underscored his legitimacy as Son of Heaven, even as he promoted order and harmony, asserted his sovereignty vis-à-vis the bureaucracy, and impressed the people with his splendor.

All rituals—state, community, and family—validated the sense of hierarchy and order, so crucial in the Confucian worldview. Rituals drove home to watchers and participants the differentiation in individual status and, therefore, of power and roles. In county seats the Confucian School-temple and the Temple of Literature featured "altars to the sages and to local historical worthies, and here as well the semiannual spring and autumn sacrifices are performed." Chen Hongmou noted significantly that "the transformation of local customary practice begins in the School-temple, with the conduct of sacrifices by the local official."[54] The rituals were the conduits by which the state asserted its political and moral authority in the locality; and the participation of local elites was a visible expression of their accepting and furthering the legitimacy of the state. Outside the county seat, in smaller towns and even the countryside, shrines—like the Shrine for the Virtuous and Kind—and temples—like that to Hu Zizheng—dotted the landscape. They served as sites for local sacrifices and traditional local festivals, which underscored Confucian values and strengthened community cohesion. There were other occasions in communities when Confucian values were in focus. In Chen Hongmou's elementary schools, for instance, the teachers took their pupils to the local Confucian temple two times a month to pay their respects to Confucius and to bow to their teachers and each other: part of the function of ritual was to contribute to one's own self-cultivation.[55]

A community ritual that asserted social hierarchy even as it promised a greater sense of community was the community drinking ceremony (*xianglin jiuli*)—a community banquet *mandated by the state* and hosted twice a year by the county magistrate at the Confucian School-temple. The objective of the drinking ceremony is to

> show the proper respect for the aged and consideration for the virtuous. . . . Persons of advanced age and outstanding virtue are to occupy seats of honor, and others are to have places proper to their ages. Men who have committed offenses against the law are not allowed to intrude upon the seats intended for good and obedient subjects.[56]

Guests were carefully divided by the magistrate into status groups: principal guest, intermediate guests, ordinary guests, and elderly guests. After 1753, the principal guest had to come from the elderly or the gentry; commoners could be invited as intermediate or ordinary guests. During the banquet, guests received testimonials and praise based on their guest level. Chen Hongmou, who was a strong supporter of the ritual, noted its goals: to stress that age and youth were placed in proper ranking, to recognize and respect those with exemplary virtue, to emphasize and carry on the Confucian norms, and to focus on and stimulate local community cohesion.[57] It was also a strategy for creating and fostering local models.

Ritual handbooks were readily available in most areas of China. The state urged the proper practice of family rituals focused on ancestor reverence, both for the family and the lineage. Lineage genealogies stressed ritual and ceremony. Funeral, mourning, and sacrifices for parents were obligatory. To fail to do these things properly would be seen as an expression of extreme unfiliality and bring great shame.

The transcendence of ritual in Chinese political, religious, social, and cultural life cannot be overemphasized. In their introduction to their edited

Culture and State in Chinese History, Huters, Wong, and Yu define the issue and its import well as they also offer a comparison with Western political decision makers.

> [A] county magistrate's response to a severe drought could include making plans to reduce the price of grain by selling grain from the government granary . . . or arranging for imports of grain through either official channels or private ones; the same official would very likely go to a nearby temple and pray to a deity . . . for rain. It is difficult for a Western perspective to embrace price reduction efforts and prayers for rain equally, but given the Chinese vision of correlative associations between events and processes on earth and in the heavens, a late imperial official might place equal faith in both types of efforts. Once we understand the embeddedness of political practices within the culture as well as the cultural commitments of the state, the moral elements in Chinese ideas of what it meant to rule take on much more complicated shadings. So, too, does the more ambiguous separation of "state" and "society."[58]

GOVERNMENTAL INSTITUTIONS AND APPROACHES

For benevolent and proper government, the Chinese state not only had to establish and preserve a balance between center and locality but also between "situational flexibility and bureaucratic standardization."[59] Standardization came via the functioning, regulation, and procedures of the bureaucracy and the application of laws; other less overriding specific institutions and policies allowed creative flexibility to ameliorate the potentially heavy encumbrances of both law and bureaucracy.

The Bureaucracy

In the modern world, the word *bureaucracy* seems weighted down with connotations of inefficiency, delay, and frustrated action. The traditional Chinese bureaucracy could also become that burden. As with the tensions inherent in the center-local complementariness, so too did tensions abound between emperor and the bureaucracy. The late Ming emperors, for example, were generally stymied by bureaucratic governance, which seemed, especially in matters of the powers of Confucian ritual specialists, to demand an emperor who was noninterventionist, almost a nonactor. The result was general government ineffectuality, and certainly not much political creativity. An important reality, however, as Susan Mann reminds us, is that "like all bureaucracies, China's state administration had many different, competing levels and was composed of individuals with competing loyalties to structures outside the government."[60]

Also crucial to understand is that the relationship between monarch and bureaucracy depended on the historical context, the personalities of the monarchs, and the proclivities of key ministers: monarch and bureaucracy were not static entities—the relationship among the historical players was continually evolving.

In contrast to the late Ming, the Kangxi, Yongzheng, and Qianlong emperors in the early Qing period were strong rulers who sought new ways to find leverage against a bureaucracy that often tended to be unresponsive. The Yongzheng emperor seemed driven in his short reign as a fervent centralizer and state builder. He cracked down on bureaucratic corruption and mismanagement. He rationalized local fiscal structures, used the palace memorial system effectively, established the Grand Council, and centralized control over the administrative levels of the Censorate, the emperor's "eyes and ears."[61] These creative institutionalizations were all important; indeed one historian has called him "the greatest centralizer and stabilizer of the Qing dynasty."[62]

Whereas challenges to the early modern Western states had come from clergy, aristocrats, and external threats, in late imperial China the challenge was maintaining and controlling a very large agrarian state that was growing larger by swallowing up heterogeneous populations. While for the West challenges meant relying on coercive and military power, for China it meant relying on a bureaucracy that could deal effectively with diverse populations and cultures. Chinese emperors thus had to regulate thousands of bureaucrats to make sure that they followed written codes and procedures.[63] It is noteworthy that over 50 percent of the provisions of the Qing Code dealt with regulating that bureaucracy.[64]

Bureaucrats had to follow detailed regulations that prescribed the format, deadlines, and routing of paperwork and individually had to function properly as supervisor or subordinate in an institution often ridden with factions and cliques.

The power and the responsibility of the father-mother official, the county magistrate, were especially great; equally great was the trust implicitly placed in him by the state. Its own reputation in counties all across China could rise or fall with the leadership of the magistrate as the state bureaucrat with whom people most had to deal. The state recognized that the key to good government was the magistrate and local government. The people's trust in magistrates in their judicial roles, and others as well, came because of their belief in the validity and general transcendence of the state ethical-educational-political system, a sense that these civil service degree holders were men "who, through learning and self-cultivation, comprehended [that the cosmos was inherently moral and hierarchical], lived their lives according to the rules of propriety that embodied these principles, and transformed those around them through the power of their moral example."[65] The comprehensive and holistic vision of state-society was part of the political genius of the system.

Personnel evaluations were part of the system and could obviously be critical in measuring someone for a new appointment or allowing him to stay on in an appointment. Magistrates had routine annual evaluations, but a "grand accounting" came triennially; in the latter, the governor and governor-general reviewed the records of all local administrators.[66] The problem with these triennial reports was that they became stereotyped and were done offhandedly; evaluative phrases inflated into meaningless platitudes; cliques and factions shaped and perverted the evaluations. Overall, bureaucrats tended to choose the least risky alternatives in approaching personnel and other matters; and, when wrongdoing was uncovered, there was often considerable reluctance to follow through with impeachment.

A preeminent reality in the bureaucracy as in Chinese society in general was social "connections." An American student of China has suggested that the Chinese "instinctively divide people into those with whom they already have a fixed relationship, a connection, what the Chinese call *guanxi*, and those that they don't. These connections operate like a series of invisible threads, tying the Chinese to each other with far greater tensile strength than mere friendship."[67] Among other possibilities, connections were built on friendship, from common native place, teacher-student relationships, and same-year attaining of civil service degrees. Whether dealing with the imperial, Republican, or Communist state bureaucracy, connections were a *must* to get things done.

Within the bureaucracy itself, these connections could play roles in appointments, personnel evaluations, career patterns, indeed in career success or lack of it. All *guanxi* were to have moral dimensions; they were not simply mechanical relationships. While the bureaucracy had various regulatory features—for example, the law of avoidance and surveillance by censors—these regulations were not attempts to eliminate *guanxi*, but rather to keep them within bounds of serving the public interest.

The Qianlong emperor's approach to the bureaucracy differed markedly from that of his father who championed autocratic methods. Instead he used various creative approaches—"informal, extra-institutional, and personalistic"—to try to obtain valid personnel evaluations, which bureaucrats were not conveying to him.[68] He initially stressed the use of the secret palace memorial, an institution begun in the 1690s under his grandfather, the Kangxi emperor, where confidential memorials were sent directly to the emperor—the bureaucracy was thus kept out of the loop.[69] The Qianlong emperor continued to rely on it though there were indications that some bureaucrats colluded with others to keep the truth hidden even under the secret palace memorial. He tried to use other bureaucratic channels to find out confidential information, but apparently interlocking bureaucratic networks made that difficult as well.

He did achieve some success in his efforts to monitor the personnel situation by using the imperial audience system to conduct personal interviews; this experience personalized appointments, giving the emperor more control over appointees through this brief personal contact. After these personalized appointments, documentary exchanges were ritualized; appointees sent flowery "gratitude memorials" and utilized words in subsequent memorials indicating their submissiveness. "These ritual humiliations were signs, not of degradation, but of special status: in Confucian terms, these gentlemen were not tools."[70] The Qianlong emperor also made high-level political appointments his prerogative, taking men who had handled routine appointments and had had substantial personal stake in decisions out of the picture. Thus, he used a variety of creative approaches beyond routine measures to gain more control over the bureaucracy.

But Qianlong's approaches were not only of the velvet glove variety; he could also come down with an iron fist. During his reign, the Grand Council replaced the Grand Secretariat as the chief policymaking body; it was totally under the emperor's control as he appointed council members. The Qianlong emperor also gave the Grand Council orders to levy secretly the so-called penitence silver fines on high provincial officials, including governors and governors-general.[71] The exaction of penitence silver was another effort outside the administrative routine to control high-ranking bureaucrats, usually men who had failed to investigate cases of corruption or who may have known about corruption but did not inform the emperor. The fines were steep, ranging from several thousand to hundreds of thousands of taels of silver. The monies were used by the Imperial Household Department for the personal use of the emperor and also for some public works projects like repairing the dikes of the Grand Canal.

The exactions peaked in the years 1778–1795, when fifteen governors-general (37 percent of the total) and twenty-two governors (26 percent of the total) were fined. The Qianlong emperor framed the fining as his "rescue" of the officials, who, if they had been subjected to routine bureaucratic procedures, would have lost their positions or worse. As with his nonroutine handling of appointments and personnel issues, the penitence silver fines were attempts "to construct a patrimonial system to replace the bureaucracy [and] to build a personal relationship and control over his high provincial officials, rather than using bureaucratic means."[72] The Qianlong emperor was a master at finding new methods and approaches to accomplish his goals vis-à-vis the bureaucracy.

Law and Society

As an indication of how important law was to the Chinese state, one of the
first actions of a new dynasty was to issue its own law codes: it was a matter of
setting its identity clearly apart from its predecessor, and of indicating that it
now held Heaven's Mandate. While it had once been commonplace in the field
of Chinese studies to downplay the "rule of law," emphasizing instead the
Confucian moral code and the "rule of men," recent work has made it clear
that codified law—administrative, penal, and civil—was important in practice. Philip Huang studied 221 civil cases heard in court session in three counties in Sichuan, Zhili, and Taiwan from the late eighteenth century up to the
end of the Qing. He found that magistrates mediated to bring agreement between the disputants through compromise in only eleven cases; however, in
the remaining 210, "formal court sessions actually generally produced un-
equivocal ruling for one or the other party" as magistrates "acted as judges
upholding the written code."[73] It is clear, however, that even with the usage of
the Qing code in these cases, the rule of men also remained a key. Huang's 221
cases ending in a formal court session came from a larger sample of 668; the
other 447 civil suits that had been filed were settled earlier presumably
through mediation of some sort. The rule of law and rule of men was "inextricably linked."[74]

Another way to treat this linkage is to consider a mere outline of the origins
and development of Chinese law. The discourse of law began with Legalists,
who promoted strict laws and harsh punishments to bring about social order.
But over time, Legalism came to be packaged with the older moralistic Confucianism, which had a very different prescription for order and harmony. It
was an unlikely pairing whose procedures and substance evolved through the
dynasties "varying with the context; duties and correspondingly, rights/rites
[were] also constantly being redefined as other actors change[d]."[75] Huang
summarizes the philosophical nature of the Qing code using the all-important
metaphor of family. The Qing code "took care to represent the state not only
as the stern and authoritarian father that the punishment-inclined Legalists
envisaged but also as the compassionate and protective mother that Confucians would have claimed it to be."[76] It was the iron fist within the velvet glove.
It is also important in this regard to note that law was only one kind of norm
for constraining social behavior in Chinese society, existing alongside canons
of ethics and propriety, religious values, and the use of models.

One of the hallmarks of codified civil law points to a pattern of Chinese
governance that we have seen repeatedly: the center spelled out the general
principles and allowed those at the local level to make the specific applications. Huang notes that stipulations regarding civil law were relatively few,

and, when they appeared, were limited to broad principles.[77] This was a contrast with the highly particularistic and specific criminal laws in the code. The generality of the civil stipulations allowed magistrates to be more flexible and therefore allowed for creative handling of cases in differing social and cultural contexts; it also kept the strong arm of the state out of local disputes.

Flexibility

Finally, flexibility in its strategies and approaches was a key to imperial state success and evidence of its political creativity in many arenas. In its construction of a multiethnic empire, for example, the Qing opted for a wide range of administrative institutions based upon the particular social and cultural contexts. They exercised direct control over banner organizations in Manchuria. A military protectorate ruled indirectly in Mongolia through Mongol banners and Lamaist monastic institutions. In Xinjiang, also ruled indirectly, various bodies played governmental roles concurrently: "military and civilian agricultural colonies, Mongol bannermen, tributary arrangements with roving bands of Kazakh and Kirghiz, and almost autonomous Islamic oasis communities ruled by hereditary or bureaucratic begs."[78] It then became a province in 1884. The Chinese sent a resident commissioner to Lhasa, as Chinese control overlaid Tibetan institutions.

Although under a common moral and legal system, the Chinese bureaucracy was not simply a rule-implementing, rational institution. "Rules there certainly were, but the opportunities for choice among them to fit a particular situation and the many possible applications for any one cluster of regulations" gave officials the flexibility to respond often creatively.[79] When Chen Hongmou, for example, looked for what sorts of units to which he could attach his community granaries, he used "community compact" units in Jiangxi, administrative subdistricts in Fujian, and even lineage organizations.[80]

CONCLUSION

The political creativity and genius of the imperial Chinese state lay in its unitary Confucian state system amid the country's vast diversity. That system was directed by a minimalist state where, when matters went smoothly, the center set out general principles for policies and let the locality work out the specifics, an arrangement that fostered flexibility and considerable pragmatism. Such decentralization of policy execution was possible because of the unity of state and society, the meritocratic bureaucracy produced by the civil service examination, and the array of "civilizing" strategies undertaken or sponsored by the state.

Finally, a secret of the Chinese state's success lay in its amalgamating potentially antagonistic systems or spheres. In addition to state/society, there were center/locality, Legalism/Confucianism, bureaucratic standardization/situational flexibility, *guanxi* and regulations, and rule of law/rule of men. The blending of each alternative sphere or strategy suggests the complementariness of yin/yang and the selection of "both . . . and," in contrast to the West's often preferred option of "either . . . or." In any case, the Chinese state's melding of these alternatives served the state well and fostered a general long-term stability in the state system.

Dialectic approach of balancing interests

NOTES

1. Philip A. Kuhn, *Soulstealers: The Chinese Sorcery Scare of 1768* (Cambridge, MA: Harvard University Press, 1990), 187–232.

2. R. Kent Guy, *The Emperor's Four Treasuries* (Cambridge, MA: Harvard University Press, 1987).

3. Quoted in Julia Ching, *Mysticism and Kingship in China: The Heart of Chinese Wisdom* (Cambridge: Cambridge University Press, 1997), 63.

4. David N. Keightley, "Early Civilization in China: Reflections on How It Became Chinese" in Paul S. Ropp, ed., *Heritage of China: Contemporary Perspectives on Chinese Civilization* (Berkeley: University of California Press, 1990), 35.

5. Pamela Kyle Crossley, "The Rulerships of China," *American Historical Review* 97, no. 5 (December 1992): 1480.

6. R. Bin Wong, "Confucian Agendas for Material and Ideological Control in Modern China" in Theodore Huters, R. Bin Wong, and Pauline Yu, eds., *Culture and State in Chinese History: Conventions, Accommodations, and Critiques* (Stanford, CA: Stanford University Press, 1997), 307.

7. See Wong, "Confucian Agendas," 307, and also R. Bin Wong, "The Grand Structure, 1736–1780" in Pierre-Etienne Will and R. Bin Wong, *Nourish the People: The State Civilian Granary System in China, 1650–1850* (Ann Arbor, MI: Center for Chinese Studies, 1991), 70.

8. Patricia Thornton, *Disciplining the State: Virtue, Violence, and State-Making in Modern China* (Cambridge, MA: Harvard University Asia Center, 2007), 29.

9. David Johnson, "Communication, Class, and Consciousness in Late Imperial China" in David Johnson, Andrew J. Nathan, and Evelyn S. Rawski, eds., *Popular Culture in Late Imperial China* (Berkeley: University of California Press, 1985), 58–59.

10. For a "not quite best practices" view, see the classic novel *The Scholars* by Wu Jingzi (New York: Columbia University Press, 1993).

11. Evelyn S. Rawski, "Economic and Social Foundations of Late Imperial China," in Johnson, Nathan, and Rawski, eds., *Popular Culture*, 12.

12. John Bryan Starr, *Understanding China: A Guide to China's Economy, History, and Political Structure* (New York: Hill and Wang, 1997), 42.

13. Jane Kate Leonard and John R. Watt, "Introduction" in Jane Kate Leonard and John R. Watt, eds., *To Achieve Security and Wealth: The Qing Imperial State and the Economy* (Ithaca, NY: Cornell University Press, 1992), 2.

14. H. Lyman Miller, "The Late Imperial Chinese State," in David Shambaugh, ed., *The Modern Chinese State* (Cambridge: Cambridge University Press, 2000), 34.

15. Calculated from Yu Keping, *Globalization and Changes in China's Governance* (Leiden: Brill, 2008), 29.

16. Philip A. Kuhn, *Origins of the Modern Chinese State* (Stanford, CA: Stanford University Press, 2002), 22.

17. William T. Rowe, *Hankow: Commerce and Society in a Chinese City, 1796–1889* (Stanford, CA: Stanford University Press, 1984), 339.

18. Kuhn, *Origins*, 23.

19. See Jane Kate Leonard, *Controlling from Afar: The Daoguang Emperor's Management of the Grand Canal Crisis, 1824–1826* (Ann Arbor, MI: Center for Chinese Studies, 1996).

20. Leonard, *Controlling from Afar*, 249.

21. James L. Watson, "Standardizing the Gods: The Promotion of T'ien Hou ('Empress of Heaven') along the South China Coast, 960–1960" in Johnson, Nathan, and Rawski, *Popular Culture*, 323.

22. John Patrick Delury, "The Mixed Constitution of Gu Yanwu" (unpublished paper delivered at the 2009 Association for Asian Studies Convention, March 28, 2009).

23. Timothy Brook, "Family Continuity and Cultural Hegemony: The Gentry of Ningbo, 1368–1911" in Joseph W. Esherick and Mary Backus Rankin, eds., *Chinese Local Elites and Patterns of Dominance* (Berkeley: University of California Press, 1990), 43.

24. *The Great Learning* in William Theodore de Bary, Wing-tsit Chan, and Burton Watson, eds., *Sources of Chinese Tradition*, vol. 1 (New York: Columbia University Press, 1965), 115–16. De Bary points out the omission of the locality in *The Trouble with Confucianism* (Cambridge, MA: Harvard University Press, 1991), 98–99; Rowe's discussion is on 377–80 in *Hankow*.

25. Brook, "Family Continuity," 45–46.

26. Prasenjit Duara, *Culture, Power, and the State: Rural North China, 1900–1942* (Stanford, CA: Stanford University Press. 1988), 15–16, 25–26.

27. See Rowe's discussion, *Hankow*, 331–35.

28. Leonard and Watt, "Introduction," 2; Huters, Wong, and Yu, *Culture and State*, 254.

29. Quoted in Huters, Wong, and Yu, *Culture and State*, 1.

30. Arthur P. Wolf, "Gods, Ghosts, and Ancestors" in Arthur P. Wolf, ed., *Studies in Chinese Society* (Stanford, CA: Stanford University Press, 1978), 143, 145.

31. This discussion is based on Rowe, *Hankow*, 406–7.

32. Pamela Kyle Crossley, *A Translucent Mirror: History and Identity in Qing Imperial Ideology* (Berkeley: University of California Press, 1999), 256.

33. Huters, Wong, and Yu, *Culture and State*, 4–5.

34. Quoted in Hsiao Kung-chuan, *Rural China: Imperial Control in the Nineteenth Century* (Seattle: University of Washington Press, 1967), 236.

35. Mao Qiling, *He yushi xiaozi ci zhufuwei lu* [A record of the reestablishment of the shrine to Censor He and his filial son], (n.p., n.d.), 3 a–b.

36. Yu Keping, *Globalization*, 29.

37. Quoted in Rowe, *Hankow*, 418.

38. Hsiao, *Rural China*, 239.

39. Hsiao, *Rural China*, 241.

40. Rowe, *Hankow*, 390.

41. Hsiao, *Rural China*, 186.

42. Victor H. Mair, "Language and Ideology in the Written Popularizations of the *Sacred Edict*," in Johnson, Nathan, and Rawski, *Popular Culture*, 343–44.

43. Quoted in Donald J. Munro, *The Concept of Man in Contemporary China* (Ann Arbor: University of Michigan Press, 1979), 136.

44. Rowe, *Hankow*, 327.

45. Munro, *Concept of Man*, 154.

46. R. Keith Schoppa, *Xiang Lake—Nine Centuries of Chinese Life* (New Haven, CT: Yale University Press, 1989), 86–88.

47. R. Keith Schoppa, "The Capital Comes to the Periphery: Views of the Sino-Japanese War Era in Central Zhejiang," in Kenneth G. Leiberthal, Shuen-fu Lin, and Ernest P. Young, eds., *Constructing China: The Interaction of Culture and Economics* (Ann Arbor, MI: Center for Chinese Studies, 1997), 122.

48. Evelyn S. Rawski, *The Last Emperors: A Social History of Qing Imperial Institutions* (Berkeley: University of California Press, 1998), 197.

49. Richard J. Smith, *China's Cultural Heritage: The Ch'ing Dynasty, 1644–1912* (Boulder, CO: Westview Press, 1983), 287.

50. Michael G. Chang, *A Court on Horseback: Imperial Touring and the Construction of Qing Rule* (Cambridge, MA: Harvard University Asia Center, 2007), 72.

51. Chang, *Court on Horseback*, 85.

52. Chang, *Court on Horseback*, 8.

53. Rawski, *The Last Emperors*, 200.

54. Rowe, *Hankow*, 440.

55. Rowe, *Hankow*, 417; Smith, *China's Cultural Heritage*, 290.

56. Quoted in Hsiao, *Rural China*, 209.

57. Rowe, *Hankow*, 384.

58. Huters, Wong, and Yu, *Culture and State*, 5–6.

59. Rowe, *Hankow*, 283.

60. Susan Mann, *Local Merchants and the Chinese Bureaucracy, 1750–1950* (Stanford, CA: Stanford University Press, 1987), 10.

61. Smith, *China's Cultural Heritage*, 42.

62. Huang Pei, *Autocracy at Work: A Study of the Yongzheng Period, 1723–1736* (Bloomington: Indiana University Press, 1974), 21.

63. See Kuhn, *Soulstealers*, 190–219.

64. Jonathan K. Ocko and David Gilmartin, "State, Sovereignty, and the People: A Comparison of the 'Rule of Law' in China and India," *Journal of Asian Studies* 68, no. 1 (February 2009): 60.

65. Ocko and Gilmartin, "State, Sovereignty, and the People," 60. See also Philip Huang, *Civil Justice in China: Representation and Practice in the Qing* (Stanford, CA: Stanford University Press, 1996), 198–99.

66. Thornton describes the system in *Disciplining the State,* 26–29.

67. Fox Butterfield, *China: Alive in a Bitter Sea* (New York: Times Books, 1982), 74–75, cited in Ambrose Yeo-chi King, "Kuan-his and Network Building," *Daedalus* 120, no. 2 (Spring 1991): 64.

68. Ting Zhang, "'Penitence Silver' and the Politics of Punishment in the Qianlong Reign (1736–1795)" (unpublished paper, n.d.), 23.

69. Jonathan D. Spence, *Ts'ao Yin and the K'ang-his Emperor, Bondservant and Master* (New Haven, CT: Yale University Press, 1966), 221–29.

70. Kuhn, *Origins,* 209–10.

71. This discussion is based on details in Ting Zhang's essay, "Penitence Silver."

72. Ting Zhang, "Penitence Silver," 40.

73. Philip Huang, "Codified Law and Magisterial Adjudication in the Qing," in Kathryn Bernhardt and Philip C. Huang, eds., *Civil Law in Qing and Republican China* (Stanford, CA: Stanford University Press, 1994), 143.

74. Ocko and Gilmartin, "State, Sovereignty, and the People," 128.

75. Randall Peerenboom, "What's Wrong with Chinese Rights? Toward a Theory of Rights with Chinese Characteristics," *Harvard Human Rights Journal* 6 (1993): 47; quoted in Stanley B. Lubman, *Bird in a Cage: Legal Reform in China after Mao* (Stanford, CA: Stanford University Press, 1999), 19.

76. Huang, "Codified Law," 174–75.

77. Huang, "Codified Law," 178.

78. Leonard, *Controlling from Afar,* 63.

79. Huters, Wong, and Yu, *Culture and State,* 9.

80. Rowe, *Hankow,* 281.

10

Political Creativity
and Political Reform in China?

Joseph Fewsmith

The political reconstruction of the Chinese state and the continuing dilemmas of reform it faces emerge from the long period of political, economic, and social trauma that followed the end of the Qing, or, to put it in the terms that Keith Schoppa uses, followed the end of the period of political creativity and genius that had held China together for so long. It was not only that imperial China ended under pressures from the outside world, but the way in which that end came is important for understanding contemporary China. Although there were mounting problems in the late Qing period—the Opium War, Second Opium War, Taiping Rebellion, Nian Rebellion, Northwest Muslim Rebellion, and Sino-French War, to name only a few—it was China's defeat in the Sino-Japanese War of 1894–1895 that galvanized the emotions that changed China's trajectory. Whereas China's sense of centrality in the world had been increasingly challenged by Western encroachments, it was its defeat by Japan, a country that China had always viewed as peripheral, that brought home to a new generation of Chinese that China was now a marginal country in world affairs.

That new generation of Chinese was led by Kang Youwei, then in Beijing with 1,200 other holders of the *juren* degree (the second level in the tripartite hierarchy of imperial exams) to take the metropolitan (*jinshi*) exam. Kang drafted a memorial that expressed a new and radical sense of nationalism. Calling for wholesale political change, Kang and his fellow examinees said, "Not a single moment should be lost. If there is delay of a whole month or a whole year . . . even a sage will not be able to deal effectively with the aftermath."[1] The nation was in crisis, and only immediate, radical action could salvage the situation.[2]

Kang's radicalism had its roots in the developing *qingyi* ("pure talk") movement that had grown up particularly in the aftermath of the Sino-French war.[3]
Zhang Zhidong (famous for his later call to "take Western learning for practical use and Chinese learning as the essence") had urged the throne not to sue
for peace; Zhang's staunch resistance was not just based on his assessment that
the war was winnable (which it was), but primarily on his moral outrage at the
temporizing, compromising approach of the Qing.[4] It might be argued that
precisely such temporizing and compromising, which under different circumstances might be seen as a moderate and flexible approach to problem solving,
had underlain much of the political creativity that Keith Schoppa describes so
well in his chapter. The problem was that that world had collapsed, unleashing
a different, moralistic and noncompromising vocabulary that would come to
dominate twentieth-century political discourse in China.

The *qingyi* discourse of political opposition found favor with mid- and
lower-level officials who were frustrated by governmental ineffectiveness and
their own inability to influence policy. Such people reached out through social
networks to like-minded officials, and subsequently to local scholar-gentry
managers, people who supported a reformist agenda and wanted broader political participation. Many of these people were highly educated, ambitious
people who had little outlet for their talents and found themselves increasingly critical of those in power. Such people supported Kang Youwei and the
Reform Movement of 1898, and then were forced to turn their energies to
provincial outlets after the reform movement failed.[5]

Without trying to trace the twists and turns of Chinese politics in this period, it is necessary to point out that China's sense of political crisis did not
end as China's imperial system gave way to the new Republic of China. On the
contrary, the new republic was quickly threatened by President Yuan Shikai's
monarchical ambitions and Japan's imperialistic ambitions in the form of the
twenty-one demands, which would have reduced China to a dependency if
accepted in full. China's descent into warlordism only heightened the sense of
cultural crisis, and a new generation sought regeneration through cultural
revolution. Although often called "China's enlightenment," the New Culture
Movement embodied an intellectual radicalism that drew on the antecedents
of *qingyi* and soon exploded into moral rage as the Paris Peace Conference
awarded Germany's concessions on the Shandong peninsula to Japan.[6]

There was thus an increasing radicalization of Chinese thought from at
least 1895 through the May Fourth Movement and the founding of the CCP
as China was increasingly marginalized in terms of world politics and as
China's intellectuals were increasingly marginalized within Chinese society.[7]
This radicalization of thought would soon be accompanied by increasingly
well-organized and violent political parties and militaries as battles were

Increased Radicalization

fought to reunify China (1927–1928), to "exterminate" internal enemies (1927–1937), to defend the country against Japan, and to vie for supremacy in China's civil war. Even the triumph of the CCP in 1949 did not end this period of radicalism as one mass movement after another was launched, culminating in the Cultural Revolution of 1966–1976. Looking at the long arc of Chinese politics, it is possible to trace this radicalization of thought and politics from at least the defeat by Japan in 1895 to the death of Mao in 1976. The intensity and duration of conflict in this period dramatically changed the state-society relationship while changing the political system from one staffed by bureaucrats thoroughly educated in the Confucian classics to one staffed by "cadres" (*ganbu*) who were specialized in mobilizing people. China's ideology may still have been based on morals, but those morals were based on class purity and class struggle, not Confucian propriety.

THE DEATH OF MAO AND THE DYNAMIC OF REFORM

When Mao Zedong finally[8] died, China could begin the long task, which continues, of trying to normalize politics and society. Given the chaos and decentralization of the Cultural Revolution years, the government's first instincts were to recentralize and to modernize the economy. With the ideological passions finally exhausted, there was a clear crisis of legitimacy. People spoke about the three crises: spiritual (*jingshen weiji* 精神危机), belief (*xinyang weiji* 信仰危机), and culture (*wenhua weiji* 文化危机).[9] And this sense of ideological disillusionment was only deepened by the very real poverty in which most of the country found itself. After a quarter century of exhausting political campaigns, the per capita income of urban residents in 1978 was only 316 yuan, while the per capita income of rural residents was a mere 134 yuan. China was one of the poorest countries in the world, and over one-quarter of China's rural population had an annual income of less than 50 yuan.[10] At the time, for political reasons, the exchange rate between the RMB and the US dollar was 2 to 1, though it was clearly much less than that if markets had been allowed to determine the rate. Economics would determine the contours of China's reforms.

The government's first instinct was to "buy" modernization. The "four modernizations" were reendorsed, and China hoped to sell oil, primarily to Japan, in exchange for a number of large-scale, turnkey projects. In 1978, China drilled 6.5 million meters of oil wells, followed by another 8.2 million meters in 1979, and another 6 million meters in 1980. Fortunately for China, the country turned out to have few oil reserves. The combined impact of those 20.7 million meters of drilling was the discovery of only one small oil field.[11]

If China had found more oil fields like that in Daqing, China's political economy most likely would have remained highly capital-intensive and state-centric. The whole pattern of decentralized, export-oriented, labor-intensive industrialization that we associate with China's economic reforms might never have materialized, or would have occupied a very different place in China's political economy.

At the same time that central planners were trying to find oil, China's peasants were trying to survive. China's senior economic policy specialist, Chen Yun (陈云), famously said that if something were not done, party secretaries in the countryside would lead peasants into the cities to demand food.[12] The something that was done was the Household Responsibility System (HRS), an arrangement that assigned land to each household, in the process shifting both risk and initiative. The economic revolution that this set off was tremendous, but the political impact was significant as well. The emergence of the HRS would herald the end of the commune system, with implications that are still echoing across the landscape.

 Moreover, China made the decision to open itself to the outside world. Given the history of imperialism and Mao's nationalistic emphasis on "self-reliance" (*zili gengsheng* 自立更生), it took more than a little political courage and the sort of dominant political power that only Deng Xiaoping possessed to move ahead with opening up. The decision to open China to the outside world worked extremely well. Labor rates in Hong Kong were increasing and the possibility of opening factories in neighboring Guangdong generated synergies that were too powerful for either side to resist.[13] Once China was open, the influx of capital and ideas proved overwhelming, which is not to say that they were not resisted.

If economics were critical in shaping the contours of reform, politics were equally important. The politics of China are important in and of themselves, but they also raise important questions for political science as a field. Although there has been a great appreciation in recent years for the role institutions play in promoting economic growth, this literature seems singularly unable to explain the process of reform in China. Most of institutional literature is shaped around themes of incremental change, path dependence, and historical legacies,[14] but, of course, what China experienced in the 1976–1980 period (or, perhaps longer, depending on one's focus) has been characterized by rather sudden change and path divergence. This is not to say that historical continuities are not important in China's reforms—which have been informed either at different times or simultaneously by traditional Chinese history, twentieth-century history, and PRC history—or that there has not been important incremental, path dependent changes. But it is difficult to explain the emergence of China's reforms, their economic or political course, or their robustness by pointing to historical incrementalism and path dependence. If the institutionalist literature has little to offer students of China, despite some important insights, China offers students of institutions a cornucopia of data and hypotheses to be explored. I hope this chapter will offer some hints as to why this is the case.

Moreover, historical explanations for the robustness of China's reforms are also surprisingly weak. Traditionally China saw itself as the center of its cultural universe. Other countries borrowed from Chinese civilization; China did not need to learn from others (the notable exception being Buddhism). Moreover, unlike, for instance, Japan, China does not have a history of reform.[15] The most famous reforms in Chinese history, those of Wang Anshi in the Song dynasty, ended in failure, as did the efforts of the Donglin faction in the late Ming dynasty.[16] More recently, the Reform Movement of 1898, led by Kang Youwei and Liang Qichao, collapsed after only a hundred days, leaving, perhaps, a legacy of frustration and political polarization but not one of reform and progress. Indeed, until the reforms of the first decade of the twentieth century, which marked a surprisingly vigorous effort coming from a dying dynasty, China's administrative organization of six boards and recruitment of officials through examination of their knowledge of the classics had continued unbroken for a thousand years, despite conquest by the Mongols in the thirteenth century and the Manchus in the seventeenth century. In short, as China embarked in reform and opening in the late 1970s, there was not much of a historical repertoire of ideas and experience to draw upon.[17]

Some leverage on the question of the transformation of Chinese politics can be gained by focusing on the issue of legitimacy. Mao Zedong had dominated the history of the PRC, and Mao Zedong Thought had been the solipsistic core around which legitimacy revolved.[18] When Mao died, it was Hua Guofeng who became chairman of the party (on the rather flimsy basis of having a note from Mao, apparently intended for different purposes, which said, "With you in charge, I am at ease" (*nibanshi, wo fangxin* 你办事我放心).[19] When Hua Guofeng famously vowed to "resolutely uphold whatever policy decisions Chairman Mao made, and unswervingly follow whatever instructions Chairman Mao gave" (which subsequently became known as the "two whatevers" [*liangge fanshi* 两个凡是]),[20] he was merely basing his legitimacy on Mao's legacy. Nevertheless, he moderated Mao's policies in practice. For instance, Hua upheld the famous Dazhai model in agriculture, but he deemphasized some of the radical aspects of Dazhai's collectivism. Hua's actions were precisely what students of Max Weber would have predicted, namely that he would engage in the routinization of charisma.

Indeed, this gentle path away from Cultural Revolution extremism toward more moderate but still identifiably Maoist policies seemed to be the logical way to proceed. Perhaps Hua could have found a way to make it work if he had been able to balance the Gang of Four against a group of veteran cadres, but Hua cooperated in the arrest of the Gang the month after Mao died, opening himself up to what would prove to be relentless pressure from the veteran cadres who had been purged in the Cultural Revolution.[21] Led by Deng Xiaoping, these veterans would take advantage of Hua's youth (born in 1921, Hua was fifty-five when Mao died in 1976) and relative incompetence to force him out of office and take over in their own right.

This deposing of Hua Guofeng is rather interesting and of considerable import for understanding the subsequent unfolding of reform. When Hua put forth the "two whatevers," Deng Xiaoping immediately responded by saying that Mao's thought had to be understood "comprehensively."[22] By comprehensively understanding Mao's thought, Deng meant that one had to test Mao's thought, or more specifically the policies that were said to derive from it, against the criterion of practice.[23] After all, Mao himself had raised the criterion of practice and had proved a master of applying Marxism-Leninism to the concrete realities of China in the course of the revolution. But even as Deng continued to uphold Mao Zedong Thought (and would enshrine it as one of the "Four Cardinal Principles"), he was suggesting that Mao Zedong Thought not be understood as an ideology but rather as an epistemology, a tool by which truth could be understood. Mao Zedong Thought was no longer a solipsistic claim to truth, but merely a way to approach practical problems. This was not, as Tang Tsou points out, the routinization of charisma but rather routinization through the repudiation of charisma.[24]

But the repudiation of charisma comes at a cost. The CCP's claim to legitimacy had always been a solipsistic claim that it alone understood Marxism-Leninism and thus had the right to interpret and implement that doctrine. But the Cultural Revolution had shown that the party's claim was less than convincing. As the regime's ideological guru Hu Qiaomu put it in a critical speech on the economy at the beginning of the reform era, there were objective economic laws and if the party did not adequately comprehend and act in accordance with those laws, there would be severe costs to pay—as the party had discovered to its chagrin in the Cultural Revolution (and, indeed, in the Great Leap Forward before that).[25] As with Deng's call to understand Mao Zedong Thought comprehensively, Hu's admission that there were objective laws external to Marxism as an ideology accepted Marxism-Leninism as an epistemology (though, ironically, Hu Qiaomu would have problems with General Secretary Hu Yaobang taking this line of thought further in his 1983 speech commemorating the centennial of Marx's death).[26] What the turn from solipsism to epistemology does is open the door to experts, who are specialists in interpreting objective laws, and expertise does not depend (at least in theory) on being a party member or an official. Perhaps non-Marxist economics had something to teach the party about those "objective laws" of economics. And given the pressing need to improve China's economy, the practice of economics became less and less dominated by Marxist ideologues—setting off squabbles about the role of Marxist economics that continue to this day.[27]

Of course, once the party admitted that its solipsistic claim was false, that opened a slippery slope for other fields to claim that they, too, were subject to objective laws, and, because of that, experts, not the party (and certainly not party ideologues), were the best interpreters of those laws. This is what Tang Tsou called the "sociological postulate," which Tsou paraphrased as "Every sphere of social life has its special characteristics (*tedian* 特点) and is governed by special laws of an objective nature. Political leadership can and should create general conditions and a framework favorable to the operation of these laws. It can use these laws to promote the desired development. But it cannot violate these laws without suffering serious consequences."[28] Thus, there were soon discussions about the laws governing journalism, sociology, writing, and other fields.

Worst of all, from the party's point of view, was the logical conclusion that politics itself might not be something the party could claim as a truth but something that should be subjected to debate. This was the conclusion Beijing University professor Guo Luoji drew, not without penalty, in his famous 1979 article. In a cleverly set up dialogue, Guo has one character say, "Opening up socialist democracy is not a matter of the public servants allowing their masters to speak but of the public servants listening to their masters speak," and arguing that "precisely because it is a political question it should be discussed."[29]

As Guo Luoji's article suggests, the price of giving up the party's solipsistic claim to truth was the opening up of the question of legitimacy, and the question of legitimacy has been a driver of China's political reforms over the past thirty years.[30] Understanding its vulnerability, the party had three responses.

First, the government responded to its ideological vulnerability with the use of a variety of measures to enforce its control, including coercion. After all, if one erects boundaries, they must be defended. Political campaigns and policy measures opened and closed political space during the 1980s. For instance, the campaign against spiritual pollution in 1983 targeted "rightist" thinkers, while the party's "Decision on Economic Structural Reform" the following year accelerated economic reform.[31] Control and coercion have also been employed to rein in the media, harass or arrest dissidents, prevent the free flow of information (such as by creating the "Great Firewall of China" to censor the Internet), and preserve "social order," often against those resisting the actions of predatory local officials. Coercion should never be underestimated in preserving authoritarian rule—it can and does prevent alternative expressions, protests, and civil society from appearing—but it cannot address the issue of legitimacy. The best it can do (from the regime's point of view) is provide a period of time while the issue of legitimacy is addressed in other ways.[32]

Economic Success   Second, more positively, the party highlighted performance legitimacy, the ability to oversee economic development and the improvement of people's lives. The argument here was that even if Marxism-Leninism was an episte-mology, the party was best equipped to employ that epistemology, and the evidence of that was the rapidly growing economy. Indeed, the Chinese economy has grown approximately 10 percent per year for the last three de-cades, a truly remarkable accomplishment for a country as large as China. Implicit, however, was the trade-off between economic development and po-litical quiescence.

The switch to performance legitimacy does not mean that the party gave up its use of ideology to frame issues, explain party goals, and identify pri-orities. Nevertheless, its function in the polity was quite different. In the Maoist era, ideology (specifically Mao Zedong Thought) was the focal point around which everything else revolved, the central rational that legitimated everything else, including private life. That is what charismatic authority means. Once charisma ends and the solipsistic claim to truth fails, however, what is left is not an animating ideological force, but simply boundaries. Against leftist opponents, Deng could raise the slogans "seek truth from facts" and "practice is the sole criterion of truth," and against rightist critics he could uphold the Four Cardinal Principles (Marxism–Leninism–Mao Zedong Thought, the socialist road, the people's democratic dictatorship, and, most important of all, the leadership of the CCP). In between lay a broad "middle way," the boundaries of which changed depending on need (whether one was fighting against spiritual pollution or promoting eco-nomic reform) but whose center of gravity shifted distinctly to the right over time. The carving out of a middle path allowed Deng to build a coalition of often conflicting political forces and personalities and to begin to create a different type of polity, one that necessarily had to have greater reliance on institutions and law, about which more will be said later. [33]

Uncertainty   Third, and most important for our purposes, opening up the question of legitimacy creates uncertainty. On the one hand, there is the issue of succes-sion. By what means could the leadership present successive leaders as legiti-mate? This was a particularly thorny issue in the 1980s because there were deeply divided interests and visions within the party and because power was inevitably passing from the revolutionary generation to the postrevolutionary generation. Struggle over succession was one of the forces that generated the tensions underlying Tiananmen, and succession has always been problematic in authoritarian regimes. Beyond the specific problems of the 1980s, there was

Succession

the issue of the very different career paths followed by the postrevolutionary successors. They were not the rebels their elders had been but rather bureaucrats who had risen step by step up bureaucratic ranks. Moreover, because their careers were generally confined to bureaucratic organizations that were "stove-piped" into the decision-making process, few had the range of experience or acquaintance that the revolutionary generation had possessed. Most particularly they had little or no military experience, and control of the military had been a prominent characteristic of Chinese politics throughout the twentieth century. Furthermore, largely because of the tumultuous politics of the Mao era, those selected as successors routinely came from engineering backgrounds. Given the stress on economic development and the potential conflict inherent in choosing successors with more political backgrounds, the choice of engineers was perhaps inevitable. To the extent that engineers tend to be pragmatic, these successors were well suited to the tasks of the times. But in their inability to articulate a public vision, the emergence of a generation of engineers meant that legitimacy issues would continue.[34]

In the post-Tiananmen period, this technocratization of the political elite appeared to smooth out relations among the elite, in part because of the homogenization of elite selection.[35] In addition, the pressures of the post-Tiananmen period, including the collapse of socialism in Eastern Europe and the Soviet Union, were very much a part of this convergence of opinion because they highlighted the dangers of leadership division and certain types of political reform. So the elite converged, albeit not altogether easily, around a program of "neoconservative" reform—strengthening the center (especially in fiscal terms) against overdecentralization, articulating the "dangers" of multiparty democracy, revising party ideology to emphasize the "Three Represents" and then, under Hu Jintao, "scientific development."[36] They were careful to distribute political positions, balancing different interests in the party, and emphasizing procedures. To a certain extent, a procedural legitimacy (at least among the elite) began to emerge. Most of all, they emphasized economic development.

On the other hand, if political pressures and generational transition worked to ameliorate tensions among the political elite, diminishing if not ending uncertainty over succession, there was another aspect of uncertainty that undermined legitimacy, namely, defining the "publicness" of the government. The solipsistic claim to legitimacy posited that the regime's legitimacy lay in its privileged claim to the truth. But if the CCP has no privileged claim to the truth, or at best a partial claim to the truth, then the regime's publicness must be demonstrated in other terms; it must be shown that those selected for high positions are not pursuing their own private or factional interests but rather the public's business.[37] This could only be demonstrated through a significant

transparency

remaking of the bureaucracy, which is largely coterminous (at least at the higher ranks) with the party apparatus.

Over the 1980s, China remade its bureaucracy, instituting rules for retirement and moving from "red" to "expert" through the promotion of technocrats. As Hong Yung Lee notes, in the reform period, "the regime cited the possession of technical knowledge rather than the ability to manipulate symbols as the intellectuals' most salient characteristic."[38] But Weberian-style bureaucracy never emerged (or, at least, never dominated). What was happening was not the technocratization of politics but the political use of technocrats.[39]

This difference underscores that in reforming its bureaucratic system, China was not retracing the meritocratic routes pursued by post-Meiji Japan or postrevolutionary France.[40] It could not without the CCP giving up its claim to legitimacy altogether. Consequently, China followed the course of building a hybrid bureaucracy: the competence of the bureaucracy was improved, in some cases dramatically, but the promotion process remained firmly in the hands of the party, and loyalty remained at least as important a criterion of promotion as competence.

ELITE SUCCESSION

Elite succession has been the bane of authoritarian regimes, and, although China has managed this issue surprisingly well, there may be reason to believe that the issue is not yet solved. China has dealt with the issue through four main mechanisms: (1) rules governing retirement, (2) an informal but nevertheless seemingly well-institutionalized practice of what might be called "overlapping succession," (3) rules governing promotion, and (4) an informal but critical effort to balance interests within the party.

The CCP began introducing retirement practices in 1980. There were at least two immediate pressures forcing consideration of this issue. One was age. Deng Xiaoping was seventy-four years old in 1978, and the rest of the senior leadership, returning to high positions in the wake of the Cultural Revolution, were similarly advanced in age. Many of them had undergone hardship in the Cultural Revolution and faced serious health issues. The other was ideology. The senior elite was composed of people who had fought the revolution to realize Marxist goals; now Deng was asking them to preside over the marketization and internationalization of the economy. Many resisted, and those who were willing often had little knowledge about how to go about the tasks Deng and the leadership set for them. There was a real need to rejuvenate the leadership. The Twelfth Party Congress in 1982 established the Central Advisory Commission as a way to retire, or at least semiretire, senior cadres honorably and open up their positions to younger, better trained leaders. Of the 210 full members of the newly elected Central Committee, 97 (46 percent) were elected for the first time.[41] In an unusual party procedure in 1985, 54 full members of the Central Committee were dropped at the Fourth Plenary Session of the Twelfth Central Committee and 56 new members elected to that body at the National Representative Conference held September 19–25.[42] At the Thirteenth Party Congress two years later (1987), 65 percent of the full membership of the Central Committee was replaced (the Central Advisory Committee was disbanded at the time of the Fourteenth Party Congress in 1992).[43] Within only a decade of the inauguration of reform there had been a complete turnover in the membership of China's formal governing bodies.

Thus, within a few years of the inauguration of reform, a process by which junior leaders were expected to serve under more senior leaders before they could move up took hold. Eventually this system was extended to the senior-most leaders. When Jiang Zemin was named general secretary in 1989 (under the extraordinary circumstances of Tiananmen), he was still a relatively junior leader; real power remained in the hands of party elders. It was not until 1994–1995 that the actuarial tables and Jiang's growing experience combined to allow him to consolidate power.[44] This pattern was repeated in 2002 when Jiang Zemin stepped down in favor of Hu Jintao, but Jiang nevertheless retained his position as head of the Central Military Commission for an additional two years and appointed several of his close associates to the Politburo Standing Committee apparently to watch over Hu Jintao.[45] Presumably Hu will do the same to his successor in 2012.

If rules governing retirement have been gradually institutionalized, so too have rules governing promotion. By specifying the age band, educational background, and experience of candidates to be considered for promotion to different posts, the party has been able to rejuvenate the party with the type of cadres it desires for the tasks at hand. This practice also sets up expectations of those who want to be promoted, so they go out and get the skills that are needed. This does not end personalism in promotion, but it does limit the pool from which higher-level leaders can plausibly promote lower-level officials. The combination of knowable criteria for promotion and enforced retirement age has done much to routinize the political system.

Finally, there has been a very realistic effort to balance these system building measures with the informal balance of power within the party, particularly at the highest levels. Thus, although China has made significant progress in institutionalizing promotions to the highest positions (Politburo and Politburo Standing Committee), one cannot but note that at every Party Congress the rules governing leadership selection change somewhat. Thus, at the Fourteenth Party Congress in 1993, the retirement age was set at seventy. By this rule, Qiao Shi, often seen as a rival to Jiang Zemin, was forced to retire. But Jiang, also seventy, was allowed to stay on because he was needed! In 1997, the age limit was lowered to sixty-eight, just old enough to catch Li Ruihuan, also a thorn in Jiang's side. Five years later, the size of the Politburo Standing Committee was expanded at the last minute permitting several close associates of Jiang Zemin to take up positions from which they could watch Hu Jintao.

The CCP has always had difficulty balancing the formal institutions and the informal rules of the game, and it appears that the combination of increasing institutionalization of some rules while allowing the informal exercise of others has proven stable. Of course, one hopes that someday rules governing leadership, especially at the highest levels, might be fully institutionalized, but that does not seem to be possible within the context of authoritarian politics.

PARTY REFORM

Because the party would not yield its dominant political position and because performance legitimacy had become so important, the party had little choice but to reform itself. This reform has taken three directions: the specification of rules for office holding (discussed above), efforts to specify performance criteria, and the limited introduction of competitive criteria.

Retirement and the gradual professionalization of the cadre ranks greatly improved administrative performance and the overseeing of economic reform. Over time, however, the party found much difficulty controlling the behavior of cadres, particularly in the lower ranks.[46] The system was geared toward encouraging economic development and it tolerated a certain amount of corruption if cadres did their jobs. But pressures to develop the economy and control corruption put local level officials in conflict with local residents. There were enormous social pressures to continuously expand the size of local government, and township governments grew by about three times between the mid-1980s and the late 1990s.[47] And these cadres needed to be paid. And local governments needed to show that they were doing things, so they built roads and put up office buildings (often for themselves!). All this required funds, so local officials kept squeezing more taxes out of peasants. By the mid-1990s there were protests and often violence as peasants engaged in what Kevin O'Brien and Lianjiang Li call "rightful resistance."[48] Central government's calls to lessen the burdens on peasants went unheeded, and the central government, its own resources increasing under the effect of the 1994 tax reform, eventually abolished the agricultural tax altogether, lightening the burden on peasants but leaving local governments even more strapped for funds.

Local officials, still under pressure to develop the local economies, responded by taking over local land, which could then be sold for high profits to enterprises wanting to invest in the area. So peasant protests changed focus, from tax resistance to demanding better compensation for land seizures, but the number of protests did not diminish.

In an effort to reduce corruption and make local cadres better comply with the center's demands, the party began to promulgate a series of measures that it hoped would strengthen organizational control over local cadres. For instance, in 1995 the party promulgated the "Regulations Governing the Promotion and Appointment of Leading Cadres (Trial Use)." These regulations, which were developed under Zeng Qinghong's auspices, were intended to combat the buying and selling of offices that had become prevalent. The core of the regulations was that each cadre being considered for promotion had to undergo a process of "democratic recommendation," "evaluation," "deliberation," and "discussion and decision." The intent of the regulations was to open up participation in the promotion process and introduce secret ballots (in the final decision phase) to minimize the possibility of bribery.[49] These regulations were subsequently adopted formally in 2002, with minimum revision.

These regulations were followed by others, including the "Trial Implementation of the Regulations of the CCP on Disciplinary Measures" promulgated in 1997, and the "Regulations on Inner-Party Supervising the CCP (Trial Use)" issued in 2004. These and many other regulations attempted to define the limits of cadre behavior.

One has to say that China's political reforms—the regularization of elite politics and the elaboration of rules governing the selection and promotion of lower-level cadres—have yielded very positive economic results. As is well known, China's economy has grown approximately 10 percent per year for three decades, an unprecedented accomplishment, especially for a large country. This growth has generated the impressive cityscapes visitors to the PRC see, and, more important, reduced the number of those in poverty by some 300 million. Economic growth has also underlain the improvement of the educational system, which has generated tremendous improvements in China's human capital.

As is apparent in the headlines of our daily newspapers, China is no longer marginalized in the world. Even if it is premature, talk of the emergence of a "G2" (the United States and China) governing the global economy suggests that China has indeed been restored to a position of centrality in the world. Moreover, the Chinese state is clearly more confident than at any time in modern history, and that confidence is reflected in its seizing back the narrative of Chinese history. While the opening ceremonies of the Olympic Games did many things, they clearly asserted state interpretations of many symbols of China—the Great Wall, the Confucian tradition, the invention of gunpowder—that had been the object of intellectual ridicule in the 1980s, particularly in the television series *He Shang*.[50]

At the same time, China's intellectuals have been restored to a place of honor (which is not to say that there are not still many intellectuals at odds with the state), often advising the government from positions in universities and think tanks as well as from bureaucratic offices in the government itself. Just as marginalization of nation and intelligentsia generated radical thought and action in an earlier era, there is some evidence that both China's reemergence as a major nation in the world and the role its intellectuals are playing are generating moderate attitudes. For instance, Iain Johnston has done survey work in Beijing that suggests that middle-class residents are more open toward free trade, oppose increases in military expenditures, and have greater feelings of amity toward the United States (a frequent target of nationalist criticism).[51]

INNER-PARTY DEMOCRACY?

Despite the economic results of China's model of reform, the elaboration of bureaucratic rules, in and of itself, was (and is) insufficient to control the behavior of cadres; indeed, the mere elaboration of bureaucratic rules can have perverse consequences: the more strongly rules of behavior are specified through vertical channels, the more lower-level cadres have incentives to curry favor with bureaucratic superiors and, consequently, ignore the very people they are allegedly serving. Demands to focus on economic development lead to ignoring environmental degradation and other consequences of rapid growth. Indeed, they even lead to noneconomic results as cadres invest in "image projects," which look good to visiting higher-level cadres but do not yield profits, or build local enterprises before market demand has been investigated. And the elaboration of bureaucratic rules do little to break up the web of interests at the local level that are vital both to ensuring control (the "stability" so valued at higher levels) and to spawning corruption.

Indeed, the interests of local cadres are often in variance with those of local residents as the increase in local protests in recent years vividly demonstrates. Such mass incidents grew from 8,700 in 1993 to 87,000 in 2005—when the government stopped issuing such statistics.[52] Although this presented no direct threat to the legitimacy of higher levels, it suggested that local problems could escalate and perhaps present serious stability issues.

Precisely because of such pressures, there has been a variety of efforts to introduce some sort of electoral process into the selection of cadres. As noted above, the 1995/2002 Regulations Governing the Promotion and Appointment of Leading Cadres included a phase of "democratic recommendation." This was still an inner-party process but it was intended to expand the number of cadres who could participate in the process of evaluating and selecting cadres (or, putting it another way, the regulations were intended to check the power of the party secretary). From this start, the party has experimented with various ways to expand "inner-party democracy." Sichuan province in Southwest China started earlier and has probably gone the furthest in promoting such systems as "public recommendation and public election" (*gongtui gongxuan* 公推公选) and "public recommendation and direct election" (*gongtui zhixuan* 公推直选). The core of these systems is that candidates being considered for particular positions be nominated (recommended) by a larger body of people, usually including leading officials at the township level, leading cadres at the village level, and some representatives of the public. Such a group might consist of two hundred to three hundred people, much greater than the handful of people who might previously have controlled nominations and selections but clearly not mass democracy. After a process of examination (there are specific requirements in terms of age, education, and experience for different positions), the candidates give speeches outlining their approaches to solving the locality's problems, and then they are voted on by a greater or lesser number of party members, depending on which system is being used.[53]

Although a seemingly promising way to introduce a degree of openness, competition, and procedural legitimacy into the party, there are many reasons why such systems have not flourished. Fundamentally, within China's hierarchical administrative system, the ability of one level to introduce reform depends on the support or at least tolerance of higher levels. And that acceptance, in the final analysis, depends on the degree to which higher-level leaders believe such reforms serve their (higher-level leaders') interests. For instance, sometimes local-level reforms are introduced to reduce frictions between local cadres and citizens, but if the crisis passes, the support for the reform is concomitantly reduced. The fiscal dependency of lower-level units on higher-level offices is another constraint. As long as funds are allocated by higher-level administrative offices (say at the county or municipal level), lower-level leaders are dependent on higher levels; they are responsible to their bureaucratic superiors, not the citizens they serve. Moreover, reforms are often introduced by local leaders, either out of idealism or the desire to distinguish oneself politically, and when that leader is transferred to another position, support for the reform tends to fade. In the absence of stronger foundations in institutions and public opinion, many of China's reform experiments remain highly personalized.

Finally, the logic of hierarchical, bureaucratic control simply clashes with the logic of electoral democracy. And the party's commitment to hierarchical, bureaucratic control, as evidenced by the proliferation of regulations governing cadre behavior, appears to be as strong as ever. The party's answer to its inability to control its lower-level agents appears to be to issue one more set of regulations to try to check the unwanted behavior. As much as the central party organization would like to constrain the behavior of local "number one" officials, it seems unable or unwilling (probably both) to take the steps necessary to break up the personal networks that dominate local politics. Ironically, one reason higher levels are not willing to take more decisive steps against local networks is that local cadres are usually reasonably well-educated and well-connected people. If their interests were hurt substantially they could become a formidable opposition force at the local level. Then efforts to control local politics would be even less effective! And so the cat and mouse game between higher-level officials not wanting lower-level officials to abuse their power (at least to the point of generating social disturbances) continues on.

CONCLUSION

This chapter has argued, first, that political reform—understood in broad terms—has been driven by the decentralizing direction of economic reform in the first decade of reform and by questions of legitimacy and uncertainty set off by the death of Mao and the subsequent repudiation of routinization of charisma. The CCP's recognition of "objective" laws outside of Marxism-Leninism, despite its argument that it was still the best interpreter of those laws, was a rejection of the solipsistic claims to authority that had guided the party since its founding. That rejection had consequences for the role of ideology in the polity, for the legitimacy of succession, and for the "publicness" of the party-state. The party has continued to assert its ability to represent societal interests rather than to accept competing claims that publicness should be driven by bottom-up representation of societal interests and views. In dismissing such claims both coercion and efforts to reshape the party have been important.

The party meets society at the local level—particularly at the village and township levels—and it is here that the decentralizing direction of economic reforms has conflicted with the statist direction of administrative/party reforms. The inability of the central state to control local officials causes social tension and instability at the local level, which potentially endangers the central state. As suggested above, the party has done considerable experimentation with increasing political participation at the local level, particularly through various forms of "inner-party democracy." Such experiments might continue to expand, but they do conflict with the party's traditional, hierarchical structure encapsulated in the prescription that "the party controls the cadres" (*dangguan ganbu* 党管干部), and there has been considerable resistance to efforts to organize even inner-party elections at the township level.

Since this discussion of reform began with the way economic reform shaped political reform, perhaps it is appropriate to end it in the same way. The tax reform of 1994 shifted resources upward, impoverishing local governments and enriching provinces and the central government. The result has been efforts to rationalize local government by merging villages and townships, to move financial accountability upward, so that village finances are controlled by townships (*cuncai xiangguan* 村财乡管) and township finances are controlled by counties (*xiangcai xianguan* 乡财县管). There has, so far, been little study of the impact of these changes, but the effect seems to be to make lower levels more dependent on higher levels, thus undermining the need for local officials to be responsible to the local citizens. In other words, after some two decades in which the trend of economic reform was decentralizing, it now appears to be centralizing. This strengthens higher levels, making the need for horizontal controls less important.

Although this conclusion must be advanced cautiously, it appears that the forces driving political reform in a decentralizing, gradually opening direction may have stalled and even been reversed, allowing a freer hand for the party's preferred method of exerting hierarchical control. If this is the case, however, it is a trend that will run headlong into the continuing need to demonstrate legitimacy at the highest levels and the need to demonstrate the publicness of the party and government to society. And those will be the tensions and conflicts that will shape politics in China in the future.

NOTES

1. Quoted in Tang Tsou, "Reflections on the Formation and Foundations of the Communist Party-State in China," in Tang Tsou, *The Cultural Revolution and Post-Mao Reforms: A Historical Perspective* (Chicago: University of Chicago Press, 1986), 259. See also Kung-chuan Hsiao, *A Modern China and a New World: Kang Youwei, Reformer and Utopian, 1858–1927* (Seattle: University of Washington Press, 1975).

2. On Tan Sitong, one of the radical young thinkers in Kang's group, see Luke S. K. Kwong, *Tan Ssu-t'ung, 1865–1898: Life and Thought of a Reformer* (Leiden: Brill, 1996).

3. Hao Chang, *Chinese Intellectuals in Crisis: Search for Order and Meaning (1890–1911)* (Berkeley: University of California Press, 1987).

4. Lloyd Eastman, *Throne and Mandarins: China's Search for a Policy during the Sino-French Controversy, 1880–1885* (Cambridge, MA: Harvard University Press, 1967).

5. Mary Backus Rankin, "'Public Opinion' and Political Power: *Qingyi* in Late Nineteenth Century China," *Journal of Asian Studies* 41, no. 3 (May 1982).

6. Lin Yü-sheng, *The Crisis of Chinese Consciousness: Radical Anti-traditionalism in the May Fourth Era* (Madison: University of Wisconsin Press, 1979).

7. Yu Yingshi, "The Radicalization of China in the Twentieth Century," *Daedalus* 122, no. 2 (Spring 1993):125–50.

8. Chen Yun once said, "If Mao had died in 1956, he would have been regarded as a very great man. If he had died in 1966, he still would have been regarded as good. But, alas, he died in 1976, and there is nothing we can do about it." Quoted in Nicholas R. Lardy and Kenneth Lieberthal, eds., *Chen Yun's Strategy for China's Development: A Non-Maoist Alternative* (Armonk, NY: M.E. Sharpe, 1983).

9. On the atmosphere at the time, see Chen Fong-jing and Jin Guantao, *From Youthful Manuscripts to River Elegy* (Hong Kong: The Chinese University Press, 1997), 13–88.

10. Wu Xiang, "Yang guan dao yu du mu qiao" [The broad road and the single plank bridge], *Renmin ribao*, November 5, 1980.

11. Barry Naughton, *Growing Out of the Plan: Chinese Economic Reform, 1978–1993* (Cambridge: Cambridge University Press, 1995), 70–72.

12. Chen Yun. "Jianchi an bili yuanze tiaozheng guomin jingji" [Readjust the national economy in accordance with the principle of proportionality], in *Chen Yun wenxuan* (1956–1985) [The selected works of Chen Yun, 1956–1985] (Beijing: Renmin chubanshe, 1986), 226–31.

13. Ezra F. Vogel, *One Step Ahead in China: Guangdong under Reform* (Cambridge, MA: Harvard University Press, 1990); Thomas G. Moore, *China in the World Market: Chinese Industry and International Sources of Reform in the Post-Mao Era* (Cambridge: Cambridge University Press, 2002).

14. Douglass C. North, *Institutions, Institutional Change and Economic Performance* (Cambridge: Cambridge University Press, 1990); Paul Pierson, *Politics in Time: History, Institutions, and Social Analysis* (Princeton, NJ: Princeton University Press, 2004).

15. Gilbert Rozman, ed., *The East Asian Region: Confucian Heritage and Its Modern Adaptation* (Princeton, NJ: Princeton University Press, 1991).

16. James T. C. Liu, *Reform in Sung China: Wang Anshi and His New Policies* (Cambridge, MA: Harvard University Press, 1959); John W. Dardess, *Blood and History in China: The Donglin Faction and Its Suppression, 1620–1627* (Honolulu: University of Hawai'i Press, 2002).

17. Rozman makes this point when comparing the historical legacy of China and Japan. See Rozman, *The East Asian Region*.

18. Philosophically, solipsism is the idea that one can only understand one's own mind (hence, Descartes famous declaration, "I think, therefore I am"). The term is extended here to mean a privileged claim to the truth, that is, something that cannot be tested by reference to something external to the ideology itself, such as voting.

19. Frederick Teiwes and Warren Sun, *End of the Maoist Era: Chinese Politics during the Twilight of the Cultural Revolution, 1972–1976* (Armonk, NY: M.E. Sharpe, 2008).

20. *Renmin ribao*, editorial, "Study Well the Documents and Grasp the Key Link," *Renimin ribao*, February 7, 1977, trans. FBIS, February 7, 1977, E1–E3.

21. See Roderick MacFarquhar on the failure of Hua and the Gang of Four to work together, "The Succession to Mao and the End of Maoism, 1969–82," in Roderick MacFarquhar, ed., *The Politics of China: The Eras of Mao and Deng*, 2nd ed. (Cambridge: Cambridge University Press, 1997), 248–339.

22. Deng Liqun tells the story of Zhu Jiamu identifying the import of the editorial and telling Deng, who promptly told Wang Zhen. See Deng Liqun, *Shi'erge chunqiu (1975–1987)* (unpublished draft, 2 vols.), 1:127.

23. Deng Xiaoping, "'Liangge fanshi' bu fuhe Makesi zhuyi" 两个凡是" 不符合马克思主义 [The 'two whatevers' are not in accordance with Marxism], in Deng Xiaoping, *Deng Xiaoping wenxuan* (Beijing: Renmin chubanshe, 1983), 35–36.

24. Tang Tsou, "Reflections," 295.

25. Hu Qiaomu, "Act in Accordance with Economic Laws, Step Up the Four Modernizations," *Xinhua*, October 5, 1978, trans. FBIS, October 11, 1978, E1–22.

26. Hu Yaobang, "The Radiance of the Great Truth of Marxism Lights Our Way Forward," *Xinhua*, March 13, 1983, trans. FBIS, March 14, 1983, K1–22.

27. See Liu Guoguang （刘国光）, "Jingjixue jiaoxue he yanjiu de yixie wenti" 经济学教学和研究的一些问题 [On certain issues in the teaching and research of economics], *Jingji yanjiu* (经济研究), no. 10 (October 2005): 4–11.

28. Tang Tsou, "Political Change and Reform: The Middle Path," in Tsou, *The Cultural Revolution and Post-Mao Reforms*, 220.

29. Guo Luoji 郭罗基, "Zhengzhi wenti shi keyi taolunde" 政治问题是可以讨论的 [Political issues can also be discussed], *Renmin ribao*, November 10, 1979. Guo Luoji was shortly thereafter banished from Beijing to Nanjing.

30. In highlighting the issue of legitimacy and (below) uncertainty, I am drawing on Bernard S. Silberman, *Cages of Reason: The Rise of the Rational State in France, Japan, the United States, and Great Britain* (Chicago: University of Chicago Press, 1993).

31. Richard Baum, *Burying Mao: Chinese Politics in the Age of Deng Xiaoping* (Princeton, NJ: Princeton University Press, 1994), 143–88.

32. Bruce Bueno de Mesquita and George W. Downs, "Development and Democracy," *Foreign Affairs* 84, no. 5 (September–October 2005): 77–86.

33. Tang Tsou, "Political Change and Reform," in Tsou, *The Cultural Revolution and Post-Mao Reforms*, 219–58.

34. Li Cheng, *China's Leaders* (Lanham, MD: Rowman & Littlefield, 2001); Joseph Fewsmith, "Generational Transition in China," *Washington Quarterly* 25, no. 4 (Autumn 2002): 23–35.

35. Li Cheng and Lynn White, "Elite Transformation and Modern Change in Mainland China and Taiwan: Empirical Data and the Theory of Technocracy," *China Quarterly*, no. 121 (March 1990): 1–35.

36. Joseph Fewsmith, *China since Tiananmen*, 2nd ed. (Cambridge: University of Cambridge Press, 2008).

37. This line of reasoning is indebted to Silberman, *Cages of Reason*.

38. Hong Yung Lee, *From Revolutionary Cadres to Party Technocrats in Socialist China* (Berkeley: University of California Press, 1991), 401.

39. Xu Xianglin 徐湘淋, "Dang guan ganbu tizhi xia de jiceng minzhushi gaige" 党管干部体制下的 基层民主式改革 [Democratic grassroots reforms under the struc-

ture of the party-controlling cadres], *Zhejiang xuekan* 浙江学刊, no. 1 (2004), 106–12.

40. Silberman, *Cages of Reason*.

41. Lowell Dittmer, "The 12th Congress of the Communist Party of China," *China Quarterly*, no. 93 (March 1983): 108–24.

42. *China Directory* (Tokyo: Radiopress, Inc., 1986), A4–5. I am indebted to Alice Miller for locating this data.

43. Li Cheng and Lynn White, "The Thirteenth Central Committee of the Chinese Communist Party: From Mobilizers to Managers," *Asian Survey* 28, no. 4 (April 1988): 371–99.

44. Fewsmith, *China since Tiananmen*, 168–71.

45. Joseph Fewsmith, "The Sixteenth Party Congress: The Succession That Didn't Happen," *China Quarterly*, no. 173 (March 2003): 1–16.

46. This statement should not be taken as implying that higher-level party cadres toe the rules. On the contrary, there is much evidence that corruption and other manifestations of noncompliance are rampant at that level as well. However, when looking at either the issue of higher levels to control lower levels (the principal-agent problem) or the impact on social stability, the wayward behavior of lower-level cadres is arguably the more serious problem.

47. Jean Oi and Zhao Shukai, "Fiscal Crisis in China's Townships: Causes and Consequences," in Merle Goldman and Elizabeth J. Perry, eds., *Grassroots Political Reform in Contemporary China* (Cambridge, MA: Harvard University Press, 2007).

48. Kevin O'Brien and Lianjiang Li, *Rightful Resistance in Rural China* (Cambridge: Cambridge University Press, 2006).

49. "Dangzheng lingdao ganbu xuanba renyong gongzuo zanxing tiaoli" 党政领导干部选拔任用工作暂行条例 [Regulations governing the promotion and appointment of leading cadres (trial use)] retrieved from www.people.com.cn//GB/channel11/11/20000804/172987.html. On Zeng Qinghong's role, see *Wen Wei Po*, September 10, 1995, A27.

50. Megan Steffen, "Visions of Chinese Nationalism: The Beijing 2008 Olympics and China's Developing National Identity" (unpublished undergraduate seniors thesis, Boston University, 2009).

51. Alastair Iain Johnston, "Chinese Middle Class Attitudes towards International Affairs: Nascent Liberalism?" in *China Quarterly*, no. 179 (September 2004): 603–28. It should be noted, however, that alongside such attitudes nationalistic attitudes have increased in the years since Tiananmen. See Fewsmith, *China since Tiananmen*.

52. C. Fred Bergsten, Bates Gill, Nicholas R. Lardy, and Derek Mitchell, *China: The Balance Sheet* (New York: PublicAffairs, 2006).

53. Lai Hairong 赖海榕, "Jingzhengxing xuanju zai sichuansheng xiangzhen yiji de fazhan" 竞争性选举在四川省乡镇一级的发战 [The development of competitive elections at the town and township level in Sichuan], in He Zengke 何增科, Gao Xinjun 高新军, Yang Xuedong 杨雪冬, and Lai Hairong 赖海榕, eds., *Jiceng minzhu he defang zhili chuangxin* 基层民主和地方治理创新 [Innovations in grassroots democracy and local governance] (Beijing: Zhongyang bianyi chuabanshe, 2004), 51–108.

VI

CONCLUDING REFLECTIONS

11

Struggle for Identity

A Political Psychology of China's Rise

Qin Yaqing – Commie, Mouthpiece, Panda Hugger

China has attained rapid economic development since the early 1980s. Currently it is the third largest economy of the world and it will surpass Japan in the foreseeable future. As the world has been hit severely by the financial crisis and most of the major countries have been struggling in the most difficult economic recession since the end of World War II, China is expected to take the lead in moving out of the economic recession and to embark on a new round of development. Scholars and policymakers even put forth a concept of G2, when discussing the new distribution of the world power and the models of governance.[1] What are the dynamics of China's thirty years of eye-catching development? It is indeed a significant question.

In this book, American scholars tackle the question from different perspectives by examining either the past or the present. For instance, Esherick in chapter 1 shows how the tribute system and the treaty system affected nationalism in China and how it impacted China's development. Dittmer in chapter 2 studies how current domestic and international factors intertwine to create a dynamic for China's rise. Other chapters too explore history or the contemporary era to analyze China's rise and its implications.

Attempting to combine the perspectives based on historical observations and present situations, this chapter argues that there is a sustained and historically developed dynamic for the persistent endeavor that has made China's rise possible and even inevitable. From 1840 to 1949, Chinese people made one attempt after another to rejuvenate the nation, such as the One-Hundred-Day Reform Movement, the democratic revolutions to establish a republic, and the May Fourth Movement, but all ended up in failure.[2] Instead of putting an end to the successive process, each failure served as the beginning of the next try. There must, therefore, be an unfailing dynamic that makes Chinese people keep exploring solutions to the rise of the nation. Although none of these attempts in the respective periods completed the mission due to the political, economic, social, and intellectual constraints, the dynamic has never died out.

This tenaciously sustained dynamic is Chinese people's strong will to reconstruct the nation's identity that was once lost in the encounter with the West. "Who am I?" Chinese people have continuously asked themselves this question when being confronted with the new international system. To reconstruct a new identity vis-à-vis international society has become a strong desire that has been driving Chinese people to take actions.[3] The dynamic is psychological and social in nature, providing sustainable energy for the struggle for recognition in international society, with which the Chinese nation had the first head-on encounter in 1840. In this sense, the will to reconstruct a new identity can function as a persistent factor that links the past and the present, a narrative that tells the story of the modern and the contemporary China, and a psychology that combines the modern history and the present reality of China's development.

IDENTITY ESTABLISHED: CHINA AS THE CENTRAL KINGDOM IN THE TRIBUTE SYSTEM

In some sense the tribute system was a pseudointernational system. It was not based upon sovereignty, and it was hierarchical in nature.[4] Thus it was not a genuine international system if judged by the Westphalian standards. But at the same time, it was an integrated whole consisting of relatively independent and interacting parts and it did contain relationships that had functions similar to the composite units of an international system, even though they could not be strictly defined as sovereign states.[5] It was somewhat like a hegemonic system in which China had an essential identity of the leading actor or even the dominant power, surrounded and respected by the peripheral vassal states. As the tribute system grew to its full maturity, these identities were highly internalized and externalized—meaning that China accepted the identity and committed to the responsibilities of being the leading actor of the system, and the other actors in the periphery acknowledged China's identity and honored China's central role in their interactions with China.[6]

It is important to note that the tribute system was a rather closed system. Geographically, it covered roughly the so-called East Asian Cultural Circle consisting of today's Northeast Asia, Southeast Asia, and other limited neighboring areas. With no agreement upon the exact origin, it is estimated that the tribute system took an initial shape roughly around Qin (221 B.C.–206 B.C.) and Han (206 B.C.–220 A.D.) dynasties, and became a full-fledged system consisting of China and the vassal states in Ming (1368–1644) and Qing (1644–1911) dynasties after two thousand years' development.[7] Since it was built on the traditional Chinese ideas on order, political institutions, and ethical norms, it is natural that China took the leading position in the system. The tribute system has the following features.

Firstly, the structure of the tribute system was hierarchical, for the Chinese power was supreme and the Chinese culture was dominant. The combination of hard and soft power established China as the central and leading actor in the system and the surrounding states as its subordinates. Qin Shi Huangdi unified China in 221 B.C., making it the largest country by land in the Chinese cultural sphere. After a further development in Tang dynasty (618–907) and Song dynasty (960–1279), China came to be the strongest power in the region, judged by any standard of land, population, military power, or economic strength. Even though sometimes minority ethnic groups ruled China as in the Yuan dynasty (1271–1368) and the Qing dynasty (1644–1911), the tribute system did not collapse. Instead of subverting the system, the ethnic rulers became successors and disseminators of the Chinese culture. Relying on its predominant power and cultural advantage, China kept the hegemonic system stable for over two thousand years, having met no real challenge until the 1840s.[8] Its unchallengeable preponderance not only undergirded a superstable systemic structure, but also guarded its identity as the Central Kingdom in the system, able to radiate toward the periphery.[9]

Secondly, the ordering principle of the tribute system was the Confucian notion of *li* (礼), or ritual. It is reasonable to say that this essential notion of Confucianism determined the ideational structure of the system. Rule by ritual preset the differentiated social positions and functions for each actor accordingly. "Different positions, different roles, and different honors." The vassal states paid tribute to show that they were following the ritual and China returned more than it received also in accordance with ritual. To draw an analogy between the tribute system and a circle, China was the center and other states were on the circumference. Different positions defined different social statues and identities. As interpreted by Fei Xiaotong, such a hierarchical configuration was "the fundamental feature of the societal structure in traditional China."[10]

However, the unequal social relations in the hierarchical tribute system were not in a bad sense by design.[11] It is, for example, different from the exploiting relationships between the slave owners and the slaves, or the proletariats and the bourgeoisie in Marxist thought. According to Confucianism, all the actors in a society could be defined in terms of five relationships, that is, father and son, emperor and minister, husband and wife, brothers, and friends. The Confucian ethics believed that social order was maintained if the differentiated positions were well defined and followed. Such ethics started at the basic unit of society—the family, where the father was the authority and the son the subordinate. But the management of the family was through authority, morality, and love, rather than mere material power and conquest: the father should love the son and the son should be filial to the father. The patriarchic love and filial affection thus constituted the nature of the relationship. The same ordering principle defined the relationships within a society, which was actually seen as an extended family.[12] In the tribute system, China, like the head of the household, had not only the honor and the authority to lead the family, but also the responsibilities to take care of the vassal states as the junior members of the family. In return, the vassal states should respect China as the senior member of the family. So the ritual constructed in the system a culture distinct from the anarchy of Hobbes, the individualism of Locke, or the moral equality of Kant, for the actors in the tribute system did not treat each other as enemies, competitors, or friends.[13] It is a unique historical experience and cultural construct that is hard to depict and represent by Western discourses. It is such a hierarchy that had helped maintain the order and stability of the tribute system for about two thousand years.

Thirdly, the governing principle of the tribute system was the Confucian morality of *ren* (仁), meaning virtue or benevolence. Although the system was based upon the superior power and culture of the Chinese and maintained through a hierarchical structure, the system in its ideal form disdained conquest or exploitation. The Confucian morality was explained by Confucius as "loving people." Take the relations between father and son as an example. Different as their social positions were, father and son did not treat each other as master and servant. Instead, they could love each other, even though they were entrenched in a hierarchical relationship. The father could punish the son out of love, for the punishment aimed to teach the son how to become a useful man. To extend to society the ethical principle of the patriarchic love of the father and the filial love of the son, it might mean to build a fiduciary society, which was not a system consisting of adversary and rival pressure groups, but a community based on fiduciary trust. The goal of politics was not only to attain law and order in society but also to establish a fiduciary community through moral persuasion and unequal love. The governing process was thus not a control mechanism based upon impersonal factors but a manifestation of the art of moral persuasion.[14]

Considering the systemic structure, the ordering principle, and the governing principle, China's leadership was accounted indispensable in the tribute system, for its political, military, and economic strength laid the material foundation, its cultural superiority produced the principles that maintained order, and its Confucian morality defined the way of governance in the system. An essential part of this narrative is that China gained an identity as the Central Kingdom and the strongest power in the system. This identity was deeply internalized through the two thousand years' development and became a collective memory and an ideational symbol of the Chinese people. Even though a hierarchical pattern is not possible in the contemporary international system, which takes equality as one of the most important norms, the ideal identity as a big and strong power in the collective memory of the Chinese people remains unchanged. To reconstruct an identity that fits into the collective ideal of the Chinese has thus become an unfailing dynamic and a strong psychology of China's rise.

IDENTITY LOST: CHINA'S HUNDRED-YEAR PUZZLE AND STRUGGLE

In the middle of the nineteenth century, the Western powers started to penetrate the China-centered tribute system and history witnessed a clash between the two international systems. On the one hand was the Westphalian international system formed in 1648, with nation-states as the basic units, sovereignty as the fundamental norm, and balance of power as the major mechanism to maintain the systemic order; on the other was the China-centered tribute system, with the Central Kingdom as the leading power of the system, the Confucian ritual as the fundamental ordering principle, and the Confucian morality as the major method to maintain the order. The West won over the East in the clash.

The clash broke out in the Opium War in 1840, but it had been brewing during the earlier trade between China and the West. From 1760 to 1834, Europe had already traded goods with China, but the trading was largely controlled and regulated by the Chinese government with a set of hierarchical rules characterized by restrictions on merchants. In the late eighteenth century, opium began to be exported to the Chinese territory, causing huge trade deficits for China. Due to the worsening situation for the Qing government, conflict over the trade problems led to a war. Not surprising, China was defeated by advanced British warships and forced to sign the Treaty of Nanjing in 1842, the first unequal treaty in the modern history of China. Following it, China was forced to sign the Treaty of Xiamen with the United States in 1844, and the Treaty of Huangpu with France in 1844.

Then, China lost the second Opium War and signed more unequal treaties with Russia, the United States, and Britain. As Fairbank has observed, in the two decades after 1840, the tribute system collapsed and a treaty system was formed in its stead, indicating the beginning of a new "international" order for China's foreign relations and a new identity for the imperial China.[15] This new order was built on the collapse of the tribute system at the cost of China's dignity, sovereignty, and territorial integrity. In this new order, China was turned into, as Chinese scholars have called it, a semifeudal and semicolonial country.[16] Thus the collapse of the tribute system and the formation of the treaty system deprived China not only of its identity as the Central Kingdom, but even worse, of its opportunity to join the international system as a full-status actor. China, therefore, had become a nation that had no identity vis-à-vis the strange, aggressive, and West-dominated international system. China was degraded from a central kingdom to a humiliated subordinate, from a leader of a system to a loser despised by foreign powers.[17] Chinese scholars even commented that the Qing court became a government serving not the Chinese but the foreigners.[18]

This new identity fell tremendously far short of the ideal picture in the collective memory of the Chinese. This huge and ever-widening perceptual and psychological gap became the source of the dynamics for China's rise. Since then, China kept on struggling for its ideal identity and status. From 1840 to 1978, it made four major attempts, all of which failed.

The first attempt was the Westernization Movement in the 1860s with the focus on technological modernization. In the interval of thirty years' peace after the Second Opium War, Chinese political elites reflected on China's failure and sought ways to rejuvenate the nation and to reconstruct its identity as a big and powerful country. They ascribed the military failure to the advanced technologies of the Western powers, which were reflected particularly by the advanced warships and weapons. This judgment made them believe that to develop a strong Chinese navy was the solution to rejuvenating the country and to regaining China's identity. So the Westernization reformists in China pushed forward to develop China's military industries. In 1868, the first steamboat was successfully built in China. In 1888, the well-armed Beiyang Fleet was established. Soon after, Nanyang Fleet and Fujian Fleet were put into service. China's naval strength soared to first place in Asia and ranked among the strongest in the world. It was also during this period that China translated a number of Western technology books and employed many foreign experts as a means to introduce and learn Western technologies.

The Westernization Movement took an approach of self-strengthening, believing that the Chinese values were superior while the Western technologies better. Taking therefore "Chinese learning as the essence, and Western learning as practical knowledge," it made no plan to change the political and social institutions of China, but merely to learn the practical technologies from the West. And the movement was a top-down reform, with senior officials of the Qing government as the major initiators and prime movers.[19] It could have been a possible way for China to regain its identity as a big and strong power, but unfortunately, the First Sino-Japanese War broke out in 1894, which shattered the reformists' rosy dream of national rejuvenation through self-strengthening, for other stronger powers seemed not to allow China to have time for self-strengthening. In the late nineteenth century, after the Meiji Restoration, Japan became the most modernized country in Asia and considered itself the only East Asian country that had caught up with the pace of the most advanced development represented by the West. China lost the war to Japan and was forced to sign the Treaty of Shimonoseki in April 1895, which not only marked the end of the Westernization Movement, but also set the whole nation thinking about how to rejuvenate itself. The political elites who had been attempting to reconstruct a new identity for China through learning from the West were left in deep despair. They were even under serious attack by the conservatives, who believed that learning from the West had done great damage to the Chinese value system. The defeat by Japan shocked the whole country, but it also provided renewed energy for the Chinese to continue to seek new ways of identity reconstruction.

The second attempt was the Reform Movement in 1898, with the ambitious mission of reforming the governing rules and institutions. It had been so unexpected that Japan, a former student of China, defeated its teacher in the war that the Chinese started to question the validity of the institutions of China. As an eminent Chinese scholar said, the defeat by Japan, "a country that China once did not take seriously," "shocked, depressed, puzzled, and desolated the Chinese nation."[20] They came to realize that the problem might not only lie in the backwardness of technology, but in the fundamental political and social institutions. Thus they began to reflect on the reform of the governing body. They wanted a fundamental change.

In 1895, when the news that China had signed the Treaty of Shimonoseki reached China, it immediately became a fuse igniting a new flame of national fury. Intellectuals all over the country were thrown into anxiety and anger. In 1898, Kang Youwei led 1,300 civil examination candidates to sign a ten-thousand-word petition to the emperor, appealing to repeal the Treaty of Shimonoseki, to refuse peace talks with Japan, to modernize the Qing Imperial Army, and to implement a reform. This unveiled the One-Hundred-Day Reform Movement. On May 11, 1989, the Qing emperor Guangxu officially proclaimed the beginning of the reform, and ordered a series of measures to be taken for developing the national economy and strengthening the state through manufacturing, railway building, and mining. The reform policies also included abandoning the old military buildup and establishing new armies, encouraging people to make candid policy proposals and discuss politics openly so as to improve governance, and abolishing the traditional examination system and setting up Western-style schools. Besides all these new policies, the most fundamental one was to stop the old way of imperial ruling and establish a constitutional monarchy.[21]

Judged by the major measures to develop the national economy and military might, the Reform Movement appeared to be more or less the same with the Westernization Movement. But its proposal to abrogate the absolute imperial rule and to establish a constitutional monarchy made a fundamental difference. The reformists considered that it was the imperial system that had caused the loss of the war with Japan, the loss of dignity because of the unequal treaties, and, most important, the loss of national identity, and thus they believed that the only way out was a profound reform that would lead to institutional innovation. Governing institutions, for the first time in China's two-thousand-year history, became the main target for the reformist elite. From questioning the backward technology to attacking the backward governing institutions, here lies the real significance of the Reform Movement.

The Reform Movement could, too, have been an opportunity for China to reconstruct its identity if it had not met with powerful conservative opposition. The reformists relied almost completely on the reform-minded emperor. Unfortunately, the movement failed in the end due to the strong opposition by Empress Dowager, who held the real power tightly in hand. The leaders of the reform were either killed or exiled. Emperor Guangxu was placed under house arrest by Empress Dowager. The reform measures were mostly abolished. But the failure, like that of the Westernization Movement, did not put out the Chinese aspirations and in fact added to the momentum of a continued struggle for a new identity. The Westernization and the Reform movements began in peace, but both ended up in violence: the former was shattered by the warships of Japan and the latter by the power of conservative opponents. So, when the next attempt was made, a violent approach was to be taken up.

The third attempt was the 1911 Revolution. After the Reform Movement had failed, China continued its misery in poverty and political instability. The occupation of China's capital city by the joint armies of the Western powers was another symbol of an identity-less China. Losing all hope in the Qing government, the new Chinese intellectuals reflected on the failure and concluded that they should set up political organizations and launch a revolution to overthrow the imperial reign of the Qing government. Dr. Sun Yat-sen put forward the famous Three Principles of the People: nationalism, democracy, and people's livelihood. The Tongmenghui (The United League), founded by Dr. Sun Yat-sen in 1905, was the most influential revolutionary organization. It advocated "expelling the Manchus, restoring the Han rule, founding a republic, and dividing equally the land ownership." The political mission of the organization clarified its goals, namely, to restore the reign of the Chinese nationals and to establish a republic in China. So the attempt it made was to wage a revolution of a nationalistic and democratic nature.[22]

The 1911 Revolution aimed at overthrowing the reign of the Qing government through radical and revolutionary action. The Wuchang Military Uprising in 1911 succeeded in establishing a government by turning to violent military action. Echoing the uprising, most of the provinces of China declared independence and secession from the Qing government. On January 1, 1912, the Republic of China was founded in Nanjing, and Dr. Sun Yat-sen was inaugurated as first provisional president. Meanwhile, the provisional parliament was established as the highest lawmaking body and the provisional government promulgated a series of policies and decrees to encourage and develop democracy and capitalism. On March 11, 1912, the provisional parliament issued the Provisional Constitution of the Republic of China, stipulating the separation of the five powers, namely, executive, legislative, judicial, examination, and censorate.[23] A parliamentary system was established, a responsible cabinet set up, and a republic born that seemed to be able to reconstruct a new identity for China.

The 1911 Revolution created an important opportunity to rejuvenate the Chinese nation. However, the conservative forces used weapons to stage a tit-for-tat comeback. Yuan Shikai seized power and was sworn in as provisional president. Later, he suppressed the Second Revolution led by Dr. Sun Yat-sen, and crowned himself as emperor, attempting to restore the absolute monarchy. Fortunately, under a nationwide condemnation, Yuan Shikai's plot did not succeed. But neither did China win a peace through all the revolutions in quick succession. It entered an anarchical era of warlords fighting against each other, dividing the country into their own fiefdoms. Finally, the 1911 Revolution faded off the historical stage when Dr. Sun Yat-sen failed to protect the constitution from being violated and smashed.

If we say that the Westernization Movement wanted to develop advanced technologies and that the Reform Movement aimed at institutional innovations, then the 1911 Revolution not only brought about a drastic institutional change, but also a cultural earthquake. Responding to the 1911 Revolution, the May Fourth Movement in 1919, the most important cultural movement in the modern history of China, put forward the slogan of "Down with Confucius," boldly and profoundly questioning the Chinese traditional culture that had existed and worked for more than two thousand years without a break, sustaining a civilization of five thousand years. The collapse of the tribute system, in a sense, triggered a cultural crisis, an identity crisis, in China, for it subverted the central position of the Chinese culture, the Confucian ethics, and Chinese civilization as a whole, not only within the tribute system itself, but also within the heart of the Chinese nation. It is thus natural that the new intellectuals negated completely Chinese culture with Confucianism at its core. Due to the repeated failures of the past attempts, the Chinese intellectuals, especially the new intellectuals educated in the West, started to question this cultural core. Seldom in human history has a nation begun to doubt its roots. The pain and the torture must have been tremendous. Some Chinese scholars, such as Yan Fu, even criticized the Chinese knowledge as completely "empty" and "futile."[24] The purpose of the questioning was to seek a practical way to reconstruct a new China. However, the endeavor was blocked by the successive wars in the coming years. In 1931 China was invaded by Japan. In 1945 China was bogged down in the civil war. China did not have peace for time long enough to revive.

The fourth attempt at restoring China's identity was made after the end of the civil war and the founding of the People's Republic of China. From 1949 to 1979, China enjoyed another thirty years of peace. The territory was largely unified; foreign forces were driven out; and social and economic construction started. It is a reasonable argument that one generation of peace and stability gives a country the chance to revive, even if it has been totally destroyed by a war. In the early 1950s, China showed a trajectory of strong economic development. It could have been a chance for China to regain a suitable status and to reconstruct an appropriate identity among the nations in the world.

However, international and domestic factors kept China from successfully entering international society. At the international level, a bipolar pattern took full shape after 1949, and China had to take a lean-to-one-side strategy to guarantee its own survival.[25] China made tenacious efforts to develop relations with the newly independent developing nations to mitigate the effect of its isolation in the world, but the situation did not change fundamentally, for the West could not accept a Soviet ally to the international community it led.[26] In the 1950s, China was engaged in the wars, directly or indirectly, against the Western powers first in Korea and then in Vietnam. In the 1960s, China broke with the Soviet Union and became an enemy to both superpowers. The Cold War configuration and the major power rivalry excluded China from the international system. At the national level, in the late 1950s, the consecutive political movements put China into severe domestic turbulences. Millions of people suffered from natural and man-made disasters. The chaotic situation eventually culminated in the Cultural Revolution, which threw China even deeper into isolation. The identity issue could not be addressed at all under such circumstances. China remained an outsider of the international system, sometimes as a revisionist and sometimes a detached power in its identity vis-à-vis international society.[27]

New Dress for an old tattered view of Chinese Victimhood.

IDENTITY RECONSTRUCTED: REFORM AND OPENING UP

If we look back at China's tortuous but never-ending struggle for identity, we can find that the failed efforts have one common feature. For various reasons, they all separated China's self-strengthening from China's integration into international society. The traditional political and intellectual elites had a long-established and embedded belief that the Western value system would not work in China and therefore they resisted such values out of their biased misunderstanding of the Western learning. They persisted in the view that China was the center of the universe and that all other nations were somewhat barbarians to be educated. "All the failures, frustrations, and pains that our nation suffered in modern times were caused by the barrier of the rigidity of the traditional mind-set."[28] On the other hand, the new intellectuals wanted to completely destroy the Chinese tradition and culture. They did want to learn everything from the West, from technology to governance, but they saw not only the resistance inside their own country, but also reluctance to accept China by the Western-led international community. Thus, opening up, for both conservatives and radicals in China, was not possible. Their way to overcome this predicament was perhaps to strengthen China first and get into international society second. Such a separation, even though caused understandably by the circumstances at the time, had kept China from solving its identity puzzle.

Finally and luckily, China set its new course to reconstruct a new identity in 1978, when it started to implement the policy of reform and opening up. The policy, as any of the efforts made before, pursues a goal of rejuvenating the Chinese nation and reconstructing a new identity for China. This time, however, the approach was completely different. The past endeavors had more or less an inward-looking nature. They tried self-strengthening, through learning advanced technologies, institutions, and even cultures, but they failed to carry out a genuine opening-up policy to go together with the self-strengthening effort. As discussed above, traditional Chinese scholar-officials, who had a strong resentment against anything Western and often observed it as harmful, constituted themselves a strong barrier to the opening to the rest of the world.[29] On the other hand, the Western-led international society refused to accept a nation that was chaotic, turbulent, and ignorant of the rules and regimes practiced in the Westphalian system they had established. Without becoming truly integrated into international society, China could not succeed in reconstructing the new identity it had long desired for.

In this sense the most significant ideational change of the reformist policy-makers in the year of 1978 was to treat opening up and reform as twins with equal importance, believing self-strengthening and identity reconstructing were two aspects of the same process. Neither could be achieved without the other. If the past attempts were to seek self-strengthening first and then regain the proper identity vis-à-vis international society, the 1978 reform was to take opening as simultaneously significant. Self-strengthening could only be realized in the process of opening China to the rest of the world and vice versa. A successful reconstruction of China's national identity could be done only through integrating itself into the international society it faced and from which it had been detached. Empirical evidence of the integration of Chinese identity with international society can be seen in three areas.[30]

The first is economic interdependence. Such interdependence indicates the level of how well a state is integrated into the international economic system. It is an important aspect reflecting the identity of the state to the international system. Since reform and opening up, China and the rest of the world have been getting increasingly interdependent. The most telling indicator is trade dependence. It shows that China has been fully integrated into the international economic system.

China's dependence upon international trade has changed dramatically in the reform era. In 1980, China's international trade made up only 12.61 percent of the GDP, but it soared to 29.97 percent in 1990, 43.92 percent in 2000, and 63.83 percent in 2005.[31] Obviously, China depends more and more upon the global economic system. China's fast economic growth benefits from its integration into the world market. Under such circumstances, China cannot remain an outsider of the international economic system. China used to be a revisionist, a detached power, and an outsider. Now it has become an important participant in the system. This is a fundamental change in China's identity.

The second is China's acceptance of the existing international regimes. The number of multilateral international organizations a state has joined reflects the extent to which the state accepts the international regimes. So memberships in the international organizations suggest a state's basic identity in international society. The international regimes include formal and informal rules and institutions constraining the behavior of international actors. Regimes set guidance for state behavior and form converging expectations among states and other international actors.[32] International organizations encourage cooperation and undergird the social structure of the international system. With interdependence developing further in international society, international organizations will continue to expand its scale, and finally might form worldwide organizational networks in relevant areas, which can improve the effectiveness of the system and stimulate cooperation among the members. According to Alastair Iain Johnston's statistics, China has obtained memberships in a large number of international organizations, far more than the world average, and at almost the same level as the United States, Japan, India, and other major powers. Johnston's research demonstrates that China has become a more active member of the international society, and China accepts, supports, and contributes to the current system of international regimes.[33]

The third is social identity. The economic indicators show how a state is integrated into the international economic system; the number of the international organizations it has joined shows how it accepts the international regimes and vice versa; and the number of the international multilateral conventions it has signed shows how it accepts international society and how international society accepts China. As discussed above, the international conventions and organizations set rules and norms binding international society together. Whether a state is content with international society or not can be observed through its attitudes toward the generally accepted rules. China's attitudes show that in the past thirty years, China did not act as a challenger to the current rules, but largely a responsible member in international society. During the more than thirty years from 1949 to 1979, China only joined 7 multilateral conventions in total. However, in 1980 alone, the first year after implementing the policy of reform and opening up, China joined 59 multilateral conventions. In 2008, the total number of multilateral conventions it joined reached 298.[34]

Looking more closely at the statistics, we can find that from 1978 up to the present there were two peak years. One is in 1984, when the People's Republic of China recognized all the international labor conventions signed by the Kuomingtang government in the 1920s and the 1930s. The other is in 2001, when China signed more than twenty relevant conventions and twenty-three multilateral conventions after joining the World Trade Organization (WTO) in 2000. The first peak year shows that China began to seek a change in its identity as a member in international society. The second peak is not only a record high, but also more significant in a practical sense. Joining the WTO was a turning point of China's relationship with the international organizations. The year 2001 was critical for China to become a full member of international society and a component part in the international system. Since then a point of no return has been reached.

Another example is energy. In the 1980s, China's dependence on international energy was negligible. Since the beginning of the twenty-first century China has imported more and more oil, reaching almost 50 percent of its oil consumption in the mid-2000s. It is natural that China's demand will continue to increase. As Downs describes in chapter 8, in facing global problems such as energy China is not simply behaving as one international competitor among many, but is trying to address global problems of energy security, to reassure its partners, and to stabilize the fluctuations in world markets. With such initiatives China goes beyond passive participation in the world system and seeks to improve its functioning.

All this shows that China and the international system are highly interdependent and China is now a stakeholder in international society. Some may argue that as China further develops, it may pay more attention to balanced growth domestically. Indeed, the recent financial crisis has forced China to start restructuring its economy in favor of domestic consumption. However, China and the world economic system have already merged into an inseparable whole. Common interest lays a foundation for further cooperation between China and the international economic system, the economic regimes, and other economies in the system. Moreover, and perhaps more significant, China has already been fully integrated into international society. The social ties are even more durable than the economic ones. China's all-around participation in the international multilateral and intergovernmental organizations proves that China is willing to abide by international rules and norms. If it is right to say that society is maintained through international regimes and social members are bonded by international rules, China's persistent efforts to join international regimes since 1978 show that it is willing to be a responsible member, contributing to the maintenance of international society.

In the past thirty years, China has been in the process of reconstructing a new identity in international society, an identity close to its ideal one—strong and prosperous, equal and responsible. China has redefined itself from an outsider to a participant in international society. Reform and opening up has spurred the development of the country and brought about tremendous political, economic, and social changes, which, in turn, have been facilitated by China's joining international society. Since 1979, China has gradually gained a full membership in international society. It is sometimes argued that this new identity is still in the process of reconstructing, but it stands firm as China further develops. It is the identity China is happy with.

With this new identity, China and international society have frequent interactions, and developments at international, national, and subnational levels are now closely interconnected. Chinese leaders have realized that "the relationship between the contemporary China and the world has experienced a historical change. China's future and its destiny are closely linked with the destiny of the world."[35] In 2005, the First Deputy Secretary of State Robert Zoellick used the term "stakeholder" in an address to the US-China National Committee.[36] In the same year, Chinese president Hu Jintao made a proposal at the UN Summit for building a harmonious world.[37] These words marked a positive solution to China's one-hundred-year identity puzzle.

CONCLUSION

Since the policy of reform and opening up began in 1978, China has made a successful attempt to integrate itself into international society. The world itself and China's views of the international system and international society have both changed profoundly, which has created favorable conditions for China to address its identity puzzle.[38] Through reform and opening up, China has changed itself and has decided to join international society. The end of the Cold War and the policy of reform and opening up have also created conditions for international society to accept China as a member. As a result, China has made a revolutionary change in its identity: from a revisionist state to status quo power and from an outsider to a full and active member.

China has acquired three important experiences during the process of reconstructing a new identity in international society. First, China's persistent and resolute struggle for reconstructing an identity constitutes an inexhaustible dynamic for China's rise. As a big country with a five-thousand-year civilization, China desires and expects to gain a proper status in the international system and a proper identity in international society, which fit and correspond to its land scale, population size, and resources. The struggle will not stop. It is an undisputable fact and common sense that any state or any nation that has such an expectation or ideal will act similarly. China does not expect to restore the tribute system or bring China back to its former position as the Central Kingdom, for it has accepted the basic norms and rules in the current international system that had been largely formed in the last century. Instead, the expectation is to seek a proper status for a nation like China. With such a political psychology, China's rise is inevitable and irreversible, and the struggle for an identity is the fundamental driving force of China's rise.

An essential aspect of identity is China's definition of itself as a unified country. Although national sovereignty and territorial integrity are concepts China has learned relatively recently from the West, they are important for the Chinese nation as it has been searching for its identity not as a civilization pretending to be a nation-state, but as a nation-state in its real sense, together with the strong belief in the "grand unity" that has developed ever since the Qin dynasty. Taiwan, Tibet, and Xinjiang are so vehemently defined as inseparable parts of China, largely because they are significant symbols of China's identity as a modern and unified nation-state.

Second, the effective way to reconstruct an identity is through nonviolent and nonradical reform. The initial attempts were made to develop China's economy and technology, and to innovate its political institutions through self-strengthening. They failed, both because of the misunderstanding by the Chinese political and intellectual elites of the self and the other, and because of the Western countries' *realpolitik* policy that might is right. In the clash between the West and the East, China was thus not ready and at the same time was given no chance to understand the contents and forms of the international system established by the West. What they saw since the 1840s' first encounter with the West was largely power politics and the law of the jungle. Due to this, China was thrown into towering rage and committed itself to a tit-for-tat mentality, believing that only warships worked for national defense and national rise. Guided by such a mentality, China overthrew the Qing dynasty and the monarchy through violent revolutions. However, instead of reconstructing a proper identity for China, the sustained wars further devitalized the nation. It became a luxury to talk about China's identity vis-à-vis the international system for almost one hundred years. As Dittmer summarizes in chapter 2, in the 1950s through 1970s, stress on uncompromising struggle and national liberation wars, as well as efforts to export revolution, made China unable to rise. It is also realized that radical approaches could not help China reconstruct its desired identity in the international system. For territories beyond its defined borders, China has no ambition; but within such borders, China will make no concession, for it concerns not only the legitimacy of the government, but also the identity of the nation.

The effective solution has proved to be reform and opening up after the fundamental ideational change in China initiated by Deng Xiaoping. China abandoned its revolutionary mentality and approached international society with a new attitude, an attitude of cooperation and integration. In due course, to integrate itself into international society, China met opposition both domestically and internationally, but persistent efforts have succeeded in the final analysis. From reform to revolution, from revolution to reform: the century-long struggle for identity illustrates a tortuous path of identity reconstruction as well as a deep reflection on the consequences of reform and revolution. The successful solution to reconstructing an identity is not violent revolutions, but reform; not radicalism, but pragmatism. This experience has become the most recent addition to the collective memory of the Chinese people.

Third, the basic strategy to reconstruct a new identity is opening up. The early attempts since 1840 neglected the importance of opening up and therefore did not place adequate emphasis on "opening to the rest of the world" as a most significant step toward the reconstruction of China's identity. Even those people like Wei Yuan, and Lin Zexu, who were considered open-minded officials and scholars, failed to understand that China could rejuvenate itself only through getting into international society. Lin Zexu even suggested, "If China shut down its markets, the British economy would collapse."[39] The Westernization Movement, although encouraging learning from the West, aimed to learn the foreign technology so as to defend China against the foreign invasion. The 1911 Revolution was legitimated by its opposition to the unequal treaties. Anti-invasion was a major theme of the revolution, and to drive away foreign powers was one of the fundamental goals of the revolution. In the early years, China was opened up under the force of foreign powers, not voluntarily. It is well discussed by Perkins in chapter 5 that China's opening up met strong resistance from the conservatives after the Opium War, followed by weakness and chaos from 1895 to 1949, and did not come true after 1949 because of the planned economy during the 1950s through the 1970s.

In 1978, opening up became a basic national strategy of the same importance as reform. It is the first time that China actively opened itself up to the international system. The institutional change, as discussed by Naughton in chapter 6, and the reform in domestic laws have been largely caused by China's integration into the international economic and social systems. It is the opening up that has encouraged China to carry out domestic reform and eventually led to ideational change. China's rise is thus a result of both reform and opening up. Without opening up, the reform could not have been so successful. Opening up is one of the core ideas guiding China to integrate into the world and to reconstruct its appropriate membership in international society.

A state's attitude toward international society and its international behavior are rooted in its identity. States with different identities have different worldviews, which, in turn, make different impacts upon its foreign policies and strategies. As a state's identity changes, its attitude and policy toward international society also changes.[40] The changes of the environment, the development of the social economic conditions, and the frequent interactions with other states in international society—all drive a state to explore new ideas and to reestablish new identities.[41] The feedback from the international system enables an actor to reexamine its attitude and worldviews. The actor adjusts or even changes its views on the self-other relationship. This is what I mean in this chapter by stating that China has been undergoing a profound process of reestablishing its identity. China's reform is not just a dramatic economic event, but also a fundamental social transformation. Reform and opening up have changed China's status and identity in international society, making it possible to interact with the world as a full member of the international community. The process of mutual influence and mutual transformation has finally addressed China's hundred-year puzzle on identity, and in a very positive manner.

Mao is not mentioned in the article

NOTES

1. Former US National Security Advisor Zibigniew Brzezinski, World Bank President Robert Zoellick and Chief Economist Justin Yifu Lin, and British Foreign Secre-

tary David Miliband have all used the term *G2*. See respectively Geoff Dyer, "How the United States and China Dance Together," www.ftchinese.com/story_ce .hph?storyid=001026716 (accessed June 1, 2009); Robert Zoellick and Justin Yifu Lin, "Recovery Rides on the G-2," *Washington Post,* March 31, 2009, 16; and *Huanqiu Shibao* [Global Times], May 20, 2009, 6.

2. China in its modern history held four elections: 1908–1909 (the Constitutional Movement), 1913–1914 (the Republic established after the 1911 Revolution), 1917 (the Second Parliament), and 1947 (after the victory over Japan in World War II). But none of them succeeded. See Li Zongtao and Wang Yuan, "Sixiangzhe Zhang Pengyuan" [Zhang Pengyuan: A thinker], *Nanfang Renwu Zhoukan* [People], 64–66.

3. On the issue of China's hundred-year identity puzzle, see Qin Yaqing, "Wenhua, Shenfen yu Zhongguo dui Guojia Anquan de Renzhi" [Culture, identity, and China's perception of national security], in Zheng Yushuo, ed., *Maixiang 21shiji de Zhongguo Waijiao* [China's foreign policy toward the 21st century] (Hong Kong: Tiandi Publishing Co., 2001), 174–92; "Guoji Guanxi Lilun de Hexin Wendi yu Zhongguo Xuepai de Shengcheng" [The core problematic of international relations theory and the formation of a Chinese school], *Social Sciences in China,* no. 3 (2005): 165–76; and "Guojiguanxi Lilun Zhongguo Xuepai Shengcheng de Keneng he Biran" [Possibility and inevitability of a Chinese school of international relations theory], *World Economics and Politics,* no. 3 (2006): 7–13.

4. It may be argued that the tributary system is not an interstate system in a real sense, but a world system, or that China is more a civilization than a nation-state. Such arguments assume that the international system should be defined as a system of sovereign states and nation-states. I argue that the tributary system is at least a quasi-international system, for the relations between China and tributary states and the relations among the tributary states show some features similar to an international system, even though they were not straightly defined as sovereign states.

5. Barry Buzan and Richard Little, *International Systems in World History: Remaking the Study of International Relations,* Chinese edition (Beijing: Higher Education Press, 2004); Qin Yaqing, "Possibility and Inevitability."

6. See John K. Fairbank, ed., *The Chinese World Order: Traditional China's Foreign Relations* (Cambridge, MA: Harvard University Press, 1968).

7. The tributary system had already come to a full maturity in the Ming dynasty. The Qing dynasty in fact inherited this system and carried out similar policies after the Manchu rulers were assimilated into the Chinese culture.

8. Kenneth Waltz, *Theory of International Relations* (Reading, MA: Addison-Wesley, 1979); Robert Gilpin, *War and Change in World Politics* (Cambridge: Cambridge University Press, 1981); Qin Yaqing, *Baquan Tixi yu Guoji Chongtu: Meiguo zai Guoji Chongtuzhong de Zhichi Xingwei 1945–1988* [Hegemonic system and international conflict: US support behavior in international conflict, 1945–1988] (Shanghai: Shanghai People's Publishing House, 1999).

9. For example, Kang maintains that the order of the tributary system could only be kept stable if China remained the predominant power in the system. Therefore, a strong China helps maintain the order in the region. See David C. Kang, *China's Rising: Peace, Power, and Order in East Asia* (New York: Columbia University Press, 2007).

However, as China's power declined, the system did not collapse. A possible reason is that the ordering principle and the governing principle persisted, even if its power declined. This, to some extent, agrees with Keohane's argument that order exists after hegemony. See Robert Keohane, *After Hegemony: Cooperation and Discord in the World Political Economy* (Princeton, NJ: Princeton University Press, 1984). In this book, Evelyn Rawski put forward a somewhat different argument that half of the 2,400 years of the tribute system witnessed a power decentralization. She argues that during three periods (fourth to seventh, tenth to thirteenth, and sixteenth to early seventeenth centuries) China could not control effectively the vassal and neighboring states. Her argument is reasonable in that it refers to territorial control and military superiority. It is true that China was sometimes less powerful and sometimes had more might and that its physical control of the land was sometimes tight and sometimes loose. But since China in the two thousand years had no such concept of sovereignty and therefore had no such an idea of complete land occupation, *jimi* (loose rein) had been the persistent policy guidelines. My argument herein is that China's maintenance of the tribute system had been mainly in terms of the normative system based upon the Chinese culture. The advantage in "soft power," or cultural and institutional attraction helped maintain the tribute system. See Brantly Womack, *China and Vietnam: The Politics of Asymmetry* (New York: Cambridge University Press, 2006), 78–79. Challenges had always been there, but the essence of the tribute system had not been changed even when a foreign power became the ruler of the Chinese.

10. Fei Xiaotong, *Xiangtu Zhongguo* [Rural China] (Beijing: Sanlian Press, 1985), 23–25.

11. This kind of inequality does not mean "control" as implied in Western international relations theories. The stronger (China) and the weaker (vassal states) existed, both understanding that such relations were normal. This is similar to what Womack describes as an asymmetric relationship. See Womack, *China and Vietnam: The Politics of Asymmetry,* 17–23.

12. Zhao Tingyang, *Tianxia Tixi: Shiji Zhidu Zhexue Daolun* [The Tianxia system: A philosophy for the world institution] (Nanjing: Jiangsu Education Press, 2005).

13. The Confucian culture defines five basic relationships, every one of which, except that between friends, is hierarchical in nature, suggesting the superior and inferior positioning as the key to the relationships. All the relationships defined by the cultures described by Alexander Wendt are equal at least in name. See Alexander Wendt, *Social Theory of International Politics* (Cambridge: Cambridge University Press, 1999), 246–312.

14. Tu Wei-ming, *An Insight of Chong-yong* (Beijing: People's Press, 2008), 47–81.

15. Fei Zhengqing (John Fairbank), "Tiaoyue Zhidu De Xingcheng" [The formation of the treaty system], in Fei Zhengqing (John Fairbank), ed., *Jianqiao Zhongguo Wanqing Shi* [The Cambridge history of China: Late Ch'ing] (Beijing: China Social Science Press, 1993), 1:234.

16. Wang Shengzu, ed., *Guoji Guanxi Shi* [A history of international relations] (Beijing: World Affairs Press, 1996), 2:227–37.

17. See Xiao Fulidelike Weikeman (Frederic Wakeman, Jr.), "Guangzhou Maoyi Yu Yapian Zhanzheng" [The Canton trade and the Opium War] and Fei Zhengqing (John

Fairbank), "Tiaoyue Zhidu de Xingcheng" [The formation of the treaty system], in Fei Zhengqing (John Fairbank), *The Cambridge History of China*, 1:175–232, 233–91.

18. Zhang Haipeng and Li Xizhu, *Zhongguo Jindai Tongshi* [A history of modern China] (Nanjing: Phoenix Publishing and Jiangsu People's Press, 2006), 5:64.

19. Wu Shiying, ed., *Yangwu Yundong Yu Bianjiang Weiji Juan* [The volume of the Westernation Movement and the boundary crisis], in Dai Yi, ed., *Zhongguo Jindaishi Tongjian* [A complete history of modern China] (Beijing: Hongqi Press, 1997), 3:6–8.

20. Wu Shiying, *Westernization Movement*, 44.

21. Wu Shiying, *Westernization Movement*, 44.

22. Li Yumin, ed., *Xinhai Geming Juan* [The volume of the 1911 Revolution], in Dai Yi, ed., *Zhongguo Jindaishi Tongjian* [A complete history of modern China], 5:24–26.

23. John Fairbank and Edwin O. Reischauer, *China: Tradition and Transformation*, rev. ed. (Boston: Houghton Mifflin, 1989), 406–13.

24. Cited from Zhang Haipeng and Li Xizhu, *A History of Modern China*, 3:475.

25. The policy of "lean to one side" means that China, as a socialist country, should stand firm with the Soviet Union and should resolutely oppose the Western camp led by the United States. See Mao Zedong, "'Yibiandao' duibudui?" (Is leaning to one side correct?), in *Maozedong Waijiao Wenxuan* [Selected works of Mao Zedong on diplomacy] (Beijing: Central Documentary Press and World Affairs Press, 1994), 278. For an analysis of the lean-to-one-side policy, see Zhang Xiaoming, "Lengzhan Shiqi Xin Zhongguo de Sici Duiwai Zhanlue Xuanze" [New China's four strategic choices in the Cold War years], *Dangdai Zhongguoshi Yanjiu* [Modern Chinese History Studies], no. 5 (1997): 42.

26. Qin Yaqing, "Guanyu Zhongguo yu Guoji Shehui de Sange Jiashe" [Three hypotheses on the relationship between China and international society], *World Economics and Politics* 3 (2003): 10–15.

27. Yaqing, "Three Hypotheses," 10–15.

28. Xiao Gongqin, *Rujia Wenhua de Kunjing* [The dilemma of the Confucian culture] (Guilin: Guangxi Normal University Press, 2006), 158–59.

29. Xiao Gongxin has made an excellent analysis of the role of this conservative force and its distorted understanding of Western ideas and things. The scholar-officials used the traditional knowledge schema to interpret things Western and concluded that China did not need to follow those strange ideas and tricks. Even the most open-minded Chinese intellectuals failed to see the world in its true sense and understand it in a proper manner. See Xiao Gongqin, *Dilemma of the Confucian Culture*, 39–55.

30. Qin Yaqing, "International Factors and China's External Behavior," in Pauline Kerr, Stuart Harris, and Qin Yaqing, eds., *China's "New" Diplomacy: Tactical or Fundamental Change?* (New York: Palgrave, 2009), 33–53.

31. *China Statistical Yearbook 2005*, www.stats.gov.cn/tjsj/ndsj/2005/indexch.htm (accessed May 18, 2009).

32. Hedley Bull, *The Anarchical Society* (New York: Columbia University Press, 1977); Robert Axelrod, *The Evolution of Cooperation* (New York: Basic Books, 1984); John Ruggie, "What Makes the World Hang Together?: Neo-utilitarianism and the Social Constructivist Challenge," in Peter Katzenstein, Robert Keohane, and Stephen

Krasner, eds., *Exploration and Contestation in the Study of World Politics* (Cambridge, MA: MIT Press, 1999), 215–45; Alexander Wendt, *Social Theory of International Politics* (Cambridge: Cambridge University Press, 1999).

33. Alastair Iain Johnston, "Is China a Status Quo Power?" *International Security* 27, no. 4 (2003): 5–56; also see Alastair Iain Johnston, *Social State* (Princeton, NJ: Princeton University Press, 2007).

34. Ministry of Foreign Affairs of the PRC, www.fmprc.gov.cn/chn/wjb/zzjg/tyfls/default/htm (accessed May 18, 2009).

35. See Hu Jintao, *Gaoju Zhongguo Tese Shehuizhuyi Weida Qizhi, Wei Duoqu Quanmian Xiaokang Shehhui er Fendou: zai Zhongguo Gongchandang Dishiqici Quanguo Daibiao Dahui shang de Baogao* [Uphold the great banner of socialism with Chinese characteristics and strive for new victory of building an all-over well-off society: Report to the 17th National Congress of the CCP] (Beijing: People's Press, 2007), 47.

36. See Robert Zoellick, US Deputy Secretary of State, "Whither China: From Membership to Responsibility," remarks at US-China National Committee on US-China Relations, September 15, 2005, www.ncuscr.org/files/2005Gala_Robert-Zoellick_Wither _China.pdf (accessed May 20, 2009).

37. Hu Jintao, "Nuli Jianshe Chijiu Heping, Gongtong Fanrong de Hexie Shijie" [Strive to build a harmonious world with long peace and common prosperity], speech at the UN Summit, September 15, 2005, www.fmprc.gov.cn/chn/gxhlzlb/ldzyjh/t212356.htm (accessed May 20, 2009).

38. Zhang Baijia, "Gaibian Ziji, Yingxiang Shijie: Ershi Shiji Zhongguo Waijiao Jiben Xiansuo Quyi" [Change China and influence the world: An outline of China's diplomacy during the 20th century], *Social Sciences in China*, no. 3 (2002): 4–19.

39. Xiao Gongqin, *The Dilemma of the Confucian Culture*, 28.

40. Ronald L. Jepperson, Alexander Wendt, and Peter J. Katzenstein, "Norms, Identity, and Culture in National Security, " in Katzenstein, ed., *The Culture of National Security* (New York: Columbia University Press, 1996), 52.

41. Martha Finnemore and Kathryn Sikkink, "International Norm Dynamics and Political Change," in Katzenstein, Keohane, and Krasner, *Exploration and Contestation*, 269.

Index

About the Contributors

Brantly Womack is Cumming Professor of Foreign Affairs at the University of Virginia and has been named an honorary professor at two Chinese universities. His publications include *China among Unequals: Asymmetric Foreign Relations in Asia* (2010), *China and Vietnam: The Politics of Asymmetry* (2006), *Foundations of Mao Zedong's Political Thought, 1917–1935* (1982, Chinese edition 2006), *Politics in China* (with James Townsend, 1986, Chinese editions 1994, 2002), and *Contemporary Chinese Politics in Historical Perspective* (edited, 1991).

Lowell Dittmer is professor of political science at the University of California, Berkeley, and editor of *Asian Survey*. His recent publications include *China's Deep Reform: Domestic Politics in Transition* (edited with Guoli Liu, 2006), *South Asia's Nuclear Crisis* (2005), *China Under Modernization* (1994), *China's Quest for National Identity* (with Samuel Kim, 1993), and *Sino-Soviet Normalization and Its International Implications* (1992).

Erica S. Downs is the China Energy Fellow at the John L. Thornton China Center at the Brookings Institution. Her publications include "Who's Afraid of China's Oil Companies?" in Carlos Pascual and Jonathan Elkind, eds., *Energy Security: Economics, Politics, Strategies, and Implications* (2009), "China's 'New' Energy Administration," *China Business Review* (2008), "Business Interest Groups in Chinese Politics: The Case of the Oil Companies," in Cheng Li, ed., *China's Changing Political Landscape: Prospects for Democracy* (2008), and "The Fact and Fiction of Sino-African Energy Relations," *China Security* (2007).

Mark Elvin is emeritus professor and visiting fellow, Division of Pacific and Asian History, Research School of Pacific Studies, Australian National University. He is also an emeritus fellow of St. Antony's College, Oxford. His publications include *The Retreat of the Elephants: An Environmental History of China* (2004), *Sediments of Time: Environment and Society in Chinese History* (edited with Liu Ts'ui-jung, 1998), *Cultural Atlas of China* (with C. Blunden, 1983, revised edition 1998), *Changing Stories in the Chinese World* (1997), *Another History* (1996), and *The Pattern of the Chinese Past* (1973).

Joseph W. Esherick holds the Hwei-chih and Julia Hsiu Chair in Chinese Studies at the University of California, San Diego, where he has chaired the Program in Chinese Studies. His publications include *Reform and Revolution in China: The 1911 Revolution in Hunan and Hubei* (1976, second edition 2002, Chinese translation 1982), *Remaking the Chinese City: Modernity and National Identity, 1900–1950* (editor, 2000), *The Origins of the Boxer Uprising,* (1987, Chinese translation 1994), *Chinese Local Elites and Patterns of Dominance* (coedited with Mary B. Rankin, 1990), *Lost Chance in China: The World War II Dispatches of John S. Service* (1974, 1975), and *Modern China: The Story of a Revolution* (with Orville Schell, 1972).

Joseph Fewsmith is professor of international relations and political science as well as director of the East Asia Interdisciplinary Studies Program at Boston University. His publications include *China Since Tiananmen: From Deng Xiaoping to Hu Jintao* (2001, second edition 2008), *Elite Politics in Contemporary China* (2001), *The Dilemmas of Reform in China: Political Conflict and Economic Debate* (1994), and *Party, State, and Local Elites in Republican China: Merchant Organizations and Politics in Shanghai, 1980–1930* (1985). He is one of the six regular contributors to *China Leadership Monitor*, a quarterly web publication analyzing current developments in China. He is also a research associate of the John King Fairbank Center for East Asian Studies at Harvard University.

Barry Naughton is So Kwanlok Professor of Chinese and International Affairs at University of California, San Diego. His publications include *The Chinese Economy: Transitions and Growth* (2007) and *Growing Out of the Plan: Chinese Economic Reform, 1978–1993* (1995), which received the Ohira Memorial Prize in 1996. Naughton is the author of numerous articles on the Chinese economy and is editor or coeditor of *The China Circle: Economics and Technology in the PRC, Taiwan and Hong Kong* (1997), *Reforming Asian Socialism: The Growth of Market Institution* (1996), and *Urban Spaces in Contemporary China* (1995).

Dwight H. Perkins is Harold Hitchings Burbank Professor of Political Economy in the Faculty of Arts and Sciences of Harvard. Previous positions at Harvard include director of the Harvard University Asia Center, associate director of the East Asian (now Fairbank) Research Center, chair of the Department of Economics, and director of the Harvard Institute for International Development. His recent publications include *The Challenges of China's Growth* (2007), *Economics of Development* (with Steven Radelet and David L. Lindauer, sixth edition, 2006), and *Under New Ownership: Privatizing China's State-Owned Enterprises* (with Shahid Yusuf and Kaoru Nabeshima, 2006). Classics include *Rural Development in China* (with Shahid Jusuf, 1984), *China's Modern Economy in Historical Perspective* (editor, 1975), and *Agricultural Development in China, 1368–1968* (1969).

Qin Yaqing is professor and vice president of China Foreign Affairs University and vice president of the China National Association for International Studies. His publications include "Relationality and Processual Construction: Bringing Chinese Ideas in International Relations Theory," *Social Sciences in China* (2009), "Structure, Process, and the Socialization of Power: East Asian Community Building and the Rise of China" in Robert Ross and Zhu Feng, eds., *China's Ascent: Power, Security, and the Future of International Relations* (2008), "Why Is There No Chinese IR Theory?" *International Relations of Asia Pacific* (2007), and *Power, Institutions and Cultures* (2005). He has coauthored and coedited many books, including *China's "New" Diplomacy* (2009) and *International System and China's Diplomacy* (2009). He also has translated E. H. Carr's *Twenty Years' Crisis*, Robert Jervis's *Perception and Misperception in International Politics*, and Alexander Wendt's *Social Theory of International Politics*.

Evelyn S. Rawski is Distinguished University Professor of History at the University of Pittsburgh and a former president of the Association for Asian Studies. Her publications include *The Last Emperors: A Social History of Qing Imperial Institutions* (1998), *Education and Popular Literacy in Ch'ing China* (1979), and *Agricultural Change and the Peasant Economy of South China* (1972).

R. Keith Schoppa is professor and Doehler Chair in Asian History, Loyola University Maryland, and president of the Historical Society for Twentieth Century China. His publications include *Modern East Asia: Regional and National Identities Amid Changing Contexts* (2010), *Revolution and Its Past: Identities and Change in Modern Chinese History* (second edition, 2005), *Twentieth Century China: A History in Documents* (2004), *The Columbia Companion to Modern Chinese History* (2000), *Song Full of Tears: Nine Centuries of Chinese Life at Xiang Lake* (2002), *Blood Road: The Mystery of Shen Dingyi in Revolu-*

tionary China (1995, Chinese translation, 2000), *Xiang Lake: Nine Centuries of Chinese Life* (1989), and *Chinese Elites and Political Change: Zhejiang Province in the Early Twentieth Century* (1982).

Michael D. Swaine is senior associate of the Carnegie Endowment for International Peace. Prior to this appointment he was research director of the RAND Center for Asia Pacific Policy and RAND Center for Asia Pacific Policy Chair in Northeast Asian Security. His publications include *Assessing the Threat: The Chinese Military and Taiwan's Security* (with Andrew Yang, Evan Medeiros, and Oriana Mastro, 2007), *Managing Sino-American Crises: Case Studies and Analysis* (2006), and *Interpreting China's Grand Strategy* (with Ashley Tellis, 2000).